Off The Beaten Track
SOUTHERN FRANCE

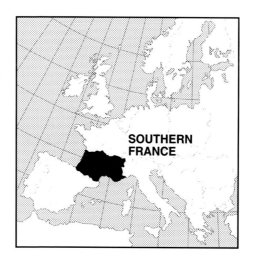

SOUTHERN FRANCE

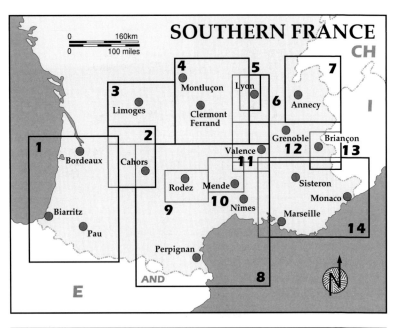

SOUTHERN FRANCE

CH

I

0 ——— 160km
0 ——— 100 miles

4 Montluçon
5 Lyon
6 Annecy
7
3 Limoges
Clermont Ferrand
2
Grenoble **12** Briançon **13**
1 Bordeaux
Cahors
Valence
11
Rodez Mende
Sisteron
Monaco
Biarritz
9 **10** Nîmes
Marseille
Pau
14
Perpignan
8
AND
E
N

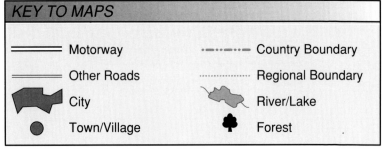

KEY TO MAPS

Motorway		Country Boundary	
Other Roads		Regional Boundary	
City		River/Lake	
Town/Village		Forest	

Off the Beaten Track
SOUTHERN
FRANCE

Rex Grizell • Barbara Mandell • Roger Penn
Don Philpott • Brian Spencer • Joy Thatcher

MOORLAND PUBLISHING

Published by:
Moorland Publishing Co Ltd,
Moor Farm Road West, Ashbourne,
Derbyshire, DE6 1HD England

ISBN 0 86190 439 7 (UK)

The Globe Pequot Press,
6 Business Park Road,
PO Box 833, Old Saybrook,
Connecticut 06475-0833

ISBN 1-56440-458-7 (USA)

© Moorland Publishing Co Ltd 1994

Note on Maps
The maps for each chapter, while comprehensive, are not designed to be used
as route maps, but to locate the main
towns, villages and places of interest.

Cover photograph:
Rural Museum near Châteux de Milandes
(MPC Picture Collection)

Black and white illustrations have been
supplied as follows:

Comite Departmentale de Tourisme
Aveyron; Comite Departmentale du
Tourisme du Rhône; Comite Regional
de Tourisme du Limousin; R. Grizell;
B. Mandell; MPC Picture Collection;
R. Penn; D. Philpott; Photo D. Viet;
Photo J-Louis Guerrier; B. Spencer;
J. Thatcher

Colour illustrations have been supplied
as follows:

Comite Regional de Tourisme du
Limousin (Arnac-Pompadour);
A. Emery (Savoie); R. Grizell (Château
de Bonaguil, La Roque Gageal);
Hoseasons Holidays Abroad Ltd.
(Aigues-Mortes, Carcassonne);
G. Irving (Agay); MPC Picture
Collection (Périgueux, Sarlat, Les
Eyzies, Rocamadour, Cahors); R. Penn
(Valleraugue, Molines); B. Spencer
(Puy Goion, Le-Puy-en-en-Velay,
Argentière, La Meige); J. Thatcher
(Aubenas)

Origination by:
P & W Graphics Pte Ltd., Singapore

Printed by:
Wing King Tong Co. Ltd., Hong Kong

MPC Production Team:
Editorial: Tonya Monk
Design: Ashley Emery
Cartography: Alastair Morrison
Typesetting & Assistant
    Editorial: Christine Haines

British Library Cataloguing in Publication Data:
A catalogue record for this book is available from the British Library.

Library of Congress Cataloging-in-Publication Data
Off the beaten track. Southern France/Barbara Mandell...[et al.].
    p. cm.
Includes index.
ISBN 1-56440-458-7
1. France, Southern—Guidebooks.   2. France, Southwest—Guidebooks.
I. Mandell, Barbara. II. Title: Southern France.
DC607.3.044   1994
914.4'04839 — dc20   93-47309
                                                                  CIP

Contents

Introduction

Western Europe is a continent of great diversity, well visited by travellers from other parts of the globe and inhabitants of its own member countries. Throughout the year and particularly during the holiday season, there is a great interchange of nationalities as one country's familiar attractions are left behind for those of another.

The sharing of cultures brings us closer in all senses to our neighbours. Yet essential differences do exist, differences which lure us abroad on our annual migrations in search of fresh sights and the discovery of unknown landscapes and people.

Countless resorts have evolved for those who simply crave sun, sea and the reassuring press of humanity. There are, too, established tourist 'sights' with which a country or region has become associated and which the manifestations of mass tourism exploit. This is by no means typical of all well known tourist attractions, but is familiar enough to act as a disincentive for those of more independent spirit who value personal discovery above prescribed experience.

It is for such travellers that this guidebook has been written. In its pages, no more than passing mention is made of the famous and the well documented. Instead, the reader is taken if not to unknown then to relatively unvisited places — literally 'off the beaten track'.

Through the specialist knowledge of the authors, visitors using this guidebook are assured of gaining insights into the country's heartland whose heritage lies untouched by the tourist industry.

From wild, scantily populated countryside whose footpaths and byways are best navigated by careful map reading, to negotiating the side streets of towns and cities, travelling 'off the beaten track' can be rather more demanding than following in the footsteps of countless thousands before you. The way may be less clear, more adventurous and individualistic, but opportunities do emerge for real discovery. With greater emphasis on exploring 'off the beaten track', the essence of Southern France is more likely to be unearthed and its true flavours relished to the full.

Tonya Monk
Series Editor

1 • Aquitaine

Variety, they say, is the spice of life — a cliché which makes Aquitaine one of the most highly-seasoned areas in France. Nor does it do anything by halves. To the west, the Bay of Biscay hurls long Atlantic rollers against the most impressive sand dunes in Europe, the high Pyrénées with their summer flowers and winter snows provide a frontier with Spain while, to the north, the Parc Régional des Landes de Gascogne maintains that its forest is more extensive than any other on the Continent. Added to this are lakes and rivers filled with fish, pastures and vineyards, ancient towns, isolated villages and coastal resorts busy planning their way into the twenty-first century.

Historically the contrasts are just as obvious. The earliest residents, who hunted mammoths in the area anything up to 20,000 years ago, have left plenty of evidence of the kind of life they lived. The Romans moved in considerably later and under the Emperor Augustus extended the northern boundary from the River Garonne to the Loire. In the twelfth century the English, united with Normandy for the time being under one ruler, added it to their other possessions on the Continent. They lost it again, together with the Hundred Years' War, at the battle at Castillon, near Bordeaux, in 1453. The kingdom of Navarre did not survive much longer. The southern part went to Spain in 1516 and the northern section became part of France in 1589. After some three centuries the British moved back without firing a shot, simply by adding Biarritz to their list of popular holiday resorts after Napoleon III and the Empress Eugénie decided that the little fishing village would make an acceptable summer residence. Biarritz is still sophisticated inspite of modern additions like camping sites but the British have largely switched their affections to the Perigord where they have settled in force and give every impression of making their invasion a permanent one.

Aquitaine, south of the River Garonne, is largely off the beaten track with few places of international repute apart, of course, from

Bordeaux itself, Biarritz and Lourdes. The bigger towns are scattered thinly over the region, interspersed with villages and hamlets which, between them, have a considerable amount to offer the visitor. Most have at least one *auberge* with comfortable beds complete with bolsters and, usually, extra pillows tucked away in the cupboards for anyone who needs them. The cooking tends to be traditional and based on local produce. Oysters are particularly good round Arcachon, the famous Bayonne hams are made in Orthez and buntings are a speciality in the Landes along with mushrooms and asparagus. Fish comes in all flavours from salmon to carp stuffed with *foie gras*, steaks are served with truffle or red wine sauces and venison, wild boar, woodcock and partridge all appear on local menus. Many of the wines are justly famous, particularly Bordeaux and Graves, but each region has its own local favourites. Madiran concentrates on red, the Béarn mostly on *rosé* and the Landes on white. Sweet wines appear as *apéritifs*, with fruit and with *foie gras* while Armagnac, the famous and ancient brandy of the country, takes pride of place with coffee. Fruit soaked in Armagnac is delicious as are the various cheeses.

Sports are very much part of life in Aquitaine. Tennis courts can be found nearly everywhere along with swimming pools, some of which are heated. Riding stables cater for anything from an hour out in the countryside to a full-blown pony trek while some experts insist that it is the best place to go in France for a golfing holiday. Fishermen can choose between salmon, trout and shad in the rivers or pike, bream and roach in the lakes and ponds and there are routes designed for long-distance hiking as well as short rambles. The Pyrénées offer plenty of opportunities for mountain climbing and, all the usual winter sports during the season. The seaside resorts are equipped for activities of every description. Surfing, especially in the Biarritz area, is said to be the best in Europe. The majority of villages in the Basque country have their own pelota courts, pool tables appear in the most unlikely places, rugby is becoming increasingly popular and there are casinos in the larger centres, especially on the coast. Bullfights pull in the crowds as do the many *fêtes* and festivals that take place during the summer.

Apart from hotels and *auberges* there are villas and apartments, *gîtes* that can be anything from a country cottage to part of a private house, holiday villages, sites for tents and caravans and, in keeping with the times, half a dozen centres where visitors need a toothbrush but no clothes to feel perfectly at home. Fortunately the weather lends itself to naturism with hot sun during the summer season

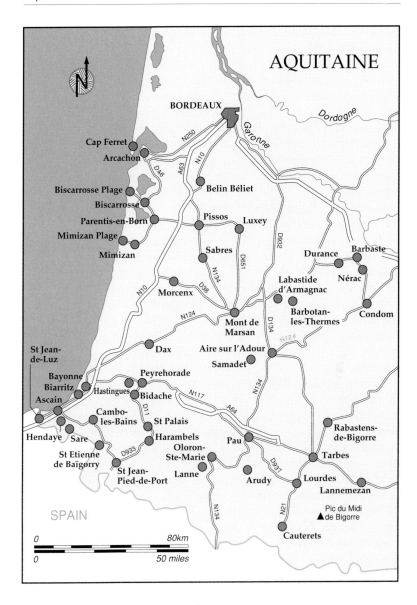

although the spring can be chilly and winter in the mountains is decidedly cold.

The traditional language is 'Oc', the word for 'yes' in southern France as opposed to 'Oïl' which was confined to the country north of the Loire. Even the *langue d'oc* varies to a certain extent from one region to another, especially where the accent and intonation are concerned. However *langue d'oil* has become the official version for the whole country.

Getting to Aquitaine presents no problems at all. Paris is an hour away by air with daily flights to and from Bordeaux, Biarritz, Pau and Agen. There are also direct flights to several European capitals and to more than a dozen French cities, among them Nice, Lille, Grenoble and Clermont-Ferrand. The train services are equally accommodating, providing daily opportunities for travel from Paris to Agen, Dax, Hendaye and Pau and back again as well as facilities for taking the car by rail if the destination is Tarbes, Bordeaux or Biarritz. Motorists who prefer to find their own way to Aquitaine have a choice of three motorways that run north to Paris, east to the Mediterranean and south to Spain. Other main roads fan out in all directions and there is an extensive network of secondary roads linking hundreds of small towns and villages. Generally speaking the surfaces are good but where road works are in progress the deviations can be bumpy to say the least of it. Some little lanes call for even lower speeds and more constant attention, particularly where there is only room for one car and a distinct possibility that another vehicle or a flock of sheep will be coming in the opposite direction.

Many people with a tour of Aquitaine in mind will probably start from **Bordeaux**. Not only is it the capital with all the advantages of an airport, a busy harbour and a goodly number of very comfortable hotels, coupled with a wide choice in the less-expensive bracket, but it also abounds in places to see and things to do. Having once set foot there, any traveller worth the name would be curious to see exactly what the city has to offer before setting out for parts other visitors often ignore. Its many churches include a cathedral, the basilica of St Michel which almost, but not quite, overlooks the river and the more centrally-situated church of Notre-Dame. Nearby is the Grand Théâtre, solid and frequently traffic-bound, where opera lovers congregate for the Bordeaux Festival. It is all of a piece with the shopping area where large windows tempt passers-by of every income and persuasion. The city is rich in museums, the two main ones being the Musée des Beaux-Arts with paintings covering every school from Rubens to the twentieth century, and the Museum of Decorative Arts where the emphasis is on the eighteenth century, exactly matching the building in which it is housed. Among the smaller ones the Musée d'Aquitaine delves back into prehistory before bringing local matters up to date; the more unusual Musée des Douanes tells the story of smuggling and the customs men who tried to stamp it out; the Centre Jean Moulin concerns itself with World War II and the large public gardens have a natural history museum of their own. Visitors with only a passing interest in matters such as these can head for the racecourse, play tennis or golf, set off along the Canal-du-Midi or opt for any of a number of water sports.

The nearest place to find both sea and sand is **Arcachon**. It is a biggish town that shares its name with a large sea-water bay-cum-lagoon where oysters take second place to tourists, but only just. The shores are a mass of small villages and camping sites, all spending their time keeping holidaymakers entertained and happy. There is a yacht harbour with boats for hire, deep-sea diving and fishing, surfing, wind-surfing and waterskiing with a choice of casinos and a museum of the sea. Apart from displaying leftovers from the Iron Age and other relics that have turned up in the area from time to time, it has an aquarium with more than five hundred different species, making it difficult to see them all at once.

There are plenty of shops, a wide range of hotels, little trains that chunter backwards and forwards to the sea and boat trips round the Bassin d'Arcachon as far as the lighthouse at Cap Ferret, stopping just short of the Bay of Biscay itself.

Behind the enormous sand dunes, **Pyla-sur-Mer** has the highest of all, a line of lagoons runs parallel with the shore, getting smaller and smaller all the time until they peter out completely a little north of Bayonne. The Etang de Biscarrosse et de Parentis, one of the larger, more northerly ones, has some difficulty in deciding whether it should be a holiday playground or concentrate on oil. As a result it has a small land-locked marina and a sprinkling of pumps that are hard at work all the time. The water can be unexpectedly rough in windy conditions and although there are places to park better spots can be found for bathing or having a picnic. **Biscarrosse Plage** takes its role as a seaside resort quite seriously and keeps a watchful eye on bathers who wander off on their own when the sun umbrellas and beach beds get too numerous for comfort. The town itself breaks new ground with a seaplane museum while **Parentis-en-Born** invites motoring enthusiasts to inspect its petroleum museum.

A large military zone, peppered with shellholes and other tell-tale traces of modern warfare, marches south with the dunes, successfully cutting off all access to the sea between Biscarrosse Plage and **Mimizan**. This is a rather self-important little town which had an abbey church back in the thirteenth century but now draws attention to local history, including traditional arts and crafts, by means of a small but carefully planned museum. It also has its own *plage* (beach) very much in keeping with all the other similar places further along the coast. As they are not linked together, special short detours are needed to inspect each one, to be greeted by silver sands, camping sites, functional shops, an occasional tennis court and, sometimes, pedalos for hire. Eventually, perhaps, they will all link hands, with hotels and high-rise buildings, villas and promenades presenting the same united front that one sees on the Riviera, but for the moment the dunes facing the Atlantic are relatively undisturbed. Everywhere the breakers look perfect for surfing but it is as well to remember that there are strong currents which make it a dangerous pastime for anyone, with or without a board. It is more sensible to keep an eye open for warning notices and stay within sight of the lifeguards.

Holidaymakers whose horizons extend beyond a mixture of sun, sea and sand will find that there are any number of attractions well away from the coast. The forests of the Landes, vast as they are, only form part of the Regional Park that begins at the Bassin d'Arcachon. At one time the area consisted largely of marshes and moorland with sand blown in by winds from the west gradually taking it over and turning it into a wilderness. The first attempts to control nature began at the end of the eighteenth century and within a remarkably short time pine forests had sprung up and large sections were drained, ready for cultivation. Today there are cornfields, strawberry patches and asparagus beds flourishing alongside the trees which, in turn, provide both wood and resin. The River Leyre runs through the park, bordered by oaks, alders and chestnut trees. However these are by no means newcomers to the region. The alder was, and still is, used almost exclusively for making *sabots* (clogs) acorns were fed to pigs and sheep and the chestnut, in company with beans, was the only source of starch before the Spaniards brought back potatoes from Peru in the early sixteenth century.

Apart from being a viable commercial proposition the area is ideal for research into the environment and for open-air holidays. Visitors are encouraged to explore on foot, by canoe, on horseback or on bicycles. To make life easier for them the authorities have provided two holiday centres and extra accommodation in half a dozen other villages round about. Anyone who could not find something to interest them in the area would be extremely hard to please. The forests are full of ferns and gorse; foxes, squirrels, deer and wild boar have their homes there and more than two hundred different kinds of birds are to be seen in residence or just passing through. Typical wattle-and-daub type houses can be discovered hidden away in isolated clearings and a request for a glass of water may lead to an invitation to share a fish soup or a pigeon pie. By way of entertain-

Stilts were once used extensively when keeping watch over sheep

ment the villagers enrich their summer festivals with calf races, their own version of bowling competitions, music and dancing and racing on stilts. These used to be everyday wear for shepherds keeping watch over their flocks and both men and women could spend hour after hour perched upon them quite comfortably. For all practical purposes this art is now a thing of the past although some young men say that they can stay up there all day, possibly leaning on a long pole or a convenient tree while they have their lunch.

Another thing that comes as a mild surprise in the Landes is the sound of bagpipes, an accomplishment which has been handed down through the ages and often accompanies traditional songs. The place to find out all about them is the Lapios Centre in **Belin-Béliet**, just off the *autoroute* from Bordeaux. It is a little place that can rustle up a tennis court, a bedroom with a private bath and some delightful home cooking. It is only one of several small hamlets in the area with something out of the ordinary to offer. **Pissos**, further south, falls into the same category although its offerings include an artisan's house, the remains of an ancient glassworks and a twelfth-century church. It holds two fairs every year, one at Easter and the other towards the end of August, and makes a practice of selling handicrafts during the summer. **Luxey**, on the other hand, focuses its attention on ecology with a most informative resin museum. This traces the story from the moment the pine is tapped and the resin collected in small clay pots, although these have been replaced by plastic bags in some cases, and follows the process through to the boilers which hive off the turpentine. The remaining mixture, once used for candles, is stored in special barrels made on the premises, and the demonstration ends with a display of the final products. They are many and extremely varied.

Sabres diversifies to a much greater extent. It is the site of one of the special holiday villages, has facilities for riding and pony trekking, is equipped for tennis and does much of its shopping at the open-air market on Thursdays. A tiny Napoleon III museum, standing alone except for a small church in the forest on the road to Solferino, is open all the year round provided someone is at home to answer the door or the telephone. However, Sabres is known first and foremost for the Ecomusée, an authentic village which has been completely restored and goes under the name **Marquèze**. There are no roads up to it and visitors have to take a small train from Sabres which is all that remains of a line that used to carry passengers and timber to Mimizan a hundred years ago. It runs at weekends and on holidays from March to November, operates on weekdays between June and September but grinds to a halt for the rest of the year.

Not unnaturally there is a certain commercial side to Marquèze, mainly confined to the reception area, where everything from aspirin to postcards is on sale, to the children's playground and the picnic area close by. These aside it is partly a research centre and partly a nineteenth-century hamlet operating more or less as it did in the olden days. Before setting off to explore what turns out to be quite a sizable area it is an advantage to see the model of the museum to get an idea of where things are and the part they play in the general scheme. The master's house, the biggest of course, has been restored and furnished with everything necessary to make it habitable; the miller's home, dating from 1834, is a trifle smaller and conveniently close to the old mill, while the cottage is typical of those provided for farm workers and other people employed on the land. There is a communal bread oven which doubled as a drying cupboard for hemp and flax, an 1857 sheepfold that is still in use and beehives with Tauzan oaks nearby, specially pruned so that the swarms can settle on them easily. The fields are sown with original crops and cultivated by traditional methods in order to compare them with modern ones and there are chicken coops and pig pens, vegetable gardens, fruit trees and vines. Specialists are on hand to explain the finer points of the enterprise, such as the reason for so many different types of grain, the importance of sheep and bees in the natural cycle

The Ecomusée of Marquèze can only be reached by train — there are no roads

and the advantages of planting root vegetables in the later phases of the moon. Two regulations are rigidly enforced — 'no smoking' and 'dogs must be kept on a lead'.

Apart from a sprinkling of *auberges* in this rather sparsely populated area there are some *gîtes*, quite a few farms identified by the sign *'Chambres d'Hôtes'* or *'Fermes d'Hôtes'* which are good for bed and breakfast and the usual variety of camping sites. In addition places like **Morcenx** qualify for a mention in the official list of country holiday resorts and have cafés and shops that are perfectly adequate for everyday needs. **Mont-de-Marsan**, further south, is quite large by local standards, possessing half a dozen hotels, a golf club with a 9-hole course and a municipal museum specialising in sculptures created between the wars. Some are dotted about the garden of the old building, which has survived from the Middle Ages and is open every morning and afternoon except on Tuesdays. A small natural history museum is housed in what was once a chapel.

Dax, on the banks of the Adour, is another matter altogether. To begin with it is an important spa with literally dozens of hotels, at least four of which are highly rated, furnished villas and apartments and sites for tents and caravans. The town with its hot water springs has been known since Roman times and it has the remains of an ancient wall to prove it. The Borda Museum goes into past history very thoroughly, collecting coins and items of archaeological interest, highlighting popular traditions and providing libraries of books and photographs. However it is not simply a choice between taking the waters or browsing about in the archives. Bullfights are staged in the middle of August, there are theatres and cinemas, concerts and festivals and a popular casino. Sports include tennis and swimming, riding and shooting with surfing at Hossegor.

The inveterate viewer of ancient buildings would find an equally short drive to the south every bit as rewarding. Across the river from Peyrehorade is the little fortified town of **Hastingues**, founded by an Englishman, John Hastings, in 1289 on the orders of Edward I, who also ruled Aquitaine. Its fortunes were bound up with those of the Abbaye d'Arthous, founded in the twelfth century and up-dated at intervals during the next five hundred years. Part of the building is half-timbered and the rest, including the church, is stone. Its present function is to give house-room to the Musée Archéologique Départemental and display a collection, the most modern part of which goes back to ancient Rome. It is open morning and afternoon and anyone who is anxious to look round is invited to ring the bell.

The Romans, who thoughtfully left behind so much for the museum, also built the baths at Sorde l'Abbaye further to the east. Although they were used as the foundations for part of a monastery established there in the Middle Ages, sections of the system and some mosaics can still be seen, along with a highly decorative mosaic in the eleventh-century church. It would also be a pity to miss the ruins of the Château de Gramont on a hill overlooking **Bidache**. The somewhat grim little fortress came into being in the fourteenth century with an extension two hundred years later for Duke Antoine III, Marshal of France and a force to be reckoned with at court.

Bayonne, as well as being a busy port, with obvious Roman connections, is worth a visit for two quite different reasons. In the first place it provides easy access to the magnificent beaches further south and in the second, it has a handful of memorable attractions of its own. The old quarter is virtually surrounded by huge stone walls protecting, amongst other things, the impressive cathedral not unlike the one at Reims. Along with a fourteenth-century cloister and sixteenth-century stained glass windows there is a distinctly twentieth-century plaque in one of the little chapels. It recalls with gratitude the Miracle of Bayonne in 1451 when the surrender of the English garrison was attributed to timely intervention from on high. No such phenomenon appears to have taken place when Wellington marched in from Spain after winning the Peninsular War but there is a monument which calls the occasion to mind and commands a spectacular view at the same time. Bayonne's Museum of Fine Arts is one that should not be missed. It includes a collection presented to the town by the artist Léon Bonnat, who was born there. In sharp contrast the Musée Basque, a couple of blocks away, is mainly concerned with the way of life, fashions, crafts and sports peculiar to the region, with special emphasis on pelota.

Getting around is really quite simple because, like a number of other towns in the south, it appears to have evolved a one-way traffic system that actually works. Parking areas are available, making it easy to leave the car and wander about inside the walls. However there has been so much expansion outside that the visitor, and probably many of the inhabitants, would be hard put to decide where Bayonne ends and Biarritz begins. There are some attractive little gardens, plenty of trees and the Rue du Pont-Neuf, linking the cathedral with the lively Place de la Liberté, provides ample opportunities to sample the local chocolate. This has been a speciality ever since cacao nuts were brought back from the New World in the seventeenth century. Incidentally, it would be difficult to find a restaurant that does not serve those very thinly-cut slices of raw smoked ham that take their name from the town. Bayonne's Grandes Fêtes at the beginning of August attract large crowds who spend the entire day, and most of the night, celebrating in traditional style.

Biarritz has a more international flavour, although it also puts on some extremely colourful Basque festivals during the season. The resort has been an exclusive holiday playground for more than a hundred years. In spite of the fact that, in some ways, it is past its glittering prime, the town has managed to update its attractions without entirely losing the original atmosphere. Empress Eugénie's summer residence is now a palatial hotel, there are thoroughfares named after Edward VII and the Prince of Wales and a château on the Lac de Brindos is beautifully decorated and serves delectable food. There is no good reason for including it amongst places which are off the beaten track save for its curiosity value and the facilities it provides for all maner of sporting activities. The absence of historic buildings and quaint, medieval streets is offset by five golf courses within easy reach, swimming pools and tennis courts, a skating rink, riding stables and, above all, superb beaches for surfing, splashing about or simply lying in the sun. There are some impressive views, especially from the Rocher de la Vierge, connected to the mainland by a footbridge near the Musée de la Mer which displays all the different scientific aspects of marine life alongside an enormous aquarium, a pool for sea lions and a section devoted to birds.

On the far side of Biarritz a road runs along the cliffs above sandy beaches and some not particularly noteworthy resorts. **Bidart** has its fair share of hotels and places to pitch a tent while **Guéthary**, an ancient fishing port on its own little inlet, is popular with people who know the area well. It has a small church of some interest, opportunities for swimming, tennis, deep-sea diving and walking and a few hotels, one with a menu that attracts gourmets from miles around. It is also the last stopping place before **St Jean-de-Luz**.

Whaling used to be the main occupation for local fishermen but these days the emphasis has switched to tuna fish and anchovies which keep the port very much on its toes. St Jean-de-Luz is a fascinating town, full of life and colour, owing as much of its atmosphere to Spain as it does to France. It is full of picturesque seventeenth-century houses, the biggest and most decorative being the Maison Louis XIV where the royal apartments are open during the summer months. The church of St Jean-Baptiste may not look very inviting from the outside, but the interior is both ornate and unusual when compared with churches further north. Tiers of galleries with wooden balustrades and long oak benches line the walls, giving it the appearance of a rather strange theatre with massive religious overtones. A ship under full sail looks perfectly at home, as do the statues of popular local saints, several angels, the decorative arches and a retable resplendent with gold. Coupled with all these treasures from the past are the many attributes so essential to a modern holiday resort. There are two golf courses, both of which call for a certain amount of skill, although if you do take your eye off the ball at the Nivelle Golf Club you can always blame the view. Apart from tennis courts there is a yacht harbour with a sailing school, deep-sea diving and a long sandy beach overlooked by the casino and by hotels of various sizes, each with a restaurant attached. The Festival of St John is held in June with a Tuna Festival a month later and a whole range of entertainments during the summer in which pelota and bullfighting play a prominent part.

Cibourne, on the other side of the river, is practically a suburb of St Jean-de-Luz. The composer Maurice Ravel was born there in a five-storey house in the shadow of the church of St Vincent which is open to view. His parents took him to Paris when he was three months old but in spite of this he was always a southerner at heart. He both spoke and wrote Basque, kept up with all the friends he made during his repeated visits to the area and wrote his *Trio* at 14 Place Ramiro Arrue. A story is told of a friend who called on him one morning when he was staying in St Jean-de-Luz. Ravel was just coming out of his bath but, nothing daunted, he picked out a few notes on the piano with one finger, saying he thought they were 'very insistent'. That is one way of describing his unforgettable *Bolero*.

From Cibourne a busy road runs through Socoa with its old fortress and along the Corniche Basque to **Hendaye**, the last resort before the Spanish frontier. It manages to deal with heavy road and rail traffic and keep holidaymakers happy at the same time. The *plage* has a leisure park, plenty of sand and so many trees and flowers that it ignored the famous Frenchmen who invariably have streets named after them and called its avenues Mimosas and Magnolias instead.

To get the best bird's eye view of the region it is only necessary to drive inland to **Ascain**, a nice little town in its own right, park the car and catch the mountain railway that winds up to La Rhune. This is an exceptional vantage point in good weather, looking across to the ocean, away to the forests and along the Pyrénées, but it is not worth bothering about in mist and rain.

An alternative to La Rhune for anyone with an aversion to climbing Pyrénéan peaks would be to follow the winding road to **Sare**. It boasts a typical Basque church, shady streets, a small hotel with an excellent restaurant and some not-too-demanding grottos a short distance away. **Aïnhoa** has just as good views, slightly more up-market hotels, a restaurant to rival the one at Sare and is on the direct route to **Cambo-les-Bains** in the valley of the Nive. As the name implies, Cambo has its own thermal establishment but the main place of interest is a museum in the Villa Arnaga, on the road to Biarritz, filled with souvenirs of poet and author Edmond Rostand.

Cambo is one of those places which mark the parting of the ways, unless of course enough time is available to follow a zig-zag course. As always the long way round provides the most variety. To begin with, a series of minor roads thread their way through undulating country where the pastures are dotted with patches of dense woodland and filled to bursting point with sheep. A sign which does not seem to be pointing anywhere in particular announces the Grottes d'Isturits et d'Oxocelhaya, down a narrow lane which would otherwise have little to recommend it. On closer inspection Isturits turns out to have been a popular residential area in prehistoric times while Oxocelhaya is full of stalactites and stalagmites enhanced by a waterfall which sparkles even though it is petrified. They are open each morning and afternoon and do not even bother to close for lunch during the high season.

St Palais, the next town of consequence along the route, makes no attempt to delve so far back into the past. Instead it is content with being the capital of the Navarre and a stopping place on the ancient pilgrims' road to Compostela. The main square, filled with trees and surrounded by old houses, has changed very little over the years. A picture in one of the hotels bears this out, the only difference being that it now has 'no entry' signs and parking space for cars. There is a sports complex with volley-ball, tennis and swimming, a camping site along the banks of the river, footpaths of varying descriptions and a tea room with upholstered seats, something of a rarity in this part of the world. Horses, fishing and pelota all appear on the list of holiday activities, there are some quite reasonable shops as well as a market every Friday and a typical Basque festival on the first Sunday after 15 August. During the summer Christmas-type decorations are festooned across the streets, everything from flowers to stars and guitars, all picked out with white lights. Tucked away in the woods to the south is **Harambels**, a little hamlet with an ancient chapel that was also on the pilgrims' way.

A pleasant small road with off-shoots that wander aimlessly about, only to end quite suddenly, leads to **St Etienne-de-Baïgorry**. On the way it passes Iholdy where the church is worth a glance because of the wooden gallery attached to the outside. St Etienne is built along the bank of the river and is a good place for exploring the Vallée des Aldudes and clearing customs before heading across the Pyrénées and into Spain. The main hotel, with river frontage, has been in the same family for generations and has an excellent restaurant which specialises in a delicious fish mousse .

A scenic road links the village with **St Jean-Pied-de-Port**, the ancient capital of the Basse-Navarre. The town has expanded considerably since the days when it was necessary to fortify in order to survive and the fifteenth-century ramparts are now surrounded by quite modern houses, garages, a railway station and a leisure park. Inside the walls the atmosphere is totally different with narrow streets, buildings that have been there since the sixteenth century, a squat stone church and an ancient hospital containing a library and a small local museum. Unfortunately the citadel is not open to the public but any time is visiting time for the Roman bridge of Eyharalerry which may well have proved useful to Charlemagne when he arrived in the vicinity with his army towards the end of the eighth century. There are a number of hotels, and provision is made for tents and caravans but it is as well to uncouple the latter if you intend to spend a lot of time exploring in the mountains.

The area to the south is a maze of steep little roads in not particularly good condition which keep doubling back on themselves in a

The square at St Palais

most neurotic fashion. There is a dearth of villages, but plenty of streams and woods with places to stop for a picnic or a gentle stroll. Exceptional views are hard to find and most of those that do exist are on the road from St Jean-Pied-de-Port, through the Col Bagargui, to Larrau which has two small inns but nothing that could really be called attractions. In order to become better acquainted with the Pyrénées it would be necessary to deviate still further through Lanne, Aramits and Arette before heading south again towards Arette-la-Pierre-St Martin, known for its cross-country skiing. The church at **Lanne** was originally a chapel attached to the Château de Isaac de Porthau who gained immortality as Porthos in *The Three Musketeers*. Dumas also drew on Trois-Villes and Aramits for his masterpiece but it is difficult to visualise those heroes against the background of twentieth-century white houses with red or brown shutters and gardens filled with flowers. **Arette**, which has the same air of apparent affluence, had to be largely rebuilt after an earthquake in 1967 so it is no good looking for any literary clues.

Oloron-Ste-Marie is every bit as delightful as it sounds. Built on a hilltop site once occupied by a small Roman settlement, it manages to combine the best of two totally different worlds. The main road through to the south, along the River Aspe, is full of little shops including some quite acceptable boutiques. Behind them a promenade marks the line of the ramparts which originally protected the domain of the Vicomtes de Béarn. Gaston IV was an enthusiastic participant in the Crusades, a fact which is illustrated to good effect on the splendid entrance to the thirteenth-century cathedral church. There are prisoners brought back in chains from the Holy Land, a statue of Gaston on horseback, wildlife both real and imaginary and a telling interpretation of St John's vision of the Apocalypse. The old quarter of Ste Croix, in a kind of wishbone-shaped area between two rivers, takes only a short time to explore even including a visit to the local church and a few minutes spent admiring the view.

The only reason for stopping off in **Arudy** would be to visit the Maison d'Ossau, a museum that complements the Parc National des Pyrénées. It takes a look at the past history of the area as well as all the flora and fauna to be seen there today. The park, which adjoins the Spanish National Park of Ordesa, is one mass of lakes and waterfalls, mountain peaks reached on foot or by cable car, deep valleys threaded through with little streams, forests and open spaces resplendent with rhododendrons, iris and edelweiss. The only trouble is that the more places you want to see the more you have to keep doubling back on your tracks. There are comparatively few roads, and some of them have stretches which can be anything from difficult to dangerous. However, with a little ingenuity it is possible to discover delightful hamlets consisting of a few houses and a small basic inn where the owner will be only too pleased to draw attention to anything of interest, be it scenic or historical. In the absence of any informed advice the temptation to branch off along a likely looking shortcut ought to be resisted whenever possible. The chances are that you will run out of road before you get where you are going, which means leaving the car, probably under a tree, and completing the journey on foot. Unless this sort of thing appeals to you it is far better to stick to the larger roads or decide to walk or go by bicycle, taking advantage of paths and cart tracks which lead to otherwise inaccessible places. There are opportunities for shooting, fishing, climbing and potholing and local information offices will provide all necessary details such as where to go, what to take and whether a licence is necessary.

Even without venturing into the wilder sections of the National Park there are just as many different activities available and as great a variety of things to see. For instance, the underground caves at **Betharram**, discovered nearly two hundred years ago, are well equipped to receive visitors. They are open both morning and afternoon during the season with boat trips along the subterranean river, a little train that cuts down walking time and a selection of fascinating grottoes to explore. The nearby sanctuaries of Betharram include a seventeenth-century church while St Pé-de-Bigorre, about the same distance away in the opposite direction, was the site of an abbey dedicated to St Peter whose name, for some reason or other, has been abbreviated to St Pé. The Wars of Religion took their toll but a fourteenth-century statue of Notre-Dame-des-Miracles has survived and can be seen in the sanctuary. Further afield there are enough forests and streams to satisfy even the most demanding open-air enthusiast in addition to several hills that are worth climbing for the view. Le Béout makes things easy with a cable car to the summit where the panorama takes in a couple of valleys, as well as many other peaks and more than a casual glimpse of **Lourdes**.

If, as the publicity brochures insist, 'all the world goes to Lourdes' one would expect to find a sprawling metropolis filled with high-rise hotels and apartment blocks, supermarkets, boutiques and souvenir shops. Naturally they do exist, but in spite of this the description is wide of the mark. By no stretch of imagination could this beguiling town with its reputation for miracle cures be described as 'off the beaten track' but it is unlikely that any traveller, however allergic to crowds, would pass by without a second glance. Lourdes was originally a stronghold belonging to the Counts of Bigorre but in 1858 young Bernadette Soubirous told her family and friends that she had seen and talked to the Virgin Mary in a grotto on the far side of the river. After the same thing had happened several times even the clergy were inclined to believe her. She went into a convent run by the Sisters of Charity and in 1933, a little more than 50 years after her death, she was canonised. In the meantime the grotto and the fields about it had changed considerably. A statue of the Virgin was placed in a niche in the rock, a rather severe altar was added, invariably surrounded by bowls of fresh flowers and lit by dozens of candles, and building work began in earnest. Three superimposed churches appeared between 1871 and 1889, followed in 1958 by a huge underground basilica which can hold 20,000 people. The miraculous water that figured largely in the visions of Ste Bernadette was directed into fountains and from there to pools designed especially for invalids. As the number of pilgrims increased so did the museums devoted to religious matters and soon a variety of places associated with her began to attract large crowds. They include her birthplace at **Cachot**, the parish church where she was baptised and the old hospital with all its pictures and souvenirs. During the season there are ceremonies every day ending with a torchlight procession in the evening. Pilgrimages are organised at intervals from Easter to the middle of

October, starting with a Festival of Music and Sacred Art.

Although the town is somewhat preoccupied with the spiritual side of life there is no reason why the out and out pagan should not enjoy a visit just as much. The fortified castle, reached by a lift, a long ramp used by the one-time owners or a formidable number of steps, dominates the scene, rising out of a tree-covered hill overlooking the river. It is open throughout the year and contains an old chapel and an extremely interesting Pyrénéan museum. There are areas set aside for football, rugby, tennis, pelota and clay pigeon shooting, not to mention judo, karate and athletics. Swimmers have a choice of two municipal pools, one of which is covered and heated, or the lake which is shared by fishermen, boat owners and water-skiers. Riding stables can be found at Benac and St Pé-de-Bigorre, the streams are stocked with trout and the mountains are ideal for climbing and walking. Some half dozen ski resorts operate well into the spring and a funicular railway up to the Pic du Jer runs at regular intervals all through the year. Excursions are available to any number of places in the vicinity including spectacular mountain passes, attractive lakes and waterfalls and spas like Cauterets that have quite a few attractions of their own.

Lourdes shares a large airport with **Tarbes**, 19km (12 miles) away. It is a much bigger town concerned mainly with commerce and industry and is decidedly short on buildings of historic or architectural interest. However it has some very comfortable hotels and anyone of a military turn of mind would probably spend a few days there most profitably. The first place to see is the Jardin Massey, partly because it is a delightful park and partly on account of the Musée International des Hussards. This covers some five hundred years of army history, with particular emphasis on the cavalry, and is full of lifelike figures decked out in the appropriate uniforms, fully equipped and armed to the teeth. Apart from Mondays and Tuesdays, it is open every day with a 2-hour break for lunch. A short walk away is the house where Marshal Foch was born. It traces his career in considerable detail from his enlistment in 1870, through his outstanding achievements on the Western Front during World War I to his death in 1929 when he was buried with due ceremony at Les Invalides in Paris. A little further down the appropriately-named Avenue du Régiment-de-Bigorre, more or less opposite the barracks, is a large stud which has been training and providing horses for the French cavalry during the past hundred years or so. There are guided tours each afternoon except on Sundays from July until early in February.

Less than half an hour's drive to the south-west is **Capvern-les-Bains**, a spa town that not only ministers to the sick but takes an interest in keep-fit fanatics. There are several hotels and *auberges*, any number of furnished apartments and a couple of caravan sites. Visitors can play tennis or golf, use the gymnasium and the sauna, go for long walks and gamble at the casino. The Château Mauvezin, which like the castle at Lourdes once belonged to the Counts of Bigorre, is an added attraction. It is open daily from May to October and has, among other things, a folklore museum and a good view of the ancient Abbaye de l'Escaladieu which is also open to the public, except during January and February.

Somewhat less inviting is the ruined fortress at Montaner, much closer to Tarbes in the opposite direction. It is described as an ancient château but in fact looks much more like an arena with a tower attached. It is reached by way of a series of little roads through countryside which is pleasant enough although not particularly scenic. Tiny hamlets pop up now and then and the traffic is much lighter than the volume that sometimes has to be contended with on the main route from Tarbes to Pau, the capital of the Béarn.

Anyone who knows **Pau** and is asked to describe it usually starts off with the word elegant, which is precisely what it is. Of course this does not apply to the suburbs which have a tendency to sprawl and are much the same as the outskirts of any other town. However, they have not been allowed to encroach on the historic centre with its beautiful parks and gardens and the famous Boulevard des Pyrénées looking out over the river towards the mountains. At one end is the Château de Gaston Fébus, designed as a fortress but transformed into a castle in the early sixteenth century by Marguerite d'Angoulême, sister of François I, who married the King of Navarre. Several other heads of state, including a brace of Louis and as many Napoleons, looked in now and again, each one adding a touch or two of his own. The result is a fascinating mixture of styles surrounding a large courtyard with a triple arch at one end and a tower at each corner. The royal apartments on the first floor have been incorporated into the National Museum with decorations and furniture that would make Henry IV feel perfectly at home. His tortoise shell crib stands in the room where he was born, there are some regal tapestries on the walls, not much in the way of carpets and several chairs are drawn up to a table beside his bed as if a few friends were about to join him for a game of Cardinal Puff. The third floor of the château is given over to the Musée Béarnais which includes a little bit of everything from folklore and furniture, through local architecture and traditional costumes to birds and bears.

The Musée des Beaux Arts has a building all to itself and has got together a varied collection spanning some four hundred years, augmented by medals and coins. Finally there is the Musée Bernadotte, the birthplace of Jean-Baptiste who rose to the rank of marshal in Napoleon's armies before being crowned King Charles XIV of Sweden in 1818.

It was shortly after this that the British began to set their seal on Pau. A certain Doctor Taylor encouraged his more well heeled patients to winter in the Béarn and they, in turn, introduced steeplechasing, with a course reputed to be second only to Aintree, fox hunting and golf. The 18-hole course, laid out beside the river in 1856, is the oldest on the Continent and has recently been joined by the Royal Golf Club du Domaine-St-Michel where members can swim and play tennis and squash as well. Apart from other tennis courts and swimming pools Pau has a motor racing circuit for Grand Prix events and a sailing school, provides routes for hikers and caves for potholing as well as an attractive casino in the tree-filled Parc Beaumont at the eastern end of the Boulevard des Pyrénées. There is no shortage of hotels of any size or of restaurants offering international cuisine alongside good home cooking. Shops can be anything from small, sophisticated and expensive to covered markets which are essentially cheap and cheerful. They are particularly useful for anyone renting an apartment or parking a caravan on one of the sites outside the town.

Several museums in the region display what they describe as 'Pièces de Samadet', one of the largest collections being in the château at Lourdes. It is a distinctive type of earthenware, decorated with fairly basic flowers, butterflies and so on, which was all the rage at court in the eighteenth century until the Revolution put a temporary stop to such frivolities. One of the best places to inspect it is in **Samadet** itself where a most informative museum has been opened in a house that once belonged to the Abbé de Roquépine. It traces the whole process with life-size figures demonstrating the various stages of their art. A potter, seated on a bench, appears to be turning a large wheel with his feet in order to rotate the smaller one on which the clay is worked. Next door a painter, using a design pricked out on transparent paper, creates various patterns with something that looks rather like a quill. The job completed, the plates are stacked in a rack, half a dozen or more at a time, and put into the old kiln in the corner to be fired. Examples of the finished articles are displayed in glass cases in an adjoining room.

The museum also provides an accurate picture of the way people lived in those days. The labourer has an all-purpose room with a fireplace, a bed covered by what could easily be taken for a modern duvet and two oxen with their heads protruding through an opening in the wall. Apparently this was the way cattle were fed during the winter, which is a trifle confusing as there does not seem to be anywhere for fodder to be stored. A bourgeois family with a much higher income possesses some excellent furniture including a superb grandfather clock, has carpets on the floor and a bed warmer which consists of a pot of live coals suspended inside a metal contraption which, hopefully, prevents the bedclothes from catching fire. In the well stocked kitchen something exactly like a ladder is suspended high up in front of the fire. It would have been ideal for airing the laundry but in fact was used for storing bread and hams. Elsewhere there are all the tools necessary for making rope-soled shoes and *sabots,* spinning hemp and flax, operating a forge, cutting up logs and running the farm.

Roughly half way along the road to Aire-sur-l'Adour there is a branch off northwards to **Eugénie-les-Bains**, famous mainly on account of a hotel run by Michel Guérard whose name is painted in large letters on the surrounding wall. Quite a few people consider it to be one of the best hotels with undoubtedly one of the most superb restaurants in the whole of France. It has all the decorative refinements of the nineteenth century allied to every modern comfort, is set in delightful gardens full of trees, ponds and flowering shrubs and provides tennis and swimming but, sadly, all this luxury does not come at bargain prices. The village is a pleasant little place with thermal baths and half a dozen other hotels.

Aire-sur-l'Adour is known as the *foie gras* capital, and you cannot get more up-market than that! Along the roadsides in every direction are signs inviting passers-by to call in for truffles, *foie gras* and, occasionally, Armagnac. Provided the visitor has had the foresight to buy some delicious fresh bread, a little butter and a bottle of Tursan wine before working out the quickest way to a shady river bank, this must surely be one of the most satisfying places to have an impromptu picnic. The town itself is small and moderately industrial with a church whose history goes back to Roman times. It contains the body of the martyred Ste Quitterie encased in marble in the crypt. There is also a run-of-the-mill cathedral, racecourse, arena, swimming pool and a handful of modest hotels.

Still heading north, a spiderweb of reliable little roads tempt the traveller into the heart of the brandy country where every second village has 'd'Armagnac' tagged on after its name. The area is fairly wooded between the vineyards and is criss-crossed by small streams that run in and out of tiny lakes and ponds. Anyone who is planning to take home a bottle of Armagnac, but whose motto is 'try before you buy', would be well advised to make for **Labastide d'Armagnac**. It is a very small town indeed, hardly more than a square surrounded by arcades attached to elderly houses with a church in one corner, but it is the nearest place to the seventeenth-century château Garreau. A road that could certainly do with some expert attention leads to the château which specialises in brandy of various ages, half a dozen different liqueurs, trains young people and runs a miniscule museum. It is open all year round with a tour of the cellars and distillery thrown in on Tuesdays and Thursdays. Machinery, some of it well over a hundred years old and showing its age, stands around the walls, leaving space for a counter where samples are offered for tasting and bottles are sold. Among the list of suggestions put forward by the management are iced Armagnac served 'on the rocks' and Floc de Gascogne, described as a liqueur but intended as an *apéritif,* well chilled and accompanied by *foie gras* or *confits*, a national delicacy made from pork or duck. These are also sold on the premises along with various fruits preserved in the appropriate manner.

Visitors feeling a bit peckish and in need of something more substantial for lunch are directed to any of three *auberges* a few minutes' drive away. Tourists on bicycles might well decide to set out fractionally early in order to visit the chapel of Notre-Dame-des-Cyclists, just off the road to **Barbotan-les-Thermes**. This is a small spa with beautiful gardens, an attractive main street lined with shops and lovely wooded country all round. It is also rather overblessed with hotels which means that it can be crowded. On the medical side it concentrates on rheumatism and its allied complaints but also provides tennis, riding and naturism for people who have no need to take the waters in search of a cure. A direct route, due east, passes through Casteinau with its little lake, Montréal complete with a ruined church and the remains of a Roman villa at Séviac about two kilometres (a mile) away and Larressingle, an ancient fortified village that has been completely restored.

Condom, more fortunate in its history than in its name, is worth a visit, partly to see the Gothic Cathédrale St Pierre. It was built in the early sixteenth century and is filled with statues, the one in St Peter's chapel looking exactly like Joan of Arc. It has been embellished quite recently and is unexpectedly light inside. Next door is the ancient Chapelle des Evêques and behind them both, a block away, are

Henry IV mill at Barbaste

streets of old houses presenting more or less the same united front as they did some two hundred years ago. The Musée de l'Armagnac has taken over part of the original Palais des Evêques and is open daily but closes on Mondays and on most official holidays. The Abbaye de Flaran, to the south, was founded in 1151 with a cloister added a couple of centuries later but it is no longer inhabited by monks. Instead it has been transformed into a cultural centre which is always shut on Mondays.

La Romieu, east of Condom, owes its existence to Arnaud d'Aux, a relative of Clement V, the first pope to hold sway in Avignon. It has not fared particularly well over the past seven hundred years but there is a good deal to see, including the tombs of the cardinal and members of his family and the remnants of a palace that was once his home. By completing three-quarters of a circle round Condom, more for the drive than anything else because there is little to recommend it apart from an odd view and a means of avoiding the main roads to the north, it is an idea to stop briefly at **Fources**. Brief is the operative word because it is an incredibly small and completely circular fortified hamlet founded by the English in the thirteenth century, and does not appear to have changed much since. The houses are built on arches overlooking an open space in the middle with their backs to the walls and that is all there is to it, but the atmosphere is worth the extra mileage. The same could be said of **Durance**, although it is decidedly angular and looks rather the worse for wear. An extremely solid tower-archway promises great things but produces nothing except two dilapidated old houses and several comparatively new ones. It is necessary to search round for the ruins of a château that belonged to Henry IV and the ancient Grange Priory on the edge of the forest. It is much easier to find the twelfth-century château at Xaintrailles which was modernised three hundred years later by Jean Poton who fought alongside Joan of Arc.

Barbaste is infinitely more rewarding for anyone who wants to come to terms with Henry IV or simply needs a shady spot to park a caravan. The king had an impressive mill on the banks of the river, reached by a fascinating bridge, built of stone and wide enough for a single horseman, with small triangles jutting out at intervals on either side. They are just big enough to hold an armed soldier or give refuge to anyone unfortunate enough to be caught in transit when the royal party arrived home from hunting or fighting a minor war. The mill, which in spite of its name looks more like a smallish palace, was well fortified and must have been a thoroughly desirable country residence in its time. The town on the other side of the river is small and friendly and the caravan park seems to be quite well equipped. Travellers in search of a bed for the night would be wise to press on to Lavardac with its little *auberge* or head south to Nérac where there would probably be less difficulty in finding a room.

Whichever way you look at it **Nérac** is an enchanting town. The old quarter is a tangle of twisted alleys with houses that have not changed very much since the castle was built back in the Middle Ages. The church of Notre-Dame is tucked away towards the far corner, almost opposite a sixteenth-century bridge and no distance from the Palais du Tribunal and a seventeenth-century town hall. Further up river is the large Garenne Parc with a profusion of trees and several fountains including the aptly-named Fountain of Daisies and the Castle of Nazareth that once belonged to the Templars. The whole area is overlooked by the castle of Henry IV, named after him in spite of the fact that it was actually built before he was born. It is a typical blending of half-timbered apartments protected at strategic intervals by high stone walls and it is not difficult to visualise Marguerite d'Angoulême, Catherine de Medici and members of the Valois family drifting through the various rooms. The museum which has taken their place brings history to life through collections of prehistoric and Roman relics and illustrates the subsequent life and times of ancient Nérac with many personal touches and some rather nice old paintings. The somewhat dour church of St Nicholas

Henry IV castle at Nérac

is right beside it and the little streets beyond are full of attractive houses but very few hotels.

The country round about is not especially interesting although Nérac is one of Aquitaine's designated holiday resorts. It puts itself out to entertain visitors, even to the extent of building two new golf courses and keeping the castle museum open all through the year. In addition it is only 30km (18$^1/_2$ miles) from Agen and the River Garonne , or a trifle more if the drive is planned so as to include the château at Estillac and the small village of Aubiac where there is an old church. **Agen** itself is fairly large and lively with arcaded streets, river frontage and an attractive bridge spanning the canal. The cathedral of St Caprais dates from the twelfth century but it is less absorbing than the Musée des Beaux Arts. The tapestries, furniture, medieval jewellery, ceramics and paintings all attract their own particular crowds and there is a natural history section to round off the visit. A few small gardens can be found quite close to the centre of the town and there are plenty of hotels and restaurants which are quite adequate without being in any way spectacular and some of them stay open twelve months of the year.

The only thing one has to decide when leaving Agen is which route to take on the journey home. There is a fairly direct road to Paris through Limoges and Orléans, a host of alternatives for anyone with enough time left to sample the delights of the Perigord, while the average driver who chooses the Autoroute des Deux Mers should take no more than two hours to reach Bordeaux where the trip began.

Further Information
— Aquitaine —

Museums and Other Places of Interest

Agen
Museum of Fine Arts
Open: daily 10am-12noon and 2-6pm. Closed Tuesdays.

Arcachon
Museum of the Sea
Open: 10am-12 noon and 2-7pm. Palm Sunday to end October. All day during July and August.

Arudy
Museum of Flora and Fauna
☎59-05-80-44 for details.

Barbaste
Henry IV Mill
Not open at time of going to press.

Bayonne
Basque Museum
Open: 9.30am-12.30pm and 2.30-6.30pm (10am-12noon and 2.30-5.30pm in winter). Closed Sundays and public holidays.

Béliet-Belin
Lapios Centre
Traditional music and bagpipes.

Betharram
Caves and Sanctuaries of Betharram
Open morning and afternoon during the season. Enquire at the tourist office in Lourdes.

Biarritz
Museum of the Sea
Open: 9am-7pm daily in summer. Otherwise 9am-12noon and 2-6pm.

Bidache
Castle Gramont
Open: no specific times, enquire from caretaker.

Biscarrosse
Sea Plane Museum
Open all day during summer, no specific times.

Bonnat
Museum of Fine Arts
Open: 10am-12noon and 4-8pm in the season. Varies in winter. Closed Tuesdays.

Bordeaux
Casa de Goya
Open: 2-6.30pm. Closed Sat and Sun.

Centre Jean-Moulin Resistance Museum
Open: 2-6pm. Closed Saturdays, Sundays and public holidays.

Contemporary Arts Museum
Open: 9am-12noon and 1-6pm. Closed Sundays.

Customs Museum
Open: 10am-12noon and 1.30-5.30pm. Closed Mondays.

Decorative Arts Museum
Open: 2-6pm. Closed Tuesdays.

Fine Arts Museum
Open: 10am-12noon and 2-5pm. Closed Tuesdays.

The impressive ruin of Château de Bonaguil, Agenais-Périgord-Quercy

Périgueux, Agenais-Périgord-Quercy

La Roque Gageac, one of the most spectacular villages along the banks of the Dordogne, Agenais-Périgord-Quercy

Musée d'Aquitaine
Open: 2-6pm. Closed Tues and Sun.

Natural History Museum
Open: 2-5.30pm. Closed Tuesdays and
mid-September to mid-June.

Cachot
Birthplace of Bernadette
Open: daily 2.30-5.30pm.

Cambo-les-Bains
Musée Rostand
Open: May-Sept 10am-12noon and
2.30-6.30pm; October 2.30-6.30pm only.

**Between Cambo-les-Bains and St
Palais**
Grottes d'Isturits et d'Oxocelhaya
Near Cambo-les-Bains
Open: mid-March to mid-November
9am-12noon and 2-6.30pm.

Capvern-les-Bains
Château de Mauvezin
Open: May 10am-12noon and 2-7pm;
June to mid-October 9am-12noon and
2-7pm; Sundays and holidays to
7.30pm; mid-October to April, Sundays
and holidays 2-6pm.

Condom
Armagnac Museum
Open: June-mid-Sept 10am-12noon and
2-6pm. Otherwise closed at 5pm. Also
closed Mon, Sundays in winter, 1
January, Ascension Day, 14 July, 15
August, 1 November and 25 December.

Dax
Musée Borda
Open: 2-6pm. Closed Saturday and
Sunday, November to May.

Hastingues
Abbaye d'Arthous nearby
Open: April to October, 9am-12noon
and 2-6pm; November to March 9.30am-
12noon and 2-5pm. Closed Tuesdays.

Labastide-d'Armagnac
Museum and brandy tasting
Open: daily 9am-12noon and 3-7pm.

Lourdes
Château and Pyrénéan Museum
Open: 9-11am and 2-6pm. Closed at
5pm September to June.

Pavillon Notre-Dame
Open: 9-11.45am and 2.30-6pm. Closed
at 5.30pm on Mondays and from mid-
October to Easter.

Luxey
Resin Museum
Open: June-mid-September daily with
tours at 10 and 11 am and 2, 3, 4, 5 and
6pm. Otherwise 10am-12noon and 2-
7pm. March-November Saturday
afternoons, Sundays and holidays only.

Mimizan
Museum
Open: mid-June to mid-September
10.30am-12.30pm and 2.30-6.30pm.
Sundays 2.30-6.30pm. Closed Tuesday.

Mont-de-Marsan
Musée Despiau-Wlérick
Open: 9.30am-12noon and 2-6pm.
Closed Tuesdays.

Musée Dubalen
Open: 9.30am-12noon and 2-6pm.
Closed Tuesdays.

Open-Air Museum
Open: 9.30am-12noon and 2-6pm.
Closed Tuesdays.

Nérac
Henry IV Castle Museum
Open: 9-11am and 2-5pm. Closed
Mondays and 1 January, 1 May, 1
November and 25 December.

Pau
Béarnais Museum (in château)
Open: 9.30am-12.30pm and 2.30-5.30pm

Bernadotte Museum
Open: 10am-6pm. Closed Mondays.

Musée des Beaux Arts
Open: 10am-12noon and 2-6pm. Closed
Tuesdays.

National Museum (in château)
Open: 10am-12noon and 2-5.30pm in
summer. Closes at 4.45pm in winter.

Parentis-en-Born
Petroleum Museum
Open: Easter to end October 9am-
12noon and 2-6pm. Closed Tuesdays.

Sabres
Ecomusée Village
Trains daily at frequent intervals when
the village is open.
Open: mid-June to mid-September
daily; March to November Saturday,
Sunday and holidays, pm only.

St Jean-de-Luz
Maison Louis XIV
Open: 10.30am-12.30pm and 3.30-
6.30pm July and August. 10am-12noon
and 3-6pm June and September. Closed
Sunday mornings.

St Jean-Pied-de-Port
Basque Museum
No specified opening times. Enquire at
the Information Office.

Samadet
Musée des Faïences de Samadet
Open: daily 10am-12noon and 2-6pm.
Closed Monday and Tuesday.

Tarbes
The Harras
Open: July to mid-February. Guided
tours 2.30-5pm. Closed Sundays.

Maréchal Foch Museum
Open: July to mid-September 8am-
12noon and 2.30-5.45pm. Otherwise 2-
5pm only. Closed Tuesdays and
Wednesday, 1 January, 1 May, 1 and 11
November and 25 December.

Musée Internationale des Hussards
Open: daily 10am-12noon and 2-6pm.
Closed Mondays and Tuesdays.

Tourist Information Offices

Arcachon
Place Franklin Roosevelt
☎ 56-83-01-69

Bayonne
Place de la Liberté
☎ 59-59-31-31

Biarritz
Square d'Ixelles
☎ 59-24-20-24

Bordeaux
12 Cours 30-Juillet
☎ 56-44-28-41

Capvern-les-Bains
Rue Thermes
☎ 62-39-00-46
Open: May to mid-October.

Dax
Place Thiers
☎ 58-74-82-33

Lourdes
Place du Champ-Commun
☎ 62-94-15-64

Mont-de-Marsan
22 Rue Victor-Hugo
☎ 58-75-38-67

Nérac
At the Mairie
☎ 53-65-03-89

Oloron Ste Marie
Place de la Résistance
☎ 59-39-98-00

Pau
Place Royale
☎ 59-27-27-08

St Jean-de-Luz
Place Maréchal Foch
☎ 59-26-03-16

St Jean-Pied-de-Port
Place Charles de Gaulle
☎ 59-37-03-57

2 • Agenais-Périgord-Quercy

Agenais

A gen, the prefecture (county town) of the department of Lot et Garonne, is one of the oldest towns in France. There was an important settlement here on the Garonne, halfway between Bordeaux and Toulouse, more than a thousand years before the Romans arrived in 56BC, called it *Aginnum* and made it the capital of the area.

But today all vestiges of its Roman occupation lie buried beneath its streets and it is a neat, modern town, with little sign of its long history. But it is still the chief market and trading centre for all the fruits and produce of the fertile land which the Romans loved so much. To the rest of France, Agen is famous for two things, rugby football and prunes. The rugby team have often been champions of France. The surrounding countryside has many plum orchards, and after California, the Agenais is the world's biggest producer of prunes, made by oven-drying the plums. Peaches, pears, apples, melons, cherries and strawberries, are widely grown, and there is a huge production of tomatoes, peas, beans, asparagus, and artichokes. Visitors who arrive in September, should try the juicy, delicious prunes called *mi-cuit* (half-dried). Not many are produced, as they are difficult to transport successfully, and they are soon snapped up.

For the tourist, Agen is a town of limited interest. Its cathedral, St Caprais, dates from the twelfth century, but was very heavily restored during the nineteenth century, and is of moderate interest compared with the majority of French cathedrals. But the municipal museum, converted from three restored mansions of the sixteenth and seventeenth centuries, which have been made intercommunicating, is well worth a visit. The pride of the museum is the *Venus de Mas*, a beautifully sculpted marble statue dating from the first century BC. It was unearthed by a farmer near the little town of Mas d'Agen, in 1876. The statue has lost its head and an arm, but the body, more youthful than that of the Venus de Milo, is sculpted with equal

35

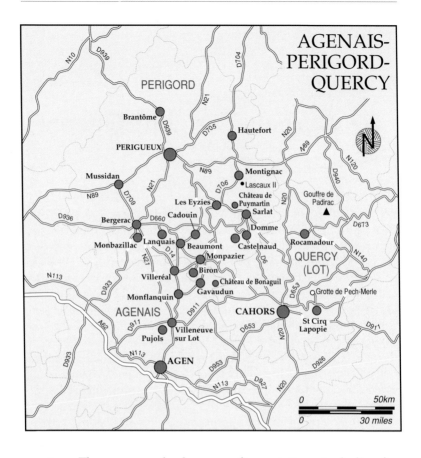

mastery. The museum also has some fine paintings, including five Goyas, the 'Pond at Ville d'Avray' by the great landscape artist, Corot, works by Courbet and Watteau, and a number of important Impressionist pictures.

Agen has a wide promenade, the Graviere, beside the Garonne. A 500m (1,640ft) long aqueduct with 23 arches carries the Canal Laterale a la Garonne over the river. The aqueduct includes a footbridge. Agen is served by the A62, the Autoroute des Deux Mers, which crosses the region from north-west to south-east linking Bordeaux and Toulouse with the Mediterranean coast, and by the N21, from Limoges to the Pyrénées, which runs north to south through Lot et Garonne. The high speed TGV trains linking Paris to Bordeaux and Toulouse, stop at Agen. The nearest international airports are Bordeaux and Toulouse, and Agen has its own airport for internal French services.

The charming scenery of this countryside is not seen at its best from the big main roads, though there are places on the N21 between Villeneuve sur Lot and Bergerac, where the villages on isolated hilltops and poplar-lined streams in the valleys make it clear why the great writer, Stendhal, described this region as the Tuscany of France. Once you get off the main roads you will find delightful secret valleys with wooded hillsides, tumbling streams and small lakes. The tiny villages are named after long-forgotten saints, St Colombe, St Julien, St Eutrope, St Pastour, and linked by narrow roads, sometimes grass-grown in the middle, and edged with banks where bees drone among the wild flowers all summer long. Keen walkers will find that this lovely and varied countryside is crossed by several of the GR (Grande Randonnée) footpaths, including GR65, GR652, GR69, and GR636.

Wherever the visitor goes there is likely to be something of historical interest, some survival from the distant past, for the whole area was in dispute between the English and the French throughout the 120 years conflict known as the Hundred Years War. This long struggle was sparked off at a village in the Agenais called **St Sardos** — another forgotten saint. St Sardos had been in English-held territory since 1303, and Edward II, King of England and Duke of Aquitaine, took exception to the fact that the French had taken it over and fortified it. Charles IV replied that he was simply defending the priory, which was dependant on the Abbey of Sarlat, which was French. In 1323, a number of Anglo-Gascon barons supporting Edward II, attacked and sacked St Sardos. The following year Charles IV sent an army into Aquitaine, and recaptured most of the Plantagenet territories. The Hundred Years War had begun.

Today, St Sardos is a tiny village lost in rustic calm. The priory has long since disappeared, and the church on the site is undistinguished nineteenth century, but there are still a few medieval houses.

It was the Hundred Years War which gave this countryside its most characteristic feature, the fortified villages, known as 'bastides', which were built as strongholds, some by the French, some by the English, at strategic points throughout Aquitaine. The bastides were built to a basic plan which, with few exceptions, varied little from one to another. They were rectangles, crossed by a road from top to bottom and another from side to side. Where the roads met, there was the market square, with the church at one side. The bastide was normally walled all round, and had four gates. Between the walls and the central roads there were narrower streets. Most of the bastides came into existence all at once, being built and inhabited within a year and they must originally, because of their uniformity, have been a good deal less picturesque than they are now.

Any visitor to the region should make a tour of some of the bastides, either of their own choice of route, or following, for example, the signposted Circuit des Bastides in the northern part of Lot et Garonne. A good starting point is **Villeneuve sur Lot**, which was the first of the bastides. It was Alphonse de Poitiers, brother of King Louis IX (St Louis), who founded Villeneuve sur Lot in 1253. Unlike almost all the others, which are on easily defended hilltops, Villeneuve was built in a valley on both sides of the River Lot. Perhaps, because of this more accessible position, at an east-west north-south cross-roads, Villeneuve is one of the few bastides which has expanded, and the old bastide, with two of its gates still remaining, is now at the heart of the town. It is a pleasant country town where markets are held in the central square, which has kept its ancient arcades, on Tuesday and Saturday mornings. From the conventional tourist point of view Villeneuve is of limited interest. Its church, St Catherine, consecrated in 1937 after many years of building, is an red brick edifice in Romanesque-Byzantine style, but has some restored four-teenth- and fifteenth-century stained glass saved from the previous church on the site. The town's Gaston Rapin Museum is undistin-guished. The bastide quarter, now a pedestrianised shopping area, still has some restored medieval buildings, one of the best of which is the Maison de Viguerie, the old court house, dating from 1369.

The nearest bastide to Villeneuve is the old walled village of **Pujols**, only 3km (2 miles) walk away. The hill you climb as you approach the village is known as Alaric's camp. When the Roman Empire in the west came to an end it was followed in the fifth century AD by an invasion of the Visigoths, who ruled Aquitaine for 100 years. During this invasion Alaric the Goth camped on this hill. Pujols itself with its thirteenth-century church of St Nicholas, and its thirteenth-century walls and houses, has been heavily restored in the past 20 years, and from being an almost complete ruin, is now a centre for craftsmen, artists, and antique dealers. On Sunday morn-ings the local farmers' wives hold a market there to sell home-made cheeses, jams, honey, ham, pâtés, country bread and cakes. Cars are not allowed in the village, and a parking place, from which there is a splendid view over Villeneuve and the valley of the Lot, is provided just outside the walls.

If you take the D676 north from Villeneuve, a 16km (10 mile) drive brings you to another interesting bastide, **Monflanquin**. Situated at the top of an isolated conical hill, and visible throughout the countryside, Monflanquin was also founded by Alphonse de Poitiers, in 1256. Its square still has all its arcades, and is surrounded by well-restored medieval houses. The village has a church in southern Gothic style, heavily damaged in the seventeenth-century Wars of Religion. The nave and the choir were rebuilt in 1673, and the fifteenth-century fortified façade has also been restored. Near the church there is a terrace with extensive views eastwards over the countryside as far as the Château de Biron, just across the departmental border in Dordogne.

Thirteen kilometres (8 miles) north of Monflanquin on the D676 there is another attractive bastide, **Villeréal**, also built by Alphonse de Poitiers. In the market square Villeréal has a splendid oak-timbered market hall built in the fourteenth century, with an upper storey which was added 200 years later.

It is a pleasant drive from Monflanquin via the D150 to Gavaudun (11km/7 miles) and on through the pretty valley of the Lede to Lacapelle Biron (7km/4 miles). **Gavaudun** is a once-fortified village, which still has its stone gateway and, high on the cliff immediately above, the keep of the ruined castle. Near the gateway at the foot of the hill there is a café which offers snacks and light meals.

Lacapelle Biron was founded only in the eighteenth century, when the local lord objected to the noise of the market which was held beneath the walls of his château at Biron, and ordered the stallholders to move further away. They moved 5km (3 miles) to the site which has become Lacapelle Biron, which is just inside Lot et Garonne. **Biron** itself is just across the border in Dordogne, but it fits naturally into a tour of this group of bastides, though it is not a bastide itself — the first castle on the site was built more than 50 years before the first bastide — and it is simply a classic example of a medieval fortress with its dependant village. Biron is particularly interesting both historically and architecturally, since it remained in the hands of the Gontaut-Biron family for more than 700 years and through fourteen generations, until it was bought by the Dordogne department about 20 years ago. Throughout that time different members of the family added to and rebuilt the castle so that it is now a massive structure reflecting a number of different periods of architecture. The Gontaut-Birons, the premier barons of Périgord, were an extremely important family, who often produced marshals and admirals of France, and were friends of the royal family. They also had a streak of treachery. The worst of them, Charles de Gontaut-Biron, was a friend of Henry IV, France's most popular king, who made him a duke and governor of Burgundy as well as a marshal of France. In return Charles de Gontaut-Biron launched a plot against the king which would have broken up France and given him a kingdom of his own. He was found out, but Henry forgave him. Undaunted, he continued to plot and was again caught out. The magnanimous Henry offered to pardon him, if he would confess his crime. De Gontaut-Biron haughtily refused, and was beheaded in the Bastille in 1602.

The de Gontaut-Birons considered themselves even greater than they were. The unique chapel is a monument to their self-importance. Having decided that it was beneath them to worship with the common people, they built their own chapel on top of the existing parish church, so that the common people should worship beneath them. So the chapel has two naves — the upper one with an entrance from the castle courtyard for the use of the family only, and a lower one which continued in use as a parish church.

The castle, which is on a height dominating the surrounding countryside for a radius of 30km (19 miles), is slowly being restored. It has the largest vaulted kitchens in France, an impressive state hall, and monumental staircase. In summer it is used for concerts, exhibitions of paintings and sculpture, and the work of different craftsmen.

From Biron it is only 8km (5 miles) by the D53 and then the D104 to **Monpazier**, one of the most attractive bastides in France. It is a short but scenic drive, but those who prefer a walk, can do it on foot by picking up the G36 which crosses Biron.

Monpazier was built in 1284 for Edward I of England as a bastion against Villefranche du Périgord, 20km (12 miles) away to the southeast (by D660), which had been built for the French king in 1261. Throughout the Hundred Years War this tit-for-tat building of opposing bastides went on, and it was not uncommon for them to attack each other. There is a story that the people of Monpazier and Villefranche planned in secret to raid each other's town. By coincidence, they chose the same night and, having marched across country by different routes, each carried out their raid, with remarkably little opposition, and returned home staggering under the weight of their booty, only to find that they, too, had been looted.

During the Hundred Years War Monpazier was captured and recaptured between the French and the English six times. During the Religious Wars of the sixteenth century it changed hands between the Catholics and the Protestants. In the early seventeenth century Monpazier was the centre of a revolt of starving peasants, led by a weaver named Buffarot. At the head of a mob of 8,000, armed only with pitchforks, he terrorised the countryside and plundered the

Monpazier, one of the most attractive bastides in France

castles. Their success was short-lived. The Governor of Aquitaine, the Duc d'Epernon, sent in troops who subdued the revolt and captured Buffarot, who was broken on the wheel in the market square of Monpazier.

If the visitor should want to see only one bastide, Monpazier, is a good choice. The layout is the same, three of its towered gateways remain, as well as many ancient houses, the thirteenth-century church with fifteenth-century additions, and the arcaded market square.

Today Monpazier is both peaceful and picturesque, and is known now as the 'capital of mushrooms' for the region. Its busiest days are during the autumn and winter, when on certain days there are 'fairs' for the sale of the delicious *cèpes de Bordeaux*, second in esteem only to the famous Périgord black truffles, which are also marketed in Monpazier. The old enemy, **Villefranche du Périgord** is less frequented, but it, too, is little changed from the original bastide. The market square has an ancient covered market with roof supported on massive stone columns, and still has its old grain measures. The circuit of this group of bastides can be completed by returning to Monpazier, and then to Villereal, Monflanquin, and Villeneuve.

Throughout the countryside of the Agenais there are numerous *pigeonniers*, or pigeon-houses. These buildings were originally status

The Château de Bonaguil in Lot et Garonne

symbols, as farmers were not allowed to have them unless they possessed sufficient land for the pigeons to find all their food on it without invading a neighbour's territory. Some of them were integrated with the house or château itself, and some were erected separate from, but close to, the main building. They vary widely in design, and some are large enough to house hundreds of birds, and unlike the usual English dovecot they had a practical as well as an ornamental value. The pigeons were kept as a food supply, and as a source of manure, which the farmer sold to lesser farmers, or used on his own fields. This pigeon guano was so rich that it had to be diluted with rainwater to avoid harming the crops, and was considered so valuable that it was divided among a farmer's heirs in the same proportion as the land itself.

There are many châteaux in Lot et Garonne, but most of them are in private hands and not open to the public. One which is open and well-worth visiting is the **Château de Bonaguil**, in the east of the department. It can be reached directly from Villeneuve sur Lot via the D911 to the Monsempron-Lisbos-Fumel complex, then after Fumel fork left on to the D673, signposted Château de Bonaguil, and then after about 4km (2 miles) turn left again. Bonaguil was the last feudal fortress built in France, finished in 1520, a time when other lords were building 'châteaux de plaisances' like those on the Loire, because the king, Charles VII, had forbidden private defence works. But Berenger de Roquefeuil, the brutal, hunchbacked owner of Bonaguil was a man who went his own way. When the king fined him for savage treatment of his vassals, he reacted by strengthening his castle. He worked on it for 40 years, determined to create a fort that no royal troops, would ever subdue. It was a masterpiece of military architecture, offering no easily attacked angles but with its own cannons covering every approach. Berenger de Roquefeuil waited in vain to prove his point, living on to 82 before dying within the walls. But the clash of arms was never heard at Bonaguil, it was never attacked, and never besieged.

Today this impressive ruin, now partly restored, belongs to the municipality of Fumel and is open to the public. In the summer season until the end of August there are hourly guided tours (closed for lunch), some in English. On summer evenings there are musical performances by international artists.

At the foot of the castle there is a small village which has three restaurants. One of them, 'Aux Bons Enfants' has a tree-shaded garden, with a small stream, and a terrace where lunch is served in summer.

Périgord

Périgord is the name of an ancient province of France, the limits of which conformed very closely to those of the modern department of Dordogne, the third largest in France. The area is still known to the French as Périgord, especially so by the people who live there. In the east the landscape is of wooded hills, which are the last outposts of the Massif Central, and, in general the land slopes down from east to west, and from north east to south-west to the plains of the Gironde. It is marked by a fantail of beautiful rivers — the Dronne, the Isle, the

Auvézère, and the Vézère, which flow down into the Dordogne itself. There is a great variety of scenery, from steep-sided river valleys to rolling hills and forested plains.

In the past it was said that there were two Périgords, the Périgord Blanc, now in the centre of the department, and named for the frequent outcrops of chalky rock, and the Périgord Noir, in the southeast, named from the darkly wooded hills. These two terms are still in common use, as well as Périgord Vert, a term invented about 20 years ago by local tourist authorities to describe the northern part of the department.

Dordogne is not a fertile department, but its mild climate enables a variety of crops to be grown here and there, so that in the past many of its people lived as subsistence farmers. By comparison it is relatively prosperous today, due to the development of tourism. This followed the discovery, towards the end of the nineteenth century, of numerous prehistoric sites, among them the painted caves, and the famous Grotte de Lascaux. The department's economic situation has also improved with the development of the wine industry, and the planting of strawberries, for which Dordogne is the chief French producer.

Apart from its scenic beauty and the fascination of the prehistoric sites, Périgord is rich in other points of interest for the visitor, medieval castles, bastides, fortified churches, picturesque villages, and in leisure resources of all kinds such as fishing, boating, walking and cycling.

From the Channel ports the natural routes to Périgord are the N20 to Limoges and then the N21 to Périgueux, or the N20 to Limoges and then the D704 into Périgord Noir, or the N10 to Angouleme and then D939 to Périgueux.

From the Agenais the N21 leads north from Villeneuve sur Lot to **Bergerac**, the main town of southern Dordogne. Attractively situated on a wide and pleasant reach of the Dordogne, Bergerac is now more interesting than it was a few years ago, since the old quarter has been successfully restored, and almost entirely pedestrianised. Among the narrow streets and old squares there are a number of medieval houses, including the fourteenth-century La Vieille Auberge in the Rue des Fontaines. In the seventeenth-century Maison Peyrarede there is a comprehensive museum of tobacco, the Musee du Tabac — Bergerac has long been the headquarters of the nationalised French tobacco industry — and the building also contains a small museum of the town's history. Nearby, the Protestant church is a reminder that Bergerac is and always was a stronghold of

Protestantism in France. During the Religious Wars of the seventeenth century the inhabitants, despite constant persecution, refused to abandon the new faith. Many of them emigrated to America or to more tolerant parts of Europe, and the population of Bergerac dropped sharply. In the nineteenth century the coming of the railway and the new roads built to link Bordeaux to Paris all favoured Périgueux, which then became the capital of the region.

In the Place de la Myrpe there is a statue of Cyrano de Bergerac. The interesting thing is that the real Cyrano de Bergerac was not a Gascon at all, he was a Paris-born Italian named Savinien Cyrano. When he became a professional soldier he was posted to a regiment of Guards, commanded by and made up of Gascons, and he added de Bergerac to his name to fit in better with them. He was a famous swordsman and was also an accomplished poet and playwright. In all his years in that Gascon regiment, he never even acquired a Gascon accent. He died in 1655. It was not until 250 years later that he was born again as a swaggering Gascon in Edmond Rostand's famous play *Cyrano de Bergerac*.

The play was one of the greatest successes ever in the French theatre, and it is not surprising that Bergerac associated itself with the hero. They brushed aside his origins, pointing out that after all he was known to everyone as Cyrano de Bergerac — so he remains the local hero, and Bergerac has its restaurants, bars and cinema named after him.

Not far from the statue is the Museum of Regional Ethnography, open every day except Sundays and Mondays which has an interesting collection of the tools and farm machinery of earlier times, things which might otherwise be forgotten as new technology takes over.

Bergerac is the centre of a region which produces sound but inexpensive table wines. The best is Pecharmant, made on the slopes of the hills north of the town. The Maison du Vin, in the old quarter, is open to the public daily in July and August. It has been arranged in the former monastery of the Recollets. These were the Catholic priests sent by Louis XIII to Bergerac with the task of converting the Protestants of the region back to Catholicism (the French verb *recoller* means to stick back). The original cloister is intact, around an inner courtyard, and there is a fine vaulted cellar. On the first floor there is a Great Hall with views across the river to the vineyards of Monbazillac.

Unlike Pecharmant, the majority of Bergerac wines are produced in the area south of the Dordogne river. The most famous of them is Monbazillac, a rich sweet white wine, second only to the best

Sauternes. In the Middle Ages it was known all over Europe and was the favourite wine of the Vatican. The wine of **Monbazillac** can be tasted and bought at the château itself, which is open to the public, and has a very good restaurant. The château was built in 1558 and is a fine example of the transitional period between the purely defensive castle — the château fort, and the more elegant 'châteaux de plaisances' of later periods. It has survived unchanged and undamaged from the sixteenth century. It has some fine rooms, and a small museum which is a good guide to the traditional life of the region.

Visitors interested in archaeology or literature may like to take an excursion from Bergerac to **Montcaret** in the extreme west of the department. Just north of the D936 about 40km (25 miles) from Bergerac, Montcaret was a thriving village in Roman times and has some Gallo-Roman remains, including mosaics and a Roman bath with designs of fish and an octopus. **St Michel de Montaigne**, a sleepy village only 2km (1 mile) from Montcaret, was the birthplace of the famous French essayist, Montaigne. All that remains of the château in which he was born in 1477 is a round tower, containing his bedroom and the library in which he worked. He had more than a thousand books, a prodigious number for those times. When he died, the books, every one of which could be worth a fortune today, were given by his daughter to the Abbot of Roquefort, but what became of them after that is a mystery. Montaigne was a great admirer of the Roman civilisation, but archaeology was an unknown science in his day and he can never have been aware that, only a short stroll from his home, fascinating evidence of that lost civilisation lay just beneath the surface of the ground. Montaigne's tower is open to the public daily, morning and afternoon (Mondays and Tuesdays, January to mid-February excepted). The rest of the château was burned down in the nineteenth century, and rebuilt by Louis Napoleon's Minister of Finance, Monsieur Magne.

Périgueux, the prefecture of Dordogne, lies 47km (29 miles) north of Bergerac on the N21. With its suburbs it makes a town of about 60,000 inhabitants, of limited interest to the visitor, but a good centre for touring the Périgord Blanc. The town was founded by the Romans, who called it *Vesunna*. Most important of the few Roman remains is a tower 24m (79ft) high, called the Tour de Vesone (Vesunna Tower), and a pleasant public garden has been created around it, set about with pieces of Roman statuary found during excavations. Nearby, the site of a large Roman villa has been excavated. It is believed to have belonged to a member of the family of Pompey, the great rival of Julius Caesar. The ruins show there were three large reception rooms, sixty smaller rooms, central heating, and galleries around a fountained courtyard, and suggest the luxurious style in which wealthy Romans lived. The remains of the former Roman amphitheatre, which could hold 20,000 spectators, have also been made into a public garden.

Périgueux has a very unusual cathedral. It is said to have been inspired by St Mark's Cathedral in Venice, which itself was derived from the church of the Apostles in Constantinople, built in the eleventh century, and since disappeared. The oriental domes and turrets of this cathedral of St Front have become the symbol of Périgueux, as the Tower Bridge is a symbol of London, and are known all over France to people who have never been to the city. As it stands today St Front is almost entirely a nineteenth-century reconstruction, and its cavernous interior is curiously lacking in atmosphere. For most visitors the most interesting thing about St Front is the view of it from across the river.

Around the cathedral and near the river there is an area of narrow streets with many Renaissance and medieval houses, full of interesting architectural features, especially in the Rue de la Constitution, the Rue Limogeanne, and the Rue Plantier. A clear plan of this area, showing the chief points of interest, is available from the Syndicat d'Initiative, in the Place Francheville, in the town centre.

Brantôme, 27km (17 miles) from Périgueux by the D939, is a jewel of a small town, most of it islanded between two arms of the River Dronne, with five bridges, riverside gardens with weeping willows, and many medieval and Renaissance houses. Its beauty brings thousands of tourists in high summer, and it suffers, but in spring or autumn, it is a wonderful place to idle around in. The buildings of the former Benedictine abbey beside the Dronne, which are now used as town hall and museum, are open to the public. They were restored in the nineteenth century by the architect Abadie, the man who over-elaborated the cathedral of St Front and was also designer of the Sacre Coeur in Paris. Fortunately he left alone the most important feature of this abbey, the bell tower, which has somehow survived 800 years from Norman times.

Only 10km (6 miles) from Brantôme and reached by the D78 which follows the winding course of the River Dronne is the picturesque village of **Bourdeilles**, with an old mill beside the river and a château on a bluff immediately above. The château is in two parts, one medieval, and one Renaissance. In the old medieval part Pierre de Bourdeille was born in 1540. He was the son of a count who was the High Sheriff of Périgord. His older brother, Andre, inherited the estates and Pierre became first a soldier-courtier. As such, he had a distinguished career, but, at 49, it was cut short by a terrible fall from his horse. As a result he was bedridden for 4 years, and never physically active again. Instead, he became a writer. His inside knowledge of the goings-on at court and among the highly-placed throughout the land enabled him to write books like *Lives of Famous Men and Great Soldiers* and *Lives of Amorous Ladies* . He had retired to Brantôme where, although he had never taken religious orders, the king had given him the sinecure post of abbot, and had chosen the name of the town as his *nom-de-plume*, Brantôme. He was not the man to let truth get in the way of a good yarn, and his books are still read today. Walkers can join the GR36 footpath at either Brantôme or Bourdeilles.

From Bourdeilles there are two attractive roads to Ribérac, the D78 and then the D710, south of the river, or the narrower D103 and then D104 north of the river, a route which offers some fine views over the valley of the Dronne.

A quarter of the Dordogne area is forested, and the wildest and least populated area of all, the lonely and mysterious forest of the Double, lies to the right of the D708 which leads south from Ribérac. This ancient forest, with many lakes and streams, was known for centuries as a hideaway for robbers and villains of all kinds. The prevalence of malaria, swamp fevers of all kinds, and vipers, tended to keep their pursuers away. On a fine summer's day it is an attractive place, but for most of the year it is dark and sinister. There are several narrow roads through the forest, any one of which will give an idea of its character and isolation. At **Echourgnac**, a road to the right leads to a Trappist monastery called L'Abbaye d'Echourgnac, Notre Dame d'Esperance. The monks came here in the nineteenth century, drained many of the stagnant pools and so got rid of malaria and other fevers, and the snakes, and started the cultivation of some of the land. The monks have since been replaced by nuns of the same Trappist Order, and from their beautifully-kept monastery grounds they produce home-made cheeses, jams, and honey which they sell in their shop. There are twenty-four modern rooms available for visitors who wish to go into retreat. The monastery is on a height and there are extensive views over the forest.

From Echourgnac the D38 leads south-east through the forest to **Mussidan**, a small industrial town, specialising in ceramics. Mussidan lies in a loop of the River Isle and on the N89 which crosses this wild area from east to west. From Mussidan the D709 to Bergerac, 25km (15½ miles), crosses another lonely and thinly-populated area, the

Lush greenery covers a picturesque building at Les Eyzies, Agenais-Périgord-Quercy

Sarlat, Agenais-Périgord-Quercy

Rocamadour, a spectacular collection of churches, ramparts and ancient buildings, Agenais-Périgord-Quercy

Forêt du Landais. This is drier than the watery forest of La Double, and has many more pine trees. In places there are large clearings where strawberries are cultivated.

There is an interesting circuit to the east of Brantôme, beginning on the D78 and then left on to the D83 to Villars and the **Château de Puyguilhem**, an early Renaissance château, very well restored by the State, which took it over after the World War II, when it was in ruins. From Villars the D98 leads to the photogenic village of St Jean de Cole, a charming place with some restored medieval houses, and a two-tier Renaissance cloister.

Thiviers, a few kilometres along the D707, is a small, unspoiled country town, famous for its food markets, especially truffles, walnuts, and *foie gras*. It has some medieval houses, and a fine Romanesque church, with impressive sculptures.

From Thiviers take the D707 eastwards across country to Lanouaille, and then turn south on the D704. This road leads to La Bachellerie and then by the D65 to Montignac and the valley of the Vézère and its famous prehistoric sites. Seventeen kilometres (11 miles) south of Lanouaille at a crossroads, the D62 leads east to the **Château de Hautefort**. This is a large and elegant château, well restored after being partially burned down in 1968, with a beautiful park and gardens well worth strolling through on a fine summer day. The château, which dominates some lovely countryside, compares with the better châteaux of the Loire Valley. Inside there are some fine tapestries, a collection of seventeenth- and eighteenth-century furniture, and the altar which was used for the Coronation of Charles X at Reims. The nineteenth-century French writer, Eugene Le Roy, was born at the castle, where his father was bailiff. Though a tax collector, Le Roy sympathised with the peasants, and his novels describe their hard lives and bitter poverty. The best-known, *Jacques le Croquant*, tells of their revolt against this misery. One of the towers of Hautefort has a small museum devoted to this writer.

If Les Eyzies 26km (16 miles) further down the Vézère Valley from Montignac, is the 'capital' of prehistory, **Montignac** is almost equally important as the base for visiting the **Grotte de Lascaux**, the most famous of all the painted caves. The original grotto of Lascaux discovered in 1940, attracted thousands of visitors. The breath, warmth, and movement of air produced by so many people changed the conditions in the cave, and the paintings began to deteriorate. The real Lascaux was closed to the public in 1963 and has remained closed ever since except to very small groups of accredited scientific experts. But since 1983 the public have been able to visit the Grotte de Lascaux II, a nearby cave which was remodelled to become a replica of the main 'Bull Chamber' of Lascaux I, and on the walls of which exact copies of the original paintings were made using the same techniques and the same materials as the prehistoric artists. No tickets are on sale at Lascaux II itself. They must be obtained at a ticket office in Montignac, and are stamped with a particular time of day, and are available only for that time. This system avoids the hours of queuing which would otherwise be necessary.

This area of prehistory can hardly be called off the beaten track, since it has been a tourist destination for the best part of a hundred years. There are sites on all sides throughout the Vézère Valley and nearby. Perhaps it is sufficient to recall some of those most worth visiting. Apart from Lascaux II, other caves with prehistoric paintings include the Grotte de Combarelle, the Grotte de Font de Gaume, both close to Les Eyzies and both with hundreds of drawings and paintings, and the vast cave of Rouffignac which has 8km (5 miles) of galleries (visit by small electric train) with many drawings of mammoths and other animals.

There are also some impressive caves without paintings but with stalactite and stalagmite and crystal formations. The best of these are the Grotte de Carpe Diem, 4km (2 miles) north of Les Eyzies by the D47, and the nearby Grotte du Grand Roc, halfway up an imposing cliff. From the steps leading to this cave there are splendid views over the Vézère Valley.

No one who finds this earliest civilisation of prehistory interesting should miss the National Museum of Prehistory at **Les Eyzies** installed in a castle on a rock above the village. There is nothing musty about this museum, which has been repeatedly updated. Its exhibits are well arranged, and a visit gives a clear idea of the chronology of the ancient past and a basis for comparison of the various sites.

There are other sights worth seeing in the Périgord Noir apart from the caves and their evidence of prehistoric man. There are several attractive châteaux in the same area, among them the Château de Commarque, a rugged and grandiose ruin of a twelfth-century stronghold, and nearby, the **Château de Puymartin**, a splendid château which has been the home of the de Marzac family for 500 years. It was restored in the nineteenth century and is worth a visit. There is fine period furniture and some superb Aubusson and Flemish tapestries, but it has that indefinable atmosphere of a continuously inhabited home, rather than that of an elegant museum, as found in most castles and great houses. Both these châteaux lie just to the north of the D47, a pretty road which runs from Les Eyzies to Sarlat, the capital of the Périgord Noir.

Sarlat is certainly worth a visit, particularly in spring or early autumn. In the high season the crowds introduce a fairground atmosphere, very foreign to the narrow streets and alleys of this remarkable old town. Until 30 years ago Sarlat was a poor, dirty, miserable town with many of its most ancient buildings in ruins, including the church. The change is due to one man, Andre Malraux, who was de Gaulle's Minister for Cultural Affairs. He introduced a law providing for the restoration of historic buildings and the most ancient quarters of certain towns.

There is plenty to see in Sarlat, and it can only be done on foot. The best plan is to pick up a route map from the Office de Tourisme in the Place Liberte or, in July and August only, also in the Avenue de Gaulle. It should be pointed out that Sarlat is very much a town of appearances, with many medieval and Renaissance façades and architectural details, but almost no interiors to be seen. This is largely because, when the period façades of the buildings were restored to their original aspect, the interiors were often divided into flats and modernised. Nevertheless, a stroll through Vieux Sarlat, with its cobbled alleys and ancient houses and chapels is an impressive experience. It is one of the charms of Sarlat that you can wander in haphazard fashion and find something of interest around almost every corner, even so it is better to have the map with you, or you might miss something only a few steps away in the other direction.

Every year from mid-July to mid-August Sarlat holds a festival of music and theatre in the Place de la Liberte. It attracts star performers and is justly renowned.

Those who want souvenirs of the region should walk down the Rue de la Republique, the most commercial street in the Périgord Noir. It is particularly good for the gastronomic products of the region. This street, known locally as the 'Traverse' was constructed in 1837 in a straight line through the middle of the old quarter, destroying everything, however old and interesting, in its way, with no attempt at preservation. It was done in the name of progress and shows the total indifference of French local authorities to their historic past before it became evident that, through tourism, there was money to be made.

In contrast with the valley of the Vézère and Sarlat, there is an area of the Périgord Noir in the valley of the Dordogne itself and also south of the river which is much less visited. The first place to see here is the bastide of **Domme**. This picturesque walled village is dramatically sited on the edge of a high cliff with unsurpassed views of the lovely river winding through its valley and across to distant hills.

The walls of Domme are pierced by three impressive medieval gateways. One of them, the Porte des Tours, has two towers, in one of which Knights Templars were imprisoned in the fourteenth century, when King Phillippe le Bel outlawed the whole of the order and burned its Grand Master, Jacques de Molay at the stake. As the flames consumed him Molay's voice could be heard cursing the king and all his descendants, a curse which largely came true. Philippe died the next year, and none of his descendants reigned for more than 6 years, and all died young. The names and coats of arms of those Knights Templars who were imprisoned at Domme can still be seen in rooms at the Porte des Tours.

Domme is a very attractive village built in golden stone, and made more beautiful by the profusion of flowers grown around their homes and in window-boxes by the villagers.

Only 3km (2 miles) west of Domme, on the north bank of the river, is **La Roque Gageac**, which has won the title of the prettiest village in France. It is built of the same golden stone, but on a series of ledges in the face of a cliff, so that from a distance the houses almost seem to be built on top of each other. Though it was largely destroyed by the Germans in World War II, the village has been carefully restored, and it is well worth a walk around among the narrow alleys with their craftsmen's workshops, and some of the higher streets have enchanting views of the river. The apparent showpiece at the western limit of the village, the white Château de la Malartrie, seemingly fifteenth century, is actually a nineteenth-century imitation of the earlier style.

Places worth seeing are close together in this area. From La Roque Gageac, the riverside D703, narrow and very crowded in high summer, leads to **Beynac-Cazenac**, another riverside village. On a crag high above it stands one of the most spectacularly-sited castles in Périgord, the Château de Beynac. It is possible to reach the château on foot from the village, but it is a steep climb. By car, you have to take a road which sweeps inland for a couple of miles and then back to the castle, and the few houses huddled round its skirts. A path leads round the edge of the castle to a viewpoint which can take you back almost a thousand years. Richard Coeur de Lion and his captain, Mercadier, stood together at this point, after capturing the original fortress, and decided how they would use the strongpoint to control the river valley and the surrounding countryside. Few places give a stronger sense of feudal power, of the lord and his castle dominating

La Roque Gageac

the lesser men below, than this great castle. It is open to the public, but the interior is somewhat less impressive than the site itself.

From Beynac cross the river via Vezac to visit the **Château de Castelnaud**, the great enemy of Beynac during the Hundred Year's War. Beynac had by then become a French fortress, while Castelnaud was owned by the Caumont family, who took the English side in the war. The castle has an interesting museum of medieval warfare, with full size replicas of the war machines in use in medieval times.

Four kilometres (2 miles) west of Castelnaud on the D53 there is another interesting castle, the **Château des Milandes**. This was another property of the Caumont family who owned it until the Revolution. After being neglected for 50 years it was very well restored during the nineteenth century and is in good condition today. Josephine Baker, the famous star of the Folies Bergere, who had lived in the area during World War II, helping the Resistance and RAF aircrew who had been shot down, bought Les Milandes to provide a home for orphan children of different races, colours and religions, where they could live in harmony. She spent a fortune in support of this ideal and kept it going for nearly 20 years but in the end bankrupted herself in the effort. The château has many souvenirs, both of her and the Caumont family, and one of the finest Flamboyant Gothic chapels in Dordogne.

Return to the D53 from Les Milandes and follow it across country to Belves, and then take the D54 to **Cadouin**, where the former Cistercian abbey was for hundreds of years one of the most famous places of pilgrimage in Europe. As a holy relic, the abbey had a piece of cloth which was believed to have bound the head of Christ at the Crucifixion, and which had been given to the abbey after a twelfth-century Crusade. The great and the famous and the humble came from far and wide to kneel in prayer before this relic, but the pilgrimages came to an end in the 1930s, when experts established from Arabic inscriptions on the cloth that it could not be older than the twelfth century; in other words it was new when given to the abbey. But as one of the best preserved abbeys in France, Cadouin is still worth visiting, and is a textbook of different architectural styles from Romanesque to Flamboyant Gothic.

Beaumont de Périgord, 17km (11 miles) by D25 from Cadouin, is an unusual bastide built by the English in 1272 in the form of an 'H' in honour of Henry III, who died in that year. It has a good example of a fortified church, with square towers at each corner, which was well restored in the nineteenth century. Guided tours of the bastide take place during July and August. It is a pleasant little town with a very good and unusual restaurant (see Accommodation and Eating Out listing at the end of this guide).

One of the most unusual châteaux in Dordogne is at **Lanquais**, reached by the D660 north for 10km (6 miles) to Couze, then left on to D37 which leads directly to this château. The interesting thing about Lanquais is that it is a combination of a fourteenth-century Gothic castle and a sixteenth-century palace. The Renaissance addition was made by Galiot de la Tour d'Auvergne, member of one of the most distinguished families in France, the men becoming bishops or generals in the service of the king, and the women the wives or mistresses of kings. Madeleine de la Tour d'Auvergne was the mother of Catherine de Medici, whose three sons became in turn kings of France. When they were young, Catherine de Medici ruled as Regent. It was at the time of the Religious Wars, and Catherine formed a 'flying squad' of beautiful and noble girls whose job was to influence powerful Protestants. One of them, Isabel de Limeuil, the sister of Galiot de la Tour d'Auvergne, was assigned to the Prince de Conde. But this attractive girl, known affectionately to the court as 'Sweet Limeuil' was a bit too enthusiastic in trying to convert the Prince, and had a baby by him. Catherine 'sacked' her, and Isabel sent the baby to him in a basket lined with a cloth discreetly embroided with the Conde arms. He behaved nobly and accepted the child, but his wife was less forgiving and he died shortly afterwards, poisoned by her. When she was not at court, Isabel who was soon forgiven by Catherine, lived at the Château de Lanquais.

The D660 crosses the Dordogne at Couze and leads west to Bergerac, 19km (12 miles).

Quercy

It is not always the case but it is very often noticeable that as you cross from one department to another in France the nature of the landscape changes at once. The two adjacent departments of Lot et Garonne and Lot are quite different. A few kilometres into Lot and the fertile fields and orchards of Lot et Garonne are replaced by a wilder, heavily wooded landscape of steep-sided hills and stony heathland, with only patches of fertility in the river valleys. The Quercy is a region which includes almost the whole of the Lot department, and it is so named from the Latin word *quercus*, meaning oak tree, which makes up most of the woodlands. It is well-known for its delicious lamb, for the black truffles which grow in the oak woods, and for its picturesque villages.

Cahors, the capital of the region, is an individual and remarkable city in many ways. It lies within a great loop of the River Lot, the narrow neck between the two arms of the loop is closed by a steep hill, which, in medieval times was walled from side to side, making Cahors an almost impregnable fortress. The only access then across the river was by three fortified bridges, but two of them were pulled down in the early nineteenth century. The third, the Pont Valentré, with its three towers, remains intact today. Cahors was captured only once in its long history. Having withstood repeated English attacks during the Hundred Years War, it fell to a Protestant army led by Henry of Navarre, later Henry IV of France, after a siege and a battle lasting 3 days and nights.

Despite its remoteness Cahors became an important town in medieval Europe. Its rise followed the election of Cardinal Jacques Arnaud Dueze, who had been born there, to the Papacy. The cardinals had not been able to agree among themselves on the election of a Pope to succeed Clement V, who died in 1314. Eventually they chose Dueze, as he was already 72 and seemed to be in very poor health, in the belief that they would soon have another election. But Dueze had deliberately exaggerated his frailty, his health improved dramatically once he was elected, and he confounded the cardinals by living another 18 years. During this time he showed that he was a born administrator and a financial genius. When he died the Church was richer than it had ever been, with 20 million gold francs in the Treasury. Jean XXII knew well the capabilities of his fellow citizens of Cahors, and he lost no opportunity to give them responsibility. As a result Cahors became in the early fourteenth century the most important banking centre in Europe.

The Cathedral of St Stephen, was started in the eleventh century and built in a grim, fortress-like style, as it was meant to serve also as a refuge for the people in times of attack. On the north side there is a very fine Romanesque doorway. It was originally in the fourteenth-century façade but was moved during renovation. The nave has two domes, one of which has some fourteenth-century frescoes showing the stoning to death of St Etienne (Stephen), which were rediscovered in the late nineteenth century after spending hundreds of years under coats of whitewash. A door in the chancel leads to a fine cloister added in the sixteenth century in Flamboyant Gothic style.

There are markets in the cathedral square on Wednesdays and Saturdays (during the winter these are well-known for truffles and *foie gras*). In the narrow streets around the cathedral those interested in architecture will find numerous fascinating details in doors, mullioned windows, and decorative sculptures. This old quarter still has a strong atmosphere of the past, more genuine than that of Sarlat, which here and there has a toy-town gloss about it.

The sight not to be missed is the Pont Valentré itself, probably the finest example of a medieval fortified bridge remaining in Europe. The towers at each end could be closed by gates and portcullises, and the central tower was used as an observation post. The bridge is remarkably photogenic, and one of the best viewpoints is from the other side of the river, near the Fontaine des Chartreux, named from the Carthusian monks who used it to bring a supply of fresh water into the city.

Apart from Cahors itself, the Quercy has a number of other attractions, each worth a special excursion. Like Périgord Noir, Quercy has a number of interesting caves. The **Grotte de Peche-Merle** is one of the finest of all the caves in France, combining prehistoric art with many of the most impressive natural features to be found in caves — stalactites and stalagmites, strange crystal concretions ranging in colour from red to a frosty sparkle, and natural 'sculptures' on the walls of vaulted, intercommunicating chambers. Scholars believe that Peche-Merle was used as a kind of temple — there is no evidence that it was ever lived in — and that men were led by its natural beauty to add their own decorations. There are drawings of horses, bison, mammoths and other animals. In one place a frieze depicting bison and mammoths which is 10m (33ft) long and 3m (10ft) high, is thought to date from 25,000 years ago. The number of visitors admitted are limited, so it is advisable to arrive as early as possible in the day. The tour of the various chambers in the huge cave covers 1.6km (1 mile) and takes 1½ hours.

A short drive from Peche-Merle by the D41 and across the river leads to one of the most attractive villages in France, **St Cirq** (pronounced Seer) **Lapopie**. The village was a fortress in medieval times, though its castle was later destroyed on the orders of Louis XI, who was afraid it might become an enemy stronghold. The site, above the village, offers panoramic views of the river valley and the countryside. The village itself built into the steep south bank of the river, looks across to the sheer cliffs where the Lot enters a gorge. There is a fortified fifteenth-century church in a dominant position in the village, and in the narrow streets and alleys around it, old houses have been carefully restored by painters and wood carvers. There are several GR footpaths in the area, including the GR36, which passes through St Cirq Lapopie.

Another attraction which no one in the area should miss is the **Gouffre de Padirac**, situated about 60km (37 miles) north-east of Cahors by the N20 and then D677. Since it is partly open at the top, Padirac is an enormous pot-hole or chasm, rather than a cave. The traditional local belief is that Satan made the hole on his way down into hell. It was not until 1889 that the great speliologist E.A. Martel discovered the underground river and linked galleries associated with the great chasm. The perennial action of water has created stalactites and stalagmites, and there are waterfalls which prevent the river from being completely navigable.

The visits to Padirac are somewhat regimented, but they have to be in order to keep control of the many people who want to make the 1½ hour tour. Without an organised system the visits would become chaotic. A steep flight of steps leads down about 100m (328ft) into the gulf, but it is usual to make the descent in lifts. Well-lit passages through the rock lead to the embarkation point. The 700m (2,296ft) boat trip on the still, translucent water, with cleverly placed lighting dramatising the strange forms of the great rock walls, is very impressive. It is all so vast that there is no sense of being shut in, but if you make the trip in the heat of summer you will find it quite cold by contrast down there, and there is a constant drip of water from above, so it is sensible to wear something warm and protective for the visit. Near the end of the boat trip you will see the Great Pendant, a stalactite which hangs from the roof 78m (256ft) above to just above the surface of the water.

After landing there is a walk back to the lifts which takes you through narrow galleries and up stone steps, and past some more interesting features, including a 40m (131ft) stalagmite known as the Great Pillar, a number of pools, a waterfall and a lake of emerald green water trapped 20m (66ft) above the level of the river. During the boat trip flash photographs are taken by the official photographer, and before you get to the lifts for the journey back to the surface there is a kiosk where you can order pictures of yourself and family in the boat to be posted to you. Padirac is open from Easter to mid-October, and during July and August only is not closed for lunch.

From Padirac it is a short drive, 16km (10 miles), to **Rocamadour**. As it has so many thousands of visitors, Rocamadour can certainly not be considered off the beaten track. But there is a way to see this lovely old town which, despite the souvenir shops, restaurants and hotels, and tourist crowds, retains its wonderful atmosphere. That is to arrive on a summer evening, stay overnight, and have a good look round first thing in the morning before the cars and coaches arrive.

The houses of Rocamadour cling like limpets to a rock cliff which forms one side of the valley of the small River Alzou, which flows far below. The visitor enters through the Porte de Figuier, the Gate of the Fig Tree, which was already an entrance to the town in the thirteenth century. From the main street, heavily commercial, alleys and steps lead upwards past old houses and towers, and eventually to the castle at the top, a nineteenth-century edifice attached to a four-teenth-century fortress. From its ramparts there are splendid comprehensive views of Rocamadour and the surrounding countryside. Like Lourdes, Rocamadour, is a place of pilgrimage, and has been one for a far longer time, since the twelfth century. Unlike Lourdes, its 'speciality' was not the cure of the sick, but the forgiveness of sinners and criminals. Pilgrims, including kings and nobles, used to climb the 216 steps to the oratory on their knees. Thieves and murderers and other criminals had to make the climb in chains, having been sentenced to do so as part of their punishment. At the top, in the Chapelle Miraculeuse, they knelt before the Virgin and asked forgiveness while the priest recited prayers on their behalf. Then he removed their chains, and gave them a certificate to prove that they had made the pilgrimage, and to absolve them from further punishment.

Pilgrims still make this climb, some of them on their knees, but no longer in chains. The chapel used now, Notre Dame de Rocamadour, was built in the nineteenth century, and is one of seven churches in the small Place St Amadour. The eleventh- to thirteenth-century St Saviour's basilica has a fine sixteenth-century carving of Christ above the altar. Another of the chapels, St Michael's, has two frescoes, considered to be twelfth century, on the outside. They represent the Annunciation and the Visitation of the Virgin.

The Tourist Office is in the Town Hall, a restored fifteenth-century house. The council chamber has examples of the work of Jean Lurcat, the greatest tapestry designer of modern times. A full tour of Rocamadour, which has to be done on foot, takes at least 3 hours and, because of the amount of climbing, can be tiring, but there are lifts to make it easier.

At Rocher des Aigles (Eagle's Rock), above the village, there is a breeding centre for birds of prey. Some of the birds have been trained to give impressive flying displays, and these take place several times a day during the season.

Further Information
— Agenais-Périgord-Quercy —

Museums and Other Places of Interest

Agen
Musee d'Agen
Open: 10am-12noon and 2-6pm daily
except Tuesdays. Admission free on
Wednesdays.

Bergerac
*Musee du Tabac and Local History
Museum*
In the Maison Peyrarede
Rue de l'Ancien Pont
Open: mornings and afternoons daily.
Afternoons only on Sundays. Closed
on public holidays.

Maison du Vin
Place de la Myrpe
Open: afternoons, and am/pm during
July and August. Closed Sunday,
Monday out of season and holidays.

Beynac
Château
Open: daily mornings and afternoons
from 1 March to 15 November.

Biron
Château
Open: daily mornings and afternoons.
Closed on Tuesdays except 1 July to 7
September. Closed 15 December to 1
February.

Bonaguil
Château
Open: daily mornings and afternoons
from Palm Sunday to end September.
Afternoons of Sundays and public
holidays at other times. Closed
December and January.

Bourdeilles
Château
Open: daily mornings and afternoons in
July and August. Closed on Tuesdays in
other months. Closed in winter.

Brantôme
The museum in the monastic buildings
of the abbey (now used as Town Hall)
are open mornings and afternoons
during the school holiday from 1 June
to 15 September.

Cadouin
Abbey
The abbey cloisters are open mornings
and afternoons daily from 1 July to 7
September. Closed on Tuesdays in
winter, and from 15 December to 31
January.

Castelnaud
Château
Open: all day 10am-7pm from 1 May to
30 September (closed on Mondays and
Saturdays in May, June and September).

Les Eyzies
Musee Nationale de Prehistoire
Open: mornings and afternoons every
day except Tuesday.

Gouffre de Padirac
Near Rocamadour
Open: daily Easter to October.

Grotte de Combarelle
Open: daily but closed on Tuesdays,
and from 1 to 8 May, 1 to 11 November,
and 25 November to 25 December.

Grotte de Font de Gaume
Open: daily but closed on Tuesdays,
and from 1 to 8 May, 1 to 11 November, and 25 November to 25 December.

Grotte de Lascaux II
Open: all day in July and August.
Mornings and afternoons from 1
February to 30 June and from 1
September to 31 December. Closed on
Mondays outside high season. No
tickets available at the site in the high
season, they must be bought in
advance at the office in Montignac.

Hautefort

Château
Open: daily mornings and afternoons
from Palm Sunday to 1 November.
Sunday afternoons at other times.

Lanquais

Château
Open: daily mornings and afternoons 1
April to 31 October. Closed on
Thursdays and in winter.

Les Milandes

Château
Open: daily mornings and afternoons 1
April to 30 September.

Monbazillac

Château
Open: daily mornings and afternoons.

Peche-Merle

Cave
Near Cahors
Open: daily mornings and afternoons
from Easter to November.

Puyguilhem

Château
Open: daily mornings and afternoons 1
July to 7 September. Closed on
Tuesdays in other months and closed
from 16 December to 31 January.

Puymartin

Château
Open: daily mornings and afternoons 1
June to 30 September. Afternoons only
in April and May.

Tourist Information Offices

All French towns have a tourist
information office, usually called the
Office de Tourisme, but sometimes still
by the old name, Syndicat d'Initiative.
In villages the local Mairie supplies
tourist information.

Agenrea
Office de Tourisme
107 Blvd Carnot
Agen
☎ 53 47 36 09

Lot (Quercy)
Office de Tourisme
Place A-Briand
Cahors
☎ 65 35 24 97

Périgueux
Syndicat d'Initiative
1 Avenue Aquitaine
Perigueux
☎ 53 53 10 63

In addition to information on sightseeing, all tourist offices have details of all
leisure activities available in their
district, canoeing, horse-riding, golf,
cycling, hang-gliding etc. Just ask.
Some large tourist offices undertake to
find and book hotel and holiday
accommodation, though not more than
five days ahead.

3 • Limousin

L imousin is a wild region with great stretches of countryside on which mankind has made little impression. Travellers on the east-west route from Paris to Bordeaux and back, or from north to south from Brittany to the Massif Central, and pilgrims on the way to St James of Compostella, all had to cross Limousin. So historically it has always been a crossroads. But the great tracts of upland, hostile in winter, the many steep-sided river valleys, meant that few travellers who passed that way wanted to stop. Apart from the high mountain regions of the Alps and the Massif Central, Limousin has the most severe winter climate in France, and this, together with its relatively infertile soil, has always kept the population thinly scattered. But the summers are warm and pleasant, and its three departments, Haute-Vienne, Creuse and Corrèze, are widely different in character and offer a constantly changing pattern of wild and lovely scenery. There are great woods where the fox, the wild boar and the deer pass more frequently than men. On the heathland and hillsides the partridge and the hare are at home. Apart from a few weeks in summer the peace of the wide lakes is disturbed only by the occasional plop of a fish or the raucous cry of a heron. In quiet stretches of the sparkling rivers otters glide, and trout doze in deep pools. It is above all a countryside for nature lovers, for walkers, pony trekkers, cyclists, photographers and artists.

In summer a few French holidaymakers come to this diverse and always uncrowded land, but there are few tourists. In the east the department of Corrèze has the plateaux of Millevaches and Gentioux in the north and the mountains of Monedieres in the south, but this is all upland rather than actual mountains, reaching a maximum height of about (3,500ft) 1,067m, and much of it is often snow-covered in winter. This wide plateau country is a great water table in which a number of important rivers, including the Creuse, the Vienne, the Vézère, and the Corrèze find their source.

In the north-west the land is less elevated, reaching about 610m (2,000ft), but is more broken up into regular hills, characterised by

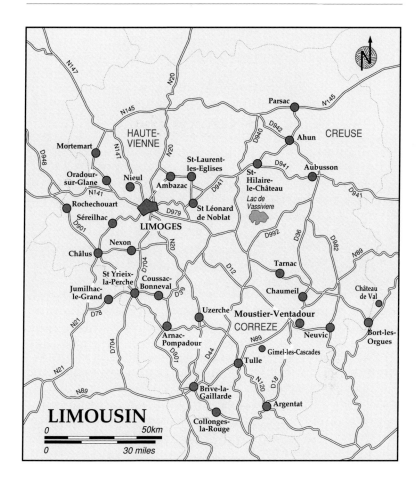

forests of oak and beech on the higher slopes, and of chestnut woods and grass pastures lower down.

In the south there are more plateaux, between the Rivers Vézère and the upper reaches of the Dordogne, and in places the land is sectioned by deep gorges and takes on the wild aspect of the adjoining Massif Central. Most savage of all is the lonely valley of the Maronne, its steep sides thickly wooded, even in the gorges.

But in addition to its unspoiled and lonely landscape, Limousin has other attractions, numerous castles, historic churches, excellent museums, and an artistic tradition based on superb porcelain and enamel work.

Limoges, the prefecture (county town) of Haute-Vienne, with a population of about 115,000, is easily the largest town in Limousin.

Decorating the famous porcelain made at Limoges

Brive La Gaillarde in the south of the region, comes next with 55,000, and then Tulle, with 20,000, both in the Corrèze department, and then Gueret, the prefecture of the Creuse department, with only 16,000. They all have good hotel accommodation but many visitors may prefer to be based in a country hotel or inn, or better still in self-catering accommodation within easy reach of one of these towns, rather than in a town itself.

Limoges is a town of modest interest but it does have some unusual and important attractions. The first thing not to miss is Adrien-Dubouche National Museum of Porcelain, which has a collection of more than 10,000 pieces of the finest French and European porcelain. At the end of the eighteenth century large deposits of china clay (kaolin) were discovered in southern Limousin near the town of St Yrieix-la-Perche. In Napoleonic times the porcelain industry in Limousin became concentrated on Limoges and has grown steadily in importance ever since. Apart from its strength in Limoges porcelain, the museum has beautiful pieces from Sèvres and many other French factories, as well as from Chelsea, Meissen, Delft, Naples, and Madrid. At Aixe sur Vienne, 15 minutes south of Limoges on the road to Périgueux, the Maison de la Porcelaine also offers guided visits showing the manufacture and decoration of fine china.

The other great product of Limoges, enamel, is strongly represented in the Municipal Museum installed in the former Bishop's
Palace, adjoining Limoges cathedral. Enamel is a much more ancient
industry in Limoges than porcelain and the earliest pieces among the
hundreds on display date from the twelfth century. The tradition is
still alive today, and though a demand from tourists has resulted in
a decline in the level of craftsmanship there are still a few studios
near the town centre which are producing high quality work. The
museum also has an Egyptology collection, French painting, modern
art including sculpture and enamels, and a Gallo-Roman collection
dating back to the second-century AD. The terraced gardens next to
the museum overlook the Vienne and have many ancient trees
framing views both of the cathedral and the former palace.

St Etienne Cathedral was begun in 1273, and was continued and
enlarged over six centuries. Its best features are the Portail St Jean, the
splendid north door, which was finished in 1530, when Flamboyant
Gothic was at its most vigorous, and the beautifully carved and
decorated stone rood-screen of the same period which originally
separated the choir from the transept. Next to the cathedral there is
an old quarter called L'Abbesaille in which the Rue de la Regle has
many ancient houses. Another unusual old quarter, called La
Boucherie, is near the Gothic church of St Michael of the Lions. As
long ago as the thirteenth century there were eighty butchers in this
district. Many of the old timbered houses have now become smart
shops, but one of them is on show as a traditional butcher's shop of
the Middle Ages.

North-east of Limoges there is a hilly region, the Monts d'Ambazac,
in which there are a number of picturesque villages well worth
visiting. Villages like Compreignac, Ambazac and St Sylvestre are
excellent starting points for delightful walks through these wooded
hills which have some lovely lakes in their valleys. The D28a, which
crosses these hills from Bessines-Gartempe in the north to St Laurent
les Eglises in the south (both these villages have inns) offers many
fine views and is a good route for keen cyclists who do not mind some
climbing. Close to St Laurent is the Pont du Dognon, a bridge across
the River Taurion at a point where it is really a long, narrow lake
formed by the barrage of St Marc lower down. The site is dramatically picturesque, and there is excellent coarse fishing in the lake.

Ambazac itself has a twelfth- to fifteenth-century church which
contains a remarkable reliquary. Made in beautifully-worked copper and champleve enámel, and encrusted with semi-precious stones,
this reliquary of St Etienne de Muret was the largest of seven

originally placed on the main altar of the abbey of Grandmont, near St Sylvestre. It was made in 1189 at a time when the abbey was a centre of craftsmanship in enamel and gold. The foundations and a few old stones are all that remain of the abbey buildings which were demolished in the early nineteenth century, after this order of monks had been suppressed by the Pope in 1772, and the abbey's treasure was removed in 1790. Another relic of St Etienne de Muret, a fifteenth-century bust in embossed silver, and a reliquary of St Junien, both also part of the original abbey treasure are now in the church of the little village of **St Sylvestre**. The church of St Martin at **Compreignac** is one of the best examples of a fortified church to be found in Limousin. It was originally built in the twelfth century but was destroyed during the Hundred Years War by English troops, and was rebuilt and fortified during the fifteenth and sixteenth centuries.

In this lonely countryside where every other village seems to have its own saint the religious traditions are strong and there are many manifestations in honour of the saints. The most important of these are the 'ostensions' which take place every 7 years (next in 1995) on the first Sunday after Easter in the departments of Haute-Vienne and Creuse. The ostensions, which date back to the tenth century, are the solemn showing of the relics of saints to the faithful, often in the beautifully-crafted reliquaries in enamel and gold for which Limousin is famous. Each locality has developed its own traditional ceremony. The streets are decorated with flags and flowers, and there are colourful processions, with drums, fanfares, costumed guards of honour, and various craftsmen's guilds in their traditional finery also take part. In as much as they are manifestations of religious fervour the ostensions have much in common with the famous 'pardons' of Brittany, and like them they have taken on a secular and tourist side.

A few kilometres north of Compreignac, the lake of **St Pardoux** is a good centre for active outdoor holidays. There are well-equipped sandy beaches for safe bathing, and the lake also offers good sailing, windsurfing, and fishing. Other amenities include horse-riding, mountain-biking, archery, hang-gliding, tennis, and walks in the surrounding woodland. There are several well-equipped camp sites, including Santrop, in hectares of woods and clearings, for caravanners.

On the 10 June 1944 one of the most tragic events of World War II took place at **Oradour-sur-Glane**, 22km (14 miles) west of Limoges. The little town was surrounded by Nazi troops who herded the women and children into the church and the men into barns and

Château de Rochechouart

garages. The buildings were then destroyed by fire and dynamite, and the people were massacred by machine guns and grenades. Only a few men survived, and one woman and a young boy who escaped from the church through a window at the back. The martyred and ruined village has been left as it was, so that its history may not be forgotten, but next to it a new, forward-looking town has been built.

The region south and south-west of Limoges is rich in historic castles. In the early Middle Ages the nobles of Limoges were vassals of the Dukes of Aquitaine who were also Kings of England but they were constantly under pressure from the King of France to support him against the English. The castles, mostly built in the twelfth century but added to and refortified later, particularly during the Hundred Years War, formed a defensive barrier on the southern limits of the Limousin. The most interesting of these châteaux can be seen by following what the Limousin tourist authorities call the route of Richard the Lionheart. Although he was King of England, Richard the Lionheart, the favourite son of Eleanor of Aquitaine, was also Duke and Governor of Aquitaine, and he spent most of his time there. This was quite understandable at the time because the richness and revenues of Aquitaine were considerably more important than those of the whole of England.

The Lords of **Rochechouart**, west of Limoges, were among those who took the side of the French king during the Hundred Years War. Their château was started in the twelfth century, but only the keep remains from that period, most of the rest is fifteenth century. It was much battered in successive wars, but the Lords of Rochechouart made a point of marrying rich wives, and there was always money to restore it. It should have been destroyed during the Revolution, but the men appointed to do it found the task too hard, and left it. In the early nineteenth century it was bought and restored by the State. It now houses administrative offices and the departmental museum.

The Château de Montbrun, hidden in a green valley near **Douarnazac** on the D213, is another château where only the square keep remains from the original twelfth-century fortress. The rest is fifteenth century but is in a remarkably good state of preservation. The rooms in the interior include an ancient kitchen with a huge spit, a guard room, and a defensive post with round holes through which the earliest form of cannons could be fired.

There is a story that at the beginning of the year 1199 a peasant discovered a splendid golden treasure buried in a field at **Châlus**, 7km (4 miles) from Montbrun. It consisted of 'a golden emperor, his wife, his sons and daughters, all seated at a table of solid gold', and the Viscount of Limoges had failed to yield this treasure to his lord, Richard the Lion Heart, as he should have done. Richard arrived at Châlus in March 1199 to claim this treasure. Whether this is the real reason for his visit no one knows for certain but towards the end of March he lay siege to the castle. On the 26 March he was standing in front of the castle when he was badly wounded in the shoulder by an arrow from a cross-bow. Gangrene developed in the wound and he died on the 6 April. He is said to have forgiven the man who wounded him and to have asked that he should be spared. But these wishes were not carried out. A few days later Richard's men captured the castle, hanged all the defenders, and flayed alive the man who shot the fatal arrow. There is no record of what became of the golden treasure.

Châlus is an extremely interesting castle which combines the partial ruins of the feudal fortress with a wing built in the seventeenth century, which now contains a room devoted to the history of the castle and the life of Richard, and another which exhibits the ancient craft of basket-making. The castle also includes part of the thirteenth-century living quarters, with ancient fireplaces and stone columns. In the oldest part of the ruins, dating from the eleventh century, there is a vaulted six-sided room which formed the base of one of the towers, the top of which can be reached by a spiral stone staircase, and a lower room, probably a guard room in which there is an eleventh-century fireplace.

About 10km (6 miles) along the D15 east of Châlus are the impressive ruins of another feudal fortress, the **Château des Cars**. Once the seat of the governors of Limousin, the castle was built in the twelfth century, and reconstructed and restored in the fifteenth and sixteenth centuries. During the Hundred Years War it was a stronghold of English troops until it was captured by the great French soldier of fortune Bertrand du Guesclin. Below and in front of the château are some fine stables with mansard roofs built by one of the lords of Cars in the eighteenth century.

From Cars a pretty road leads south through the forest of Cars. Turn left after a few kilometres at a place called Brumas on to a road which leads to another picturesque feudal ruin, the **Château de Lastours**. The ruined keep is twelfth century, and most of the living quarters date from the thirteenth to fifteenth century, but the Lastour family were famous and powerful long before then. Gouffier de Lastours was one of the knights who took part in the first Crusade and entered Jerusalem alongside Godefroy de Bouillon. A strange tale was told about de Lastours and sung by the troubadours. He is said to have saved a lion from death in the desert, and in gratitude the beast followed him everywhere and refused to leave him. When de Lastours eventually left for France the lion died from drowning as he swam after the ship taking his master away.

Still on the D15 and only 10km (6 mile) east of Cars at the small town of **Nexon** there is a more elegant château set in an attractive public park. The Château de Nexon was built in the fifteenth and sixteenth centuries, but was allowed to deteriorate at the time of the Revolution. It was completely restored during the nineteenth century. Nexon was one of the original breeding places of the pedigree Anglo-Arab horses which became the backbone of horseracing throughout the world. This little town has another unusual distinction, it has had a long association with the circus and now has a National Circus School.

Twenty kilometres (12 miles) south of Nexon, is the old town of **St Yrieix-la-Perche** where deposits of kaolin were found in the eighteenth century, leading to the establishment of a porcelain industry in Limousin. Uranium has been found in the region, and the reserves are estimated at 26,000 tons, the energy equivalent of 230 million tons of oil. The town's Collegiate church is of more than usual interest. It is a vast building in a mixture of Romanesque and Gothic styles. An eleventh-century porch and bell tower survive from the original building, and the wide nave, the vast transept and its side chapels, and the spacious, vaulted choir were added from the end of the twelfth century. The church treasure includes a fine fifteenth-century bust of St Yrieix in embossed silver over sculpted wood, the beard and eyebrows in engraved gold. The heavy jewelled necklace is thirteenth century. A superb Bible, made in Limoges in the eleventh century, is on show in the Hôtel de Ville.

There are two interesting castles within easy reach of St Yrieix. To the west, 12km (7 miles) by the D78, the **Château de Jumilhac-le-Grand** stands on a rocky height above the River Isle overlooking the town of Jumilhac. The château has as many towers and turrets as a castle in a children's book of fairy tales, and there are some striking features in the interior, including a Great Hall with a monumental chimney-piece with sculptures representing the four seasons, and a stone staircase with Louis XIV balusters. In one of the towers a spiral staircase leads to a room built within the thickness of the walls. It is called the Spinner's Room, and legend has it that a former chatelaine of the castle was imprisoned there by her husband in punishment for her infidelities. She is said to have passed her time spinning wool and weaving tapestries to decorate the room. The legend also says that the wool was brought to her by one of her noble lovers who had disguised himself and obtained work as a shepherd on the estate.

Twelve kilometres (7 miles) to the east of St Yrieix by the D901 is the **Château de Coussac-Bonneval**, one of the most impressive and interesting of all the châteaux of Limousin. Originally it was a fortified manor dating from the eleventh, twelfth and fourteenth centuries, which was rebuilt and added to in the fifteenth, seventeenth and eighteenth centuries. The interior is beautifully furnished with antiques dating from the Renaissance to post-Napoleonic times, and has some fine tapestries and carved panelling. The castle has its own charming little twelfth-century church, restored in the fifteenth century. There is also a twelfth-century Lanterne des Morts, probably restored about the fourteenth century. Only a few of these strange towers remain in France. They were surmounted by a cross and had windows on all four sides of the 'lantern' at the top. A small door allowed a lamp to be placed inside and raised to the 'lantern'. The light burned in honour of the dead (the tower was often at the entrance to a cemetery) and as a reminder to the living, and also as a reference point for anyone lost.

There is a good story associated with almost all the old castles of France, and at Coussac-Bonneval the story is actual history rather than legend, which is not always the case. Claude-Alexandre de

Bonneval was born in the château in 1675. He became a professional soldier and commanded a regiment in the Italian campaigns from 1701 to 1706. Next he offered his services to the Emperor of Austria, and became a general of the Austrian army and a friend of Prince Eugene. But in 1717 after a disagreement with the Prince he was banished to Dalmatia, then part of the Ottoman Empire. In order to continue his career as a soldier in Constantinople he converted to the Muslim faith, and offered his services to the Sultan of Turkey. He reorganised the Turkish army and won some brilliant victories over the Austrians. As a general of artillery, he was known as Achmet-Pasha, and was given precedence over all other pashas. He longed to return to France and Coussac-Bonneval but never managed to do so, and died in Constantinople.

Take the D126e south from Coussac-Bonneval to **Segur-le-Château**. This delightful old village nestles in a deep gorge of the Auvézère river. Its narrow and tortuous streets with many timbered houses dating from the fifteenth, sixteenth and seventeenth centuries, and the ruins of a twelfth-century castle, create a fascinating and picturesque ensemble which appeals strongly to painters and photographers.

From Segur-le-Château take the D6 south and then the D7 east to **Arnac-Pompadour** where there is an interesting and unusual castle. In 1745 this château of the twelfth, fourteenth and fifteenth centuries was given by Louis XV to his mistress, Madame de Pompadour, together with the title of marquise. In 1761 the king also established at Pompadour a stud for the breeding of horses, which became, during the nineteenth century, a famous source of pedigree Anglo-Arab horses. Today it is of considerable interest to horse lovers, with more than a hundred thoroughbred stallions of the Arab and Anglo-Arab races, as well as some magnificent specimens of draught horses — percherons, bretons, and from the Ardennes. The thoroughbred mares used in breeding are kept in a separate establishment at **Beyssac**, 4km (2 miles), to the south-east. Visitors can tour both places on weekday afternoons, and from the beginning of July to the end of September, horse races are held at Pompadour on Sunday afternoons.

The château of Pompadour, now lived in by the officials of the stud, was well-restored in the nineteenth century, and is an imposing structure. The terraces and exterior can be visited by the public.

Some of the most imposing natural sites are in eastern and southern Limousin. The Plateau de Millevaches is a lonely upland where the winters are long and rigorous, and the rainfall heavy.

Millevaches translates as 'Thousand Cows' but linguists believe that the *vaches* is a corruption of an older Celtic word *batz*, meaning 'springs', and it is a fact that the plateau is a huge watershed from which streams pour down towards the Loire, the Dordogne, and the Gironde. It is also a fact that the few people who live there permanently are often stock farmers, raising sheep and more rarely cattle. The area was once well forested but in 1575 during the Wars of Religion the forest was burned and it was not until 1860 that the first steps were taken in reafforestation. Now there are some large areas of pine forest covering almost half the plateau, but there are still great stretches of monotonous heathland with little variety but outcrops of granite rocks. Nevertheless, the space and the purity of the air increasingly attracts people from the towns to set up summer holiday homes in the area, often by converting neglected farm buildings into cottages, and this trend helps to counteract the economic loss to the area caused by the decline in farming brought about by the steady expansion of the forests.

For walkers, cyclists, and horseriders the plateau offers a variety of routes on quiet roads and paths. Motorists, too, can enjoy the great open spaces, leaving their cars where the countryside appeals to them to go for long walks through the forest and across moorland. A good starting point is the village of **Peyrelevade** in the centre of the plateau. Hotels are few and far between but there are one or two camp sites and a number of guest houses, details of which can be obtained from any local Mairie. In some ways the absence of facilities and the general lack of tourist or commercial enterprise in the mountains and plateaux of Limousin adds a lot to the appeal of this lonely area. For walkers the signposted Grandes Randonnées footpaths (GR440 and 44) cross the Plateau de Millevaches, passing through Peyrelevade. For cyclists a map showing a number of attractive routes through Limousin, including the Plateau de Millevaches, with indications of places with possible accommodation, is available. Accommodation and stabling for horseriders and pony-trekkers is easier to find in south-eastern Limousin than in the north and west. Maps and details covering these activities, and also fishing, as well as camping and self-catering accommodation can be obtained from the Comité Régional de Tourisme du Limousin (see Further Information). Although there are no ski resorts in Limousin, the snow cover in winter on the Plateau de Millevaches and around Mont Bessou and the Puy Pendu offers good cross country skiing with equipped tracks. The town of Meymac is a good base.

For the more conventional holidaymaker who is nevertheless a lover of the open air, the **Lac de Vassiviere** is one of the most interesting and varied destinations in Limousin. North-west of the Plateau de Millevaches and 60km (37 miles) due east of Limoges, Vassiviere is an artificial lake of about 1,000 hectares created by a barrage on the River Maulde, but the hills which surround it and the irregularity of the 45km (28 miles) of shoreline with numerous inlets, beaches and several islands, make it a scenically very attractive place.

The direct route from Limoges to Lake Vassiviere is east by the D941 to St Léonard de Noblat, and then by the D13. There is a church of considerable architectural interest at **St Léonard de Noblat.** It was built in the twelfth century and has since been restored. Its most remarkable feature is a massive belfry-porch in the Limousin style with four square storeys topped by two octagonal storeys and a spire. The interior of the church has some fifteenth-century carved oak stalls, and a reliquary casket of St Leonard. Near the church there are a number of old houses from the thirteenth, fifteenth and sixteenth centuries.

The D13 from St Leonard to Lac de Vassiviere is a picturesque route, with the possibility of an even more picturesque diversion by the D14, which passes alongside several barrages on the River Maulde before rejoining the D13 about 20km (12 miles) before reaching the lake via Peyrat le Château. Accommodation around the lake varies from hotels, to self-catering *gîtes*, holiday villages, and camp sites. Facilities include sailing clubs and schools, windsurfing, boat launching ramps, equipped beaches, golf, riding, tennis, canoeing, and bicycles and boats can be hired. There are also some very good walks with signposted footpaths through the woods and hills on all sides of the lake (the GR44 and GR46 pass close to the lake).

Only 10km (6 miles) away to the east is the second largest lake in Limousin, the **Lac Lavaud-Gelade**, but, unlike Vassiviere, this lovely lake has not been developed touristically, apart from a single basic camp site.

The town of **Aubusson**, famous for its tapestries, lies 86km (53 miles) east of Limoges and about 30km (19 miles) north-east of Lac de Vassiviere. The making of tapestries was introduced to Aubusson from Flanders in the fourteenth century, and reached its finest level in the sixteenth and seventeenth centuries, but the industry was ruined at the time of the religious wars. Many of the best craftsmen were Huguenots who emigrated from France when the persecution of Protestants started again after the revocation in 1685 of the Edict of Nantes, which had given them some protection. During the

Aubusson is famous for its tapestries which can be seen in exhibits in the town

nineteenth century the industry revived slightly, but it was not until the 1930s that it was revitalised, when the great French artist, Jean Lurcat, began to design tapestries and was joined by a number of other fine painters. Today the Jean Lurcat Cultural and Artistic Centre includes the Departmental Museum of Tapestry, which exhibits in turn different tapestries from its stock of works by Lurcat and his contemporaries. There are also rooms devoted to the history of tapestry, and to the different looms and methods of weaving.

The Maison du Vieux Tapissier, next door to the Syndicat d'Initiative, is a fine sixteenth-century house which was once the home of a family of weavers. It contains objects and furniture relating to traditional life in Aubusson, and on the first floor a weaver's workroom is fitted out as it would have been in the past. In the same street, La Rue Vieille, which is pedestrianised, the ancient houses have been restored and are now art galleries, antique shops, and craftsmen's studios. Not far from La Rue Vieille, on the other side of the Grande Rue, is the Hôtel de Ville where a major exhibition of modern and classical tapestries is held throughout every summer.

On the D942 from Aubusson north to Gueret, is the small town of **Ahun** (25km/15½ miles) situated on a hill above the picturesque valley of the Creuse. At the foot of the hill, beside the river, the village of Moutier d'Ahun contains one of the artistic treasures of France. The village church is a mixture of Romanesque and Gothic, the transept, bell tower and choir are of the earlier period, and the rest is

Gothic or Flamboyant Gothic. The impressive architecture and fine sculpture alone make the church worth a visit, but what makes it exceptional is the carved panelling which covers the walls of the apse and the choir. Moutier d'Ahun was originally a Benedictine abbey, and these carvings were commissioned by the monks, and carried out between 1673 and 1681 by a master sculptor from Auvergne, called Simon Bauer. The monks' stalls, twenty-six of them, are decorated with fantastic themes, while those of the wall panelling are taken mostly from nature, and often seem to oppose symbols of good and evil. The most striking single piece of carving is the lectern with two lions back to back, each holding a reading tray in its front paws.

The department of the Creuse, in which Aubusson and Moutier d'Ahun are situated also includes the eastern part of the rugged Plateau de Millevaches, but for the most part it is a gentler countryside than the uplands in the south and in the department of Corrèze. The Creuse is characterised by lower, sweeping wooded hills, and valleys with fields and meadows through which countless rivers and streams wander. There are many pretty villages but no town of any size, and very few major roads. This sympathetic landscape is ideal for all forms of open-air activity and leisure. You can do your own thing based on some quiet village inn of the Logis de France style, or you can book an organised activity holiday which includes accommodation and food, and often a local guide. These vary from one night up to 6 nights (7 days), and the activities covered include walking, cycling, canoeing, fishing, shooting, cross-country motor cycling, and horse-riding, as well as more specialised walks to identify mushrooms, or to see the fauna and flora around remote lakes, and bird-watching expeditions. Of a more unusual kind there are short stays in which visitors learn country cooking, or just enjoy life on a working farm, others where you learn how to make bread in the traditional way, and one week and two week courses introducing people to the art of weaving tapestries.

South of the Creuse and east of the Haut-Vienne, the third department of the Limousin region, Corrèze, is altogether more rugged than either of them. It includes much of the Plateau de Millevaches, the deep valley of the Corrèze river, which gives the department its name, and the beautiful valley of the upper Vézère. Between these valleys there is another lofty plateau, the Massif of Monedieres. These ancient hills, rounded by erosion, and nowhere higher than 1,000m (3,280ft), are outposts of the bigger mountains of the Massif Central. The 'capital' of this upland is **Chaumeil**, a pretty little village of granite houses roofed with slates, or *lauzes*, the heavy stone tiles used throughout the Massif Central. West from Chaumeil the D121 crosses the Monedieres, via the hamlet of Freysselines, by a picturesque route of about 20km (12 miles). After Freysselines turn right on to the D128. At a point called the Col du Bois a short road to the right leads to the Suc-au-May, a height which can be reached in a quarter of an hour's walk there and back after leaving the car. From the orientation table a vast panorama can be seen, with the massif of Monedieres in the foreground, the mountains around the Puy de Dôme and the Monts Dore to the east, the mountains of Cantal in the south-east, and the Plateau de Millevaches in the north-east.

The Vézère rises near the village of Millevaches itself, and its upper valley crosses some beautiful countryside, on its way to the charming little towns of Treignac and Uzerche. From Millevaches the D164 keeps in touch with the river valley almost all the way to Bugeat and Viam (23km/14 miles). At Viam cut across country by the D160 to join the D940, another pretty road which leads south to Treignac beside the lake formed by the barrage on the Vézère. From Treignac the river flows almost entirely across country away from roads to Uzerche, and can only be seen from the road near the villages of Peyrissac and Eyburie, where there are bridges. From Uzerche the Vézère flows south past Brive-la-Gaillarde, where it is joined by the Corrèze, then south-east to Montignac and Les Eyzies in Dordogne, where its valley is the site of so many famous prehistoric caves.

Though Corrèze has so much wild country it does have its fair share of things to see, among them castles, museums, ancient churches, and some of the loveliest villages in France. **Treignac** is a charming little place with old slate-roofed houses, the ruins of its ancient castle on terraces overlooking the river, a fifteenth-century market place in granite, and a church (restored) which has some interesting modern stained glass. There is a pleasant walk (¾ hour there and back) by a signposted footpath from the south-west limit of the village to a height which gives fine views of the town and the rocky gorge of the Vézère, particularly from a spot below the top where a group of granite rocks is known as the Madwomen's Rock (Rocher des Folles).

The D16, the road which passes close to the Suc-au-May, also leads, 20km (12 miles) to the north-west of Treignac to another height, Mount Gargan, from which there are panoramic views to the hills in the north, the Limousin hills to the west, and the Massif des Monedieres in the south-east.

There is an old saying in Corrèze that 'he who has a house in Uzerche, has a castle in Limousin'. This is a comment on the number of imposing old private houses and mansions, solidly built in granite, and often with slated towers or turrets, which there are in this small town. **Uzerche** was often attacked and besieged in the Middle Ages, but never once surrendered. In the eighth century at the time of the Moorish invasion from Spain, it was besieged by the Arabs for 7 years. Protected by stout walls and fortified towers, the town held out, but eventually the inhabitants had almost no food left. Rather than surrender, they tried one last ruse. They fattened their last calf and sent it as a present, with the last of their barley, to the commander of the Saracens. Discouraged at this show of plenty, the Arabs raised the siege and went away.

It is worthwhile taking a stroll through the old town. The church of St Pierre is an ancient foundation. The choir dates from the eleventh century, as does the crypt, reckoned to be the oldest in Limousin, and the nave and the bell tower from the twelfth. The church was fortified during the Hundred Years War, and was restored during the seventeenth century and again in the early part of the twentieth century. The pillars in the choir and deambulatory have some finely-sculpted capitals.

In the Rue Pierre Chalaud and the Rue Gaby Furnestin is the only one remaining of the ancient gateways. There are other old houses in the Rue Gaby-Furnestin, including one in which Alexis Boyer, surgeon to the Emperor Napoleon I was born.

Accommodation in Uzerche is limited, and if you want to stay in the area, it is worth knowing that there are Logis de France hotels in Vigeois, 9km (6 miles) to the south-west, and in the village of **Chamboulive**, nicely situated among wooded hills, 16km (10 miles) to the east of Uzerche. Chamboulive has an interesting Romanesque church, restored in the fifteenth century.

If, instead of taking the road west from Treignac to Uzerche, you take the D16 to the south-east, passing the Massif des Monedieres on your right, an attractive drive of 35km (22 miles) brings you to Egletons. A few kilometres south-east by the D991 brings you to the hamlet of **Moustier-Ventadour**. Nearby, on a rocky promontory above the gorge of the Luzege river are the impressive ruins of the Château de Ventadour. It is famous not for its military history but as the birthplace of Bernard de Ventadour, who became one of the most renowned of the troubadours and exponents of courtly love. The Viscounts of Ventadour were a literary family, several of them accomplished poets, but Bernard took his name from the château, not from the family. He was the son of a castle servant, and was born in 1125. At an early age he showed a natural gift for poetry and song, and was educated and encouraged by the family. As a well-built, handsome young man, who wrote love songs and sang them well, he was encouraged rather too freely by the viscountess. The viscount expelled him from the château, and kept a closer eye on his wife.

Bernard was equally well received by a much greater lady, Eleanor of Aquitaine. When she became Queen of England, as the wife of Henry II, she took him to London among her courtiers. After some disagreements with her husband, she returned to France, again taking Bernard de Ventadour with her. Henry II sent soldiers to bring her back to England, pointedly leaving Bernard behind, and kept her under house arrest. Bernard de Ventadour stayed 10 years with another noble, the Count of Niort, without further amorous involvement, and towards the end of his life retired to a monastery in Dordogne. He died at the turn of the century, leaving a collection of songs which were sung by other troubadours in the Middle Ages.

From Moustier-Ventadour a narrow road offers good views of the castle and takes you closer to the ruins. A footpath leads up to the site (½ hour there and back), where two towers, the high walls, rooms and courtyards of the interior, and a barbican, make it easy to recreate in imagination what was, for most of its history, an impregnable fortress. When at last it was captured, by the English during the Hundred Years War, it was by treachery, not frontal attack.

The D991 carries on eastwards by a winding and picturesque route through wooded hills and crossing the gorge of the Vianon to the old hillside town of **Neuvic**. Its narrow lanes lined by ancient granite houses give Neuvic a lot of character, which is enhanced by the lovely islanded lake, the second largest in Corrèze, created by a barrage on the River Triouzoune. The lake has a beach and facilities for sailing, windsurfing, and fishing, as well as bathing. Horseriding, cycling, and walking on signposted footpaths are among other amenities available. There is a lakeside camp site and hotel accommodation in the area. During World War II the Resistance movement was very strong in the Corrèze area, and Neuvic has an interesting museum with souvenirs and documents relating to these activities. The Musee Henri Queuille is named after a local politician who was thirteen times French Minister of Agriculture, and founder of the Credit Agricole, now one of the most important banks in France.

Travellers who enjoy wild scenery and who do not mind tortuous roads should press on from Neuvic along the D20 and follow its twists and turns until it joins the D979. About 3km (2 miles) from the Barrage of Neuvic d'Ussel, which forms the lake of Neuvic and from which there is a good view, there is an optional diversion of 4km (2 ½ miles) down a very picturesque road into very wild country leading to the Barrage de Mareges, a well-known but little visited

A typical farmhouse in Limousin

beauty spot. Beyond this the roads become extremely narrow and complicated and it is probably wiser to return to the D20. At the junction with the D979 turn right and follow the road towards Bort-les-Orgues. There are three remarkable things to be seen just before you reach the town itself. First, a turning to the right, the D127, takes you to Chantery and just outside this village there are some steps and a path leading to the foot of the 'Orgues'. These are huge blocks of basalt about 2km (1 mile) long and 100m (328ft) high, produced by the cooling of a particular kind of lava in the days when the Massif Central was volcanic. They were given the name of Orgues because of their supposed similarity to organ pipes. It is true that they are tall and narrow, but they are not especially regular in pattern. There are similar formations in other parts of the Massif Central, but these are the most impressive and are of particular interest to geologists.

Instead of following the D127 all the way to Chantery, you can take the road ahead through the villages of Sarroux and St Julien to the Site de St Nazaire, another famous beauty spot. This is a half-hour walk there and back from the car park along a path of the Stations of the Cross. At the end of the promontory a Calvary marks a point from which there is a glorious view of the gorges of the Dordogne and the Diege.

Return to the D979 and continue towards the town for another kilometre or so, where the road crosses the top of one of the greatest barrages in France. There is a car park and from the barrage there is a splendid view up the lake, 18km (11 miles) long, created by the retention of the waters of the Dordogne. This huge wall of concrete is the first step in the water staircase of the Dordogne which controls the flow of this great river. There are four others of almost equal importance, Mareges, which you may have already seen, L'Aigle, Chastang and Sablier. Between them, the hydro-electric stations at these barrages produce about 5 per cent of all the electricity used in France. At this barrage there is a model, with sound commentary, of the whole hydro-electric system of the Massif Central. During the summer season boat trips on the lake are available and there is a regular motor boat service to the Château de Val (10km/6 miles).

Bort-les-Orgues has a number of hotels but is not itself an especially interesting town, but anyone in the vicinity should consider making the short trip to the **Château de Val**, one of the most beautifully-sited castles in France. To reach it take the D922 towards La Bourboule. Just after leaving Bort-les-Orgues there is a fine view on the left of the great concrete wall of the barrage, all 700,000 cubic metres of it, much bigger and higher than might be expected. It gives a clear idea of what it needs to hold up, even partially, the force of a great river. About 5km (3 miles) after leaving the town a road on the left, with the village of Lanobre on the right, leads to the Château de Val. Left high and dry on its promontory as the waters of the Dordogne rose to fill the valley, when the barrage was completed in 1954, the Château de Val, can justly claim to look like a fairy-tale castle, and it is one of the most photographed in France. The interior of the château does not have the dramatic quality of the exterior, but there are some impressive staircases and two fine Renaissance fireplaces. Every summer it is used as a setting for exhibitions of different kinds, and the château is floodlit every night. The only supervised bathing beach on the lake is next to the château, and it is also a base for boat trips on the lake.

Brive-la-Gaillarde, the largest town in southern Limousin, is served by motorail, and as such it is a useful arrival and departure point for motorists intending to tour southern Limousin by car. It is a lively town, an administrative centre, with good restaurants and shops, but little else to interest the visitor.

In the extreme south of the department of Corrèze the small town of **Argentat** is an excellent base for a country holiday. The town itself with its picturesque old houses is beautifully placed on the upper Dordogne. It has its own small barrage a mile above the town, which helps to control the outflow from the great Chastang dam and hydro-

The Pont Valentré at Cahors is a fine example of a medieval fortified bridge, Agenais-Périgord-Quercy

One of the many picturesque river-valleys in Limousin

Arnac-Pompadour the 'Horse Lover's City', Limousin

A rural market in the Auvergne

electric station 10km (6 miles) upstream. A mile beyond the dam a signposted footpath leads off the D29 to a belvedere with fine views of the dam and the reservoir. The D29 crosses the barrage to the village of St Martin and from there the D18 to Marcillac la Croisille (14km/9 miles) and then the D978 lead (a further 30km/19 miles) to the Barrage de l'Aigle, another very impressive dam with a belvedere and views of the lake and the valley.

Of a wide choice of interesting sites, picturesque villages, and beauty spots which can be visited in easy excursions from Argentat the Tours de Merle, Collonges la Rouge, and Gimels-les-Cascades are among the best.

The Tours de Merle, the ruins of a medieval fortress in the spectacularly wild landscape of the Maronne valley, make it easy to imagine how medieval lords secure in an impregnable castle could dominate the surrounding countryside. But the development of cannons changed its fortunes, as the fortress was vulnerable to bombardment from surrounding heights, and the site was gradually abandoned. From Argentat take the D980 to St Privat and then the D13 south to St Cirque-la-Loutre and continue on the D13. On a left-hand bend there is a parking place from which there is a dramatic view of the towers immediately below, and they can be reached by a footpath leading down to them. For walkers the GR480 has some beautiful stretches in this southern part of Corrèze.

Collonges-la-Rouge is reached by the D12 south from Argentat. The route follows the picturesque Dordogne for 20km (12 miles), then just before Beaulieu-sur-Dordogne (which has a fine Romanesque church) turn north on to the D940 and then after 6km (4 miles), left on to the D38, which leads direct to Meyssac and **Collonges-la-Rouge**. This small, but lovely village is built entirely in red sandstone, and has four splendid sixteenth-century mansions, the House of the Siren, the Hotel de la Ramade de Friac, the Castel de Vassignac, and the Castel de Maussac, built by powerful local families, and a fine eleventh- to twelfth-century Romanesque church with two naves, one in Flamboyant Gothic style. Next to the church there is a former Penitent's Chapel built in the fifteenth century. Near the chapel there is a narrow, winding street with more old houses, turreted and balconied and decorated with flowers and climbing plants.

Gimel-les-Cascades is a beauty spot, one of the most wild and picturesque in all Limousin, where the Montane river has carved out a gorge and then hurls itself over a series of waterfalls not far from the village. A signposted path leads through Vuillier Park to the best places to view the waterfalls. The first, the Grand Cascade, drops 45m (148ft) to a pool from which the second, called the Redole, falls another 27m (89ft), and further on the third, the Queue de Cheval (Horse's Tail) pours from a little promontory among the rocks and drops 60m (197ft) on to the jumbled rocks of an impassable ravine. The total fall is 140m (459ft). The walk to the viewpoints, there and back, takes about an hour and may be tiring for those who are not fit and good walkers.

The village church contains an eighteenth-century pulpit and a fifteenth-century pieta, and also has a wonderful treasure. The most remarkable item is the reliquary of St Stephen. Made in the late twelfth century and decorated with Limoges enamels and precious stones, with the heads of the figures in relief. It depicts the stoning of St Stephen, and is one of the finest of all the Limousin reliquaries. The treasure also includes a fourteenth-century silver gilt bust of St Dumines, a hermit who lived in the Montane ravines, a thirteenth-century monstrance in gilded copper, a fourteenth-century champleve enamel pyx, and a curious eighteenth-century plate for the host.

The village of **Gimel**, hidden away in its wonderful setting, with a church containing treasures from the medieval past, symbolises the strange, remote character of the Limousin region. Nearby, just beyond the next village Touzac, reached by the D53, there is a small lake set in a romantic setting of pines, birches, and oaks. It has a bathing place, and is a good spot for a picnic lunch.

Further Information
— Limousin —

Museums and Other Places of Interest

Arnac-Pompadour
Château
Visit of the château terrasses am/pm. The stud is open to visitors on weekday afternoons from 1 July to the end of February.

Aubusson
Tapestry Museum
Centre Culturel Jean Lurcat
Open: am/pm all year round (closed Tuesday, mornings only in high season. Also closed one week in June and one in October.

Maison du Vieux Tapissie
Open: am/pm mid-June to end September.

Tapestry Exhibition in Hotel de Ville
Open: am/pm mid-June to end September.

Châlus-Chabrol
Château
Accompanied visits am/pm from 1 July to mid-September.
☎ 55 58 18 69

Château des Cars
Haute-Vienne
Open: all year round. Admission free by appointment.
☎ 55 36 90 22

Château de Val
Open: am/pm for accompanied visits
from mid-June to mid-September.
Closed December-June.

Coussac-Bonneval
Château
Open: from mid-March to the end of
November for accompanied visits on
the afternoons of Wednesday, Saturday
and Sunday.

Douarnazac
Montbrun Château
Open: am/pm for accompanied visits
in summer. Afternoons only in winter.

Jumilhac le Grand
Château
Accompanied visits am/pm from 1
July to mid-September. At other times
on afternoons of Sundays and public
holidays.

Lastours
Château
Accompanied visits from mid-July to
end August.

Limoges
Adrian Dubouche National Museum
Place Winston Churchill
Open: all year round (closed on
Tuesdays).

*Municipal Museum of the Palais de
l'Eveche*
(Next to cathedral)
Open: am/pm all year round (closed
on Tuesdays except from 1 July to 31
August). Admission free.

Nexon
Château
Open: am/pm all year round. Guided
tours in summer including stud.

Rochechouart
Château (including Musee Departementale)
Open: am/pm during July and August.
Afternoons only at other times (closed
on Tuesdays and also on Mondays
outside high season).

Boat Trips
Available in summer on Lake St
Pardoux, Lake Vassiviere, and from
Bort-les-Orgues/Château de Val. Also
on the Dordogne from Pont du
Chambon, or Spontour, or Chastang.

Tourist Information Offices

Aubusson
Office de Tourisme-Syndicat
  d'Initiative
23200 Aubusson
☎ 55 66 32 12

Gueret
Creuse Expansion Tourisme
43 Place Bonnyaud
23000 Gueret
☎ 55 51 93 23

Limoges
Comité Régional de Tourisme du
  Limousin
27 Blvd de la Conderie
87031 Limoges
☎ 55 45 18 80

Office de Tourisme-Syndicat
  d'Initiative
Boulevard de Fleurus
87000 Limoges
☎ 55 34 46 87

Tulle
Office de Tourisme-Syndicat
  d'Initiative Tulle (Correze)
Quai Baluze
19000 Tulle
☎ 55 26 59 61

Ussel
Office de Tourisme-Syndicat
  d'Initiative Ussel (Correze)
Place Voltaire
19200 Ussel

4 • Auvergne

The region known as the Auvergne fills most of the central and northern part of the Massif Central in southern France. Divided into four *départements*, Allier, Puy-de-Dôme, Cantal and Haute-Loire, it is a region created mostly by volcanic action. Wild rugged uplands are cut by deep winding gorges, often accessible only by the narrowest of roads. But, far from being an arid landscape, the Auvergne is gentle. Beneath the rocky summits, rolling moorlands and forests give way in their turn to lush meadows and fertile valleys. With the exception of the northern industrial belt, there are few towns of any size. Most of the settlements tend to be small groups of ancient villages and hamlets sited on sunny uplands. It is these villages and their surrounding countryside which will offer the greatest reward to anyone seeking places off the beaten track.

To preserve its special natural beauty, the Auvergne has two nature parks within its boundary. The largest is the Parc Régional des Volcans d'Auvergne which covers the highest parts of Puy-de-Dôme and Cantal, and includes Puy-de-Sancy, at 1,886m (6,186ft), the highest point not only of the Auvergne, but of the Massif Central. The other park is to the east, the Parc Régional du Livradois-Forez. Slightly smaller than the Parc des Volcans, it takes in the Monts du Forez, Plaine d'Ambert and the countryside around La Chaise-Dieu.

The region's main volcanoes formed 10,000 years ago, were the size of Vesuvius or Mount Etna. From vantage points around Mont-Dore and Cantal it is possible to trace the outline of a crater about 64km (40 miles) in circumference, together with the remains of smaller eruptions in the middle. Pinnacles, lava flows and cones, some rising to a height of 1,860m (6,101ft), dot the area, creating an often strange landscape. A number of the more prominent lava flows and volcanic stumps have been used for the protection offered by their inaccessibility. The Chapelle St Michel d'Aiguilhe for example, is built on the very summit of a high rocky pinnacle, the stump of a long dead volcano.

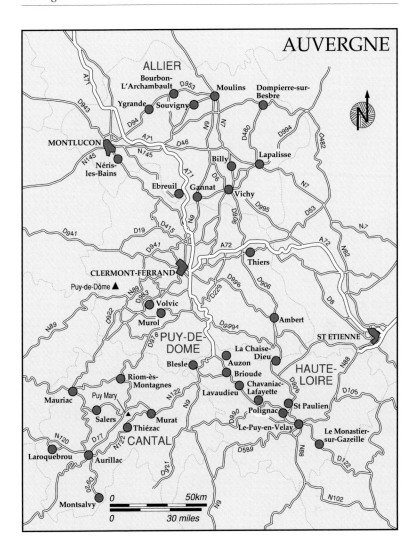

Glaciers honed the landscape, carving deep and mysterious gorges. Three major rivers and numerous minor streams flow through the Auvergne. The Allier is the only true Auvergnat river; it rises to the south of Le Puy and flows north through the region. The Dordogne which rises from the Puy-de-Sancy soon leaves the region. The Dordogne which rises from the Puy-de-Sancy soon leaves the Auvergne, flowing south and west towards the Atlantic Coast at Bordeaux. The Loire on the other hand starts by issuing from a pipe beneath the slopes of the Gerbier de Jonc in the Ardèche before again flowing north, past Le Puy before it reaches the plains north of the Massif Central and on towards the Atlantic.

The volume and quality of waters flowing out of the region have been exploited since before Roman times. Spas, with Vichy the most famous, developed over the years, using the properties of waters which flow from the volcanic rocks of the region. Reservoirs created in the narrow gorges of the surrounding hill country now provide hydro-electricity for a large part of central France.

The Romans did not have an easy time conquering this part of their steadily growing empire. Originally known as *Arvenia*, the local Gauls led by their chief Vercingétorix, put up a strong resistance and the territory did not submit to Roman rule until 27BC, when it became part of Aquitaine.

Christianity came to the region in the third century, introduced by St Nectaire and St Austremoine, together with Ste Marie. Later missionaries moved into the hilly districts and literally carved settlements out of the surrounding forest. Villages which eventually sprang from these settlements are usually named after their founder. Where the missionary was particularly active in a locality it often lead to confusion if all the villages were to be named after him. The problem was overcome by the addition of some simple description of the site. From these names we can chart the progress of an ancient saint as he spread the gospel amongst the heathen dwellers of what are still remote corners of the Auvergne.

English history has close links with the Auvergne. Part of Aquitaine, it became an English possession when Eleanor of Aquitaine married Henry Plantagenet. The Bourbons and Médicis all had strong interests in the land of this region, but their descendants were brought to heel by Cardinal Richelieu. A terror to any seventeenth-century landowning gentry who disobeyed his will, he destroyed many of their castles. These ruins now gently moulder on commanding hilltops, or deep within silent forests, poignant reminders of abandoned power.

In 1940 the collaborationist government under Maréchal Pétain moved to Vichy, but many of the local inhabitants continued the struggle against their German oppressors. Taking their name from the *maquis*, or scrub-covered hillsides, the local resistance tied down large numbers of German troops during the occupation.

Anyone visiting the Auvergne today will be met by a totally different reception. Friendly and kind, Auvergnats welcome strangers and villagers in the remotest settlements will cheerfully while away the day. To foreigners their dialect may not be easy to under-

*Bilberry picking in the
Auvergne*

stand, but these are a people who suffer fools gladly and will go to great lengths to make themselves understood. Sleepy though the countryside may be, a region where you might still find oxen yoked to the plough, but backward it is not; all the Auvergne asks is that you enter it on a voyage of discovery.

Many of the ancient crafts are kept alive by enthusiasts in the larger villages. Folk dance, local costume and lace making are just three of the crafts where local interest keeps them alive, handing them down from one generation to another. It is not uncommon to see a young girl being taught the intricacies of lace making by an elder.

Accommodation is as you find it. Large hotels are few and far between, especially away from the major towns. Although many prefer to camp these days, the best places are the small unpretentious rural hotels one finds in most of the villages. Often run by the same family, handed down generation to generation for over a hundred years, these are the places whose discovery is the highlight of any trip into a little publicised area. Food tends to be simple but well cooked and with pride. *Coq-au-vin* is a regional speciality, as is mutton (*brayaude*), as well as pork stews and potato cakes cooked with cream. Fresh-water fish dishes are popular, especially with the growth of trout farms. The moors abound with *myrtilles* (bilberries), which are used in mouthwatering tarts. The local cheeses are many and varied, ranging from almost rock hard to soft and runny. There is a *Bleu d'Auvergne*, or the white and creamy *Cérilly* and *Savaron* which has a yellowish tinge and a sharp bite. Wine from the surrounding area can be varied, but quite drinkable. The locals also make *eaux-de-vie* from almost every plant that grows in this hilly region, but beware their potency!

Exploring the remoter parts of the Auvergne can be one of the easiest, yet most fruitful voyages of discovery. Even the so-called major roads twist and wind in an almost haphazard fashion, following the dictates of a land formed jointly by volcanoes and ice movement. Side roads meander to unspoilt villages; villages where the pace of life goes on much as it has done for centuries. Wandering across heather moors is a delight and climbing the remains of the dead volcanoes is an airy exercise in ridge walking. Fortunately without the hazards associated with alpine excursions. Many of the ruined châteaux are not even signposted, only the map will show their whereabouts, and their romantic history will only be revealed to those with the imagination to fill them with long-dead people.

It does not matter how you explore the Auvergne, either by car, bicycle, on foot, or by emulating Robert Louis Stephenson who together with Modestine his donkey, explored the Cévennes to the south of Le Puy.

There are few of the awesome passes one finds in the Alps, but some of the roads, especially in the centre of the region around the Monts du Cantal, or crossing the narrow valleys, do need care. As a result, road cycling can be tough and distances deceptive, but off-road cycling on mountain bikes has its rewards. It is possible to hire bicycles, either mountain or standard, in all the main towns and many of the larger villages. The 'Star of the Auvergne Summits' is a cycle-way that starts near St Etienne and follows a high-level route to St Flour.

The network of footpaths is limitless. There are thirteen main hiking routes, the Grandes Randonnées, covering 1,000km (620 miles) throughout the Auvergne. The GR3 follows the Loire and the GR4 crosses the Parc des Volcans. Others are of a shorter duration such as the GR400 round the volcanoes of Cantal, the GR441 near Le Puy, or the GR30 which visits a series of lakes. Accommodation can be found along the way in simple *gîtes* or *relais* without the need to carry a tent.

Footpaths and quiet lanes throughout the region offer pleasant rambles well away from the noise of traffic. La Chaise-Dieu is just one of the numerous villages which make ideal centres for quiet pedestrian exploration. Brian Spencer's *Walking in the Alps*, published by Moorland Publishing, has a section devoted to La Chaise-Dieu and describes seven easy walks around the village, together with a list of things to do.

Canoeing, white water rafting and hang gliding top the list of exciting ways to explore the Auvergne.

Allier

This *département* in the northern corner of the Auvergne has none of the dramatic volcanic hills of its sisters to the south, and it is far less forested. This is a countryside given over to both the plough and grazing animals. The rural scene is only broken by a handful of towns of any size, with the famous spa town of Vichy the best known.

Herds of cattle browse in quiet watermeadows beside gently flowing streams meandering unrestricted of the rocky confines to the south of the province. In other places vineyards line the sunny hillsides, where well drained soil grows some highly drinkable wines. Once part of the Duchy of Bourbon, this is countryside for quiet wandering to sample the benefits of the land in both village restaurants and *auberges*, or bought from the local store for a picnic.

The A71-E11 autoroute more or less cuts the department in half. To the east the land undulates gently towards the River Allier. The spa town of **Vichy** is on the east bank of the now widening River Dore. It still retains much of its turn-of-the-century grandeur, though a little faded. Used by Pétain as the headquarters of his collaborationist government during World War II, Vichy's name was once linked with cowardice. However, it was not the town's fault and once its misdeeds were forgiven, people again flocked to Vichy to drink the slightly fizzy waters. It is worth visiting Vichy if only to wander round its colourful municipal gardens, or maybe drink the waters first discovered by Roman settlers; there are over 400 springs in and around the town for you to choose from.

The countryside around Vichy is probably the most rewarding part of Allier. **Gannat** is about 19km (12 miles) to the west, along the N209, it has two ancient churches and a medieval château. The latter houses a local museum and the town holds a music festival from time to time where the accent is on ancient melodies and folk songs. **Ebreuil** a few miles further west across the autoroute, sits beside a widening of the Sioule and where long distance canoe trips are organised.

Beyond Ebreuil, the land begins to rise and the road enters one of the few forests in the Allier. This is the Forêt des Colettes and where the ancient ramparts of **Charroux** lead the way to the Gorges de

Chouvigny. Charroux has a number of picturesque houses and an interesting fortified church.

To the north of Vichy, there is a twelfth-century fortress at **Billy** built at the command of the Sire de Bourbon to guard the east bank of the Allier. In fact the whole village is surrounded by ramparts, making it one of the most heavily fortified places in the region.

East now along side road to the N7 and to **Lapalisse**. The town sits beneath the benevolent gaze of its 700-year-old château. Enlarged by Jaques de Chabannes, a marshall of France in the sixteenth century, the château has a collection of fine tapestries, exquisite furniture as well as portraits of past owners. The history of the place is re-enacted in a production called *La Memoire du Temps* each Friday and Saturday evening in summer.

Children and châteaux hunters will enjoy visiting **St Pourçain-sur-Besbre**. A minor road the D480, follows the River Besbre north from Lapalisse. There are two châteaux nearby; the Château de Beauvoir only allows visitors into its grounds, but it is the **Château de Toury** which will interest children most. This is a castle straight out of a fairytale, complete with toy-like towers and turrets, which, according to legend, was built in one night and is guarded by a ferocious red dragon! There is a small open-air zoo, the Zoo du Pal, a little further up the road to complete a day out for children and adults alike. Cars are not allowed inside the zoo and visitors are transported in a small train. There is also a theme park in the adjacent Parc d'Attractions which is reached by monorail.

About 5km (3 miles) further on the quiet town of **Dompierre-sur-Besbre** makes a good base for anyone exploring the valleys of the Besbre and nearby Loire. To its west is the old market town of **Moulins**, marking the northern edge of the Massif Central and once the capital of the Ducs de Bourbon. Though surrounded by industry and commerce, the ancient heart of the town an unspoilt enclave huddled close to its magnificent cathedral. There are three interesting museums in and around Moulins devoted to local art and archaeology as well as the folklore of the district. The Musée du Folklore et du Vieux Moulins is housed in a fifteenth-century mansion which has a curious free-standing clock-tower. Four small figures of a mother, father and two children take turns to draw attention to each quarter hour.

North of Moulins is **Villeneuve-sur-Allier** where Le Rau, an ancient fort, guards the roadway through its portals. Nearby is the nineteenth-century château of Balaine which is surrounded by an extensive botanical garden, the oldest private arboretum in France.

Westwards is the other major area of forest. This is the **Forêt de Tronçais**, once owned by the Ducs de Bourbon. Forestry and wildlife live side by side, the forest is the home of a great many deer, and in one corner an oak grove, said to be the finest in France, was established in the fourteenth century. South-east of the forest is the popular little spa town of **Bourbon-L'Archambault** where the waters are said to cure rheumatism.

Souvigny still more to the south-east, has a priory church dating from the eleventh century where a number of Ducs de Bourbon and their ladies are buried beneath marble splendour. In the nearby Eglise-Musée St Marc there is a beautifully carved *Calendrier* (Calendar) which shows the appropriate task for each season, such as treading the grapes in autumn, or thawing out before a blazing midwinter fire.

The smaller Forêt de Gros-Bois surrounds the ruins of the Abbaye de Gramont and not far away is **Ygrande** and its attractive church and rustic museum.

South of the Forêt de Tronçais is Hérisson, a fortified village supported by the now ruined castle built in the thirteenth century.

Montluçon though industrialised, the largest town west of the autoroute in this part of the Allier, has managed to preserve its ancient town centre and still huddles beneath the shelter of a fortress built by Louis II during the Hundred Years War. There are two museums: the Musée Folklorique is devoted to local industry and ceramics, and not terribly interesting, but the Musée International de la Vielle has a fascinating collection of old musical instruments.

Néris-les-Bains is about 8km (5 miles) south-east of Montluçon along the N144. Nowadays a pleasant little spa town with a full programme of entertainments, Néris's waters were first discovered by the Romans. Little remains of the once gracious Roman settlement, but what has been found is on display in the local museum.

Puy-de-Dôme

This is the largest of the four *départements* of the Auvergne. The centre for all commerce for the region is the industrial city of Clermont-Ferrand, home of the Michelin Tyre Company and to which all major roads in the area are heading. Despite the surrounding industry, Clermont-Ferrand is worth the odd hour or two spent admiring its municipal gardens and its ornately decorated churches and museums. The Musée de Ranquet in the Petite-Rue-St Pierre is particularly of interest to anyone with a mechanical inclination.

Those who seek the out of the way places will naturally gravitate to the central part of Puy-de-Dôme. To the east is an area of gently rolling forested hills which is designated as the **Parc Naturel Régional du Livardois-Forez**, one of the most recently created natural parks in France. West across the valley of the River Allier is the more rugged Parc Naturel Régional des Volcans d'Auvergne, which Puy-de-Dôme shares jointly with its neighbouring department of Cantal.

The Parc Naturel Régional du Livardois-Forez is made up of two main ranges of hills; Monts du Forez and Livradois. Two major rivers, the Dore and the Allier, run through these hills, fed by a multitude of tributaries. The climate is drier than the western part of the Massif Central and often warmer.

With the exception of Thiers, in the north of the park, there are no towns of any size in the area; Ambert in the centre and Billom on the north-western boundary, the only other places of any size, are small market towns and centres of local industry.

Much of the Forez mountains which mark the north-eastern limits of the regional park, are covered in wild moors, a paradise for botanists and naturalists. The area's sub-glacial conditions support unique forms of peat-bog vegetation. It is home to a number of rare and protected species (short-toed eagles, crag martins, etc). It is here too that visitors will find *jasseries*, mountain farms where Fourme d'Ambert cheese is still made by traditional methods.

The Livardois hills are softer and more gentle. The area around Billom is rich in medieval remains, with a large number of castles, in varying states of repair, perched on volcanic outcrops, witnesses to a troubled past. During the Hundred Years War this part of France lay on the border with English possessions in France and frequently suffered from incursions by warring parties and *routiers*. Billom is also home to Gaperon cheese, flavoured with garlic and pepper.

The majority of the population work in either farming or forestry — woods account for approximately 40 per cent of the Livardois Regional Park — and the forests around La Chaise-Dieu are among the most productive in France. The farmland in the valley around Ambert is particularly rich, but you will also find small dairy farms in the hills, and unlike other parts of the Auvergne a certain amount of sheep farming. It is here that the old-fashioned 'Fourme d'Ambert' cheese is produced, the closest equivalent to Stilton you will find in France.

The area offers a wide variety of holiday possibilities ranging from gentle touring to fairly extreme white-water sports and bungee jumping in the gorges. There are a number of well-kept two star hotels and the overall reputation for good cooking enjoyed by the

Boules, a popular rural pastime

Auvergne is in no way belied by the local cuisine. An increasing number of local people also offer visitors meals and accommodation in their farms and houses.

The area is ideally suited to walking, horse riding or cycling holidays; the best way to discover the out of the way places. A large number of waymarked tracks exist (GR3 and GR412 pass through the department); the latter are long distance tracks and will need several days to complete. Others have been signposted to enable the visitor to circuit a particular village in a few hours, with walks of varying difficulty.

The region is rich in craft industries: Thiers is famous throughout France for its cutlery; a visit to the Maison des Couteliers is recommended. Le Moulin de Richard de Bas near Ambert, is an old paper mill, and museum, where paper is still produced using traditional techniques. Local lace is also famous (see the Musée de la Dentelle at Arlanc and the Hôtel de la Dentelle at Brioude in the neighbouring department of Haute-Loire). In Ambert the Musée de la Fourme et des Fromages traces the history of local cheese making and offers visitors the chance to see cheese actually being made. The Livardois-Forez natural park has assembled a list of local crafts people, whose workplaces may be visited or whose food may be enjoyed 'in situ', and built this into a holiday circuit; *La Route des Métiers*.

Descending the ridges of Puy Mary

charged waters of the Fontaines Pétrifiantes to turn inanimate objects to stone. Nearby **Murol** has a lake, Lac Chambon where you can swim, fish, hire a pedalo or bicycle, or visit the prehistoric Grottes de Jonas and the rural museum at Moulin-Neuf. Murol itself has some ancient ruins of fortifications built in the thirteenth century.

Cantal

The *département* of Cantal shares the southern half of the Parc Naturel Régional des Volcans d'Auvergne with its neighbour, Puy-de-Dôme. From Puy Mary 1,787m (5,863ft), the highest point in the Monts du Cantal, something like a dozen valleys radiate with an almost clockface precision. The peak, like the others of this chain is part of an ancient volcano. Its summit is bare rock and lower down the boggy hillside, moorland gives way to sub-alpine meadows. In turn they lead to the lush pastures of the valleys. Forests cloak most of the lower slopes, forests where nature holds sway, regenerating woodlands felled in careful rotation. Animal life is plentiful, and you should see deer in the woodlands as well as marmots sunning themselves on the higher ridges.

Two high-level roads reach the Pas de Peyrol, making an ideal starting point for anyone who wants to explore the ridges and summits around Puy Mary. Cantal has some excellent walking country.

Walking in the Auvergne is a popular pastime

The natural beauty of the Auvergne

Le-Puy-en-Velay, Auvergne

Finding accommodation can be the highlight of a tour of Cantal. Almost every village has its small, family-run hôtel or *auberge*, and even some of the restaurants will have one or two bedrooms available. The cuisine is simple, but excellent as befits this rural, but far from backward district.

Salers is at the bottom of one of the roads crossing the Pas de Peyrol, the D680. The houses built from the local black lava, still seem to huddle behind long defunct fortifications. Narrow streets and even narrower alleys offer ideal photo opportunities, or simply somewhere to wander and maybe admire the glass engravers' craft. The village church was consecrated in 1552 and is well worth visiting, as is the Maison de Barques, about a block away, a house furnished in seventeenth-century style. Salers hosts a colourful pilgrimage dedicated to Notre-Dame-de-Lorette on Trinity Sunday.

Mauriac a little further west and outside the park, also has a special pilgrimage, this one is held in early May and is in honour of Notre-Dame-des-Miracles. The church is twelfth century and there are three modest hotels. About 3km (2 miles) south-west of the village, the Cascade de Salins is but one of the dramatic waterfalls in the Gorges d'Auze.

Moving clockwise around the base of the Monts du Cantal, by roads which climb in and out of the steep valleys draining towards the Dordogne, the D678 leads into **Riom-ès-Montagnes**. Built on the foundations of a Gallo-Roman settlement, this unpretentious holiday resort is an ideal centre for walking the forested lower slopes of the Cantal hills. The Maison de la Gentiane et la Flore has an attractive display of local vegetation and medicinal plans.

North of Riom, the Gorges de la Rhue are carved deep into the lower and softer rocks and although a road, the D679 follows the ravine for most of its length, the only way to explore the side valleys is on foot. Above the hamlet of Cornillou, a waterfall which takes its name from the settlement, can only be reached by way of a disused cart track.

Apchon is to the south-west of Riom along a quiet side road, the D49. Built of stones carved from the local volcanic rock, the village sits below the benevolent protection of a ruined fortress. Visit the castle, if only to enjoy the view. Continue south of Apchon to **Cheylade** where there are two spectacular waterfalls, the Cascade de la Roche and Cascade du Sartre in close proximity to each other.

Following the D62 south, the road climbs a series of tight hairpin bends to join the Pas de Peyrol road (D680), on the Col de Serres. The road winds its way down the Santoire Valley to Dienne where it turns right and crosses the river. Climbing a low col, the road descends, in and out of forest to **Murat**, an important centre for cheese production. Look out for the ruined castle, demolished on the instructions of Cardinal Richelieu. The site is known locally as the Rocher de Bonnevie and is topped by the statue of Notre-Dame-de la Haute-Auvergne. From it there is a splendid view of mountain and forest.

A right turn outside Murat joins the N122 as it climbs towards **Laveissière** and its reconstructed *buron*, a typical hill farm of the *département*, then on towards the purpose-built ski resort of Super Lioran. Here the main road tunnels beneath the col, but an older way climbs in a couple of hairpins, past a memorial to the local maquis of World War II, then rejoins the N122 descending into the upper reaches of the Cère Valley.

St Jaques-des-Blats shelters in the valley bottom, where a handful of old, but well run *auberges* make ideal bases for walking expeditions on either side of the valley.

Grass covered ridges high above the forested slopes, lead to startlingly abrupt rocky summits, the tangible remains of the huge volcano which once dominated this part of Cantal. To the east of the valley, the summit of Plomb du Cantal 1,855m (6,086ft), can be reached by cable car from Super Lioran. South-west from the summit a high ridge can be followed, over the slightly lower summit of Puy Gros and onwards as long as time, or energies allow. To your right, side ridges lead downward into forest and the main valley. The crowded summit of Plomb du Cantal is far behind and with the exception of a friendly shepherd, it is unlikely you will meet a soul all day. This route and the one following are part of the GR400 long distance footpath, the tour of the Volcans du Cantal.

There is another high-level walk which can be followed by arranging to take a locally hired taxi to the top of the Pas de Peyrol. A path, steep in places, but easy to follow, climbs Puy Mary to join a ridge route to a col, the path climbs Puy de Peyre-Arse and turns right, skirting the dramatic rocks of Puy Griou, the remnant like the other outcrops, of a lava spewing vent. Gradually losing height, the path reaches the high pastures where a left turn joins a steadily improving track down to St Jaques des Blats.

Thiézac is about 6km (4 miles) further on down the valley where there is a pilgrimage every August to the Chapelle de Notre-Dame-de-Consolation. It was built on the orders of Anne of Austria who thought she would never have any children. Her prayers were answered by the birth of a son who became Louis XIV, the 'Sun King'.

From Aurillac the 'capital' of Cantal, a minor road, the D35 climbs high to the north-east and above the Jordanne Valley. Known as the Route des Crêtes, it follows the lower ridges of the Monts du Cantal by winding in and out beneath the higher summits and visits tiny villages such as **Fontanges**. This is where the now ruined Château de Cropières was the birthplace of Mademoiselle de Fontanges, one of Louis XIV's mistresses.

The Route des Crêtes is just one of the almost limitless routes to be enjoyed in the byways around **Aurillac**. The town is an interesting mixture of ancient and modern with sufficient old churches and museums to detain the visitor.

Laroquebrou is about 21km (13 miles) to the west of Aurillac, and is reached by a side road to the left of the N120. The medieval village is at the head of the Gorges de la Cère which are carved deep within the forested slopes leading out of Cantal. There is no road along the valley, but a railway line follows the river and can be used to explore its leafy inner recess.

The countryside of the southern portion of Cantal tends to be lower and less dramatic than the area around the volcanic Monts du Cantal. The land here though still mainly forested, is more tamed and gently rural. However, deep gorges continue the overall character of the Auvergne.

Montsalvy on the winding D920 south from Aurillac, is the most southerly town of any size in Cantal. It fits snugly beneath the wooded plateau of La Châtaigneraie, where it has quietly watched the march of time for at least 1,000 years. From the Puy de l'Arbre above the town you can enjoy a view of the whole of the Massif du Cantal, and fully appreciate its volcanic origins.

Following the departmental boundary north-eastwards, the man-made lake of the Barrage de Grandval makes an interesting stop on the way into Haute-Loire.

Haute-Loire

Following the southern boundary of the Auvergne, the border between Cantal and Haute-Loire passes through the Forêt de Margeride, an area of bloody fighting between the Germans and the local maquis during World War II. A poignant monument beneath Mont Mochet commemorating this brave resistance can only be reached along a remote back road, the D41/D48 south-west of Langeac.

Chavaniac-Lafayette to the north-east of Langeac, is of special interest to students of American history, for this was the birthplace of the eighteenth-century liberal and soldier of fortune, Marie Joseph Paul Yves Roch Gilbert du Motier, Marquis de La Fayette, better known as Lafayette, the general who did much to help the American colonialists win their independence. The village also makes an ideal base for anyone visiting the Gorges de l'Allier.

No roads of any size follow the river through the gorge, but there is a railway which makes one of the most dramatic journeys in this part of France, and runs between Langogne in the south and Langeac. The only way to fully explore the gorge is by a combination of train journeys, getting off at the handful of stations, and filling in the gaps by using a car to reach places accessible by road.

Continuing to move north-eastwards, a diversion should be made to Lac du Bouchet, an almost completely circular lake filling the crater of an extinct volcano. Nearby is the line of a Roman road which can still be traced as a ridge road along the summits of the Monts du Delvès. The road, with side turnings twisting and turning in all directions, eventually leads to Arlemdes, an ancient hamlet built on a hilltop high above the infant Loire.

About 10km (6 miles) as the crow flies to the north-east of Arlemdes, but considerably more by road, **Le Monastier-sur-Gazeille** has an ancient abbey which has still not fully recovered from its destruction during the Hundred Years War. More or less due east of the village, Mont Mezenc at 1,753m (5,752ft), marks the south-eastern limits of the Auvergne and offers some excellent high-level walking.

All roads in this part of the Haute-Loire converge on **Le-Puy-en-Velay**, the *départemental* capital. Hardly coming into the category of being 'off the beaten track', nevertheless, its strange outcrops topped with churches and monuments, make it a place to visit. Venerated since pre-Christian times, it has long been a place of pilgrimage and as a consequence has a wide range of comfortable hotels, *auberges* and excellent restaurants. A little to the north-west, is **Polignac** where a massive basaltic outcrop is dominated by an ancient fortress which once housed an army numbering 800 men along with their families and retainers. The Maison de Bilhac-Polignac encourages after many of the traditional crafts of the area and holds exhibitions and courses including the art of lace making.

The road moves north into the southern portion of the Parc Naturel Régional du Livardois Forez. A few miles short of the boundary is the Château de la Rochelamert which George Sand used as the setting for her novel, *Jean de la Roche*. Nearby are a series of caves which were inhabited in pre-historic times.

The Chapelle St Michel d'Aiguilhe is an outstanding attraction at Le-Puy-en-Velay

The D13 leaves the busier D906 at **St Paulien**, founded by the Romans who knew it as *Ruessium*, then moves on to cross the national park boundary where Allègre sits uncomfortably beneath the ruins of an ancient fortress which look as though they would collapse in a moderate wind, but have stood for centuries. Northwards again, a side turning leads down to Lac de Malaguet, another of the little lakes filling ancient volcano craters which are features of this part of the region. The lake is well stocked with trout and other fish, but permits have to be bought if you fancy catching your supper.

The main road must be rejoined to reach **La Chaise-Dieu**. Fortunately the village is by-passed, leaving it to slumber in almost medieval tranquillity. The Abbaye St Robert dominates this little town and was built in the fourteenth century on the instructions of Pope Clément VI who is also buried there in a splendid tomb. The church is famous for its ornately decorated organ, the centre piece of an annual music festival. Probably the most impressive monument the church possesses is the *Danse Macabre* mural. This compelling painting depicts medieval people from all walks of life dancing with skeletons. Magnificent sixteenth-century Flemish tapestries decorate the opposite wall, and outside, beyond the cloister, the Salle de l'Echo was designed so that the softest whisper of confessing lepers could be easily overheard in a nearby room.

La Chaise-Dieu has a number of small, but comfortable hotels where old-world charm does not mean old-world inconvenience, and where the cuisine is second to none. The village has plenty to offer anyone looking for easy forest walks, a number of long distance footpaths, Grandes Randonnées pass close to the village, or short cycle rides. Bicycles can be hired locally and there is a programme of events ranging from folk dance evenings, to organised walks.

La Chaise-Dieu sits on a ridge-top and the westward flowing streams drain towards the Allier. Mountain roads lead down to the valley and one of them the D561, leads past the Château de Domeyrat to **Lavaudieu**. The village is a scattering of farmhouses and pretty cottages on the banks of the River Senouire which flows into the Allier a few miles to the west. Completing the picturesque setting are an attractive bridge and alleys leading to the ruins of a Benedictine abbey founded almost 1,000 years ago.

Brioude is an important market town for this part of the department. Steeped with legends, this is where St Julien is said to have been hidden shortly after being converted to Christianity. St Ilpize is to the south along the D16 which leaves the main N102 at **Veille-Brioude**. The village seems prepared still to repel attackers who came this way during the Hundred Years War. Its houses are built on the bare strata of the valley sides above the Allier, their cellars carved from the living rock. A little further on is **Blassac** where the fourteenth-century frescoes in the church are kept under lock and key; however if you enquire locally they can be unlocked.

Blassac is at the most northerly section of the Gorges de l'Allier. This part of the river is one of the few accessible by road, as are two short side valleys, both of them remote and ready for exploring.

To the west and north of Brioude the countryside begins to rise towards the Monts du Cezallier, part of the Monts Dore chain. Wooded at first, then giving way to moorland, the area is cut by the Gorges de l'Alagnon. **Blesle** sits in a side valley high above the gorge. Founded by Benedictine monks in the ninth century, the village retains much of its medieval atmosphere.

Auzon is more or less due north of Brioude, just outside the border of the Livardois-Forez National Park. The village and its château suffered at the hands of Cardinal Richelieu's men, but time has healed the scars and in fact has left us with a number of statues dotted about the romantic walls of the ivy-covered ramparts.

East now to the far corner of Haute-Loire, across the deep cleft of the Loire, almost into Ardèche. The N88 linking St Etienne with Le-Puy-en-Velay cuts through the middle, and also two or three fairly important roads wind their way across its rolling hillsides.

From the industrial town of St Etienne a single track railway winds its way up steep gradients, calling at remote halts before coming to a stop in the middle of a timber yard at **Dunières**. The rail journey sets the scene for further exploration of this gentle land; land where in villages like **St Bonnet-le-Froid** a mile or two to the south-east of Dunières, the pace of life goes by without acknowledging the twentieth century. In St Bonnet the only time the village comes to life is during its two festivals, devoted to garlic sales in summer and wild mushrooms in late autumn. For the garlic festival the village street is lined with stalls selling these pungent bulbs. St Bonnet goes back to sleep for a month or so, waking up to the frenetic activity of connoisseur and commercial buyer alike picking over the huge piles of wild fungus which block the single village street.

With the tiny market town of Yssingeaux as the only place with more than one street, the rest of this delectable corner is waiting to be explored. Most villages have their small inn, a few of them offering food, but armed with a map and a picnic, this is the territory of those who prefer to find their own way round.

Further Information
— Auvergne —

Museums and Other Places of Interest

Ambert
Moulin Richard-de-Bas
Open: daily with guided tours 9am-7pm July and August. Otherwise 9-11am and 2-5pm. Closed 1 January and 25 December.

Parc Zoologique du Bouy
Open: daily June to September. Otherwise Saturdays, Sundays and holidays.

Aurillac
Maison des Volcans - Château St Etienne
Open: 10am-12noon and 2-7pm July and August, except Sunday mornings. Otherwise 8.30am-12noon and 2-5.30pm. Closed Monday mornings, Saturday afternoons, Sundays and holidays.

Balaine
Château and Botanical Gardens
Open: 10am-12noon and 2-7pm May to October. Closed Tuesday, Friday and Saturday mornings. (Open 2pm on those days).

Château de Toury
Near St Pourçain-sur-Besbre
Open: 10am-12noon and 2-6pm, April to November.

Dompierre-sur-Besbre
Zoo du Pal
Open: 10am-7pm.

Plomb du Cantal (mountain summit)
Cable car operates 9.30am-6.30pm in summer and 9am-5.30pm in winter.

Puy-de-Dôme
Château de Cordès-Orcival
Open: 10am-12noon and 2-6pm throughout the year.

Puy-de-Dôme (Mountain)
Exhibition on summit.
Open: 10am-12.30pm and 2.30-7pm mid-June to September.

Puy-de-Sancy
Cable car operates from 9am-12noon and 1.30-5.30pm.

Riom-ès-Montagnes
Maison de la Gentiane et la Flore
Open: 10am-12.30pm and 2.30-7pm mid-June to mid-September.

Volvic
Maison de la Pierre
Conducted tours 10am-1.30pm and 2.15-6pm mid-March to mid-November. Closed Tuesdays.

Tourist Information Offices

Allier
Bourbon-l'Archambault
Syndicat d'Initiative
1 Place Thermes
☎ 70 67 09 79
Open: April to mid-October.

Besse-en-Chandesse
Office de Tourisme
Place Grand-Mèze
☎ 73 79 52 84

Billom
Syndicat d'Initiative
13 Rue Carnot
☎ 73 68 39 85
Open: June to August.

La Bourboule
Office de Tourisme
Place Hôtel de Ville
☎ 73 81 07 99

La Chaise-Dieu
Syndicat d'Initiative
Place Mairie
☎ 71 00 01 16
Open: Easter to October.

Le Chambon-sur-Lignon
Office de Tourisme
Place Marché
☎ 71 59 71 56

Châteauneuf-les-Bains
Office de Tourisme
☎ 73 86 67 86
Open: afternoons only May to September.

Cantal
Aurillac
Office de Tourisme
Place Square
☎ 71 48 46 58

Châtelguyon
Office de Tourisme
Parc Etienne Clémentel
☎ 73 86 01 17
Open: April to early October.

Chaudes-Aigues
Office de Tourisme
1 Avenue Georges Pompidou
☎ 71 23 52 75
Open: May to mid-October.

Clermont-Ferrand
Office de Tourisme
69 Boulevard Gergovia ☎ 73 93 30 20
Also at the station ☎ 73 91 87 89
A.C. Place Galliéni ☎ 73 93 47 67

Cusset
Syndicat d'Initiative
Rue St Arloing
☎ 70 31 39 41
Open: mornings only July and August.

Ebreuil
Syndicat d'Initiative
Hôtel de Ville
☎ 70 90 71 33
Open: July and August.

Haute-Loire
Brioude
Office de Tourisme
Boulevard Champanne
☎ 71 50 05 35
Open: mornings out of season.

Issoire
Syndicat d'Initiative
At the Mairie
☎ 73 89 03 54
Also on the Place Général De Gaulle,
mid-June to the beginning of September.
☎ 73 89 15 90

Lapalisse
Syndicat d'Initiative
Place Charles-Bécaud
☎ 70 99 08 39
Open: mid-June to mid-September.

Le Mont-Dore
Office de Tourisme
Avenue Général-Leclerc
☎ 73 65 20 21

Murol
Syndicat d'Initiative
At the Mairie
☎ 73 88 62 62

Massiac
Office de Tourisme
Rue Paix
☎ 71 23 07 76

Mauriac
Office de Tourisme
Place Georges Pompidou
☎ 71 67 30 26

Montsalvy
Office de Tourisme
☎ 71 49 21 43

Murat
At the Mairie
☎ 71 20 09 47
Open: June to mid-September.

Montluçon
Office de Tourisme
1 Avenue Marx-Dormoy
☎ 70 05 05 92
Also Place Piquand
Open: afternoons July to September.
☎ 70 05 50 70
A.C. 128 Boulevard Courtais
☎ 70 05 15 52

Moulins
Office de Tourisme
Place Hôtel de Ville
☎ 70 44 14 14
A.C. 62 Rue Pont-Guinguet.
☎ 70 44 00 96

Néris-les-Bains
Office de Tourisme
Carrefour des Arènes
☎ 70 03 11 03
Open: early May to late October.

Puy-de-Dôme
Ambert
Syndicat d'Initiative
4 Place Hôtel de Ville
☎ 73 82 01 55
Open: mid-June to mid-September.

Le-Puy-en-Velay
Office de Tourisme
Place du Breuil
☎ 71 09 38 41
Also 23 Rue Tables during July and
August.
☎ 71 09 27 42

Riom
Office de Tourisme
16 Rue Commerce
☎ 73 38 59 45
Open: afternoons only November to
March.

Royat
Syndicat d'Initiative
Place Allard
☎ 73 35 81 87
Closed November.

Riom-ès-Montagnes
Office de Tourisme
Place Général de Gaulle
☎ 71 78 07 37
Open: afternoons only except in July
and August.

St Flour
Office de Tourisme
2 Place Armes
☎ 71 60 22 50

St Nectaire
Office de Tourisme
Anciens Thermes
☎ 73 88 50 86

St Pourçain-sur-Sioule
Syndicat d'Initiative
Boulevard Ledru-Rollin
☎ 70 45 32 73
Open: mid-June to mid-September.

Thiézac
Syndicat d'Initiative
☎ 71 47 01 21
Open: mid-June to end of August.

Vic-sur-Cère
Office de Tourisme
Avenue Mercier
☎ 71 47 50 68

Vichy
Office de Tourisme
19 Rue Parc
☎ 70 98 71 94

5 • Lyonnais-Bresse

Tourists from all over Europe know of **Lyon**. Every summer they pass through it in their hundreds of thousands, slowly, cursing the traffic jams, on their way to the Mediterranean resorts. Very few of them know that Lyon is itself a place well worth stopping in, one of the oldest and most fascinating cities in all Europe, packed with interest, with superb restaurants and comfortable hotels.

Lyon was founded in 43BC, by one of Julius Caesar's lieutenants, on the Fourvière hill overlooking the confluence of two great rivers, the Rhône and the Saône. It was meant just as a haven for refugees who had fled from an attack on Vienne, 30km (19 miles) to the south, but the settlement spread rapidly down to the peninsula between the two rivers, and within 30 years it had grown to become the capital of the Roman province of Gaul.

Over the centuries Lyon steadily prospered, spreading along the banks of the gentle Saône and the utterly different, tumultuous Rhône which flooded the town regularly and sometimes disastrously. Lyon was one of the first places to establish, in the early fifteenth century, regular Trade Fairs, which attracted merchants from all over Europe, whose currencies were exchanged at their full value and who had no taxes to pay on their sales. These favourable conditions soon made the city a centre of international trade and banking. As well as being a centre of banking Lyon became famous for its early production of printed books, the first was produced nearly 20 years before Columbus discovered America. When the Renaissance came in the sixteenth and seventeenth centuries Lyon was in the vanguard, attracting not only goods and wealth, but thinkers and philosophers from all countries. By the end of the eighteenth century Lyon was a city where industry, particularly textiles, and arts and sciences all flourished.

But all this crashed with the French Revolution. Although the population at first welcomed the Revolution, they were moderate in their views, and when King Louis XVI was executed in January 1893, they rebelled and sent the chief officer of the Revolution in Lyon,

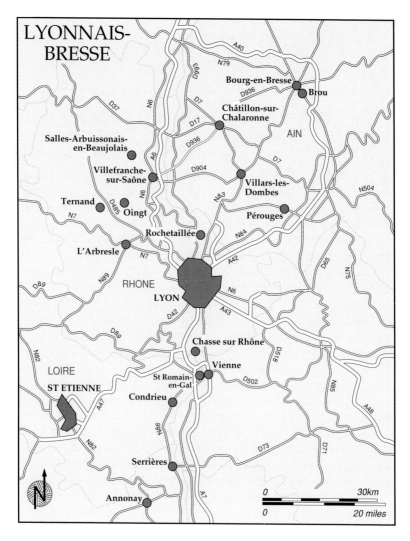

Maire-Joseph Chalier, to the guillotine. In retaliation, the destruction of Lyon was ordered by the revolutionary commanders in Paris. Lyon was besieged, and surrendered after 2 months, and the destruction of the heart of the city commenced, and suspects were slaughtered by the thousand.

But after the Revolution the Emperor Napoleon recognised the importance of Lyon and encouraged its redevelopment, laying the first stone in the reconstruction of the city centre himself, ordering two new bridges to be built across the Saône, and founding the Museum and School of Fine Arts.

The beautifully-restored Maison des Avocats, Lyon

During the nineteenth century Lyon became one of the world's most important centres of silk production, and remains so today. It also has a very important manufacture of synthetic fibres, huge chemical factories, specialising in the manufacture of dyes, and large metal industries, including wire manufacture. A third of all the electric motors produced in France are made in Lyon.

There is so much for the tourist to see in Lyon that a choice has to be made. There are, for example, twenty-four museums, all interesting, some remarkable. In the old quarter there are whole streets of medieval and Renaissance buildings, many of them beautifully restored. Lyon was the first town to benefit from *La loi Malraux* introduced in 1962 by Andre Malraux, de Gaulle's Minister for Cultural Affairs, to authorise the preservation and restoration of historic old quarters.

The heart of the Presqu'ile, between the two rivers, is the Place Bellecour, which has a huge underground car park, and from here it is a short walk across the Pont Bonaparte over the Saône, to **St Jean Cathedral** and the old streets surrounding it.

The cathedral itself was started in 1180 and was finished 300 years later, so it is a mixture of architectural styles, Romanesque for the apse and the transept, Gothic in some chapels and for the façade. The choir, with the apse the oldest part of the cathedral, has some fine thirteenth-century stained glass in the lower windows, the higher

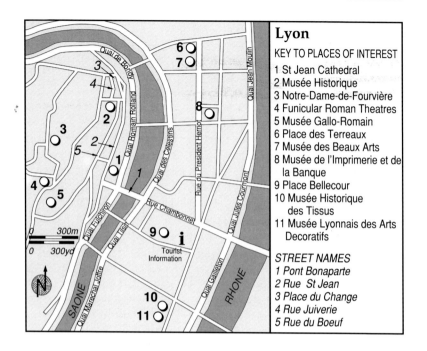

Lyon

KEY TO PLACES OF INTEREST

1 St Jean Cathedral
2 Musée Historique
3 Notre-Dame-de-Fourvière
4 Funicular Roman Theatres
5 Musée Gallo-Romain
6 Place des Terreaux
7 Musée des Beaux Arts
8 Musée de l'Imprimerie et de la Banque
9 Place Bellecour
10 Musée Historique des Tissus
11 Musée Lyonnais des Arts Decoratifs

STREET NAMES
1 Pont Bonaparte
2 Rue St Jean
3 Place du Change
4 Rue Juiverie
5 Rue du Boeuf

ones have been restored. Near the choir on the left there is a remarkable fourteenth-century astronomical clock. Four times a day, at hourly intervals beginning at noon, it becomes convulsed with activity, bells ring, cocks crow, little doors open and puppet figures pop out and engage in various activities said to represent the Annunciation. It is all impressive but rather confused to the uninitiated. It certainly bewildered Charles Dickens when he saw it in the 1840s, as he mistook the Archangel Gabriel for the Devil!

This old part of Lyon has an unusual feature which adds interest and a touch of mystery to its exploration. Many of the Renaissance houses have an interior courtyard which is reached by a vaulted passage from the street. In many cases this vaulted passage is continued on the far side of the courtyard and passes under the houses to emerge in another street. These passages are called *traboules* and the verb *trabouler* means to take short cuts from one place to another by using them. They are common in this old quarter of St Jean and also in the silk weaver's district on the hill of La Croix Rousse, where they were much used to carry about the bolts of silk, protected from the weather. The cobbled Rue St Jean, which passes in front of the cathedral, was the main thoroughfare of the medieval and Renaissance city, and following its length, with one or two side tracks makes a fascinating walk. As you face the cathedral, the building on your right is the Manecanterie, the old choir school, which dates from the same period as the earliest part of the cathedral. Turn to your left and walk along the Rue St Jean, keeping an eye out for interesting architectural details from the past. Look into the courtyard at number 27, and then at number 19 take the *traboule*, which brings you out into the Rue des Trois-Marie, where you turn left. Numbers 6 and 7 in this street have statues of Christ and the Virgin Mary flanked by female saints, set in niches in the façade. Cross the Place de la Baleine to rejoin the Rue St Jean where number 11, on the far side of the Place du Gouvernement, has one of the most impressive courtyards in old Lyon, with an eight-storey staircase in the Flamboyant Gothic style. Two doors away number 7 has a splendid façade in the same style. Continue to the Place du Change and on through the St Paul quarter via the Rue de Lainerie, where numbers 10, 14 and 18 are fine examples of Renaissance architecture. From the Place St Paul return via the Rue Juiverie, which has several fine Renaissance houses, numbers 8, 10, 13, 20 and 23. Cross back over the Place du Change and take the Rue Soufflot into the Rue Gadagne, where the Gadagne mansion (numbers 10 to 14) is the largest Renaissance building in Lyon. It was built in 1445 by the Gadagne brothers, who had made an enormous fortune from banking, and today houses the Historical Museum and the International Museum of the Marionette.

From the Rue Gadagne carry on into the Rue Boeuf, where the first building carries the small sculpture of an ox. This is a survivor of a system used in medieval times to indicate the name of a street to those many people who could not read. Next door there is a *traboule* which leads back into the Rue St Jean at number 24. At number 17 Rue du Boeuf the Maison du Crible is famous for its round tower and rose-coloured roughcast, from which the restaurant at the corner, La Tour Rose, one of the finest in Lyon, takes its name.

One of the charms of this old quarter is that there are bars, cafés, and restaurants at intervals wherever you walk, many of them with terraces where you can sit outside and enjoy the old-world atmosphere at leisure.

There are streets and staircases leading up the hill of Fourvière to the extraordinary basilica which looks down on the old town, but the less energetic may prefer to take the funicular which starts from near St Jean Cathedral. Built after the Franco-Prussian war of 1870, at the height of the nineteenth-century piety, the basilica of **Notre-Dame-de-Fourvière** is worth a quick look both inside and out. As a

monument to the poor taste and over-elaboration of the worst of
nineteenth-century art, it is difficult to beat. One French critic has
likened it to a big, fat girl overloaded with frills and flounces and
ornaments of every style. Another has said that 'in the name of Art,
it is better to avoid detailing the hollow and heavy magnificences of
the building'. Yet another has said that the best thing about the
basilica is the view of Lyon spread below you as you stand with your
back to it.

The original Roman settlement was on this hill, and the original
Roman Theatre, now very well restored is the oldest in France. It was
built in pre-Christian times and enlarged in the second-century AD
by the Emperor Hadrian, so that it could hold 10,000 spectators. It is
used for modern performances, and adjacent to it is a similar, but
smaller theatre, the odeon. These smaller theatres, from which so
many modern cinemas took their name, were used for musical
concerts and conferences.

The splendid **Gallo-Roman Museum** (Musée Gallo-Romain) on
the same hillside, and partially built into the hill with great picture
windows looking out on to the Roman theatres, is a must for anyone
with the slightest interest in Roman times. The exhibits include the
unique bronze tablet, found in La Croix Rousse in 1538, beautifully
engraved with the speech which the Emperor Claudius made to the
Roman Senate in AD48, asking for the inhabitants of Lyon, the city
where he had himself been born, to be granted Roman citizenship.
There are also mosaics and statuary, including a complete statue of
the god Neptune, found in the Rhône, silver goblets, Roman glass,
and everyday objects of Roman life.

Lyon has a very fine **Museum of Fine Arts** (Musée des Beaux
Arts), housed in the Palais St Pierre, which occupies the whole of the
south side of the Place des Terreaux. It has rooms devoted to Italian
and Dutch old masters and others covering the whole range of
French painting from the seventeenth century on, and particularly
strong in Impressionists and contemporary artists of the past 50
years. The animated café terraces of the Place des Terreaux, much
used by the Lyonnais for romantic and business meetings, offer a
contrast to the dignity of the Palais St Pierre and the impressive
eighteenth-century façade of the Hôtel de Ville which takes up the
whole of the east side of the square. The monumental fountain in the
centre of the square was the work of Bartholdi, who also made the
Statue of Liberty. Its four prancing horses symbolise the four great
rivers of France, the Loire, the Rhône, the Garonne, and the Seine,
dashing to the sea.

The Roman theatre at Lyon is the oldest in France

Among the unusual museums in Lyon, not to be found in other places, is the **Museum of Printing and Banking** (Musée de l'Imprimerie et de la Banque). In the fifteenth and sixteenth centuries the development of banking in Lyon made it one of the most important financial centres in Europe, and this museum illustrates the growth of commerce in this city, the first to set up a stock exchange and the first to issue a cheque. A number of rooms are also given over to the history of printing, from the first wood block engravings to the development of typesetting, paging and book-binding techniques, and the most modern methods of printing. At the time of the Renaissance printers came from all over Europe to Lyon and set up their own quarter in the Rue Merciere and adjoining streets, so that they could work together and exchange ideas. The collection includes many rare and ancient volumes.

The **Museum of Decorative Arts** (Musée Lyonnais des Arts Decoratifs), in the Rue de la Charite, is another remarkable museum. Set in an eighteenth-century mansion, it concentrates on the elegance of eighteenth-century life and has a fine collection of antique furniture from the great French makers, tapestries from all the great centres, porcelain from St Cloud, Sevres, and Meissen, and *objets d'art* from the great goldsmiths and silversmiths.

But the star of all Lyon's excellent museums is in the building next door, the **Historical Textile Museum** (Musée Historique des Tissus) founded more than a hundred years ago. This very unusual museum is probably the finest of its kind in the world, and illustrates the development of fine textiles from the beginning of Christian times, and from many parts of the world. Coptic tapestries from the fourth to the eighth centuries, luxurious cloths from the great days of Byzantium, splendid Persian and Turkish carpets, are among the rarities from the East. European cloths include some from thirteenth-century Sicily, velvets from Genoa, Florence and Venice, sixteenth-century materials from Spain, and the beautiful silks made in Lyon from the seventeenth century to the present day. Among the best of these are wall hangings with pheasants and peacocks made in Lyon in 1771 for Catherine the Great of Russia. Both these museums are within easy walking distance south from the Place Bellcour.

In addition to its other points of interest, Lyon is a place of pilgrimage for lovers of good food. The Lyon area is the gastronomic centre of France, some would say of the world, and there are more good restaurants in and around Lyon than in any comparable area. Michelin stars abound, and there are a dozen of the greatest chefs in France in the region. Lyon also has a tradition of great women chefs, *les 'meres' Lyonnaises*. If only a few of their restaurants survive, the reputation they had for producing the best regional dishes at a consistently high standard helped to create the gastronomic tradition of the city, still maintained and enhanced by the famous chefs of today. But the traveller does not have to go to one of the distinguished and expensive restaurants to enjoy a typically Lyonnais atmosphere. There are numerous small cafés where the regional wines can be enjoyed together with the local cuisine. Known as *bouchons*, some of these little café restaurants have achieved a reputation and are moderately expensive, though not in the same league as the famous.

Another point of great interest to tourists who are garden lovers is the beautiful **Parc de la Tete d'Or**, which gets its name from the legend that a golden head of Christ was found buried there. The park, which is to Lyon what Kew Gardens are to Londoners, is best visited in early summer when its famous roses, there are said to be more than a million flowers, are in bloom. There are also glasshouses with tropical and sub-tropical plants, a botanical garden, an alpine garden, a zoo, and an aviary full of exotic birds.

Lyon is surrounded by many other places well worth visiting. Vienne, a town which attracts tourists from all over Europe is only 30km (19 miles) to the south. After Marseilles, **Vienne** is the oldest city in France, and was already rich and prosperous in Roman times.

It has interesting early Christian churches, a splendid cathedral, and some of the finest Roman remains in France, including a theatre which could hold 13,000 spectators, making it larger than those in Orange and Lyon. This theatre was completely buried until 1922, when work began on removing the earth. It took 6 years just to uncover the 46 tiers of seats and the stage, before restoration to make it usable could begin. It is now used for performances in summer.

Directly across the river from Vienne, at **St Romain-en-Gal**, a prosperous suburb of the Roman town, with paved streets, the foundations of luxury villas, shops, a market, craftsmen's workshops, and a spa has been excavated. All this was discovered in 1967, when plans were made to build a new school there. Mosaics from the site are on show in a small museum. But the finest of all the Roman ruins at Vienne is the temple of Augustus and Livia. This is a very similar design to that of the famous Maison Carre, at Nimes, and the two of them are the best preserved examples of Roman temples in France. The excellent condition of the temple at Vienne is partly due to the fact that in early Christian times it was converted to a church and had the spaces between its pillars walled in, protecting it from the weather. It was not until the late nineteenth century that the temple was restored to its original state.

The most impressive of the Christian buildings at Vienne is the cathedral of St Maurice, which took from the twelfth to the fifteenth century to complete, and so combines the earlier Romanesque (Norman) style with the later Gothic, all in harmony. The splendid west front is 30m (98ft) high and 38m (125ft) wide and includes three portals in the Flamboyant Gothic style. The central arch is a brilliant example of the beautifully detailed carving of this period, and the whole ensemble is one of the finest examples of this period in France. The vast interior, nearly 100m (328ft) long, has a triple nave in which Roman and Gothic elements co-exist, notably in finely-carved capitols from both periods. On the left-hand side of the nave there is a thirteenth-century bas-relief showing Herod and the Three Wise Men, and a little further down the nave there are early twelfth-century statues of St Peter, on the left, and of St John and St Paul. To the right of the choir there is a superb Renaissance stained-glass window depicting the Adoration of the Magi, and the upper windows of the Choir are also sixteenth century.

The former church of St Pierre, now transformed into an archaeological museum, merits a visit not only for its contents, but as one of the oldest Christian churches in France, going back to the fifth-century AD, and the existing walls on the north, west, and south

Pottery in the Archaeological Museum at St Romain-en-Gal

sides date from the sixth century. The four-storey bell tower, which includes the entrance porch at ground level, is a classic example of the Romanesque style dating from the twelfth century. The archaeological exhibits include a Roman marble statue of Tutela, the goddess-protector of the town, and some mosaics of athletes in action.

At the other end of the town there is another church, almost equally old, St Andre-le-Bas. The nave was rebuilt in 1152 by Guillaume Martin, who signed and dated his work at the base of the second column on the right. Adjoining the church is a charming twelfth-century cloister, particularly attractive in the morning sunshine, and with a terrace which gives a good view across the Rhône.

As a change from looking at ancient churches the Henri Malartre Vintage Car Museum will fascinate car enthusiasts, and makes an enjoyable outing for all the family. The museum is based in the château of **Rochetaillée** and its grounds, and is reached by the D433 beside the Saône north from Lyon for 12km (7 miles). It was founded by a man whose business was breaking up old cars. In 1931 he decided to restore an 1898 model whose engine still worked, instead of breaking it up. Now more than half the 200 cars on show date from before 1914. Other notable cars include Hitler's armoured Mercedes, and the 1936 Hispano-Suiza used by de Gaulle after the liberation of Paris. There is also a selection of early racing cars, and trams, buses, and trolley buses, including a horse-drawn tram to which the horses could be harnessed at either end to avoid having to turn the tram around.

The Monts du Lyonnais, to the west of Lyon, offer good opportunities for scenic drives and walks (the GR76, and GR7 cross these hills). At **Courzieu** on the D30, approached via Vaugneray and the Col De Malval, then the D50 for 2km (1 mile), then 2km on an unmade road there is an interesting game park specialising in European animals such as the chamois, lynx, wolf, ibex, and revived species such as the auroch, Tarpan horses, and European bison. A botanical footpath wanders through 20 hectares of woods and park where the animals live in semi-liberty.

Follow the D113 south from the Col de Malval to Yzeron, and then take the D122 to St Martin-en-Haut, turn east on the D34 for a short distance and then fork right on to the D113 for St Andre la Cote. About 1 km (½ mile) before the village a footpath leads up to the summit (934m/3,063ft) of the Signal St Andre, a walk of about ¾ hour there and back. There are panoramic views from this mountain towards the valley of the Rhône and the Alps.

On the northern limits of the Monts du Lyonnais near **L'Arbresle**, the Couvent d'Eveux is of interest to students of modern architecture. It was built between 1957 and 1959 to the designs of the famous French architect, Le Corbusier, and is one of the few examples of modern architecture applied to the needs of a life of religious seclusion.

To the east of Lyons an excursion worth making is to **Pérouges**, an ancient fortified village so picturesque that it has often been used as a setting for period films such as *The Three Musketeers* and *Twenty Years After*. In the Middle Ages Pérouges prospered from the production of hand-made linen cloths of high quality but the industrialisation of the nineteenth century never reached the village, it was too far from the new railways, and the craftsmen could not compete with factory-made cloths. The population fell to less than a hundred and the village was on the point of becoming a complete ruin. But a few enthusiasts and lovers of the past, aided by the Ministry of Fine Arts, began the restoration of Pérouges. The cobbled and tortuous streets of the village, its ancient houses, and attractive market place, have been given new life by artisans who have set up their studios and sell their goods to tourists.

Pérouges lies just to the south of one of the most unusual landscapes in France, La Dombes, a misty and mysterious country of a thousand lakes, almost all of them artificial. It is a sad and silent countryside, created long ago by the monks of the twelfth century.

They realised that this poor land was impermeable, so that rainwater just lay on the surface. They took advantage of this to enlarge natural hollows to form artificial ponds, filled only by rainwater. They then used them for farming fish, mainly carp. Over the centuries the system has developed and the ponds, some of them more than 1km (½ mile) long, as large as small lakes, have increased in number. At **Villars-les-Dombes** in the centre of the area, just off the N83 from Lyons to Bourg-en-Bresse, there is a first-class ornithological park where more than 400 different species of birds can be seen, the majority of them waterfowl, but there are also many exotic species including tropical birds, emus, ostriches, flamingos, and vultures.

This whole area east of Lyon was part of the kingdom of Savoy from 1272 to 1601, when it was annexed by France. Its most important town was **Bourg-en-Bresse**, the centre for the administration of justice in Savoy. Today it is a quiet country town famous for only two things, poultry and the church of Brou. The chickens and other table birds of the Bresse region are renowned throughout France. Like wines, they have their own *appellation crontrôlée* and must be produced and marketed under strictly controlled conditions. They must belong to the Bresse breed, which has steel-blue feet, white feathers and a red crest. They must be raised for at least 16 weeks in liberty in the open air in grassy conditions, and fed on maize and dairy products, and then fattened for 2 weeks indoors. After slaughtering they are prepared for the market in a milk bath. Not surprisingly they are used by restaurateurs all over France, and have done much to contribute to the gastronomic reputation of the Lyon area.

On the outskirts of Bourg-en-Bresse, the church of **Brou** is a splendid jewel of the Flamboyant Gothic style. It was commissioned by Archduchess Marguerite of Savoy, as a memorial to her husband, who died in 1504, aged only 24. It was constructed between 1506 and 1532 and so is a harmonious whole, with a particularly impressive interior. The triple-arched rood screen, one of the few left in France, which separates the nave from the choir is famous for its intricate and graceful stone lattice work. Seventy-four monks' stalls carved in dark oak line the entry to the choir. Finest of all the splendid marble sculptures are those of the three royal tombs in the choir itself, exquisitely carved with small statuettes and life-size figures of the noble family in life and death. The stained-glass windows of the church are the originals made on the spot by craftsmen from Lyons.

Serious art lovers may like to make a short deviation between Villars-les-Dombes and Bourge-en-Bresse to visit **Châtillon-sur-Chalaronne**. In the council chamber of the Town Hall of this attractive little town, one of the *villages fleuris* of France, there is a remarkable triptych on wood showing the taking down of Christ from the Cross and the Resurrection. This work, completely restored, is said to date from 1527 but the artist is unknown, though the harmony of the figures and the rich colours suggest a master. Châtillon has several monuments to its historic past. The Porte de Villars, all that remains of the former ramparts, is a good example of fourteenth-century military architecture. The fifteenth-century church of St Andre is unusual in that it is of red brick with a red tile roof, and a white limestone interior. The covered market, originally built in the fifteenth century was destroyed by fire in 1670, but was rebuilt through the generosity of La Grande Mademoiselle, the niece of Louis XIII. The thirty-two pillars are from the trunks of oak trees given from one of her estates. It is the only ancient covered market remaining in the department of Ain.

It has often been said that three rivers flow through Lyon, the Rhône, the Saône, and Beaujolais. Certainly any wine lovers in the Lyon area would enjoy the short trip north to the Beaujolais area, both for the possibility of tasting wines at the vineyards and for the lovely scenery (see also chapter 6). The roads are narrow and winding but the distances are not great, and it is an area in which you can do your own exploration. One possible route is to leave Lyon by La Croix Rousse and the D485 for a rather busy 20km (12 miles) and then turn off north at Le Bois d'Oingt, a village famous for its 10,000 rose bushes, and then to **Oingt** itself which is entered by the Porte de Nizy, all that remains of a once formidable fortress. This area is known as the 'country of the golden stones' where the houses seem to glow with summer sunshine all year round, and this effect is at its best in Oingt where the narrow alleys of the village are bordered by lovely old houses with accoladed and mullioned windows, making a harmonious ensemble. The church, the former chapel of the castle, has a tower from which there are panoramic views of the hills of Tarare and Beaujolais.

From Oingt take the road to St Laurent d'Oingt and then across the D485 to **Ternand**, another ancient and attractive village, built on a promontory overlooking the valley of the Azergues. From Ternand take the D31 north back across the D485 to le Saule d'Oingt by a very picturesque route, turn right on the D116 to La Maladiere and then left on to the D19 to Cogny, St Julien and the magnificently named **Salles-Arbuissonais-en-Beaujolais**, a little village with an old priory with some interesting buildings, including a cloister, from the eleventh and fifteenth centuries. Follow the D20 to Blaceret and turn left

A cloister garden in the village of Salles-Arbuissonais-en-Beaujolais

on to the D43 for about 10km (6 miles) to Mont Brouilly whose slopes
have the most southerly of the Beaujolais vineyards, Côte de Brouilly.
From the village of Cercie fork left on to the D68e, then left on to the
D119e and to the old town of **Corcelles**. Just outside the town, the
Château de Corcelles is a fifteenth-century castle, refined by Renais-
sance additions. The chapel has some remarkable Gothic panelling.
In the main building the ancient kitchen can be seen, and the former
guard's room has been transformed into a wine-tasting room.

Two kinds of Beaujolais wine are produced, standard Beaujolais
and Beaujolais Nouveau. All Beaujolais is made from the Gamay
grape as distinct from the Pinot Noir of Burgundy, but only Beaujolais Nouveau is produced by accelerated fermentation, and should
be drunk within a few months of being made. Normally fermented
Beaujolais are those of the nine *grand crus* which carry the name of the
village which produces them; Brouilly, Chenas, Chiroubles, Côte de
Brouilly, Fleurie, Julienas, Morgon, Saint Amour, and Moulin a Vent.
Some of these will improve for several years in bottle, particularly
Saint Amour. In Julienas the tasting room, decorated with scenes
showing the god Bacchus, is in the cellar of the former church. For
those who want to enjoy tasting these wines several of the estates are
within easy reach of Corcelles, including Morgon, Fleurie, Chiroubles,
Chenas, and Brouilly. A few kilometres west of Fleurie by D26, D32
and D18e is **La Terrasse**, a viewpoint at 660m (2,165ft) altitude with

a magnificent semi-circular panorama across the valley of the Saône, the plains of the Bresse, the mountains of the Jura, and in clear weather to the Alpine massifs of Mont Blanc, the Vanoise, and the Pelvoux. An orientation table indicates the direction of the main points of interest.

Beaujolais is by no means the only wine of the Lyonnais region. The Côtes du Rhône begin at Vienne and stretch south for a hundred miles or more, producing even more wine than Beaujolais. Just south of Vienne on the west bank of the Rhône two rare and expensive wines are produced. On the steep south facing slopes of the communes of Ampuis and Tupin are the vineyards of the red wines of the Côte Rôtie. The quantity is small, only about 12,000 cases a year, and long-lasting but the quality is remarkable. A little further south the small town of Condrieu produces one of the great white wines of France from a vineyard of only 15 hectares planted with a very unusual kind of grape, the *viognier*, which has been grown there for hundreds of years. Unlike the wines of the Côte Rôtie, the slightly sparkling wines of Condrieu should be drunk young.

For 700 years before the mid-nineteenth century the only bridges across the Rhône were those at Lyon and Pont St Esprit 200km (124 miles) to the south, and sometimes, when it had not been washed away by floods, at Avignon, and there were no railways. From time immemorial goods of all kinds were transported up and down the Rhône by horse-drawn barges. The town of **Condrieu** was the chief base of the tough sailors who formed these barge crews. Steam tugs, railways and new suspension bridges put an end to their trade, but in Condrieu the river traditions are kept up, and races and jousting tournaments in boats are held there on the last Sunday in July.

About 25km (15½ miles) further south on the same bank of the Rhône as Condrieu, **Serrières** is another town famous for the sailors who faced the dangers of navigation on the Rhône, the most tempestuous big river in Europe. Navigation was only possible for 8 months of the year, and then the current was so strong that the voyage downstream was ten times faster than the voyage upstream to Lyon, which took a month and could only be completed eight times in a year. The risks of sailing the Rhône were so great that no pilot would start a voyage without a prayer to St Nicholas for the safety of the boat and the crew. Each boat carried a mariner's cross, with a large one on the front of the leading boat. Each morning the captain would bless this cross with water from the river as he said his prayer. The Museum of the Mariners of the Rhône at Serrières has several examples of these crosses, which were always made by the sailors themselves in their off-duty hours, as well as numerous other items from their daily lives, special tools, harness for the draft horses, loud-hailers, embroidered waistcoats worn on special occasions. The museum is housed in the disaffected thirteenth-century chapel of St Sornin, and in the loft above the choir there is a particularly grue-some exhibit, an ossuary containing more than 350 skeletons, four of them mummified and in an upright position. They are believed to be about 300 years old and there is no official record of why they are there. It is thought that at that time it was planned to move the cemetery of St Sornin, because it was repeatedly flooded by the Rhône, and that the bodies were removed from their graves in readiness for reburial which, for unknown reasons, never took place.

Boat trips of all kinds are available on the Rhône from Lyon and other towns. They vary from trips in quite small boats to those in which there are restaurants, and even hotel boats in which it is possible to make long trips on the river.

Annonay, a small town 16km (10 miles) from Serrières, is a place worth a visit as much for its associations as for its old town and picturesque corners. It was at Annonay on the 4 June 1783, that the first step was taken in man's conquest of the air, when the Montgolfier brothers demonstrated their new invention, the first hot-air balloon. It was a relative of the Montgolfiers, Marc Seguin, one of the nineteenth-century's great engineers, also born in Annonay, who changed the whole economy of the Rhône Valley. He was the first man to realise that the old Chinese invention of rope suspension bridges could be adapted to steel, and to use woven steel cables to support bridges. His first was across the Cance, a small river which runs through Annonay. The next was across the Rhône at Tournon, and he and his four brothers went on to build 186 suspension bridges in France and around the world. By 1850 there were eleven across the Rhône, and the times were changing. The sailors of the Rhône threatened to hang Seguin from one of his own bridges. In 1828 Seguin had made another enormous contribution to progress, when he patented a tubular steam boiler, which led to the building of faster railway engines. He had already helped to promote the construction of the first railway line, started in 1826, from Lyon to St Etienne, and the new invention meant that both railways and steam tugs, devel-oped more rapidly.

St Etienne, at 60km (37 miles) the nearest large town to Lyon, is an industrial sprawl with little to recommend to tourists in general. It does, however, have two things which will appeal the enthusiasts. Its Museum of Arms is of great interest to all those fascinated by the history and development of weapons and armour. It has numerous examples of beautifully engraved sets of pistols, and magnificently ornate rifles of Napoleonic times, many of them made in St Etienne. There is also a fine collection of armour and helmets, going back to the sixteenth century, as well as a collection of African, Oriental and Oceanic weapons. St Etienne also has a remarkably good Fine Arts Museum with many Old Masters, and a very high quality collection of the greatest modern painters, right up to the present day.

The Lyonnais region has produced a surprising number of inventors and scientists in addition to the Montgolfiers and Seguin: Andre Marie Ampere, who discovered among other things the relationship between electricity and magnetism; Thimonnier who invented the sewing machine and sold his rights for almost nothing at the Great Exhibition at Crystal Palace in 1851; Jacquard, who invented a new kind of loom which would do the work of five silk weavers; Guimet, who invented an artificial ultramarine cloth dye which could be sold for 2 francs a kilo instead of 3,000 francs for the natural product, and Antoine Lumiere, the inventor of moving pictures, and father of the cinema.

Six kilometres (4 miles) from Annonay is the safari park of the Haut Vivarais which can be visited in a closed car (or a park minibus) along a surfaced road which winds among large enclosures where different animals live in relative liberty, baboons and zebras, lions, bears and bison, camels, yaks and buffalos. Another part of the park can be visited on foot. Here there are giraffes, wolves, antelopes, ostriches, and many aquatic birds, as well as tigers and different kinds of deer. There is also a vivarium with lizards, caymans, crocodiles, and large snakes.

In addition to the wine and the food, and the numerous antiquities, the Lyonnais-Bresse region is rich in facilities for all forms of holiday leisure, particularly walking, cycling, horse-riding and fishing. There are several Grand Randonnée footpaths in the region, as well as countless signposted local paths for shorter walks through attractive scenery. For long cross-country walks the appropriate maps and guides published by the Comité National des Sentiers de Grand Randonnée are essential.

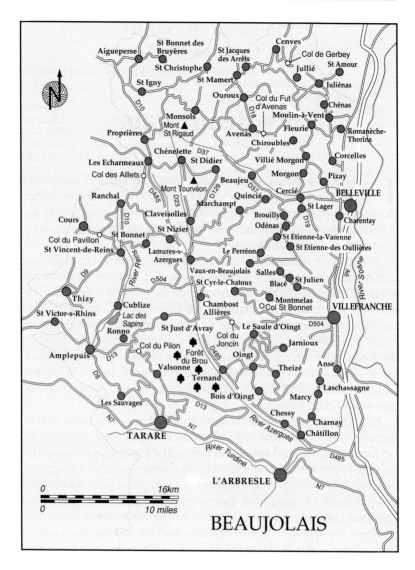

BEAUJOLAIS

0 ———————— 16km
0 ———————— 10 miles

textile industry of, originally, wool, later silk and finally cotton. Thus there are many isolated manors, scattered hamlets, village clusters and in the western valleys several small textile towns.

The regional capital is Villefranche on the N6 Paris-Lyon road, and close to the *autoroute* A6. It is the centre of the wine trade, and in spite of being busy, its older architecture is worth investigating. In the Turdine Valley is Tarare, a textile town famous for its muslins, and on the 'Route de Sapins'(firs) in the western hills are the small textile towns of Amplepuis, Thizy and Cours. In the north is the old capital (until 1592), and town of Beaujeu, in a narrow valley surrounded by vines and forests. Finally, near the N6 from Mâcon is Belleville, a wine centre convenient for seeing the northern vineyards.

The attractions of the region lie in the landscape contrasts as between the southern vineyard villages of golden stone, often perched on hills, and those of the *Grands Crus* in the north. Higher up, above 500m (1,640ft), in the hills where the vines give way to field and forest, walking in the pure air gives a supreme pleasure, along with horseriding, fishing and *ski de fond* in Haut Beaujolais. As for exploring, although the region is not vast, it is possible to believe oneself lost in the narrow valleys, steep winding hill roads and the green ocean of vines. A splendid landscape to wander in without a fixed route, the nuances of the scenery are many with discoveries round each corner in the remoter parts of the region.

The climate is seasonal, with variations due to aspect and altitude. The summers are sunny, often hot (21°C/70°F) with frequent hailstorms. Winters are cold (2-3°C/36-7°F) and sometimes misty. Springs are bright and often rainy, with occasional disastrous frosts. Autumns by contrast can be truly golden, and are a good time to see the landscape colours. Rainfall is moderate with 800-1,000mm (31-40in) on the slopes, and heavier 1,000-1,500mm (40-60in) in the granite uplands.

The region is very accessible, as the eastern borders are parallel with two main roads (N6 and A6), and a rail route from Paris to Lyon.

Road: From Paris (Orly or Charles de Gaulle airports) A6 *autoroute* (463km, 287 miles). From Lyon (Satolas airport), *autoroute* A43, then A6 to Villefranche (55km, 34 miles). From Marseilles (Marignane airport) A7 *autoroute* to Lyon (315km, 195 miles).

Rail: TGV (high speed) Paris (Gare de Lyon) direct to Lyon (Part Dieu) 2hr Marseilles (St Charles) to Lyon (Perrache) TGV ($2^1/_2$hr); then change trains to Belleville or Villefranche.

A route exists from Paris to Lyon via Nevers, Moulins, Paray-le-Monial and down the Azergues Valley through spiral tunnels, but there is only one train a day in each direction.

Haut Beaujolais

This northern hilly district is centred on the historic capital of an ancient barony which gave its name to the region, and guarded an important route via the narrow defile of the Ardières Valley.

The long, narrow main street (Rue de la République) of **Beaujeu**

Beaujeu, with its Syndicat d'Initiative, 'Temple of Bacchus' and museum

seems to hide its best buildings, but once abreast of the fine Romanesque twelfth-century church, and within the Place de la Liberté, the
town shows itself. Opposite the church is the well preserved Ren-
naissance Maison du Pays, which, with its tower and its neighbours
at differing heights, presents a remarkably harmonious group. Moving on to the Place de l'Hôtel-de-Ville with its drinking fountain and
trees, there is a building which houses a very efficient Syndicat
d'Initiative (tourist office). Upstairs is a museum containing sections
devoted to dolls, wine and geology. Underneath is a *caveau* (cellar),
called 'Temple of Bacchus', where one can sample and buy by glass,
bottle or box, 'Beaujolais Villages', for Beaujeu is a centre for this
Appellation Contrôlée. Return to the main street with its many good
restaurants: Anne-de-Beaujeu for example, in a fine old house (No
28), named after the daughter of Louis XI, is excellent for cuisine,
décor and service.

Eastern Haut Beaujolais

From Beaujeu a route which explores eastern Haut Beaujolais leaves
the main street by the D136 past the ancient Hospice de Beaujeu and

climbs steeply with hairpin bends past vineyards, and then quite wild scenery of heather, bushes and stone blocks to the Col du Fut d'Avenas (762m, 2,499ft). Here is an immense panorama embracing the plain of Bresse and, in clear weather, the Alps and Mont Blanc — the area surrounding the col is well named La Terrasse. Nearby is the *caveau*/restaurant Vignerons de Chiroubles (*Grand Cru*). Turning left onto the D18, soon the village of **Avenas** is reached with its delightfully small restored old stone church (1180). This has a superb limestone altar, and fine modern stained glass. From here one can explore a variety of routes to St Mamert: via D18 to Ouroux (Grosne Oriental Valley), or along D18e and off on the right (D32) or continue via D18e to the Col de Crie, where there is an information point (panel). Then the D23 goes through the Forêt de l'Hospice de Beaujeu and intensely green fields to **St Mamert** which seems full of turkeys. In the fields roundabout are goats grazing like cattle, and overlooking it all is a huge red-tiled Romanesque church with a central tower and presbytery attached.

On to **St Jacques-des-Arrêts** which has a beautiful church with classical windows. It maybe noticed that this area has a great variety of trees: ash, oak, chestnut and acacia, along with ferns, briars and hedged fields. Keeping on the D23 through high country the attractive village of Cenves, with its large farmhouses, is reached. A typical farm hereabouts is 15ha (37 acres), with goats, cattle and sheep. The road(D23) now descends sharply and rises to the D68 and the Col de Gerbe (610m, 2,000ft) with goats everywhere in high fields. Then to the Col de Siberie — it must be cold here during winter — and a sharp winding descent to the pleasant village of Jullié, past the seventeenth-century château of La Roche, with its swing bridge (unique in the world) pivoting on a pillar in the middle of the moat.

Jullié is surrounded by mountain slopes and trees. It has a *caveau* (Juliénas wine, *Grand Cru*), with a fine avenue of plane trees to the church, and in the village square is a plan of local walks. The restaurant, La Vigne Gourmand, can be thoroughly recommended with its *sorbet vigneron* (*cassis* and *marc*). From Jullié the narrow D68e is taken, threading through the dispersed vineyard village of Emeringes to the D26, which is followed via the Col de Durbize (550m, 1,804ft with information point) and the Col du Truges (445m, 1,460ft) with good views above the vines to St Joseph. Here the church has twin towers, and the Stations of the Cross are through a vineyard. Then the road descends to arrive back at Beaujeu.

Western Haut Beaujolais

To explore western Haut Beaujolais, leave Beaujeu by the main road (D37), up past Les Dépôts to **Les Ardillats**, a high, pretty wine village; then right to a narrow road (V4) along the Ardières Valley past fish farming ponds. Here is superb scenery of hills, high vineyards, hedges and stone farmhouses, changing to a leafy lane with ferns, Douglas firs, spruce and pine. The road joins the D23 to the Col de Crie, where an ascent can be made of Mont Rigaud (1,012m, 3,319ft) by a paved forest track.

Continue from the col by the D43 to the large village of Monsols, a disappointing place with too much obtrusive new building. Then the route goes via the D22 and the Grosne Occidental Valley to **St Christophe-la-Montagn**e, with its simple tenth-century church high up with good views. Then by D52 to the hamlet of Vaujon, turning right on to a side road via Mussery and a landscape of rural France at its best, to **St Bonnet-des-Bruyères**. The church here is large with an interesting combination of granite plus sandstone quoins and pillars. From here, by the D5, pick up the headwaters of the Sornin, and reach the main N487 and the pleasant village of **Aigueperse**, whose church has a central tower. A short way westwards along the main road, the route turns left on to the D66 through green and wooded granite country with oak, beech and ash.

Go on to the D43 and the village of St Igny-de-Vers (information point), where *ski de fond* can be practised in season, and along to the Col du Champ Juin (742m, 7,434ft). The route here turns right (D52), into much rougher country with conifers and meadows. To the east are the slopes of Mont St Rigaud, and after the hamlet of Ajoux is a viewpoint. Next, the road passes near the impressive château of La Farge — white with red tiles — half hidden amid the trees. Soon **Propières** appears, a large village (information point) on the D10; from here the western outposts of Haut Beaujolais can be explored — Azolette and St Clément-de-Vers. Then the route continues southwards on the D10 to **Les Echarmeaux** (information point), an important road junction, and viewpoint, from where the D37 can be taken direct to Beaujeu, Belleville or Villefranche.

From Beaujeu there is an interesting walk of 8km (5 miles), leaving the main street and crossing the Ardières by a small bridge, then under the main road, and climbing up steeply to the hamlet of Château St Jean. Thence by the farm of Ruettes, past the remains of the château, through forest to the Les Laforêts farm, and descending on a paved road to the hamlet of Longefay, then turn left to reach Beaujeu (GR76). These farms sell wine and cheese.

La Vallée d'Azergues

The long valley of the Azergues marks the frontier between southern Beaujolais and the forests to the north and west. It offers many chances to explore steep winding side roads, lanes, forests and high cols.

Haute Azergues

The first route begins at **Chénelette**, a high village (661m, 2,168ft) almost at the head of a tributary valley, surrounded by forests, including chestnuts, and overlooked by Mont Tourvéon (953m, 3,126ft) on the D23 (D37 Haut Beaujolais). The road is followed down to Claveisolles, and in the nearby Forest of Corcelles are the twenty oldest Douglas firs in Europe (1872). From here, turning left on to the D129, the road climbs to the Col de Casse Froide (741m, 2,430ft). Here is a good view of Mont Soubrant (878m, 2,880ft), and at the col, maize and wheatfields with a large lime tree.

Continuing on the D129, there is a long, winding, wooded descent to the pleasant village of **St Didier-s-Beaujeu**. Here is an unusual church tower with a broached spire, but the village is better known for bottling wine for export. Sometimes children can be seen on bicycles, driving goats with huge wooden crosses around their necks. From St Didier the route goes up the narrow, steep D129e and D139 past the southern slopes of Mont Tourvéon to Chénelette.

The second route starts at **Les Echarmeaux** (D37 Haut Beaujolais). Turning sharp right on to the D110 at La Scierie, the route follows the river, and the railway after Poule, to Le Prunier (D485). Then it descends along the main road, a steep-sided valley with much wood-working, past the entrance to the spiral tunnels, and arrives at **Lamure-s-Azergues**. This small town has the fifteenth-century Château de Pramenoux in a wood off on a steep road to the right, but the route is to the left on the D44, a very picturesque road to the Col de Croix Montmain (737m, 2,417ft). Then take the D88e, narrow and wooded, to the Col de la Croix-Rosier — the visitor might be surprised to find a night-club (Le Pressoir) in this remote spot. There are also good views over the vineyards. Continue on the D72 to the village of **Marchampt,** nestling in the fold of two valleys surrounded by vineyards, orchards and forests. From here much may be explored, but an excursion along the D9 to see the Château de Varennes with turrets on the walls and towers amid the trees is well worthwhile. Returning from here on the D9 via the Col de la Croix de Marchampt (685m, 2,247ft) the route continues through to Pont Gaillard, near the other side of the spiral tunnel, and so to **Le Gravier** on D485, where in the Café Gravier some interesting walks are

Girl with goats at St Didier-sur-Beaujeu

advertised, ranging from semi-Marathon du Beaujolais (22km, 13½ miles) in April to Corrida de Beaujolais Villages Nouveau in November. Then continue to Lamure.

St Cyr and Corniche du Val d'Azergues

From Lamure the D485 descends to Chambost-Allières, a small industrial outpost (metals and plastics). Here the D504 is joined, rising steeply to **St Cyr**, where there is an interesting forest walk along a *Sentier Botanique* to the Source Font-Froide in the Cantinière Forest. Then, on the D504 at Le Parasoir, there is a good view of Vaux and the Vauxonne Valley ('Clochemerle', which will be visited later); a short way on and the D44 is taken to the village of **Montmelas**. From here Mont-St-Bonnet (680m, 2,230ft) can be climbed, from where the Alps may be seen — weather permitting!

Outside the village on the D44 the fortress Château of Montmelas, restored by Viollet le Duc in the nineteenth century, presents a majestic sight. After this the D19 is joined, and taken through Cogny to reach **Le Saule d'Oingt** on the D116 where the Corniche begins. All along this crestline past the Col du Chêne (720m, 2,362ft), and Col du Joncin (735m, 2,411ft) to Chambost is a splendid wooded landscape of oaks and conifers, with panoramas on both sides at Buisson

Pouilleux, after La Cantinière. At the village of **Chambost**, just off the road, next to the small honey-coloured stone church (this is the fringe of the 'Pierres Dorées') is a large old lime tree planted in the reign of Henri IV, four centuries ago. The road then descends steeply to Chambost Allières (D485).

The Lower Azergues Valley and Le Pays de Pierres Dorées

The latter is a relatively new n ame for an old distinctive region of forty-one communes which have their own Syndicat d'Initiative at Châtillon d'Azergues. The name arose from the setting sun shining on the stone of the villages where the houses, churches and châteaux are built of ochre-coloured Jurassic limestone. The typical house is of vaulted construction, and the living room is above the cellar, reached by an outside staircase with a wrought-iron or stone balustrade — the more beautiful houses are protected by a porch with stone or wooden columns. It is impossible to do justice to this area quickly, and exploration has to be on foot or slowly by car.

An 8km (5 mile) walk in and around **Theizé** begins at this well sited and most picturesque village (D96). Starting from the centre of Theizé, by an old column with a cross built in 1567 (La Croix des Enfants de Theizé), take the track called Le Boîtier to the Clos de la Platière. Here is the house of Madame Roland, a famous writer guillotined in the Reign of Terror. It is now a small museum. Then through the vines to the chapel of St Hippolyte (1662). From here a footpath leads to the Frontenas road (D19). At the village, in passing, note the French Revolution inscription on the fifteenth-century church door. The route turns right to Moiré, and up the hill from here, one can see typical Beaujolais countryside. The descent towards Theizé is by a track, past woods and vines and a wayside cross. Below Theizé on the right, is the massive fifteenth-century fortified manor of Rapetour. Returning to Theizé there are two buildings which should be seen: the old fifteenth-century church (deconsecrated), which has a gallery connecting the adjacent Château of Rochebonne (seventeenth century), with its two huge towers and beautiful stair-case. Both buildings can be visited and although they have been neglected, they are still superb and are being voluntarily restored.

The medieval village of **Oingt** (D96/D485), perched on its knoll, is a jewel, and full of beautiful buildings. There is the remaining fortified gate of Nizy, a tower providing a fine panorama, a thir-teenth-century church with old sculptures in the apse, and a six-teenth-century village hall with exhibitions. In addition to its viticul-

The chapel of the château at Theizé

ture, the village has a tile works just outside the village, where a road leads to the Château de Prosny (fourteenth century), for a long time believed to be haunted by 'La Dame Blanche', the unfaithful wife of its seventeenth-century proprietor who put her in a convent for two years. Oingt's strange name is believed to be Graeco-Roman from *Iconium*. Leaving by D96, **St Laurent-d'Oingt** is soon reached with its *cave co-opérative*, and then the way descends steeply to the Azergues Valley. The route turns right along the D485 to Les Grandes Planches where, after turning left across the river, is the ancient village of **Ternand** on its conspicuous hill, reached by a winding road (D31e). This was fortified by the Archbishops of Lyon, and its tenth-century church is above a strange, far older fifth-century crypt with ninth-century frescoes, where an exiled eleventh-century Archbishop of Canterbury stayed. In its narrow alleys are some old houses of the fourteenth and fifteenth centuries. From here, a few kilometres away westwards, is the Forest of Brou with many paths.

Returning to the base of the hill, the route remains on the right bank of the Azergues, by turning right on to the narrow V206 by the river. After a few kilometres join the D39 to cross the Azergues, and continue to **Chessy-les-Mines** on the D485. This village has a twelfth-century church connected with the great French financier,

Jacques Coeur (fifteenth century), who owned the copper mines here, exploiting the mineral chessylite (copper pyrites). Mining began in Roman times, and only ceased in the last century, but the red spoil heaps can still be seen, away from the old medieval streets and buildings, towards the river.

A short distance further is the village of **Châtillon d'Azergues**, with its remarkable fortified château (twelfth century) and keep, now privately restored from ruin, and lived in. The château chapel can be visited, but the main feature is not its age, but the beautiful ornate restoration of the nineteenth century with its paintings. In the village is the headquarters of the Syndicat d'Initiative of the Pierres Dorées, housed in a fine building where exhibitions are held and wine tasting takes place. From Châtillon the route takes the D70e on the left from D485, towards **Charnay** on D70. Here is an old feudal château, an extremely fine eleventh-century church, and good views.

Continue on the D70 to **Marcy-sur-Anse**, an interesting place not only for its ruined château on Montézain summit, but also for a tower overlooking the Saône Valley, restored by the French Post Office. This is the only example left of the Chappe telegraph system using mechanical arms (similar to flags), constructed in 1799, which revolutionised communications in France, and was used until the invention of the electric telegraph and the Morse code. Near the quarry and Lafarge cement works is a 'Geological Path', which shows a geological fault in a clay/limestone junction after the fault was eroded, and also the local rock succession starting with the Pierres Dorées (Jurassic limestone: the Inferior Oolite of the English Cotswolds). The path is laid with stones to keep visitors' shoes clean.

Now move on to Lachassagne, where, in the church, there is a celebrated crib that took 11 years to make. Then the route turns left on to D39, and climbs to the D38, which is crossed through to Le Boiter (D19), and D96 to **Pouilly-le-Monial**, a village with a fine fifteenth-century church, and a traditional restaurant, La Forge. A side road leads the village of **Jarnioux**, dominated by its château, which is one of the most remarkable in the south-east of France. It was thirteenth century originally, but rebuilt in Renaissance times, and has six 'pepper pot' towers, and a majestic entrance. The courtyard can be visited and nearby are some fine old houses. Beyond is Ville-s-Jarnioux, which has a church with Austrian frescoes, relating to their occupation in 1814. From here the route (D116) goes to St Clair, then back down the D120 to Oingt, and on to **Bois d'Oingt**, a large village with a *cave co-opérative*, and particularly beautiful houses in the famous golden stone.

The Beaujolais Vineyards
Villefranche

Not as old as its neighbours, and of humble origin, Villefranche has long been of commercial importance. The architecture of the houses in the Rue Nationale was curiously determined by a measurement tax, making for narrow façades, but leading to courtyards, galleries and spiral staircases which are gems of the fifteenth to eighteenth centuries. Some of the best preserved, interesting, and beautiful include No 834 (fifteenth century) with superb vaulting and the arms of Anne of Beaujeu; No 790 (eighteenth century), Madame Roland's house with three storeys and wrought-iron balconies; No 528 Auberge Coupe d'Or (oldest inn), with splendid seventeenth-century stone and ironwork.

The town is also the home of a unique and curious *fête*, 'Des Conscrits' in January, which is well over 100 years old. All conscripts aged 20, the new 'class' and those in multiples of 10 years, take part in celebrations both religious and festive over several days, which has its centrepiece on Sunday morning. This is a defile, known as *'la vague'* (wave), when, in evening dress with tricloured buttonhole and ribbons (green for 20, yellow for 30, orange for 40 etc), white gloves and top hats, each class is arranged in age order and arm in arm, carrying bouquets of flowers, they sway in a vast movement behind fanfares and flags, occupying the entire Rue Nationale.

Beaujolais Villages (Appellation Contrôlée)

Leave Villefranche by the D43, and after passing Quilly, turn left on to D35, through fields of maize and sunflowers, and before reaching St Julien, turn right for a short way on the D76 to the Claude Bernard Museum. Situated in a pleasant old country seat, amid a sea of vines, this is a memorial to a pioneer of experimental medicine.

Returning to the D35 the village of **St Julien** soon appears, and on the left is the thirteenth-century Château de Rigaudière. Go along the D19 for a short way through vineyards to Blacé where there is a later classical (eighteenth century) château with an huge flight of steps. This is already the land of Beaujolais Villages, where it is said the wine engenders good humour, actions, and leads to paradise.

Back on the D35 again, approaching Salles, there is a panorama ahead of the Monts de Beaujolais, and far off, the spurs of the Morvan. **Salles** is a village with some elegant Louis XVI houses, one of which is connected with the French poet Lamartine, adjacent to the old Benedictine monastery. The twelfth-century cloisters, and eleventh-century church are worth a visit to see their sculptures.

Climbing out of Salles, join the D49e to reach **Vaux-en-Beaujo-lais**. This is probably the best known village in the region thanks to the novels of Gabriel Chevallier. It is a very attractive place built on terraces, and in a small square is a tiny, elegant building known as La Pisotterie. There is a good wine-tasting cellar here, La Cave de Clochemerle, and a less well known building, Les Balmes, where one can taste the waters of a mineral spring. The twelfth-century church has a fine door, and a fifteenth-century triptych.

The route leaves here by the D133 for **Le Perréon**, a large village with a wine co-operative, one of eighteen in the region, which produce about third of all the wine in Beaujolais. There is a small, simple, but very good restaurant here called La Cloche. Continue on the D62 to the hill village of **St Etienne-la-Varenne** on the right, rather like an Italian village in Umbria. Near here a large stone house at the top of a nearby hill, called Champagne, with a vineyard of 7.25ha (18 acres) could well represent the typical 'Villages' *vigneron* (vine grower) who does not own, but leases and cultivates the vineyard, sharing the proceeds with the landowner who provides all the equipment, under a very old form of contract. Fifty per cent of Beaujolais is worked by *vignerons* in this way

The D62 is followed to **Odenas**, where some way off amid the vines is the fine Château de la Chaise (1675), which was built by the nephew of Père La Chaise, the confessor of Louis XIV, who gave his name to the cemetery in Paris. The château has a vaulted wine cellar 104m (341ft) long but this cannot be visited.

After Odenas (D43), the Col de Poyebade is mounted, and a steep little road on the right leads to the summit of Mont Brouilly (483m, 1,584ft), with superb views, and a small chapel (1857). This was dedicated to the Virgin by *vignerons*, after the disease of oïdium had been cured by sulphur treatment and every year on 8 September there is a rather vinous pilgrimage by *vignerons*. These slopes lower down form the Côte de Brouilly, typified by the small Château Thivin, once the home of a famous *viticulteur*, Claude Geoffray, and with the hamlet of Brouilly below on the D43e, 'Côte de Brouilly' and 'Brouilly' are two of the Beaujolais *Grands Crus*, rich fruity wines.

Return to the D43, and follow it until just before the junction with the D37, where the route turns sharp left, onto a side road following a stream, and goes up to **Quincié**, a pleasant village with the rather dilapidated fifteenth-century Château de la Palud, which has great charm. From here take the D9 to the hamlet of St Vincent, and cross the Beaujeu road (D37), to reach on the left a narrow road leading to **Lantignié** (D78). Just north of this small village is Château de Tholon which has two fine courtyards, a vaulted kitchen, and beautiful

*Vaux-en-Beaujolais
('Clochemerle')*

staircases. On by D135 to **Regnié**, where there is large farm, La Grange Charton, belonging to the Hospices de Beaujeu. The buildings built at the beginning of the tenth century, form a quadrilateral around a courtyard of 3,000sq m (32,275sq ft). It is remarkable for its fermentation vats, cellars and housing for *vignerons*.

Keep on the D135, which soon meets on the right, the D68, and reach the village of **Cercié** where the chapel of St Ennemond (D68e) and the Château de la Terrière (fourteenth century) can be visited. The château still has the great door and machicolation (openings in the parapet) in front of the ancient moat. The wine from this commune is known as Pisse-Vieille, after an old legend.

After this visit St Lager (D68), where one can taste Brouilly at Le Cuvage des Brouilly, and then on to the village of **Charentay**, where there are interesting and curious buildings. First, on the right, is the eighteenth-century Château de Sermézy, and then in the village itself are the houses of the *tonneliers* (coopers), with their glass roofs. After this, in the Domaine des Combes, is the Tour de la Belle-Mère (mother-in-law), built in the last century by a very possessive woman, who wished to watch the activities of her son-in-law. Built of brick, it is no less than 35m (115ft) high! Continuing on D68, the once huge fortress of the Knights Templars, the incredible Château d'Arginy, is reached. Built and fortified in the twelfth and thirteenth centuries, all that remains of the original twenty-two brick towers is a single one called 'Sept Béatitudes', where new knights were initiated. When the Templars fell, the château was abandoned, then rebuilt in the sixteenth century, only to become a victim of the Revolution.

Château de Varennes, Quincié

After this the route joins, on the right, the D19 to **St Etienne-des-Oullières**, where there is a *cave co-opérative* and two châteaux : Milly, rebuilt in 1840, and Lacarelle with parts dating from the sixteenth century. The D43 can be taken back to Villefranche.

Northern Beaujolais and the Grands Crus

A tour of northern Beaujolais and the *Grands Crus* begins at **Belleville**, a very ancient place of Roman origin (*Lunna*), which was eventually burnt by the Saracens in 732, and rose from the ashes in the eleventh century under the name of Bellavilla, hence Belleville. It became a wine centre, and was noted for cooperage (barrel making), but the trade has recently died out. The Romanesque church (1158) is a very fine building, particularly the tower, apse, door and the nave with nine bays. The other interesting building is the pharmacy of the Hôtel-Dieu (Sisters of St Martha, Order of Beaune), where there is a remarkable collection of old pharmaceutical pottery, glass and instruments which can be visited.

Leave Belleville by the D37, and after crossing the N6, turn right on to the D18, over the Ardières River to **Pizay**. Here there is the Aero Club de Beaujolais (established in 1931 from Belleville), and a fourteenth-century château and ornate square keep and a garden by Le Nôtre. This can be visited as it is a restaurant and hotel.

From here the D69 is taken to **Morgon**, then D68 to **Villié-Mor-**

gon, a village that was on the old Roman road from Lyon to Autun, and it is around here that geology contributes, not for the first time, to the taste of wine. For the *cru* of Morgon has the nuance of kirsch, due to the ancient schists that make up the 707ha (1,746 acres) of its *vignoble*, termed *roche pourrie* by the local people.

The route now winds up by the D86 to **Chiroubles**, where its 320ha (790 acres) of vines grow on a natural terrace to 750m (2,460ft) and the *caveau* for tasting is appropriately named La Terrasse. It is a silky, light wine, and is drunk younger than any of the other *crus*. Victor Pulliat, one of the saviours of the European *vignoble*, was born here and following the epidemic of phylloxera in 1860, he grafted on native American vine-stocks.

The route descends next to the D68, and **Fleurie**, which lives up to its name both in the pleasantness of its site, with superb views, and also in its wine, which is scented, flowery and light. Strange that the acid granitic soil of its 800ha (1,976 acres) should produce a wine of which it is said: 'One glass pleasure, two joy, three good luck, and beyond — the dream.' Fleurie has a *cave co-opérative*, as well as a *caveau* — both for tasting. Before the Revolution Fleurie used to be a frontier town between Beaujolais and Mâconnais.

The route continues to **Chénas**, a curious *appellation*, because its 220ha (543 acres) of *vignoble* covers only the west and north of the commune, the smallest of the *Grands Crus*. The name comes from its ancient oaks (*chênes*), from the time of the Druids, but the oak one seen in Chénas now is not from the district for it forms the medieval arches of the château which is the *cave co-opérative*, as well as the barrels in it.

For the eastern and southern parts of the commune, move down the slope of oak trees to near the hamlet of Les Thorins on the D266 to the only remaining windmill in Beaujolais. For not only is it a classified monument, but it also gives its name to the most prestigious *cru* in the region: **Moulin-à-Vent**. Once again geology seems to be significant for the 560ha (1,383 acres) of its *vignoble* are planted in friable pink granite soil rich in manganese, which gives a deep, rich iris-scented wine that has a longevity exceptional for Beaujolais. It can be tasted in the *caveau* at the base of the famous mill itself.

Returning to the D68 the route continues via the D95 to **Juliénas**, whose 520ha (1,284 acres) of *vignoble* are spread through this and two other communes, Jullié and Emeringes (see Eastern Haut Beaujolais). There is an ancient château here with huge cellars, that once belonged to the Lords of Beaujeu, most of which was rebuilt at the beginning of the eighteenth century. But the building to see is the

Maison de la Dîme (1647), with its two storeys of arcades. Here the tithes were collected, half to the Chapter of St Vincent de Mâcon, and half to the parish priest. There is a *caveau* for tasting this rich, fruity, full-bodied wine at Le Cellier de la Vieille Eglise here.

From here take the D169 to **St Amour**, and cross from the Rhône department into the department of Saône et Loire, where its 240ha (593 acres) of *vignobles* is around the picturesque flanks of the Mont de Berrey between Beaujolais and Mâconnais. Viticulture here has been known from times immemorial, and was under the patrimony of the Canons of Mâcon, so it is surprising that the commune did not get its *appellation* until 1946, due to a former mayor and *vigneron*. The name, St Amour,would appear to have originated from the amorous propensities of the visiting canons from Mâcon. The wine is soft, delicate and fine, and can be tasted at the *caveau* in the village.

From this northerly village follow the D31 until it meets the D186 on the right. Take this to the D166, then turn left to the N6. Follow the N6 to the Maison Blanche, and take the D95 to **Romanèche-Thorins**. Here a typical Beaujolais house has been transformed into a museum, which shows the work of Benoît Raclet on the protection of vines early in the nineteenth century.

From here the route south is by the D486, and the D9e to **Corcelles**. The château here is one of the best in the region, a Renaissance jewel, altered in the nineteenth century, and restored a few years ago with intelligence and taste. Particularly worth seeing are the wells in the courtyard, the armoury and the fifteenth-century chapel. From Corcelles the D119 is taken to the N6, and via this road either Belleville or Villefranche can be reached.

The Monts du Beaujolais

This is the high land west of the Azergues Valley, between the Rhône and the Loire, a landscape of forests and steep valleys with plenty of opportunities to explore the wild and isolated uplands.

The Route de Sapins (The Road of Firs)

This route begins from Lamure-s-Azergues on the D485, which is followed northwards to the D9 on the left above Le Gravier. This road winds up steeply to **St Nizier**, a pleasant little village perched on hillside bends.

From here the road climbs through forests with occasional views to La Croix Nicelle (786m, 2,578ft) with a distant view northwards of the conical Mont-St-Rigaud which appears like a coniferous volcano. Then on to St Bonnet-le-Troncy, and a winding descent (D9) to **St**

Moulin-à-Vent, now sailless and the only remaining windmill in Beaujolais,
which gives its name to the most prestigious cru *in the region*

Vincent-de-Reins, which, although an industrial village with several outlying hamlets, is really quite beautifully sited in the valley of
the Reins. There is a 17km ($10^1/_2$ mile) walk starting from the church,
which gives good views of the valley, and then goes via the Col
Burdel (680m, 2,230ft), climbs to a high point above La Chapelle de
Mardore (748m, 2,453ft), continues through forests to above Les
Filatures, and returns to St Vincent above its valley.

From here the route follows the D108 along a very wooded up-
and-down way with a great variety of trees: Douglas firs, Norway
spruce, beech, oak, chestnut and ash to the Col du Pavillon (695m,
2,280ft). Then follow the D64, and climb to the small textile town of
Cours-la-Ville, in an area which is quite scenic, with several local
walks of varying lengths (10, 20 and 35km, 6, 12 and 21 miles) marked
yellow and white. From here the Trambouze Valley (D8) is followed,
and the fir forests tend to be above the villages on the crests, which
are good walking areas.

The route reaches the outskirts of Thizy, which, with Bourg-de-
Thizy, is a rather confused sort of place, but old and picturesque with
the interesting eleventh-century Chapelle St Georges. However, the
town can be skirted by turning left on the main D504d for a short way,
then turning right on to D9e, thence D9a to the pleasant village of **St
Victor-s-Rhins** dominated by a huge and rather fine railway viaduct. (Reins changes to Rhins because it is in the department of

Loire.) The church (eleventh century) is from the priory of Cluny, and the route continues along D9/D13 (same road) to the important textile town of **Amplepuis**, which has a museum (Place de l'Hôtel-de-Ville) named after the inventor of the sewing machine, Barthélémy Monnier. There is a walk here of 18km (11 miles) from the Place Belfort, taking in woods and the Château de Rochefort; path marked yellow.

From Amplepuis there is a very pleasant wooded route (D8) climbing steeply up to Les Sauvages (723m, 2,371ft) Here was an historic meeting between François I and James IV of Scotland to which a monument can be seen. From here, on the left, is a narrow wild high winding route with conifers and deciduous trees to the Col de Cassettes (622m, 2,040ft). Then the D56 is joined and followed with forests of beech and firs, and high open meadows with isolated plots of beans and cabbages. Later there are tremendous views on either side, before the D13 is reached and traversed. The D56 is again joined to **Ronno**, a picturesque village, where all services (electricity, water etc), are put underground. From here the D56 goes through woods to Bancillon in the Reins Valley (D504), which widens out into the large artificial, but very scenic Lac de Sapins, which can be walked round.

And so to the pleasant town of **Cublize** with three walks (marked yellow), and a long walk of 31km (19 miles) (blue and white, part GR7) high and wooded. From Cublize take the D504 to the junction with D10. Follow this road up the very picturesque valley of the Reins via the village of Magny to St Vincent. Then, the road continues northward past Les Filatures (textile village) to the upper Reins, now very wooded and rural, to Ranchal. From here the road (D10), climbs steeply to a viewpoint off the road on the right: Notre Dame la Rochette (where there is a shrine). Still going upwards the route reaches the high Col des Escorbans (853m, 2,798ft), and then plunges down through forests, and up again to the Col des Aillets (716m, 2,348ft). From here one can see eastwards over to Mont Tourvéon (953m, 3,126ft) wooded to its summit and reflect upon these dense forests of Haut Beaujolais, and how, in the 1950s, a British aircraft mysteriously disappeared and was only found by chance in November 1960. From the col the road descends, and mounts again to Les Echarmeaux, where one can go direct to Beaujeu (D37) or by D485 to Lamure-s-Azergues.

Alternative Routes into the Monts du Beaujolais (Route de Sapins)
The visitor could go from Chambost-Allières on the D485 to the D98 on the right, then to St Just d'Avray. Before the village there is the

fairy-tale château of La Valsonnière. At the village there are splendid opportunities for walking with two of 11 and 14km (7 and $8^1/_2$ miles Pierre Plantée and Roches Fayettes walks), the route then goes on to either Ronno or Amplepuis.

Alternatively, go from Les Ponts-Tarrets on the D485 by D13 to St Clément-s-Valsonne, and Valsonne, both amid forests and meadows. Then climb to the Col du Pilon (727m, 2,385ft) and from there it meets the route from St Just d'Avray.

Further Information
— Beaujolais —

Museums and Other Places of Interest

Amplepuis
Sewing Machine Museum
Open: Sat and Sun 2.30-6.30pm all year.

Beaujeu
Museum
Open: April-June, October and November daily except Tuesday, 2.30-6pm, also 10am-12 noon Saturdays and Sundays; July -Sept 10am-12 noon, 2.30-6pm.

Châtillon d'Azergues
Château Chapel
Mme Givel
Esplanade du Vingtain
69380 Lozanne (key)

St Julien
Bernard Museum
Open: November-February 10am-12 noon, 2.30-5pm; April-October 10am-12 noon, 2.30-6pm, daily except Mondays. Closed Christmas week, New Year, all of March and 15 August.

For vineyard *châteaux* (except *caveaux*) enquire Mairie (town hall) of commune.

Tasting Cellars of Places not Mentioned in Text
St Jean d'Ardières; Pommiers; Chasselas; Leyres.
Also *cave co-opératives* Bully and Létra.

Tourist Information Offices
Belleville
105 Rue de la République
☎ (74) 66 17 10

Beaujeu
Sq de Grandhau ☎ (74) 69 22 88
Mle Lauterbach: information on *châteaux*.
Open: mid-March to mid-December.

Bois d'Oingt
Mairie (town hall) ☎ (74) 71 60 51
For *châteaux* enquire at Mairie of commune (Jarnioux, Montmelas, Charney)

Châtillon d'Azergues
Place de la Mairie ☎ (74) 65 27 58
Open: early May-early November, Sat and Sun 10am-12 noon, 2-6pm.
Mme Faure (Présidente)

Monsols
☎ (74) 65 43 51
Open: Saturday morning all year; afternoons also in summer.

Theizé
Office (old church)
For visit to church and *château* contact M. Guillot ☎ (74) 71 64 27

Villefranche
290 Rue de Thizy ☎ (74) 68 05 18
Open: April-September 9.15am-12.15pm, 2.30-7pm; October-March 9.15am-12.15pm, 2.30-6pm. (Houses in Rue Nationale include Nos 816, 761, 706, 673, 594, 588, 494, 476, 465, 407, 375.)

Wine
210 Boulevard Vermorel ☎ (74) 65 45 55
Headquarters of wine co-coperatives, many wine associations and Les Compagnons du Beaujolais.

A typical Auvergne hill farm

The distant peaks of Mont Blanc, Savoie

In the Savoie the walker has a great variety of terrain to explore and scenery unparalleled anywhere else in Europe

Flowers take root in the Alps despite the seemingly inhospitable terrain, Savoie

7 • Savoie

Sheltered by the mightiest summits of the Alps, the ancient province of Savoie lies between the Franco-Italian border and the Rhône Valley on the one hand, and its northern boundary is the south shore of Lac Léman (Lake Geneva). The boundary with Switzerland continues eastwards, high above the Rhône as far as Mont Dolent, a mountain summit shared by three countries, France, Switzerland and Italy. Narrow hidden valleys, often reached only by tortuous roads, criss-cross the map as far as the boundary with the Dauphiné region.

Savoie, or Savoy to most English speakers, only became part of France in 1860. An independent state until then, it was ruled by counts of Savoie from the eleventh century, although frequently fought over by neighbouring states. In 1720 Savoie was joined with Sardinia serving as the nucleus for the formation of a unified Italy, but at the time of the unification (1860), Savoie itself was ceded to France. One of the conditions stipulated at the time was that the name Savoie should be retained as the name of the then new *département*. The locals are proud of this fact and will tell you that they are Savoyard first and French second.

Despite the incursions of tourism, the region is still very rural. Here one can still find farm houses built in the traditional style with roofs capable of bearing immense weights of snow every winter. Styles and materials differ widely. High mountain dwellings above the Maurienne valley to the south-east of Chambéry fit snuggly into the hillside and have shallow pitched roofs made of stone slabs and are called *lauzes*. Houses in the gentler climes of Chablais to the south of Lac Léman are made of horizontally-laid planks of pine or larch with interlocking corners. Originally the roofs were tiled with wooden slates, *tavaillons*, but regretfully corrugated iron is now more widespread. Savoie churches, even in the remotest villages, tend to be richly decorated, a link with the region's Sardinian history.

Food and drink of Savoie very much reflects the farming traditions of the region, and as with all mountain areas, cheese making has

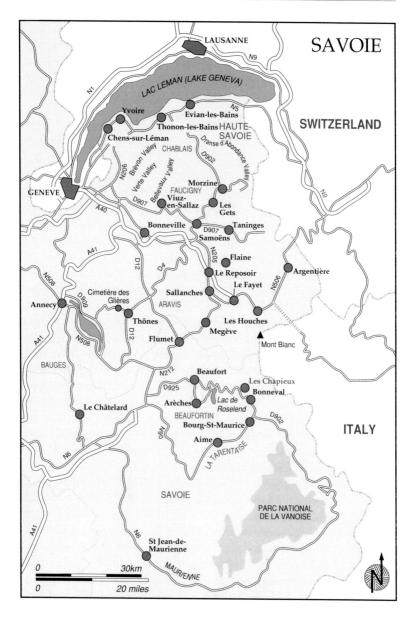

been honed to a fine art. Tomme and Reblochon are the most common cheeses made from cows' milk, but perhaps goat cheeses are the finest product to find its way down from the high alpine pastures. There are some exquisite blue-veined goats' cheeses, such as Sasenage, and a beautiful Emmental-type known as Beaufort. Try to visit a Sunday market where these will probably be on sale. Do not be afraid to ask for a sample tasting, but in any case the farm wife in charge of the stall will more than likely offer you a sliver to tempt you into buying some of her produce. Other things on sale are likely to be home-made strawberry or bilberry tarts, but beware if you need to watch your waistline!

Because mountain weather is generally cooler than say in Burgundy, wines of Savoie rarely receive the *grand cru* accolade, but nevertheless there are some very pleasant vintages grown in the more sheltered valleys. Both red and white wines come from the hillsides above the Combe de Savoie south-east of Chambéry, but the area south of Lac Geneva specialises in reds.

Eating out in Savoie again reflects the mountain character of the region. Smoked meats and sliced sausages, specialities of the area, make an interesting start to any meal. River and lake trout make alternative starters, together with much rarer pike or char, the latter being found only in deep mountain lakes. Cheese-based dishes are common and often make the meal an event designed to break the ice with the locals. With a *raclette* meal, the word comes from a French word meaning 'to scrape', the edge of half of a large cheese similar to English farmhouse Cheddar, is placed towards a special upright facing grill. As the cheese melts and becomes runny it is scraped on to guests' plates one at a time and eaten with bread and salad. The process is repeated until the diner either bursts or capitulates, again a meal not for slimmers. Another popular meal is the *fondue Savoyard*. The recipe varies from place to place, but basically it is a mixture of cheese, white wine, garlic, kirsch and nutmeg melted into a bowl, which is kept warm over a low flame. Armed with long forks, guests dip chunks of bread or pieces of spicy sausages into the *fondue*. Anyone losing their lump of bread must pay a forfeit. Traditionally one should drink either kirsch or Marc de Savoie (a wine-based spirit), with *fondue* in order to help digest the cheese. However, anyone determined not to end up with unlimited forfeits should beware the potency of these seemingly innocent spirits. Accommodation as befits a mountain region tends to be simple but comfortable. Ranging from *gîtes d'étape* where spartan facilities are provided for self catering mountain walkers, to bed and breakfast in *chambres d'hôtes*, an excellent way of getting to know the local people, and small family-run hotels and *auberges*. There are also numerous well appointed campsites throughout the region and for the more ambitious, the extensive range of mountain huts, mostly run by the Club Alpin Français (CAF) provide meals and basic sleeping accommodation. The local tourist associations will be able to provide all the necessary details of availability and cost.

Wildlife, especially in the mountains, is abundant. Since 1960, reserves both national and regional have been designated in remote areas. The most famous is the Parc National de la Vanoise, its symbol is the ibex. Covering over 50,000 acres of valleys and mountains in the Maurienne and Tarentaise districts of south-eastern Savoie, it is joined via the national border with the Italian Gran Paradis National Park. Through this international co-operation, some of the finest mountain scenery in Europe is protected from development. Well signposted footpaths and a series of mountain huts encourage the park's use by caring visitors. As well as rare alpine flowers, animals such as the ibex (*bouquetin* in French) and chamoix are making a steady return since hunting was discontinued. Gregarious marmots can be seen sitting on their hindlegs, sunning themselves outside their burrows, but keeping a wary eye open for marauding eagle.

The Réserve National des Bauges to the east of Chambéry and Aix-les-Bains, covers a range of pine and larch-clad hills where you might see wild sheep with their magnificent spiral horns.

Basically two motorway systems serve the region; both link in the west with the north-south A7/E15, Autoroute du Soleil. The busiest is the A40/E25, Autoroute Blanche which leaves the A7/E15 at Mâcon and runs via Bourg-en-Bresse and Geneva to Chamonix before disappearing under Mont Blanc on its way south into Italy.

Since Albertville grew in stature by hosting the 1992 Winter Olympics, it is now served by an easterly arm of the A43/E70, Lyon to Chambéry motorway. Beyond Albertville the N90 dual-carriageway, follows the Tarentaise valley to Bourg-St-Maurice before climbing the long winding hairpins to the Little Saint Bernard Pass. At the foot of the pass a spur road leads into Val d'Isère, and the only road access for visitors to the Vanoise.

From Chambéry another motorway, the A41/E712 links the A40/E25 via Aix-les-Bains and Annecy. Other access roads are the N37 Geneva/Thonon-les-Bains road beside Lake Geneva in the north; the N508/N512 between Annecy and the Chamonix valley and the N6/E70 Annecy-Turin road which skirts the south side of the Vanoise National Park.

By using these roads as rough boundaries and for the sake of clarity, we can split the region into three areas. In the north the Chablais and Faucigny districts are bounded by Lake Geneva and the Chamonix valley. South as far as the A43/E70 and N90 lie the Arvais, Beaufortin and Tarentaise districts. South again across the

N6/E70 as far as the southern boundary of Savoie is the Vanoise with the Maurienne district filling the valley of the Arc.

Summer visitors must beware of French ski resorts with their bulldozed hillsides festooned with a multiplicity of abandoned lifts and tows, the skylines broken by lego-like apartment blocks, every room with its own sun balcony, marvellous in winter, but abominations in summer. Fortunately most maps indicate the whereabouts of these winter resorts with a snowflake symbol, or by the black lines of ski-tows.

Chablais

Rolling forested hills cut by streams draining into the Dranse de Morzine. To the south is the deep cleft of the Chamonix valley with its backcloth, the pristine snows of Mont Blanc.

From Thonon-les-Bains on the south shore of Lake Geneva, the only through road to penetrate the area, follows the narrow Dranse valley almost to its source before the road divides at Taninges. Here one arm climbs by twists and turns across a high ridge, continuing south, then down to Cluses and the industrial part of the Arve valley. A second arm takes a more westerly and gentler route to Annemasse and the Swiss border.

Taninges stands at a cross-roads, with the fourth road following the valley of the River Giffre through Samoëns as far as Sixt nestling below the high peaks of the Cirque du Fer à Cheval.

By using this road along the Dranse, the D902 and its many side roads, it is possible to find enough out of the way places to occupy several days of quiet exploration.

The resort town of **Thonon-les-Bains** lines a sunny bay on Lake Geneva, a little to the west of the Delta de la Dranse, making an excellent base for exploring Chablais. The town's shopping centre being pedestrianised allows quiet strolling, maybe to visit the Basilica of St François de Sales, where there is a rather fine painting of *The Way of the Cross*, by Maurice Denis. The ivy-clad Château de Sonnaz houses an interesting folk museum covering the long history of the town, from Stone Age lake dwellers to more recent times.

The factory where the internationally acclaimed Evian water is bottled is at **Amphion-les-Bains** near Thonon. Every month over 50 million bottles are filled with water which has filtered its way through the rock strata of the nearby mountains. Visits can be made by prior arrangement at the Hall d'Information in the Rue Nationale in nearby Evian itself.

Returning to the valley of the Dranse, or to give it its full and correct title, the Dranse de Morzine valley. A road follows the river, along the Gorges de la Drance, then into the exciting Gorges du Pont du Diable (Devil's Bridge). Here a walkway takes visitors along the side of a towering cliff 60m (197ft) high, where they can admire the maze of strangely shaped, deep channels cut into the rocky gorge. The gorge gets its name from a massive boulder blocking the chasm. According to local legend, it was used by the Devil in order to cross from one side to the other.

At Bioge a short distance downstream from the Gorges du Pont du Diable, a left turn along the D22 follows this minor road as far as Châtel before climbing the Pas de Morgins and descending into Switzerland and the Rhône. The road follows the Dranse d'Abondance Valley. At first the road climbs steeply, through a tunnel and past spectacular waterfalls, towards the middle section of the valley. Here the fertile land supports a special breed of cattle the Abondance, whose rich milk is used to make the local cheese. The huge Haut Chablais farmhouses are covered by a single roof with shippons and hay-lofts reached from the all-weather shelter of long balconies.

At **Abondance** there are the extensive ruins of a once powerful abbey which owned the whole of this lush valley. The cloisters are worth visiting to see the frescoes and a small museum of religious art, or simply to enjoy the tranquil atmosphere.

From Châtel near the valley head, it is possible to take a cable car to the top of the Pic de Morlan. Ridges on either side of the peak wander along the Franco-Swiss border with their uninterrupted views into Switzerland, especially those of the craggy north face of the Dents du Midi, to the south-east.

There is an alternative road out of Thonon, the dramatic D26, which follows a corniche high above the Gorges de la Dranse. Skirting Mont d'Hermone, it enters the Brévon Valley and a little way beyond Vailly a side track to the right leads to Chapelle d'Hermone, a place of pilgrimage every 16 August.

About 2km (1 mile) along the valley, the road climbs past a ruined castle overlooking the sleepy village of Lullin, and then crosses the Col de Terramont. Below is the beautiful Verte Valley and the community of **Habère-Poche**, a centre for wood carving and painting. The valley is ideal for easy walking and picnicking, and the local tourist office organises a programme of guided walks. Habère-Poche's annual fête is held on the second Sunday in August and there is a firework display and dancing in the streets on the 13 July.

A left fork on the other road out of Vailly leads into another valley, the Bellvaux. Like the Verte, the Bellevaux Valley is a good centre for easy walking. One excursion leads to a limestone gorge in the Brévon Valley where a landslip in 1941 created an almost hidden lake.

Before leaving Chablais, it is worthwhile taking a look at a few of the villages towards the western end of Lake Geneva. This area is known as The Garden of Savoy (Le Jardin de la Savoie). Vineyards and fruit trees fill this sheltered corner. The local wine is Crépy, and the centre of *appellation contrôllée* for the district is Douvaine on the N5 close to the Swiss border, inland from the western end of the lake. **Chens-sur-Léman** is on the lakeside at the end of the D20 from Douvaine. Here there is an interesting little museum specialising in the local rural life throughout the ages. Pine trees shelter a pleasant stretch of beach between Chens and its neighbour Tougues. You might get a tantalising view of the Château de Beauregard on the lakeside, but it is private and not open to the public except on rarely advertised days.

The D25 follows the lake north around a wide promontory. A side turn leads to **Nernier** where there is another museum, this one specialising in contemporary art and the natural history of Chablais. **Yvoire** is at the tip of the promontory, the loveliest village, certainly on the French side of Lake Geneva. A fishing port of sloping narrow streets surrounded by a town wall with gates dating from 1316, it still retains a street pattern laid out in the early Middle Ages. Cars are banned from the town centre, making it easy to wander at will, maybe to visit the traditional Savoyard church with its bulbous bell-tower, or maybe admire the floral displays which have gained Yvoire the accolade of 'Lauréat International du Fleurissement'. Excenevex on the sheltered bay of the Golfe de Coudrée, has the largest continuous beach on Lake Geneva.

Using the D902, the Route des Alpes, again from Thonon-les-Bains, the valley of the Dranse cuts its way through higher and higher hills towards the administrative district of Faucigny. On the way it is worth stopping off at the Barrage du Jotty, a short distance upstream of the Gorges du Pont du Diable. This reservoir though only 22m (72ft) wide, because of the depth of the gorge, is able to hold over a million cubic metres of water to drive turbines at Bioge lower down the valley. Following the narrow gorge through the Défilé des Tignes, the road is tunnelled through a massive boulder blocking its path. When passing through the wide St Jean d'Aulps Valley, the ancient ruins of the Abbaye de Notre-Dame-d'Aulps should not be missed. Taking its name from the Latin word for Alps, the monastery sheltered a pious order of monks from 1904 to 1823.

Morzine, the capital of Haute Chablais, marks the boundary with Faucigny. Together with its higher neighbour Avoriaz, it is the centre of a popular winter sports area, with hang gliding and paraplaning all year round. **Les Gets**, a busy and highly developed summer resort, though hardly off-the-beaten-track, does have an interesting Museum of Mechanical Instruments (the Musée de Musiques Méchaniques). Reputed to be France's finest collection of musical boxes, pianolas and phonographs, visits can also be made to the workshop where the instruments are restored.

Taninges spans the important junction of four roads. Venerable old houses, a hump-backed bridge and a pretty market place evocatively tell us that its foundations are medieval. The road east from the crossroads in Taninges follows the Giffre valley almost to its source beneath the dramatic ramparts of the Cirque du Fer à Cheval.

The main valley road, a continuation of the D907, keeps mostly to the north side of the valley, but a more attractive alternative, the D4, leaves the D902 at a hair-pin bend a mile or so south of Taninges. Wandering through forest and across alpine meadows, the road runs via Morillon where they hold a fair on the first Sunday every August, and a cross-country cycling rally at the end of the month.

The D4 joins the D907 at **Samoëns**. Once it ran to the staccato clamour of stonemasons' hammers, but nowadays the little town makes an ideal centre for exploring the quiet valleys radiating around the headwaters of the Giffre. Usually decorated by floral displays, Samoëns town centre is dominated by a magnificent 15m (50ft) high lime tree, said to be over 500 years old. The church has a twelfth-century clock tower which acts as a memorial to the skills of the local stonemasons. The ornate tower is embellished with sculptures, and its portico is supported by carved lions, with the doorway sheltered by an awning covered in tiny copper tiles. Beside the church, an elaborately decorated fountain dates from 1763, and a sun dial on the old presbytery shows the time in several different countries.

There is an attractive alpine garden on a hillside above a side street close to the church. The Jardin Jaÿsinia, was created in 1905 by Madame Cognacq whose maiden name was Jaÿ. Administered by the Natural History Museum in Paris, the garden is an important centre for the study of Alpine flora. Zig-zagging paths take the visitor past beds where plants are displayed according to their region of origin; their sunny stroll cooled by the idyllic sound of tiny waterfalls.

Above Sixt, the road ends beneath the towering cliffs of the Tennenverge. Part of the Cirque du Fer à Cheval (Horse-shoe Ampitheatre), the whole area is now a nature reserve. The road enters the reserve past a sign asking us 'not to cull the flowers uselessly'. A delightful message which only the most uncaring would ignore. A café and car park mark the road end, but footpaths wander off in all directions to where the only sound is the trill of mountain streams or the murmuring of pines.

Faucigny

At first sight one might be forgiven for thinking that the Arve Valley is so crowded as to make quiet exploration impossible. Within its narrow confines of its valley bottom are crowded industrial towns, a railway, arterial roads, busy side roads and a motorway, the A40/E25, the Autoroute Blanche, one of the major commercial arteries between France and Italy. But the enquiring traveller will find many interesting venues in both the lower and upper valley.

Proof that the valley was inhabited in prehistoric times can be found at Reignier, about 9½km (6 miles) south-east of Annemasse, where a group of dolmens and standing stones named La Pierre aux Fées, creates the enigma as to their purpose.

Bonneville, the chief town of the Faucigny district, has an attractive square surrounded by shopping arcades, and where the riverside Quai de l'Arve's plane trees look their best in late spring. As with many Savoyard towns, the war memorial is to the dead of the Franco-Prussian War as well as World Wars I and II. The activities of the local resistance in World War II is commemorated by a museum open on Wednesdays and Saturdays.

A motorway exit to the east of Cluzes marks the start of a tricky mountain road to **Flaine**. Another settlement with historical links with clock-making, Flaine lies at the foot of the Désert de Platé. The barren limestone hills are part of the Réserve Naturelle de Passy, and are served by three mountain huts spaced suitably for several day's exploration of this remote area. A cable car from Flaine to the summit of Les Grandes Platières 8,137ft (2,480m), takes a lot of the effort out of the initial climb.

Returning to the Arve, **Magland** is a village renowned for its smoked sausages. Next is **Oëx** where two spectacular waterfalls cascade from the western ramparts of the Tête du Colonney. One of them, the Cascade d'Arpenaz, falls vertically for 228m (748ft) and if the wind is blowing directly up the valley, is blown away in a plume of spray.

Industry and holidaymaking manage to co-exist at **Sallanches**, where the evening view of Mont Blanc makes a stop-over worthwhile; the town centre is particularly attractive. There are campsites to the east of the town, beside Lac de la Cavettaz and although there

Summit of the Col de Balme on the Franco Swiss border

is excellent bathing facilities, the proximity of both a railway and the motorway take away much of the solitude. Two villages to the south of Sallanches, Cordon and Combloux, can be reached by the D113 in order to enjoy the exceptional views which have given them the title of Le Balcon du Mont Blanc. On 15 August, the inhabitants dress in Napoleonic costume and celebrate the epoch with mock-military manoeuvres.

Moving into the Upper Arve Valley where both the railway and modern road cross the Gorges de Servoz on spectacular viaducts, enter an area of popular tourism centres upon Chamonix.

Le Fayet where the Mont Blanc tramway starts, is the industrial appendage of St Gervais-les-Bains, a town which still retains the atmosphere of *la belle époque*, with the continued interest the French have in spas and health centres.

If you want somewhere to stay near Chamonix, but without the crowds and pavement stall boutiques, then **Les Houches** has much to offer. Family-run *auberges* and *gîtes* can make a stay in this quiet mountain village a pleasant way of exploring the mountain paths high above the Arve.

Cable cars on both sides of the valley take the strain out of any climb. It is hard to say which is the best, but perhaps the system which reaches the summit of Le Brévent takes a lot of beating.

Footpaths leave the summit in all directions and two long distance footpaths cross there. One is the GR5, from the North Sea to the Mediterranean; the other is the Tour of Mont Blanc, a walk of constantly changing views of spectacular mountain scenery, around the highest summit in Europe. For anyone staying in the Chamonix area, it is possible to follow two sections of the tour of Mont Blanc. Both paths have the advantage of being downhill from Le Brévent! One goes east to Argentière to connect with the excellent bus service to Chamonix and Les Houches. The other path again downhill, follows the westerly ridge from the summit to a friendly mountain hut at Bellachat before it descends through pine forest to reach the valley bottom conveniently close by the railway station below Les Houches. The path passes a mountain zoo at Merlet which can only be reached on foot, the nearest road end being that from Le Coupeau a mile or so to the west.

Villages near the valley head make suitable bases for exploring the ridges and glaciers feeding the headwaters of the Upper Arve. If you can ignore the constant grind of traffic along its single street, **Argentière** is a quaint village of old and new hotels and cafés for climbers . A little way above the village, where the road beings the first hairpin in the climb towards the border col, a side road leads off on the right towards Le Tour. Here a gondola lift will wisk you up to the breezy heights of the Col de Balme. From the small mountain restaurant which sits astride the border, easy walks can be made to the summit of the Croix de Fer, 2,343m (7,687ft), or a more ambitious excursion to the Albert 1st hut beside the Glacier du Tour, or simply to take in the view of snow-capped mountains rising above the Arve Valley.

From Argentière, both the road and railway make for a narrow gap marking the Franco-Swiss border above Vallorcine, the last village in eastern Faucigny. At the Col des Montets we have left the Arve behind and the last French section of both the road and railway follows the Vallée d'Eau Noire (Black Water Valley). The valley was one of the last places where bears survived and was originally le Val aux Ours (*ours* meaning bears in French), Vallorcine is a corruption of the old name. There are no bears there now, but there is much scope for high level walking, such as along the path to the Bérard hut, beneath the high walls of the Aiguilless Rouges to the south-west of the village.

Aravis

Strictly speaking Aravis is part of the Faucigny district, but to aid the continuity of this guide to out of the way places, this part of Savoie south of the Arve Valley is treated as a separate entity.

Aravis takes its name from the Chaîne des Aravis, a long ridge running roughly south-west and starting high above Cluses and the Arve Valley. An area of contrasts, it starts on the eastern bank of the Rhône and finishes along the summit ridge of the Mont Blanc massif.

Moving westwards from the Chamonix area, a side valley above St Gervais-les-Bains the Bon Nant, is worth investigation. The valley road serves **Les Contamines-Montjoie**, a popular, but reasonably undeveloped ski resort. Side roads lead to tiny farm settlements, many interconnected by a series of ancient paths and trackways. The road ends at the attractively decorated chapel of Notre Dame de la Gorge. The gorge in question is a mile or so upstream and is crossed by a venerable arched Roman bridge at Nant Borrant. Hannibal's army are supposed to have come this way together with their elephants.

Both the Tour of Mont Blanc and the GR5, North Sea/Mediterranean Long Distance Footpath, follow this Roman way out of the valley. About 6km (4 miles) from the road end the Châlet de la Balme offers simple accommodation to those who can discover the rather curious system of prebooking demanded by the *guardienne*. Unlike most mountain huts where pre-booking is unnecessary, one must book in advance in Les Contamines-Montjoie, either at the Tourist Information Office, or the Bureau des Guides. The problem is that as with most French offices, they are closed for at least 2 hours at lunch time, the very time walkers are passing through the town! How ramblers travelling in the opposite direction are meant to book in is not explained, but at least they can walk on into Les Contamines for more favourable accommodation.

Beyond the valley head and standing remote on the Col de la Croix du Bonhomme, there is another mountain hut; its friendly atmosphere in marked contrast with the one at La Balme. This is a large, modern establishment built around the partial ruins of an hotel dating from the turn-of-the-century. The original guests were ferried up on the backs of mules, then as now, to enjoy a view which ranges from Mont Blanc to the Vanoise further south. A ridge, the Crête des Gîttes runs south-west from the Col de la Croix du Bonhomme and is followed by a well engineered path built by the French army in the early 1900s. It was built so that troops could command one of the alpine routes into Italy. Now it makes an easy way towards the Lac de Roselend, a reservoir created for hydro-electric use.

Moving north-westwards, back across the mountains towards the Chaîne des Aravis, the high ground is cut by the River Arly, its valley followed by the N212 Sallanches to Albertville road. **Megève** is on this road, one of the original French ski resorts, it has none of the brashness associated with more modern purpose-built ski-villages. By-passed by the main road and with traffic banned from the town centre, it retains much of its early charm. The town is old, its charter was granted in 1282, and there is still a medieval pattern to its narrow, central streets. Explore its alleys, church and *donjon* (keep). There are also two museums devoted to local life, art and traditions. The top of Mont Arbos to the east of Megève can be reached by cablecar, where there are good views of the Arly Valley and the Mont Blanc range.

To reach the west side of the Chaîne des Aravis you must drive back to Cluses and turn left along the D4 by way of Scionzier. There is a nunnery at **Le Reposoir** with an interesting history; originally a Carthusian monastery which was abandoned, it became an hotel, but in 1932 it was taken over by a very strict order of Carmelite nuns. Casual visitors are not allowed, but the impressive building can be viewed from outside.

The road from Le Reposoir climbs to the rolling limestone Plateau des Glières, an important centre of Resistance activity during World War II. A simple granite stone with a bronze sword set in the Cross of Lorraine in the Cimetière des Héros des Glières in Thônes commemorates their activities. A museum in their honour tells of the time when 465 Resistance fighters held off 12,000 German and Vichy troops for almost 2 months, keeping the plateau open for Allied parachute drops. A plaque in front of the onion-domed church lists those killed during reprisal bombing raids on 3 and 4 August 1944.

Each year a much happier festival is held in **Thônes**, over the weekend nearest 15 August. This is the Foire St Maurice to mark the descent of sheep from the high alpine pasturage. The town is also an important centre of cheese making and is the headquarters of the Société Savoyarde des Fromagers du Reblochon.

The D12 runs south from Thônes, with a left fork on to the D16 into the Manigod Valley, eventually petering out beneath the Chaîne des Aravis and the start of several forest and mountain paths at the head of this delightful valley.

Viuz-en-Sallaz on the northern outskirts of Faverges where the D12 joins the N508, Ugine to Annecy road, has some Roman remains and an ancient church. An archaeological museum traces their history.

The countryside to the west of Annecy fills an inverted triangle between the A40 and A41 Autoroutes and the River Rhône. This is an area for quiet motoring, along winding forest roads and past sleepy vineyards. The N20, the road between Annecy and Geneva makes a suitable starting point for this area. At the **Ponts de la Caille**, about 16km (10 miles) north of Annecy, the road crosses the deep cleft of the River Usses. Two bridges span the gap, the first was built in 1839 on the instructions of King Charles Albert of Sardinia (Savoie was then part of the Kingdom of Sardinia). One of the wonders of engineering of its time, the bridge is supported by 24 cables, each 183m (600ft) long, suspended between two 18m (59ft) towers. At its side, the more modern bridge which now carries road traffic, was built in 1925, and has a single span of 148m (485ft).

To the west of Annecy and near the Château de Montrottier via the N508 and D14, are the impressive Gorges du Fier. Although the site is signposted, it is necessary to walk from the road. A woodland path leads to the railway, then over a narrow footbridge. You will need a good head for heights if you want to look into the 74m (243ft) gorge where the river has created fantastic rock-scape.

Annecy has its own mountain, the Crête de Châtillon, the highest point of the Semnoz ridge. A road takes the effort out of its ascent, but there are many footpaths and a good view towards Annecy and its lake when you get there.

Beaufortin

The most northerly point of the district shares the 2,539m (8,328ft) summit of the Tête Pelouse, one of the highest points of the Chaîne des Aravis. The River Arrondine starts beneath this ridge and flows towards La Giettaz on the D909 winding mountain road from La Clusaz. Below La Giettaz, the spectacular Cascade du Dard warrants more than a passing glance before moving on to **Flumet** on the N212. This alpine town developed around a twelfth-century castle which commanded movement along the Arly Valley, but only its bell-tower remains. Beyond the town, the road follows the deep gorge cut by the Arly. About a mile down the road, take a side turning to the left over an ancient bridge, the Pont de l'Abine, leads to the spectacular village of **Notre-Dame-de-Bellecombe** which is built on a ledge 46m (151ft) above the river. Adventurous motorists should try the D218. This mountain road continues beyond Notre-Dame-de-Bellecombe, climbing over the Col des Saises and then winding its way down to Hauteluce. From here there is a choice of route down the valley, but perhaps that to the left is the more attractive. This is the D70 linking a series of mountain villages to **Beaufort**. The town is the 'capital' of Beaufortin, which once commanded ancient mountain routes around the Doron Valley. A little to the south of the town, the Arèches road

The mountain range as seen above the tiny hamlet of Les Chapieux

leads to the ruins of a medieval castle, the Château de la Grand Salle, but perhaps the ornately-carved pulpit in Beaufort's church is the jewel of this ancient settlement. Gruyère is made at the Beaufort Cheese Co-operative near the main car park, and where visitors are made welcome.

Beaufort sits astride the D217, the 'back road' between Albertville and Bourg-St-Maurice at the foot of the Little Saint-Bernard Pass. From Beaufort, the road climbs 1,200m (3,936ft) in 5km (3 miles), by a series of hairpins to Lac de Roselend, the largest high-altitude reservoir in France. A side road to the right, leads to the dam and its scenic car park. Continuing uphill, the road reaches **Boudin**, an unspoilt village of mountain farmhouses built in the traditional Savoyard style. Boudin has been declared a conservation site to prevent any modern, intrusive building. Below the village is Arèches, the site of the 1924 Winter Olympics and an excellent centre for summer walking tours.

From the Lac de Roselend, the road winds its way, steeply downhill into the Vallée des Chapieux. Once the centre of slate mining, the valley takes its name from the tiny hamlet of **Les Chapieux**, an old word meaning 'the place where tools are kept'. Walkers following the Tour of Mont Blanc find Les Chapieux very much to their liking. At one time the only accommodation to be found was in an ancient *auberge* where uneven floors and massive

The view towards France from the Col de la Seigne

beds gave the impression of being part of a French farce. It no longer acts as an *auberge* but the bar is still open. Still furnished with high-backed antique settles, and with notices years out of date, it makes a visit something out of time. Visiting the *auberge* is like stepping back into the 1940s. Today's travellers passing through Les Chapieux will probably stay at the hospitable and family-run Auberge de la Nova just around the corner.

About 8km (5 miles) further on, the valley road ends beneath the wild terrain of the Aiguille des Glaciers. Here there is another shelter for walkers and mountaineers, the Châlet des Mottets. Thwarted by the Tour of Mont Blanc path missing the refuge by a few hundred metres, the owners have gone to great lengths to attract custom. A notice attached to a group of unattended donkeys beside the path junction on the way up the valley, indicates that they will carry your rucksacks to the hut free of charge. Anyone travelling in the opposite direction, over the Col de la Seigne from Italy will, unless they are particularly determined to ignore its charms, be diverted away from the main path by a fence and several notices offering food and accommodation at the chalet.

The Savoie provides skiing of the highest quality and variety

A panoramic view above Argentière, Savoie

Aigues-Mortes, Languedoc-Roussillon

Carcassonne, Languedoc-Roussillon

La Tarentaise

Basically, La Tarentaise is the mountainous district which drains into the Isère. The N90 follows the valley from Albertville to a little way beyond Bourg-St-Maurice. Here it divides with the main road climbing the gentle, but seemingly endless hairpins of the Little St-Bernard Pass. The other section now the D902, continues along the Isère Valley, giving limited access to the eastern part of the Parc National de la Vanoise.

Cable car and landscaping projects designed to turn Val d'Isère into a perfect ski resort, do rather spoil it for the summer visitor, but some of the mechanical aids can be used to advantage by mountain walkers exploring the Vanoise. The only road to cross the National Park is a continuation of the D902 across the 2,762m (9,062ft) high Col d'Iseran.

Bourg-St-Maurice, the major market town for the Upper Tarentaise, has commanded an important cross-roads since Roman times, when it was known as *Bergintrum*. The exciting drive to the Little St-Bernard Pass follows, some say, the route Hannibal took out of Italy. The 2,188m (7,179ft) road summit is an ideal starting point for several short and fairly easy high-level walks. There is also an alpine garden created by Canon Chanoux, rector of the now abandoned Hospice between 1859 and 1909. Bourg-St-Maurice holds several summer fairs when the richly adorned Tarentaise costumes are worn. The most important fair, the Fête des Edelweiss takes place every July.

Ski resorts fill almost every nook and cranny of north-facing Tarentaise valleys. Few are particularly attractive in summer, but most do have the saving grace of being stepping stones into the Parc National de la Vanoise, offering cable car access to the surrounding peaks.

About half way downstream between Bourg-St-Maurice and Moûtiers is **Aime** where the Romanesque Basilica of St Martin stands beside the main road. Originally a Roman temple, the basilica dates from the eleventh century, confirming Aime's venerable foundations. Many of the Roman and Dark Ages objects found in and around Aime are housed in the Musée St Sigismond. Assisted by a cable car from Bellecôte at the end of the mountain road south of Aime, it is now possible to reach all-year-round glacier skiing at around 3,000m (9,840ft).

Another winter sports area useful for summer mountain wanderers is the Trois Vallées district south of Moûtiers. Each of the valley roads ends at a cul-de-sac and all can be used as a starting point for high-level tours of the Parc National de la Vanoise. From Pralognan at the end of the D915, footpaths climb to the top of the Col de la Vanoise and beyond to the Félix Faure hut, the classic way into this lonely mountain region. Alternatively, the mountain hut of Peclet-Poiset can be reached from Les Priaux a little to the south of Pralognan, and where you are likely to find marmots and chamois, or even ibex.

Bauges

Geographically part of southern Jura, the Bauges is the southern two-thirds of that heart-shaped area of rolling forested hills surrounded by A43-E70 Autoroute in the south and east; the A41-E712 in the west, and the N508 linking Albertville and Annecy by way of Ugine. It also extends to the south of Chambéry into the Massif de la Chartreuse, and west towards the Rhône.

Frequently ignored by travellers en-route either to the Alps, or the south of France, the Bauge will reward those seeking out of the way places. Wild boar (*sanglier*) still roam many of the remoter forests, and this is where its truffle hunting domestic counterpart is used to search for that expensive delicacy.

The main town of the Bauges is Le Châtelard on the D911, the continuation of the D5 which winds its way south from Annecy by way of the Pont du Diable. Side roads lead into dead-end valleys, still untouched by tourism and where it is possible to walk, or simply explore with only the locals for company.

Maurienne

This the most southerly part of Savoie and is the mountainous district on either side of the Arc Valley. The N6-E70 follows the valley, carrying heavy traffic between the industrial heartland of eastern France and northern Italy. The N6 still follows an alpine route across the 2,083m (6,832ft) Col du Mont Cenis, but the trans-European E70 is tunnelled beneath the Col de Fréjus to create an all-weather route into Italy. The Massif de la Vanoise lies to the north of the valley, the eastern end of this range designated as a national park, the Parc National de la Vanoise. To the south the skyline is dominated by a line of glaciers tumbling from a ridge marking the border between France and Italy. Summits on both sides of the valley do not diminish or become snow-free until the lower reaches of the River Arc. The river which begins its life as melt-water from the Glacier des Sources de L'Arc makes a curve, south-west then north-west, to join the Isère about half way between Albertville and Chambéry.

Purpose built ski resorts fill the high combes south of St-Jean-de-

Maurienne. The French army holds live firing exercises in the re-moter regions along the border with Dauphiné, but there are still many places worth visiting.

The D927 follows the Villards Valley south-west from Ste-Marie-de-Cuines to the Col du Glandon. Here a left turn joins the D926 to ascend the 2,068m (6,785ft) Col de la Croix de Fer where there is a fine view of the glaciers and peaks of the Grandes Rousses to the south. On a clear day the summit of the 3,983m (13,068ft) high Meige can be seen to the south-east. The car park at the col makes a good high-level start for walks of all standards, from easy strolls to more ambitious climbs. The mountains surrounding the Col de la Croix de Fer are renowned for their rich variety of alpine flowers. If you walk quietly enough you will almost certainly be rewarded by the sight of marmots, or at least hear their penetrating warning whistle.

The D926 follows the Arvan Valley, almost from its source to its confluence with the Arc at **St Jean-de-Maurienne**. A fifteenth-century cathedral confirms St Jean as the ancient capital of Maurienne.

A remote mountain road the D83, leaves Termignon near the start of the climb to the Col du Mont Cenis, and penetrates the southern boundary of the Parc National de la Vanoise. Accommodation is sparse at the end of this road, but there are one or two good camp sites and refuges which make an ideal starting point to explore the surrounding higher valleys.

The valley road continues to follow the Arc to Bonneval before climbing steeply to the 3,041m (9,977ft) Col de l'Iseran. **Bonneval** is a pretty village of stone-built houses whose mellow colours range from light grey to brown. A mountaineering centre, tracks from it and along the upper valley lead to dramatic alpine viewpoints.

With heavy traffic favouring the tunnel route, the N6 across the Col du Mont Cenis now makes a pleasant way into Italy. From the 2,083m (6,832ft) summit the road follows the east bank of a man-made lake held back by one of the largest dams in Europe. The dam wall is best appreciated from a viewpoint about 9km (6 miles) beyond the col.

Another road the D902, climbs rapidly in a series of twists and turns from St Martin-d'Arc, gaining height above the Valloirette to reach the Col du Galiber, then onwards into the Romanche Valley across the Col du Lautaret. Favoured as one of the mountain sections by organisers of the Tour de France, this alpine road conveniently leads us towards the Dauphiné, see chapter 12.

Further Information
— Savoie —

Museums and Other Places of Interest

Annecy
Château
☎ 50-51-02-33
Spans four centuries from the twelfth, includes regional museum.
Open: daily 10am-12noon and 2-6pm.
Closed on Tuesdays.

Les Gets
Musée de Musiques Méchaniques
Open: December to April and July to September every afternoon except Sunday, 3-7pm.

Thonon-les-Bains
Château de Ripaille
☎ 50 26 64 44
Open: daily from June to September 10am-12noon and 2-7pm. Closed Mondays.

Samoëns
Jardin Jaÿsinia
Open: daily 8am-12noon and 1.30-5pm, but open until 8pm in July and August.
Admission free.

Tourist Information Offices

Savoie
Comité Régional de Tourisme
Alpes-Savoie-Mont Blanc
9 Boulevard Wilson
73100 Aix-les-Bains

Chambéry
Gîtes de France
24 Boulevard de la Colonne
73000 Chambéry

Haute Savoie
Association Touristique
Départementale
56 Rue Sommellier
74012 Annecy

Annecy
Gîtes de France
52 Avenue des Iles
74037 Annecy

Isère
Maison du Tourism
14 Rue de la République
38019 Grenoble

St Lairent
Gîtes Ruraux
Maison de la Chartreuse
38380 St Laurent

Vanoise
Parc National de la Vanoise
135 Rue du Docteur Julliand
73007 Chambéry

8 • The Midi

Lower Provence, Languedoc-Roussillon and Pyrénées Orientales

The Midi is the name given to this sun-drenched part of southern France which stretches from the Rhône estuary westwards to the Spanish border, and the southern foothills of the Massif Central down to the Mediterranean. Each year it attracts millions of visitors but most head for the coast and the thirty resorts along the 200km (125 miles) of sandy beaches leaving huge areas inland almost deserted. The coastal resorts have everything the tourist could want with casinos, restaurants, cinemas, theatres and discos and a huge range of sporting activities from scuba diving to para-gliding, and tennis to caving. For the traveller who wants to get off-the-beaten-track there are many treasures to explore, some great food to be eaten and good, honest wines to wash it down with. There are canals to cruise, cycle paths to pedal, quiet lanes shaded by plane trees to drive along, and well-signposted paths to hike along. There are mountain trails to walk in the summer and good skiing to be enjoyed in the winter. You can take a canoe high into the Cévennes (see chapter 8) and paddle down through the spectacular Gorges du Tarn, or kayak at a more sedate pace along the many rivers that flow through the area, such as the Hérault, Orb, Aude or Cèze. Travel by boat along the Canal du Midi, Canal du Rhône or Canal de la Robin under the shade of centuries-old plane trees. There are the signposted walking paths, the Sentiers de Grandes Randonnées, and nature discovery paths, several hundred signposted riding trails, riding centres and equipped night stop-overs. Two large nature parks have been established, apart from the Camargue, the National Park of the Cévennes and the Regional Natural Park of the Haut-Languedoc, north of St Pons.

During the winter there is skiing in the Cévennes, the Massif du Mont Lozère, and the Pyrénées. The region has been popular for centuries. The Romans built some of their greatest cities here and

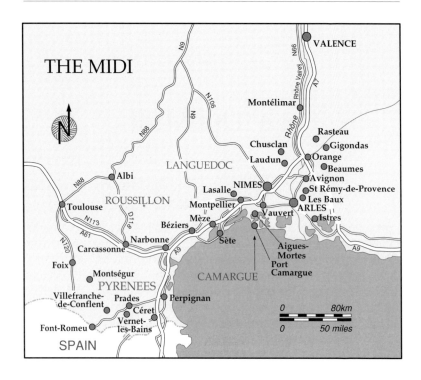

many spectacular monuments still remain. As one stands at the foot of the towering Pont-du-Gard, just west of Villeneuve-lès-Avignon, one can really appreciate the colossal engineering feats of the Roman builders. Stroll around the ancient towns of Arles, Nîmes, Avignon, Perpignan and many others and you can breathe in their past.

You can drive through the Camargue, still one of the wild places of Europe, and watch the white horses and black bulls running through the shallow waters of the salt lakes disturbing the flame red flamingoes. The Camargue is still a mecca for naturalists, especially birdwatchers, but while the horses and bulls still roam on huge ranches, vast tracts have been fenced off to create pseudo cowboy riding ranches, and some of the lakes have been drained for rice production. One advantage of progress, however, is the eradication of the mosquitoes which used to breed there in their millions. Thanks to a government blitz, the nuisance from these irritating pests has been massively reduced.

While the coastline suffers from new developments, marinas and resorts, much of the hinterland of this area has not really changed for hundreds of years. If you really get off-the-beaten-track and travel up into the Pyrénées, there are walking trails where you may not see any one else for hours, and sometimes days at a time. The villages have a sleepy atmosphere and little stirs during the hottest part of the day. The old women dressed in their black clothes sit outside their houses on rickety old wooden chairs in the cool of the evening as the men folk play *boules* on the dusty square. The intense heat in the summer means few crops can survive but olive trees and grape vines abound. This region produces more wine than any other in France and has specialised in making honest, everyday table wines. You can still buy a litre of very drinkable red for a few francs to accompany a picnic feast of french bread, *charcuterie* and olives.

In the foothills of the Pyrénées, one of the hottest and driest regions of France, cherries, oranges and lemons ripen months ahead of anywhere else. One of the interesting ways of getting away from the crowds is to spend a little time visiting some of the vineyards and sampling their wines. As the price of wines from the prestige regions of Bordeaux and Burgundy continue to rocket, regions such as Languedoc-Roussillon are improving their standards by leaps and bounds in order to compete and there are some real bargains to be hunted out. If you are near Sète pop in and visit Listel, by far the largest vineyard owner in France. The winery is surrounded by thousands of acres of vineyards, many of them planted in the sand dunes. And, after a day's exploring away from the tourists what better way to finish off than by dining out at a little restaurant sampling the culinary delights of the region.

You can spend a few days travelling along the Rhône which can offer the tourist almost everything he could wish, from excellent food and drink to spectacular scenery, from majestic castles and antiquities to cathedrals and museums. The constrast from the sleepy villages and historic buildings to futuristic developments like La Grande Motte on the coast makes the area so exciting. No matter what your interests, you will find something to your taste as you explore. The region is rich in culture, not just its history. It is perhaps the warm climate and rich atmosphere that has attracted so many writers and artists. It is the land of the poet Mistral; van Gogh immortalised many scenes around Arles in his paintings; Robert Louis Stevenson and Gauguin spent a lot of time in the area and Kathleen Mansfield lived here for a short time.

Travelling around the region is best done by car if you want to cover a lot of ground, although there are bus and train links between the major towns. Bus services in country areas can be a little hit and miss however. There are daily air services to Avignon, Mende, Perpignan, Nîmes, Montpellier or Béziers from Paris and weekly air

A typical village scene in the Midi

services between London and Montpellier and Perpignan (Dan Air). Or travel down by rail or car. The *autoroutes* are the fastest way of motoring down but most have toll sections and these can add considerably to your costs. Most of the *autoroutes* in Languedoc-Roussillon also have toll sections. If time is not too important, it is always better to stick to the secondary routes. You will not travel so fast but you will see more of the countryside. If you don't want to drive all the way down to the south of France, it is possible to put your vehicle on a train as far as Avignon, or you can pick up a hire car at any of the region's airports or main towns. Even bikes can be hired in some towns, especially those on or near the coast.

Languedoc-Roussillon stretches from the Cévennes in the north to the snow-capped Pyrénées in the south-west, from the bare plateaux in the Causses across the vine-covered plains to the Mediterranean, with its 200km (125 miles) of sandy beaches, dunes, lagoons and resorts. The Camargue, Arles and the towns around the Rhône delta really come under Lower Provence but it is convenient to deal with the whole of this region together.

There is evidence of the presence of early man dating back 300,000 years but most early settlements are now to be found west of the Rhône delta. The Greeks colonised the area around Marseilles 600 years before Christ and spread both east and west, but it was the Romans who had the greatest influence on the region, one that still remains today. The Rhône was the natural transport system into the interior, and settlements were started along its banks which grew into great towns such as Arles and Avignon. As the Romans fanned out, Nîmes became a regional centre, as did Béziers, Carcassone and Narbonne to the west. After the Romans left the area, the coastline in particular was attacked by pirates and then the Saracens, and these raids and incursions lasted for nearly 500 years. The eleventh to the thirteenth century was a period of religious fervour. It was the time of the Crusades and the seventh left the magnificent Aigues-Mortes in 1248. Splendid churches were built throughout the area, including the St Trophime in Arles, which can still be seen with its carved stone façade. The fourteenth century saw the growth of prosperity and culture in the area, as the papal court moved to Avignon; 200 years later though the area was torn as Protestants and Catholics fought the bloody Wars of Religion, followed by religious persecution. As the area settled down and a period of prosperity appeared to be on the way, the plague struck and the population was decimated.

Today, this part of the Midi has everything for the tourist from its sheer natural beauty to historic monuments, from skiing in the winter to sunbathing in the summer. If you want something more active you can play golf, tennis or horse-ride. You can go yachting, river cruising or rambling. There are mountains to scramble up, wine cellars to explore and even thermal cures to take if you have overdone it.

Its great charm, however, is the atmosphere that you cannot avoid. In the summer it is usually too hot to move too quickly so everything settles down into a gentle, relaxing almost sleepy pace. Only the towns really bustle and even these seem to sleep Spanish-style during the afternoons, when it really is too hot to work. It is the time to enjoy a quiet drink in the shade and prepare yourself for the wining, dining and maybe dancing in the evening ahead.

The Pyrénées

The impressive Pyrénées with its towering peaks soaring to more than 3,000m (9,840ft) is the natural barrier between France and Spain. From its highest peaks it falls down to the plains of Gascony in the north and the Mediterranean in the east. It is a walker's, climber's paradise in the summer and offers some excellent skiing in the winter. Despite all this, it still has not really been discovered and therefore it is the ideal place to get away from the crowds. There are climbs that demand a great deal of mountaineering skill, but there are many walks that are well within the range of most hikers. You

The pilgrimage town of Lourdes

could follow the GR10 which traverses the lower levels of the Pyrénées from the Mediterranean to the Atlantic, much of its course taking you through the Pyrenean National Park. Or, you could walk and occasionally scramble your way to the top of Canigou, one of the most impressive peaks in the range rising to just under 3,000m (9,840ft). And, if you like fishing there are scores of well-stocked mountain lakes to try.

Because the Pyrénées has not been developed as a tourist area, prices are still reasonable and basic bed and breakfast accommodation is available at very reasonable rates. Along many of the walking trails there are mountain huts where again you can stay overnight very cheaply. The facilities are basic but more than adequate. And, if you want to camp there are many sites in glorious, unspoiled countryside. Unlike most highland areas of Europe which have been developed to cash in on the skiing trade, there are few signs of this in the Pyrénées. Most of the area has not changed for thousands of years, and there are very few cable cars to take you to higher altitudes. If you want to travel about in the upper ranges of the mountains you will have to do it on foot. Although travel through the mountains is slow it is very enjoyable. There are scores of fertile valleys supporting their own communities to visit, and where you can get get basic accommodation and a hearty meal.

Because of their isolated position, the people have developed their own cultures, folk lore and customs. Many do not speak French at all and this coupled with their special style of food and architecture could lead you to believe you were not in France at all.

Apart from the rather mysterious Andorra which most people have heard of, but few know where it is, the most famous town in the Pyrénées must be Lourdes, which attracts millions of pilgrims every year. It is now world famous because of its miracle cures of the sick. Although Lourdes sprang to fame when a peasant girl saw repeated visions of the Immaculate Conception in the middle of the nineteenth century and the healing spring on the site miraculously appeared, the area has long been famed for its springs and wells with special properties. The Romans used to travel into the Pyrénées to take advantage of the sulphur springs and some are still incorporated into small spa villages where you can breathe the clean air and take a cure.

In the National Park, which runs across the high ground of the Pyrénées and extends into Spain, it is still possible to see a wide range of wildlife, but some of the most famous Pyrenean species are now sadly threatened. You can still see Egyptian vultures, and the occasional soaring eagle together with the Pyrenean chamois, or izard, but the bears have become nocturnal and been driven deep into the forests while the lynx and wolf are becoming rarer. The Pyrénées is, however, very rich in plant-life.

Man has lived in the Pyrénées for centuries and there is evidence of very early cave dwellers. Although the villages are often remote, travellers and pilgrims have been crossing the mountains for centuries on their way to the shrine of St James of Compostela. There are still wonderfully picturesque pilgrimage churches along the route. The Cathars who challenged many of the basic principles of the Roman Church were centred around Toulouse in the twelfth and thirteenth century. In 1209 the Pope, backed by the King of France, sent an army to destroy the heretics. Many of the Cathars (named after the Greek word for 'pure') fled into the Pyrénées to escape the terrible carnage of the Albigensian Crusade. Their long-since abandoned fortresses still stand in seemingly totally inaccessible spots. All the inhabitants of Béziers were slaughtered, the imposing fortress at Carcassonne capitulated after a month-long siege and there were many atrocities ordered by the Crusade's leader, Simon de Montfort. For almost 70 years the Cathars resisted, more than 400 communities were wiped out, and thousands of people killed or executed by the Inquisitors. In 1271 the final resistance was overcome and the lands of the Counts of Toulouse and Languedoc transferred to the Crown.

Because of the ferocity of fighting, few of the Cathar castles remain intact, but many can still be explored, despite their inaccessibility. Most are to be found to the east of Foix and the best examples are to be seen at Montségur, the Cathar capital for a time, Roquefixade, Usson and Puivert, formerly a troubadour court. **Foix** and its surrounding countryside is worth exploring, especially the churches with their Romanesque façades. One of the best vantage points in the whole region is from the Sommet de Portel, reached by driving along the D18 over the Col de la Crouzette and the Col de Péguère. There are a number of largely deforested valleys in the Pays de Foix, once famous for its open cast iron mines. Most of the timber was cut down to provide fuel for the furnaces. There are many caves in the surrounding hills. **Foix** is the principal town of the region, dominated by the castle with its three towers built on the hill above, and a good place from which to set out to explore this part of the Pyrénées.

To the south is the Grottes de Niaux, near the village of Tarascon-sur-Ariège, famous for its cave paintings. Although open to the public it is as well to book your visit in advance to see the magnificent animal and hunting scenes drawn about 15,000 years ago. There are other caves to visit including those at Lombrives, also near Tarascon, where a tour takes up to four hours; and Labouiche, to the north of Foix where you can take a boat trip along the underground river.

As the mountains slope down to the Mediterranean plain one could again be forgiven for thinking that you had taken the wrong turning and were in Spain. This region is even known as French Catalonia, and it has its own dialect, cuisine and customs. As the land drops from the Ceragne plain to the lowlands of Roussillon you travel through one of the most fertile, yet hottest and driest parts of France. At higher levels there are the vineyards hugging the terraces, but as you descend there are acres of fruit orchards. The high mountains here are rugged and forested but provide excellent walking, and are perhaps the most popular tourist spot in the French Pyrénées. Having said that, however, it is still possible to spend hours walking here without seeing anyone else. The resort of Font-Romeu has developed to cater for this tourist trade, walking in the summer and skiing in the winter and it boasts more than 3,000 hours of sunshine a year.

The roads here are good but tortuously bendy and as you drive down to **Villefranche-de-Conflent** from Mont Louis you can appreciate just how steeply the mountain falls away. If driving the mountain roads does not appeal, take the narrow gauge railway from Latour-de-Carol. Villefranche is a medieval fortified town which still guards the entrance to the Têt valley. There is an underground staircase with 750 steps leading through the cliff to the massive fortress which perches 155m (500ft) above the town on the mountain side. To the south is the charming spa town of **Vernet-les-Bains** and the nearby tenth-century Abbaye de St Martin-du-Canigou with its Spanish square. After centuries of dilapidation, the abbey and its cloisters with its magnificent carvings, have been restored and is now used as a retreat. It is possible to take a tour to the abbey but if you are driving go as far as Casteil and then walk up. It is a reasonably stiff walk but the views are your reward, especially if you walk on past and above the abbey. Villefranche was famous for its marble and it was widely used in the construction of the many Romanesque churches in the area under the auspices of the Abbaye de St Michel-de-Cuxa, near Prades, which is worthy of a visit.

As you descend further into the orange and lemon groves and cherry orchards you can see why this area, known as Vallespir, was so popular with artists. Picasso used to frequent the attractive town of **Céret** and there is a modern art museum there as well as a restored fourteenth-century bridge spanning the valley. Between Céret and the coast is the ninth-century abbey church at **Arles-sur-Tech** which was added to for the next four centuries. It contains a fourth-century sarcophagus, revered locally because it is always full of pure water. Near Arles is the Gorges de la Fou which affords some great walks.

Finally you must visit **Perpignan**, capital of Roussillon and the fortress home of the Kings of Majorca who reigned here from 1294 to 1344. Although in Roussillon it is more sensible to visit it as part of a tour of the Pyrénées, because it is still part of French Catalonia. The locals speak Catalan and in the bars they still dance the Spanish *sardana*, Catalonia's national dance. Buildings of interest to see are the palace and fortress of the Kings of Majorca, the town fortifications, the Gothic cathedral, and the Loge de Mer which dates back to the time when Perpignan was a flourishing sea port.

There are literally hundreds of miles of walking in the Pyrénées, especially the eastern area around Céret and Latour-de-France. The valleys of the Têt and Tech are especially beautiful, particularly in the spring when the first of the wild flowers blossom and the fruit trees burst into blossom. Long-distance paths include the GR36 which runs through the Pyrénées Orientales and the GR10, the Sentier des Pyrénées. You can plan walks lasting from a couple of hours to several days depending on how energetic you want to be. Take advantage of the narrow gauge railway from Perpignan to get to Cerdagne, a good place to start a number of walks. You can even

A courtyard in the fortifications at Salses, north of Perpignan

walk across into Spain from here. There are also a lot of good routes
for the serious backpacker who wants to get up into the mountains.

Because the frontier is vague in places and you can not always be
sure you are still in France, it is a good idea to carry your passport
with you.

Nîmes and the Surrounding Area

The whole of Nîmes and the surrounding countryside is worth
exploring either on foot, by bike or car. A detour to **St Rémy-de-
Provence**, birthplace of astrologer Nostradamus is essential. His life
is chronicled at the Museé Alpilles Pierre de Brun. The museum, in
a sixteenth-century château, also has a collection of local art, and
souvenirs of Mistral. His home was at **Maillane**, 4 miles away, where
there is another museum to his memory. Also in St Rémy is an
archaeological museum housed in the Hôtel de Sade, once owned by
the family of the notorious Marquis. If you have time, visit the
Roman excavations at *Glanum* about a mile to the south. There is an
archway from the second century BC, the oldest surviving in southern France, and an early mausoleum. Digs at *Glanum* have revealed
the presence of man as far back as Neolithic times.

Les Baux, some way to the west, attracts visitors in their hundreds
of thousands, and the cliff-top fortress carved out of stone, and its
unspoilt village (apart from the racks of postcards everywhere), are

still very appealing. There are many buildings from the fourteenth century, and the castle dates from the thirteenth. This area is so rich in history that one could spend days exploring. Most of the tourists driving in make straight for the car parks just below the village, but you can park off the road much farther down the hill and walk both to and around the village. By starting your journey on foot lower down the hill, you can get a much better understanding of why the castle was so impregnable. When you climb up the battlements of the fortress itself, it is necessary to exercise care if strong winds are blowing. The authorities have now provided handrails in some areas, but the winds can still prove a hazard. As you drive your way through the hills to Les Baux look out for the massive gun emplacements that were carved out into the slopes by the Germans.

Nîmes is again rich in antiquity, and as in Arles, it is possible to buy a season ticket giving access to all the main sights saving you a lot of money. These attractions include the magnificent amphitheatre, not as large as the one in Arles, but in much better order. It is used for French-style bullfights and throughout the summer mock gladiator fights and chariot races are also staged for the tourists. In the Blvd Hugo is the Maison Carrée, a temple built just before the birth of Christ, in Greek style. It is the finest remaining Roman temple of its type, and has a museum within the sanctum containing antiquities. Also make time to see the ornamental French gardens dating from the eighteenth century in the Quai de la Fontaine. It also contains remains of a Roman bathhouse and the ruined Temple of Diana. Next to the gardens is the Tour Magne, an octagonal watchtower built in the first century BC: it is worth climbing up to the platform at the top with your camera for the views.

In the Rue de la Lampèze there is a Roman collecting basin for water bought in from the Pont-du-Gard. From here it was distributed by ten canals to various parts of the city. The only other structure like it has been found at *Pompeii*. Also see the Porte d'Arles, a Roman gateway in the town walls dating from 16BC. Nîmes has some excellent museums; for instance the Museum of Old Nîmes, with its history of the town, as well as a history of bullfighting, the museum of archaeology, and the museum of fine arts.

Montpellier to Carcassonne

From Nîmes you can journey south-west to Montpellier, which is a thriving town and university centre, but on the way a stop off at **Aigues-Mortes** is essential. It is a perfectly preserved walled town. It is best to park outside between the canal and the Saracen's Tower and to enter the town through the massive archway. Note how thick the walls are. The town is now a tourist trap full of souvenir shops and cafés, but one can still imagine what it was like 800 years ago when the armies started to assemble before setting sail on the Crusades. There are magnificent views from the ramparts and you can walk right round the town along the walls. While travelling from Nîmes, spend some time in the Camargue. It is possible to cut down and use the coastal road which runs between the Etangs but be warned, the surface is extremely bad.

It is still possible to drive down to the sea in the Camargue, and if you are interested in birdwatching, you will be amazed at the variety of wildlife. You can see perching ospreys that seem to have no fear of humans at all. There are bee eaters, rollers, hoopoes, storks, almost all the herons, waders, ducks and a confusing collection of warblers that will have you scrambling for your bird guides. Although parts of the Camargue now constitute a national nature reserve and access is limited, it is still possible to see almost all the species from good vantage points along the road.

Montpellier is an old university town and capital of the Bas (Low) Languedoc region. It is still possible to walk round the roads that ring the old town, and these have been built on the site of the original fortified walls. One must walk down the Promenade du Peyrou, with its seventeenth- and eighteenth-century mansions. The terraced walk also offers views of the Mediterranean. The botanical gardens, founded by Henry IV in 1593, are the oldest in France. Another essential visit is to the fourteenth-century Gothic cathedral, and the fabulous Fabre museum which houses one of the best collection of paintings in France. The university dates back to the eleventh century, when a school of medicine was founded. The law school dates from 1160, and the university proper was given its charter by Pope Nicholas 1 in 1289. Montpellier is also a good base from which to visit the many vineyards in the area, including Listel, which is just a short distance off the Montpellier to Béziers road.

Béziers is an agricultural and wine town, set in the heart of the vineyards. It produces table wines, especially Muscat, the grape said to have been introduced by the Romans. The town stands on a hill overlooking the River Orb. It was a former Roman town and there are still the remains of the amphitheatre. It was fortified in the twelfth century by the Lords of Carcassonne, but this did not prevent a bloody massacre in 1209, when a force sent by the Pope killed all the inhabitants to stamp out heresy. The Roman-Gothic church of Ste La Madeleine was the scene of some of the bloodiest fighting. In the thirteenth century, the city walls were rebuilt, and at the same time the cathedral church of St Nazaire was constructed on the hill over the town. It is a fortified church and well worth visiting.

Narbonne was founded by the Romans in 118BC, although it then stood on the Mediterranean and became a flourishing port. When the Romans left in the fifth century, it was captured by the Visigoths who made it their capital. Their rule lasted for 300 years, until 719, when the Saracens invaded and took control. Then, the town was controlled by the Counts of Toulouse who ruled one half, and the bishops who ruled the other. It was not until the beginning of the sixteenth century that it was united under the French crown. The thirteenth-century cathedral of St Just was never completed, but the 'choir' and two square towers can still be seen. Additionally, the twelfth-century basilica of St Paul-Serge, and the three square towers of the fortified Palais des Archévêques are worth looking at. The Gothic-style town hall was added to the palace in the nineteenth century. The palace now houses two fine museums, one of art and history, and the other archaeological. It is also worth exploring the narrow, winding streets and alleys of the old town, with its many fine old buildings. Narbonne is another wine town and there many opportunities to taste them both inside and around the town. There is also a wine centre.

Carcassonne, due west of Narbonne, is the capital of the Aude *département*. The River Aude divides the town into three, the town, the lower town and the city (Ville, Ville-Bas and Cité). The Cité contains the finest remains of medieval fortifications in Europe, so is a must for any visitor to this region. The hill that comprises the Cité was certainly occupied in the fifth century BC by the Iberians, then by the Gallo-Romans. The inner ramparts were built in the late fifth century by Euric 1, King of the Visigoths. The fortifications resisted all attempts to breech them for almost 300 years until the Saracens stormed them successfully. Other things to be seen are the Basilique St Nazaire, from the eleventh century; the Château Comtal, incorporated into the fortifications in the twelfth century and now a museum; and the Porte Narbonnaise, surrounded by its twin towers, guarding the entrance to the Cité. When peace was restored to the region in the mid-seventeenth century, the fortifications were no longer needed and fell into disrepair. Work restoring them started in 1844 and continued for 120 years. Today, the city is a living museum to the past. In the Ville-Bas, see the church of St Vincent and the cathedral of St Michel, both from the thirteenth century. Carcassonne is quite magnificent, and it has the additional pleasure of being

Narbonne, where boating is popular

primarily a wine town, so it is possible to sit in one of the shaded street cafés, sip a glass of the local wine, and drink in the history at the same time.

The Camargue

Although the Camargue gets a brief mention in other sections it is so important that it deserves its own passage. Apart from fabulous birdwatching, it offers great walking or cycling, horse riding and even cruising. What better way of unwinding than by gently cruising the waterways of this vast wilderness area, one of the richest wildlife habitats in Europe. It is possible to arrange hire of your boat through British travel agents. The advantage of this sort of holiday is that it really allows you to get off-the-beaten-track. The boats come equipped with bikes, so if you want to explore you simply moor and pedal off. However if you choose to explore the waterways, canals and tributaries of this 800sq km (300sq mile) delta, you will not be disappointed.

The Camargue is the area of the estuary of the Rhône which divides in two just above Arles to form a triangular arm ending at the Mediterranean. The fringes of the Camargue are bordered by rich farmland where corn, vines and now rice grows. As you move into the Camargue, and especially as you move towards the sea the landscape changes dramatically. The reedbeds camouflage what is land and water, and the lakes give no hints as to whether they are fresh or salt water. It is a natural fusion of land, river and sea.

The Camargue is known worldwide for its 'wild' black bulls and white horses but as more land is drained to make way for tourist developments or farms, the area available for these proud animals diminishes. They can still be seen roaming through the salt flats but barbed wire fences mark out their territories. It is the birds alone that now have the freedom to roam unfettered. Horses and bulls, however, have been bred for sport in the Camargue since Roman times although during the Middle Ages most of the land was owned by the monasteries. Most of the farms, or mas, still operating were established between the sixteenth and eighteenth centuries. They grew corn and reared sheep, bulls and horses. Only over the last 130 years have effective dykes been built to stop the devastating floods which occurred regularly.

Today, the wildlife of the Camargue has to compete with the farmers. It is Europe's largest rice producing region, there are large scale salt pans but it still leaves something over 34,400ha (86,000 acres) for the birds and animals. The area enjoys hot, dry summers, and warm, wet winters although it is possible for stagnant water to freeze during particularly cold spells. It is possible to walk or drive down to the sea and enjoy the sand dunes which cover a wide area. There is also an expanse of dune in the heart of the Camargue in the national nature reserve. This area of dunes supports Phoenician junipers growing to a height of 6m (20ft), while in the spring the ground is carpeted with wild narcissi, rock roses, rosemary and gladioli.

The waters are very rich in fish and most private owners lease out the rights to commercial fishermen who use nets and traps. Eels are caught in large numbers, as well as carp. There are opportunities for private anglers to fish from the dykes, if they get permission first. Hunting is more popular than fishing and there is a great wealth of game, from wild boar, hare, rabbit, wild duck, pheasant and partridge. Some species, however, like the flamingoes, egrets and avocets are protected. The bulls of the Camargue are bred for fighting, but usually take part in the French *course à la cocarde*, when young men try to snatch rosettes from the animal's horns. Spanish bullfights, or *corridas*, are held in the Camargue, but the animals as well as the bullfighters normally travel from Spain. Other animals of the Camargue include the wild boar, fox, badger and otter.

St Trophime, Arles, a pilgrimage church built on the route to St James of Compostela, Spain

If you want to see the flamingoes, the best route is to travel along the *étangs* (lakes) along the coast between Les Stes Maries and Salin-de-Giraud. Here, hopefully, you will not only see flamingoes in their tens of thousands but as many as 330 other different species of birds from Europe and North Africa. Some of the rarer species as far as British and US birdwatchers are concerned, include roller, black-

winged stilt, bee-eater hoopoe, purple heron, spectacled and mous-
tached warbler, pratincole, little egret, night and squacco heron, and
stone curlew. One of the best spots for birdwatching is along the
Digue de la Mer. Although a much less welcoming place in the
winter, a trip into the Camargue can be just as rewarding then, with
up to a quarter of a million wild duck in temporary residence. The
area is equally rich in insects, amphibians, reptiles and wild plants.
Whatever time you visit the Camargue a good bird book and powerful pair of binoculars or telescope is a must. And, if you are there
in the summer have a good insect repellent as well.

The hot Mistral wind is, of course, famous in this area. It can last
a few hours or a few days. When the mistral blows, people are said
to do strange things, tempers flare and it was once a defence against
a murder charge to blame it on the winds.

Port Camargue is on the western coastal tip of the Camargue, it
is a new resort built round a massive marina. Although there is still
considerable building going on, the village has been subject to strict
planning controls, and unlike developments further along the coast,
has not blighted the area. The other town to visit is **Stes Maries-de-
la-Mer**. According to local legend the sisters of the Virgin Mary
landed here to avoid persecution after the Crucifixion. While pilgrims have come to pray at the tomb of the two Marys since the
Middle Ages, gypsies revere Sarah, their Egyptian maid, and every
year in May (24 and 25)they assemble from all corners of Europe for
their festival. In olden days, when the gypsies travelled by horse and
wagon, they would back their vehicles into the sea in an act of ritual
purification.

The fortified church is the other main attraction and for a small
charge you can climb the steps up to the ramparts for magnificent
views over the Camargue and town. In the crypt is the statue of Sarah
which is paraded annually at the head of the gypsies' procession.
Although the town with its fine beach and bustling marina does get
very busy during the summer, it is worth a visit, because isolated as
it is by the Camargue and the Rhône delta, it does not seem to have
fully caught up yet with the twentieth century. If the idea of a guided
boat trip attracts you, you can take one from Stes Maries, and if you
want to cruise yourself from the Camargue, the boats normally start
at St Gilles, the other gateway to the Camargue. You can even follow
the Canal du Rhône west to Aigues-Mortes and moor in the shadow
of the city walls.

One of the many historical sites in Arles

Arles and Area

If you have driven down from the north via Lyon, **Arles** makes a good base. There are many good hotels to suit all tastes and pockets as well as very well equipped camp sites. You could spend several days just exploring Arles itself, especially the quaint narrow cobbled back streets with their curious shops and bars frequented by the locals. You can hire bicycles to get further afield but walking, apart from in and around the town, is not a good idea because of the distances that need covering. There is a good local bus service but it is not too frequent, so you can't afford to miss the last bus back.

Arles was the first major Roman settlement in Gaul and almost everywhere you look there is something of its rich history to be seen. At one stage it was even called 'The Granary of Rome', and later the 'Little Rome of the Gauls'. If you have driven in by car, park it because the only way to explore this town is on foot. There is a Roman obelisk in the Place de la République made from Egyptian stone. It used to stand in the suburb of Trinquetaille in the centre of a chariot-racing arena. The square also houses the famous twelfth-century church of St Trophime with its elaborately carved Romanesque west porch. Researchers have found symbols used in Syrian, Persian, Nordic and ancient Roman art. It is worth stepping inside the church because the narrowness of the nave makes the vaulted ceiling look much higher. There are many fine paintings, carvings, tapestries and sarcophagi. The church is famed both for its antiquity and its carvings, in stone, wood and ivory. It was one of a string of pilgrimage churches built along the route to the shrine of St James of Compostela in Spain. Close by is the Tourist Information Office in what used to be the Archbishop's Palace, and the Hôtel de Ville.

Just an alley away is the Place du Forum with its statue of Frédéric Mistral, perhaps the most famous son of the Camargue. He was not only the region's most outstanding poet, he gave his name to the fierce wind that sweeps the area, and founded a splendid museum, the Museon Arlaten, dedicated to all things Provençale. You can also see, incorporated into the Hôtel Nord-Pinus, two Corinthian columns which, almost 2,000 years ago, formed part of a temple next to the Roman forum.

There are many other historic monuments to visit in Arles, the most important of which is the amphitheatre. All the Roman sites and museums are open to the public and if you are a culture buff, it is worth buying a season ticket which allows you to visit them all at reduced prices. The amphitheatre is still remarkably well preserved, and is supposed to be the twelfth largest of the seventy known from the Roman world. It was built in the first century on the site of an original wooden arena. It could hold up to 15,000 spectators and it is still possible to walk down into the dark depths of the buildings where the cages housed the animals and slaves ready for combat in the arena. During the Middle Ages it was used as a fortress, and two towers remain. It is used now regularly for bullfights, both the Spanish sort and the French. In the Spanish bullfight the animal is killed, while in the French version, young men try to capture rosettes draped over the bull's horns. The latter version is far more exhilarating and enjoyable.

In the Rue du Cloître is the Roman theatre, built in the reign of Augustus. It has many well preserved statues. It could seat 7,500 and it is still an excellent auditorium with wonderful acoustics.

Other things to see are Les Alyscamps, a path lined with sarcophagi with a ruined Romanesque church; the St Trophime cloisters dating from the twelfth century, around an enchanting garden; and the Roman baths of Trouille, said to date from the fourth century and part of Constantine's great palace. The water was carried 15 miles to the baths by aqueduct. There are also many museums, such as the museum of Christian art, in Rue Balze, with the finest collection of sarcophagi outside Rome; the museum of pagan art and the museum of fine arts in the Rue du Grand Prieuré, which includes a collection of old drawings by Picasso. Vincent van Gogh lived in a house in the

Place du Forum for about 16 months between 1888 and 1889 and this was the subject of his painting *Café Terrace at Night*. The house is now a shop. He also shared 'the Yellow House' in Place Lamartine with Gauguin for short time but this was destroyed during bombing in 1944. Other scenes he painted which can still be visited are the cemetery of the Alyscamps and the drawbridge over the Marseilles au Rhône canal just south of the town. The bridge was actually demolished in 1926 but was such a popular tourist attraction that it had to be rebuilt. After a day spent tramping the streets, stroll up the Boulevard des Lices in the early evening and enjoy a drink at one of the scores of bars and cafés, and decide which restaurant you will return to later that night.

About 16km (10 miles) west of Arles is **St Gilles**, definitely worth a visit, and it makes a pleasant cycle trip. It was another pilgrimage stop on the road to Compostela and has a fine abbey church with carvings dating from the twelfth century depicting the life of Christ. In the crypt is the tomb of St Gilles, which dates from the eleventh century. There is a museum to be visited and a spiral staircase with fifty steps to be climbed to the belfry.

Tour of the Rhône Delta

Greek travellers settled at the mouth of this great river in about 600BC. They founded a settlement called *Massalia*, which has continued to flourish and is today one of France's major ports and trading centres, although it is now known as Marseilles. The Greeks established vineyards and these gradually developed inland following the banks of the Rhône. Some of France's greatest red wines are still grown along the Rhône and Hermitage and Côte-Rôtie have been grown for at least 2,000 years. Throughout this time the river has been used as the natural means of transport. As the Greeks influence waned and they were forced to abandon their settlements after attacks from the Gauls, the Romans took over. They named the region *Provincia*, the origin of Provence. They built most of the great towns of the region and most of the bridges and fortifications along the river.

If travelling down from Lyons one should stop off to visit **Vienne**, about 32km (20 miles) south of this great city. There is the Cathédrale St Maurice, the Champ de Mars, the Temple d'Auguste, Roman theatre and many fine churches, buildings and museums, as well as statues everywhere. Across the river is the village of **Ampuis**, famous as the home of one of the world's great wines, Côte-Rôtie. As you travel south you can take in the village of **Condrieu** nestling at the foot of the hills at a bend in the river and thus its name, an abbreviation of Coin du Ruisseau, literally 'corner of the river'. Try the marvellous white wine produced here since Roman times.

Other places to see include Château Grillet, the smallest *Appellation Contrôlée* in France. The 3ha ($7^1/_2$ acres) of vineyards are near the village of **St Michel-sur-Rhône**. The château dates back to the reign of Louis XIII when it was a hunting lodge. Since then much has been added. The façade is Renaissance, and some of the walls are 1m (3ft) thick, showing that defence was an important consideration in this trouble-torn region.

The tour proper of the Rhône estuary should start in the spectacular town of **Orange** with its Roman theatre and impressive Arc de Triomphe. It has hotels to suit all pockets and many good restaurants. About 19km (12 miles) north-west on the N575 is **Rasteau** which produces one of France's most unusual and least known wines. It is made in the same way as port and is very popular in all the bars of the region. While in the village have a look at the communal wash-house where the women gather all day it seems, to scrub their family's laundry. To the south is **Beaumes**, another Roman town which became established as a spa resort because of the sulphur springs at Montmirail. There have been many archaeological digs in the area, uncovering Roman swimming pools and plumbing, and above the village a sculpture was discovered depicting winemaking and the treading of the grapes. The village is the now the centre for the production of the fortified, sweet wine, Beaumes-de-Venise, which is becoming increasingly popular with drinkers both in Britain and the United States.

Just to the west of the village is its neighbour **Vacqueyras**, and between the two is the church of Notre-Dame d'Aubune, built on the site where, in the eighth century, the Saracens were defeated by the Gauls. The surrounding hills are filled with caves, and the Saracens are said to have taken refuge in these for months after the battle. Beaumes actually gets its name from an Old Provence word meaning grotto, and every year on 8 September there is a pilgrimage to the church to celebrate the victory. Between Rasteau and Beaumes, close to Mont Ventoux, is **Gigondas**, on the east bank of the river, and like everywhere else along the Rhône a wine centre. The village makes a fine red wine and you can try it in the tasting centre. Most of the houses of the vineyard owners are built on the sites of Roman villas. The area is steeped in Roman history and it is thought that Roman officers chose Gigondas to retire to after seeing service in Orange.

If you return to Orange and cross the river you can travel to

Chusclan and Laudun, both wine making villages. **Chusclan** has a tradition dating back to Roman times although Benedictine monks established many of the vineyards that now surround the village. Their best rosé, the Cuvée de Marcoule is named after the nearby atomic power station. **Laudun** is a beautiful old village although it is blossoming with new housing to accommodate the workers who commute to Orange. Earthen wine jars dating back to the third century BC have been found on the flat hilltop above it, known as the Plateau du Camp de César.

The next port of call is **Châteauneuf-du-Pape**, famous for its wines and its place in religious history. This part of Provence came into its own in 1305 when Bertrand de Got was elected by the College of Cardinals as the new pope — Pope Clément V. His first decision, to end the feuding in Rome, was to move the seat of the papacy to his native France. Avignon became the new seat of power for the Roman Church, and for the next few decades there was feverish activity both in and around the city. New buildings, churches and palaces were built, bridges were constructed and country estates with fine houses surrounded by vineyards sprang up. Because summer in Avignon was, and still can be hot and oppressive, the Pope decided to build a summer palace. He chose a spot about 16km (10 miles) upstream from Avignon on a plateau overlooking the river, and as it was the Pope's new palace it was known as Châteauneuf-du-Pape. The palace was built on the site of a castle destroyed in 1248. It took 15 years to build and was completed in 1333, a year before Pope John's death. Today, little remains of the palace, apart from a tower and some walls, but the village itself is fascinating and a delight to stroll around. It is not known whether it was Pope Clement or his successor John XXII who developed the vineyards, although grapes had certainly been growing there for centuries. While the reign of the Popes in Avignon only lasted for sixty or so years, the vineyards continue to survive and prosper.

In the area it is worth a detour to **Roquemaure**, named after a fort built by the Saracens which has long since vanished. History records that it was here that Hannibal floated his elephants across the Rhône on rafts. The other village to seek out is **Villeneuve-lès-Avignon** which dates back to at least the thirteenth century. Many of the nobles attending the papal court in Avignon chose to build their summer houses here. There are many fine old buildings as well as the imposing fort, the Fort St André, and several excellent eating establishments. Finally, you must spend as much time as possible in and around Avignon itself. As with Arles, it is best to park your car and walk round the town exploring the enormous treasures it has to offer. Its wealth is overwhelming, from the splendour of the Popes' Palace, the impressive city defences, the famous bridge, and the many old buildings. For a small payment you can still walk out on to what is left of the bridge which juts out into the river.

Among the things to be seen are: the Palais des Papes, Pont St Bénézet, the ramparts and fortifications, the palace gardens, the cathedral with its cupola, church of St Pierre, the frescoes in the church of St Didier and the museums of the Petit Palais, Calvet, Lapidaire and Louis Vouland. While travelling through the area, do take the opportunity of tasting the local wines. There are tasting centres in most big villages, and vineyards which have their own tasting facilities advertise this prominently along the roadside.

The Gastronomy of the Midi

The land between the Rhône and the Spanish border plays host to a wide variety of cuisines, many of them reliant on garlic and olive oil which is available in plenty throughout. The sea provides the ingredients for many traditional dishes, while there is lamb from Roussillon, beef from around Albi and Carcassonne, and the magnificent *cassoulet* originated in Toulouse but can now be found, with many variations, throughout Languedoc-Roussillon. *Cassoulet* is perhaps the region's most famous dish, traditionally made from mutton, pork, preserved goose, and any other meats that come to hand, together with haricot beans. Vegetables are plentiful, especially tomatoes and aubergines which figure in many recipes. Because of the poor pasture, much of the meat can be tough unless cooked slowly, but the people realised this long ago and have developed special cooking skills in making casseroles and stews. In the south-west small birds, especially thrushes are roasted and eaten head and all. In the south-west *foie gras*, duck, goose and truffles figure on the menus, and snails everywhere.

There is excellent *charcuterie*, and the Toulouse sausage is especially famous. Offal, including tripe is favoured in the northern districts, while soups of all types can be found. Collioure is noted for its anchovies and sardines. Sète has its famous offshore oyster beds, and Palava has created its own speciality tuna dishes. Rice from the Rhône figures in dishes influenced by Spanish cuisine, while along the coast there are fish soups and stews, and a wide variety of fresh and salted fish.

Desserts include *cruchades*, fritters or pancakes made from maize flour, and *pescajou*, a sweet pancake from Languedoc. *Petit pâtés* are small sweet pastries, and *marrons glacés* are candied chestnuts. It is also worth looking for *pinu*, a small aniseed cake from Languedoc and *touron*, an almond pastry with other nuts, marzipan and chrystallised fruits.

Some of the cheeses of the region include Bleu de Loudes, a blue cheese from the Languedoc, made in the Velay region; it has little smell but quite a strong flavour; Les Orrys, a cow's milk cheese from the hills around Foix, on the River Ariège, to the north of Roussillon, which is strong and tangy. Then there is Passé l'An, really from Quercy, a hard, strong cheese aged usually for at least 2 years, and Pélardon des Cévennes, a Languedoc soft cheese made from goat's milk, which has a nutty flavour. Finally, there is Picodon, goat's milk cheese made in Provence.

Further Information
— The Midi —

Museums and Other Places of Interest

Aigues-Mortes
Saracen's Tower
Open: April-September 9am-12noon and 2-6pm; October-March 10am-12noon and 2-4pm.
Alleés des Sarcophages
Open: 9am-12noon and 2-5.30pm (7pm in summer).

Arles
Amphitheatre
Rond Point des Arènes
Open: 9am-12noon and 2-5.30pm (7pm in summer).

Church of St Trophime
Place de la République
Open: daily.

Museum of Christian Art
Rue Balze
Open: 9am-12noon and 2-5.30pm (7pm in summer).

Museum of Pagan Art
Rue de la République
Open: 9am-12noon and 2-5.30pm (7pm in summer).

Museum of Fine Arts
Rue du Grand Prieuré

Open: 9am-12noon and 2-5.30pm (7pm in summer).

Roman Baths of Trouille
Rue D. Maïsto
Open: 9am-12noon and 2-5.30pm (7pm in summer).

Roman Theatre
Rue du Cloître
Open: 9am-12noon and 2-5.30pm (7pm in summer).

Avignon
Palais des Papes
Open: July-September 9am-6pm; October-Easter 9am-11am and 2-4pm; Easter-June 9am-11.30am and 2-5.30pm.

Museum of Medieval Painting and Sculpture
La Place du Palais
Open: April-September 9.30am-11.45am and 2-6.15pm; October-February 9.15-11.45am and 2-6pm.

Bridge of St Bénézet
Open: 9am-12noon and 2-6pm.

Rhône Lapidary Museum
Open: 10am-12noon and 2-6pm, closed Tuesday.

Calvert Museum
Open: 10am-12noon and 2-6pm, closed Tuesday.

Les Baux
Museum of Contemporary Art
Open: 9.30am-12noon and 2-6.30pm, closed Thursdays.

Béziers
Wine Museum
Open: daily 9am-12noon and 2-5pm.

Bollène
Church of St Martin
Open: July-September 9am-12noon and 3-7pm.

Museum
Open: April-September 9am-12noon and 2-7pm.

Carcassonne Cité
Château Comtal and Museum
Open: daily 9am-5pm April-September.

Châteauneuf-du-Pape
Père Anselme Wine Museum
Open: Monday-Saturday 8am-12noon and 1.30-6pm.

Glanum
Prehistoric and Roman Excavations
Open: 9am-12noon and 2-6pm.

Narbonne
Cathedral of St Just
Open: daily except Wednesday.

Fine Arts Museum and History Museum
Open: May-September 9am-12noon and 2-5pm.

Nîmes
Amphitheatre
Blvd Victor Hugo
Open: 9am-12noon and 2-5pm (2-7pm in summer).

Maison Carrée
Blvd Victor Hugo
Open: 9am-12noon and 2-5pm (2-7pm in summer).

French Garden
Quai de la Fontaine
Open: daily to 11.30pm in summer.

Tour Magne
Mont Cavalier
Open: 9am-12noon and 2-5pm (2-7pm in summer).

Museum of Archaeology
Blvd Amiral Courbet
Open: 9am-12noon and 2-6pm.

Museum of Fine Arts
Rue de la Cité-Foulc
Open: 9am-12noon and 2-6pm.

Museum of Old Nîmes
Place aux Herbes
Open: 9am-12noon and 2-6pm.

Orange
Ancient Roman Theatre
Open: April-September 9am-6.30pm; October-March 9am-12noon and 2-5pm.

Museum
Open: 9am-12noon and 2-6.30pm.

St Rémy-de-Provence
Musée Alpilles Pierre de Brun
Open: 10am-12noon and 2-6pm, April-October; 10am-12noon and 2-7pm July/August. Closed Tuesday.

Serrières
Museum of Batellerie
Open: weekdays.

Sérignan
Museum of National Entomology
Open: weekdays.

Valence
Museum
Open: daily 9am-12noon and 2-6pm.

Valréas
Old Château, Church and Chapel
Open: June-August 10am-12noon and 3-7pm.

Town Hall
Guided tours 10am-12noon and 3-7pm.

9 • Rouergue-Albigeois

This is a region of wild and often spectacular landscape, of granitic and limestone uplands and plateaux through which torrential rivers have carved canyons and dramatic gorges. It is a region of small and scattered towns whose very stones are soaked with ancient blood. Historically, its people have always taken a minority view in religion. In the thirteenth century they were Cathars, Christians who did not accept the doctrines of the formal Catholic church, and did not believe in the divinity of Christ. Pope Innocent III accused them of heresy and launched the Albigensian Crusade against them. It was led by Simon de Montfort and was joined by many nobles from the north of France, a few of them strongly religious but others who saw the chance of being rewarded with the lands and castles of those lords who had supported the Cathars. In the name of religious prejudice whole populations, men, women and children were put to the sword and wiped out. 'God will know his own', said the leaders of the Crusade. On one occasion Simon de Montfort captured a small town, and took one hundred of its people, cut off their lips and noses, and put out their eyes, and sent them to the next town led by a one-eyed man, to terrify its defenders.

The Cathars were defeated, but an Inquisition accompanied by torture and burning at the stake went on for many years.

Again, in the sixteenth and seventeenth centuries there were cruel and bloody wars. This time between the Catholics and the Protestants. In this region and throughout the south-west the people again took the minority view and many of them became Protestants. Every town was attacked and counter attacked, massacres were common.

In the end the different factions came to live in peace together, and nothing much was achieved. Even today there are still Cathars in the region of Albi and Carcassonne, and there is a strong Protestant minority throughout France.

Physically, the region is as varied and violent as its history. Its towns and villages are unusual, its landscape requires adjectives like harsh, majestic, weird, chaotic, as well as beautiful.

190

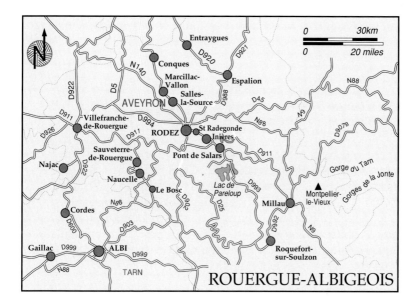

ROUERGUE-ALBIGEOIS

The near barren moorlands known as *causses* are strewn with eroded rock formations which from a distance look like ruined villages. Among the dramatically picturesque gorges are those of the Lot, the Aveyron, the Truyere, the Dourbie, and the Tarn. The countryside lends itself to many forms of open-air leisure, walking, cycling, riding and pony-trekking, and first-class fishing among them.

Albi, sometimes called 'Albi la Rouge' because much of it is built in dark, rose-red brick rather than the stone so common in France, is a city whose impact and interest far exceed its modest size. The symbol of this unique city, the soaring and lovely Cathedrale St Cecile, dominates it from all sides. The cathedral is characterised by a rare combination of fortress-like strength, graceful beauty, and a remarkable elaboration and richness of detail which verges on the ornate without ever camouflaging the masterly lines of the building itself.

The splendour of the cathedral was initially due to the importance which the Catholic church gave to reasserting its strength in a region which had for nearly one hundred years been swept by the winds of heresy. When Bernard de Castanet became bishop in 1277 he at once planned a new cathedral which would symbolise the wealth and power of the Papacy. The two preceding bishops had already shown this aspect of the Church in building a bishops' palace, the Palais de la Berbie, which was also a fortress quite clearly built to withstand military attacks. The cathedral was also conceived as a fortress. Work on it was started in 1282 and the major part of it was completed within 100 years.

Subsequent bishops added refinements and made alterations. The scourge of the Black Death in which almost half the population died in the mid-fourteenth century had delayed the completion and it was not until 1480 that the cathedral was consecrated. The huge organ was built in the eighteenth century, and the roof was redesigned in the mid-nineteeth century. As it is today St Cecile is a cathedral which it is possible to visit repeatedly, and constantly find some new contrast between the austerity of the exterior and the sheer splendour of the interior. The main entry is in the middle of the south side. A battlemented stone arch links the cathedral to a round brick defence tower. Beyond the porch a shallow stone staircase, added 100 years later, leads to a canopied porch and doorway all in stone carved in the Flamboyant Gothic style in strong contrast to the plain brick walls of the main building. Above the door the elaborate tympanum has a Virgin and Child in the centre, and figures of angels and saints in pairs in the sides of the arch. The whole external aspect of the cathedral was changed at the end of the sixteenth century when Bishop Louis I d'Amboise added three graceful storeys backed by two minaret -like towers to what had been a square bell tower no higher than the roof of the nave.

At about the same period this bishop had the choir constructed and closed off from the rest of the nave by a magnificent rood screen which shows Flamboyant Gothic carving at its most advanced. There is even, to modern eyes, a touch of humour in the figures of Adam and Eve, adorned with fig leaves considerably larger than those that later became fashionable among self-respecting nude statues. The choir stalls are magnificently carved, with a frieze of seventy angel musicians. Even the locks on the splendid wrought iron gates which form the entry to the choir are works of art. The choir is surrounded by a deambulatory in which each of the pillars supporting the arches which enclose it has a figure from the Old Testament. These carvings show the naturalism of Gothic sculpture at its finest, among the most impressive are the figures of Judith, Simeon, Jeremaiah, Isaiah, and Esther.

Beneath the organ at the west end of the nave, facing the rood screen, is a fifteenth-century painting of the Last Judgement. When it was done it was the largest fifteenth-century painting in the south of France, but at the end of the seventeenth century a bishop had a chapel installed in the base of the bell tower, and cut away the middle of this painting in order to make the doorway to it. Even so, what remains is large, impressive, and full of interesting detail.

Above all this the great, vaulted roof is conceived as a blue sky in which designs of arabesques, foliage, pastoral scenes, mingle with the major characters of the Old Testament, and Christ in Glory surrounded by symbols of the four Evangelists. Elaborate, detailed, and colourful as it is, the interior of St Cecile Cathedral is everywhere elegant and controlled, and it is one of those buildings which show unmistakably that from time to time Man can surpass himself.

Next door to the cathedral is Le Palais de la Berbie, the former Bishop's Palace. When it was built in the late thirteenth century, a time of religious upheaval, the palace was also a fortress, but after the Edict of Nantes ins 1598, which brought a measure of agreement between warring religious factions, some of its towers and fortifications were taken down, and the succeeding bishops concentrated on making the interior more comfortable, and creating gardens and shady walks around the palace. Since 1922 the Palais de la Berbie has housed the finest collection in the world of the works of the great painter, Toulouse-Lautrec, who was born in Albi in 1864. As a small boy he broke one leg and then the other, and they ceased growing. He was not a dwarf, he reached 1½m (5ft), but his legs were less than ½m (2ft) long, so that he was a grotesque figure. But Lautrec was charming, amusing, and had delightful manners so that he made friends easily. But his love of life led him to eat too much, to drink far too much, and to make love to far too many women, all of the wrong sort. He died of the effects of drink and syphilis at the age of 37 in 1901.

His mother, the Countess de Toulouse Lautrec, died in 1922 and left a great many of his works to the city of Albi and more were donated by other members of the family. The museum was opened in the Palais de la Berbie in the same year. It contains 215 paintings, 31 of the famous posters, and a large number of sketches and lithographs. Between them they show all aspects of Lautrec's life, his mother and father, their château at Celeyran, his mother's property, harvest scenes there, the château of the Toulouse-Lautrec family, and the people of the bars and brothels which he frequented so tirelessly. On the upper floors of the museum there are rooms devoted to post-impressionist artists and friends and contemporaries of Lautrec, including Gauguin, Serusier, and Bonnard, and the later schools of the early twentieth century, Fauvisme with Matisse, Marquet, Vlaminck and Dufy, and Rouault representing Expressionism, and some contemporary artists of the region. Like the cathedral, this museum is remarkable for its quality and individuality, and should not be missed by anyone with the slightest interest in painting. One of the largest of the rooms, the Salon Rose, which contains some famous portraits and works illustrating Toulouse-Lautrec's life in Paris, has a terrace with fine views of the Tarn, the Pont Vieux, and the formal French gardens of the Palais de la Berbie.

Near the cathedral and the Place St Cecile there is an old quarter with a number of interesting houses, some open to the public. At the corner of two picturesque old streets, the Rue de la Croix Blanche and the Rue Puech Berenguier, the Maison du Vieil Alby. A restored medieval house has exhibitions of various crafts and documents relating to the history of Albi. On the adjoining Rue Toulouse-Lautrec, the Hôtel du Bosc, the birthplace of Toulouse-Lautrec, can also be visited. The rooms have some fine period furniture, and souvenirs of the painter's childhood, and some of his earliest drawings and paintings. Next door there is a waxwork museum featuring people who have been important in Albi's history from the earliest times. This house was originally the home of Admiral Jean-François de Galaup de Laperouse, who was drowned at sea in 1788 while exploring the Pacific north of the New Hebrides.

Return to the pedestrianised Rue St Cecile and turn right into the Rue de l'Hôtel de Ville. The Town Hall itself is an impressive Renaissance building, with a splendid beamed council chamber. Behind the Town Hall at the junction of the Rue des Penitents and the Rue Timbal there is another fine building, the Hôtel de Reynes, now used by the Chamber of Commerce and Industry.

It is a Renaissance structure in red brick with stone mullioned windows. The interior has an attractive stone galleries, one above the other and a fourteenth-century round tower. Sculpted stone busts of King Francois the First, and Eleanor of Austria, are set in the wall of the courtyard. Immediately opposite this building is a sixteenth-century house in Albigeois style with a red brick and timbered façade, known as the Pharmacie des Penitents or the Maison Enjalbert. The main structure of the house is Gothic in style, but its transition in style to the Renaissance is shown in the carved wooden pillars and frames of the tall windows. The imposing doorway on the Rue des Penitents is both massive and elegant and shows carving of high quality.

Students of architecture will be fascinated by the St Salvy Church, near the cathedral. It was modified and added to over the centuries and is a mixture of styles from the tenth century on, with, for example, the remains of a Norman church and cloister of the eleventh century. In the thirteenth century after the Albigensian Crusade, work was resumed in Gothic style, and later a fifteenth-century brick storey was added to the round Norman and Gothic watch tower, which adjoins the square bell tower. The only remaining part of the cloister, reached by a door on the south side of the interior of the church, is the west gallery, which gives on to a charming little garden with cypresses and an ancient wellhead now planted with flowers.

Albi is an inexhaustible source of pleasure to the artist and photographer, or just to those with a sharp eye: the variety of gables and turrets and towers, some roofed with Roman tiles, some with slate; the detail of windows and doors; the mix of medieval and Renaissance façades in the old quarter; the thirteenth-century Pont Vieux and the majesty of the cathedral, all contribute to the interest of this sunny riverside city. Even the brick railway bridge has style and is in harmony with its setting.

It should also be said that Albi is a gastronome's delight, with some very pleasant cafés and restaurants tucked away in its old streets. The local wine is Gaillac, and right next door to the Musée Toulouse-Lautrec is the Maison du Gaillac, where a selection of these wines can be tasted, and right opposite is Le Bateau Ivre, one of the best restaurants.

A few kilometres north of Albi the church of **St Michael Lescure** has some points of interest. The twelfth-century Romanesque porch has pillars with historiated capitals with scenes including the temptation of Adam and Eve, the sacrifice of Abraham, and the damnation of the moneylender. An exhibition of photographs and postcards is presented in the interior of the church every year.

Cordes, 26km (16 miles) north of Albi by the D600, is believed to be the oldest of the bastide villages, and it is certainly one of the most picturesque. It was built by Raymond VII Count of Toulouse as a first step in strengthening the region after the devastation caused by Simon de Montfort's soldiers during the Albigensian Crusade. Although it can loosely be called a bastide, in as much as it is a fortified village, Cordes is in no way typical of the bastides which were built later in the thirteenth century. Almost all of them had a formal plan, rectangular with two parallel streets the length of the rectangle, and two parallel streets at right angles to them across the width.

In the centre was the market place, usually with the church to one side. In contrast, Cordes, built on the top of an isolated hill, is a rough oval in shape. It has one main street, which is not straight, although it is called the Rue Droite, and irregular lesser streets and alleys. It

Cordes, believed to be the oldest of the bastide villages

was surrounded by ramparts, vestiges of which remain, and had three fortified gateways, all still standing. Unlike most bastides, its church had no bell tower and there was no keep.

The impressive thirteenth- and fourteenth-century houses, many very well restored, face the street with graceful arcades at ground level with two storeys above in Gothic style with arched windows. The Maison du Grand-Fauconnier in the centre of the village is now the Mairie. In the interior a fifteenth-century spiral staircases leads to the first floor where there is a small museum devoted to the works of the painter, Yves-Brayer. Another fine house in Rue Droite is the Maison du Grand Veneur, easily recognised by the hunting scenes sculpted on the façade at second storey level. The covered market still has its fourteenth-century appearance though its twenty-four pillars have been restored several times and the roof was rebuilt in the nineteenth century. The well nearby is said to be 113m (3,71ft) deep.

Inside one of the gateways, the Portail Peint, so called from the painted image of the Virgin which decorates it, there is a museum which has some interesting items relating to the past of Cordes, including the town register from the thirteenth to the seventeenth century, as well as Gallo-Roman pottery, jewels from Merovingian times (seventh century AD), and medieval pottery from an archeological dig at Vindrac, near Cordes.

Cordes is a pleasant place to stroll in. Painters, sculptors, engravers, and weavers have their workshops the steep, narrow old lanes, and contribute to the revival of the village. There are panoramic views from the streets that follow the line of the original ramparts.

Cordes lies within the area where the wines of Gaillac are produced. These are some of the oldest vineyards in France. In the tenth century they already had a wide reknown and were cultivated by Benedictine monks of St Michael's Abbey beside the Tarn in Gaillac, and who set very high standards to ensure the quality of the wines. Today the vineyards cover 20,000 hectares and produce red, white and rosé wines. Some of them, both red and white, are very slightly sparkling, and are particularly good summer wines. Though Gaillac itself, 24km (15 miles) south of Cordes by D992, or 22km (14 miles) west of Albi by N88, has no major points of interest, it is a pleasant place with old squares and fountains, and a small terraced park overlooking the Tarn which was laid out by the famous French lanscape gardener, Le Notre, who planned the gardens of the Palace of Versailles.

North of Cordes the D922 leads to a region of wild and lovely scenery where the Aveyron and Viaur rivers cut and wind through thousand foot hills in a series of spectacular gorges. This is a countryside of old and picturesque villages like, Laguepie, Najac, and Villefranche-de-Rouergue.

Najac is dramatically sited on a spur above a loop in the Aveyron. Its single main street is lined with flower-decked houses and has two ancient fountains, one of them carved from a single block of granite in 1344. A little apart from the village, towering above it on a height of its own, are the impressive ruins of the royal fortress of Najac, built by Alphonse de Poitiers, brother of King Louis IX (St Louis), in 1253. It was constructed on the ruins of another fortress built in 1100 by the family of the Counts of Toulouse. Many of the houses in the village were originally built with stones taken from this older ruin.

The nature of the landscape is such that there is no direct road from Cordes to Najac. At Laguepie, where you enter the old province of Rouergue, now the department of Aveyron, the D922 heads northeast and at the village of La Fouillade, there is a left turn on to the D39 south-west to Najac, about 6 km (4 miles). An alternative is to turn left at Laguepie on to the D958, follow it for 6km (4 miles) to the hamlet of St Vincent then turn right on to the D106. After 3½km (2 miles) turn left and after another kilometre fork right on to the D954, and carry on across the next crossroads to Najac. These are narrow, winding, uphill and down dale roads, a more difficult route than by the D922 to La Fouillade, but through very attractive scenery. There are no motor roads on this section of the Aveyron Gorges, but the GR36, a signposted footpath which crosses France from Cherbourg to the Mediterranean, and which passes closes to Cordes at Les Cabannes, does follow the western rim of the gorge from Laguepie to Najac, about 15km (9 miles). Beyond Najac the GR36 carries on to Villefranche-de-Rouergue. The whole of western Rouergue is wonderful country for lovers of the great outdoors. It is ideal for and is discreetly organised for all types of walks from long-distance and difficult, down to short and easy, all in lovely scenery. Cycling, pony trekking, rock climbing canoeing and kayaking on the Aveyron, and horse-drawn caravan holidays are among other activities available, with planned accommodation, if desired.

Unlike Cordes, **Villefranche-de-Rouergue**, which lies 25km (15½ miles) north of Najac via La Fouillade and the D922, is a more classical bastide village, built on the right bank of the river between 1252 and 1256 by Alphonse de Poitiers. The settlement had been founded on the left bank in 1099 by Raymond IV, Count of Toulouse, and the new bastide brought increased population and prosperity to the village. Although the surrounding ramparts have been replaced by boulevards, the characteristic parallel roads and alleys crossing at right-angles and the central market square remain to this day. This square, the Place Notre Dame, is unusual in that the north side is a terrace, and in front of this terrace there is a large wrought iron Christ. Notre-Dame Church itself is chiefly remarkable for its high (54m/177ft) and massive bell tower which dominates the town centre. A few kilometres south of the town by the D922 the fifteenth-century charterhouse of St Sauveur, founded in 1461 and completed within 8 years, is a fine example of the pure Gothic style, and has a charming small cloister with a chapel on one side and the refectory on the other, and also an impressive Grand Cloister, according to some authorities the largest in France.

Rodez, the prefecture of the Aveyron department and the old capital of the Rouergue, lies about 50km (31 miles) due east of Villefranche. It can be approached either by the Dl or by the more southerly D911 as far as Baraqueville and then the N88. The latter route is to be preferred as it allows two interesting side trips. On the D911, 9km (6 miles) beyond Rieupeyroux, there is a turning to the right, the D997 which leads to **Sauveterre-de-Rouergue** (12km/7 miles), one of the most attractive of all the bastides. It was built in 1281 to the formal rectangular plan but with a particularly large central square. Its defensive walls have disappeared but two of the gateways remain as well as a corner bastion in ruins. The basic layout has remained virtually unchanged for seven centuries. Until the early seventeenth century Sauveterre-de-Rouergue was known as a cloth-making centre, but it was stricken by the outbreak of the plague which swept France in 1628, and it is said that only one of its inhabitants survived. Well off the beaten track, the old village slept away the centuries almost untouched. It took generations for people to return there and it never recovered its prosperity, even today its population is only about double what it was in the thirteenth century.

About 15km (9 miles) south of Sauveterre-de-Guyenne via Naucelle, and on the other side of the N88 is the **Château de Bosc**, a property of the Toulouse-Lautrec family, where the painter spent much of his youth. The château, set pleasantly among fields and woods, has been much transformed over the years from the original twelfth-century fortress. Today it is a large, flat-fronted house of three storeys with red shuttered windows, and with stone pepper-pot towers at the corners. It is still occupied by the family of Toulouse-Lautrec's mother. The interior has some fine Aubusson tapestries, a small museum with many souvenirs of the painter, and some of his drawings.

Rodez itself is a town of moderate interest to the visitor, though it is a good centre for several interesting excusions. In the town itself Notre Dame Cathedral, all in red sandstone, is worth a visit. It was built from the thirteenth, to the fifteenth century as a fortified church conceived as part of the town's defences. This can best be seen from the Place d'Armes, where the west face is bare, with no door, windows or decoration for half its height. The remarkable bell tower 87m (285ft) high, with six storeys, was added to at various times over three centuries. Massive and Gothic at the base, it demonstrates the changes in architectural style on the way up, becoming steadily more elaborate, through Flamboyant Gothic to Renaissance. The interior has fine fifteenth-century pillars and vaulting, beautiful retables of the fifteenth and sixteenth centuries, and an intricately carved organ case of the seventeenth century.

A pedestrianised route indicated by arrows links the most interesting sites in the town, the cathedral, the seventeenth-century Bishop's Palace, the Canons' House, and a number of imposing sixteenth and seventeenth-century mansions in the old quarter behind the cathedral.

A short drive to the south-east of Rodez by the D12 there are two villages with remarkable fortified churches. **Ste Radegonde** is dominated by the keep-bell tower and the defensive towers of its church, built in the thirteenth century and fortified a 100 years later, so that it could shelter the villagers. Sixty rooms were available to villagers to install themselves together with their sheep, forage and food. A few kilometres on at **Inières** there is another fortified church, also with rooms for villagers. It has a fine fifteenth-century Annunciation in polychrome stone.

No one staying in the Rodez area should fail to make an excursion to Conques. Leave Rodez by the D901 to **Salles-la-Source**. This is an unusual village built in three tiers on the flank of the upland of Comtal. It gets its name from the fact that an underground river burst out of the rock in the middle of the village as a 20m (66ft) waterfall, now harnessed by the French Electricity Authority. The village also has an interesting Arts and Crafts Museum, exhibiting early examples of the machines driven by wind or water to provide energy for industry, as well as the tools and crafts associated with agriculture and forestry.

Seven kilometres (4 miles) further on by the D901 is **Marcillac-Vallon**, a village so sheltered in its valley between the uplands that long ago the monks from the abbey of Conques planted vines there. The red wine made there today has its own *appellation contrôlée*, and is known for its fruitiness and a special flavour due to the red soil in which it is grown.

The D901 continues through the valley of the Dourdou, by way of Nauviale and St Cyprien, and then follows the gorge of the Dourdou to **Conques**, 39km (24 miles) from Rodez, in a splendid and remarkable site on the steep slopes of the Ouche near where that river joins the Dourdou. The site itself is said to be in the shape of a shell, which is said to be the origin of the name (from the Latin *conchylium*, a bivalve shell). But it is not its position and its fine golden-stone, timbered houses which make it such an extraordinary place. The village itself has been carefully restored and beautified since 1974, because it contains one of the finest examples of Romanesque architecture in France, the abbey church of St Foy which also contains unique treasure.

St Foy was martyred in Agen in AD303 and his relics were jealously garded there for 600 years. One of the monks of the Abbey at Conques thought so much of these relics that he made up his mind to steal them. According to legend, he went to Agen and passed himself off as a pilgrim, and joined the community of St Foy where he inspired such confidence over a period of 10 years that he was put in charge of the relics, and promptly made off with them, back to the Benedictine abbey at Conques.

The existing abbey church was started in the eleventh century though most of it dates from the twelfth century. Above the crossing of the nave and the transept there is a fine octagonal, lantern-type bell tower. The church was partially restored in the nineteenth century, notably the two towers flanking the façade. The west door has a tympanum which is a masterpiece of twelfth century Romanesque sculpture depicting the Last Judgement. Christ is seated in the centre in glory, the panels on his right show the blessed, and those on his left, the damned. Altogether 124 characters are shown in clarity and detail, despite their great age, and some touches of colour of the original polychrome are still to be seen.

The interior of the church, impressive in height (22m/72ft) gives an overall impression of austerity but nevertheless has more than 200 sculpted capitals, a fine sculpted group representing the Annunciation in the north transept, and the vast choir is enclosed by beautifully worked wrought iron made in the twelfth century. The eleventh to the thirteenth centuries were the great ages of the pilgrimages to St James of Compostella. Pilgrims were the tourists of their day, and in the guide prepared for them Conques was indicated as the recommended stopover for those coming from the north-east and Le Puy. Like all pilgrim churches the choir was surrounded by a deambulatory from which the faithful could see the relics of St Foy then shown in the choir.

Nothing remains of the original Romanesque cloister but one series of arches and a basin made of serpentine used by the monks for ablutions.

Conques has a kind of dramatic quality, first the lonely beauty of the site, next the impressive church, and then the remarkable treasure contained in it. This is the finest collection of examples of the goldsmith's craft in religious objects in medieval times. The oldest exhibit is a ninth-century reliquary covered in filigree gold, which is said to have been given to the abbey by Pepin, a member of the family of Charlemagne. The tenth-century seated figure of St Foy, carved in wood but entirely covered in gold leaf and studded all over with a profusion of semi-precious stones, is considered to be the absolute masterpiece of medieval goldsmith's work. There are several other works, in gold, silver, and champleve enamel of the twelfth and thirteenth centuries.

As part of the revival of the village a modern Tourist and Cultural Centre was opened in 1988, which is used for artistic exhibitions in the summer season. Every summer in July and August Conques hosts a festival of sacred and Baroque music performed by first-class soloists and orchestras.

Espalion, a picturesque town on the River Lot

North of Conques the D901 leads to the River Lot, which is the northern boundary of the region. The road which runs eastwards along the right bank of the river is narrow but picturesque, and it makes a pleasant drive to follow this route to **Entraygues**, an old town nicely situated at the confluence of the Lot and the Truyere rivers. Here, turn south-east on to the D920, a road which follows the spectacular Gorges of the Lot for more than 10km (6 miles), then the valley opens out on the approach to the charming village of Estaing. Ten kilometres (6 miles) further on, still by the D920, is **Espalion**, an attractive and picturesque town which has some good restaurants.

From Espalion the D920 leads back to Rodez (30km/19 miles), across the barren upland of the Causse de Comtal.

South-east of Rodez two lakes have been created by hydro-electric barrages, the Lac de Pont-Salars and the Lac de Pareloup. Both are large and scenically beautiful and have all the amenities for water sports holidays, equipped sandy beaches, boating centres, and holiday accommodation. Every 30 years the lakes are emptied so that engineers can inspect the condition of the barrage. This took place in the summer of 1993 for the Lac de Pareloup, but since then the lake has been refilled and things are back to normal.

Aveyron boasts one of the most unusual tourist attractions in France, of great interest both to gourmets and geologists, the village of **Roquefort-sur-Soulzon**. This large village is situated on the lower slopes below the limestone plateau of Cambalou. Thousands of years ago the north-east corner of the plateau fractured and slid away from the main part, and the movement created numerous caves in the broken off part of the plateau. The story goes that many years ago a shepherd was taking his lunch of bread and cheese in one of these caves out of the heat of the sun, when he saw a shepherdess he fancied crossing a field nearby. He left his lunch to go and dally with her and it was several weeks before he returned to that cave. The bread was rock hard and the cheese mouldy but being hungry he wiped it and took a small bite; to his surprise it was delicious. This, people claim, is the origin of Roquefort, one of the world's finest cheeses, some would say *the* finest.

It must have been a great many years ago, since Roquefort was already considered a delicacy by Roman emperors, and was eaten at the court of Charlemagne more than a 1,000 years ago. Today 7 million Roquefort cheese are produced every year. Every one of them is aged in these caves, which are the home of a penicillin mould, called *Penicillum glaucum roquefortii,* which is dispersed by currents of air through the galleries, and which thrives in the steady temperature of 7°C (45°F) to 9°C (48°F). The 3 month's ageing can only take place successfully in this unique environment, and that it why a Roquefort cheese can only come from Roquefort. The demand is so great that the great flocks of sheep on the Causses of Aveyron and Cantal cannot supply enough ewes' milk to satisfy it, about a third has to be imported from Corsica and the Pyrénées. Conducted tours of the caves explaining the whole process take about ¾ of an hour. In summer, when the outside temperature can be 30°C (86°F) or more, and the caves only 9°C (48°F), it is a good idea to wear a pullover.

Roquefort lies about 20km (12 miles) south west of Millau by the D992, and Millau itself is about 65km (40 miles) from Rodez via N88 and the D911 through **Pont de Salars**. This busy little town, a *sous-prefecture* of the Aveyron department, was once even more prosperous than today. As long ago as the twelfth century it was a centre of the glove-making industry, using the leather from the moorland flocks of sheep. For hundreds of years Millau remained the most important glove-making centre in France, producing up to 700,000 pairs a year until the World War II, including those for the rich and fashionable which were sewn finger by finger. Since then, society has become a lot less formal and people wear gloves much less than they used to. Millau's economy went into decline for several years but recovered by supplying good leather jackets, skirts, and trousers to the high quality fashion market. Many fine items are to be seen in the shops in the town.

With the development of tourism **Millau** has become a useful base for many excursions, notably to the different Causses, and the Gorges du Tarn and the Dourbie. Near the Notre Dame church in the town centre there is an Archaeological Museum which contains an interesting collection of Roman pottery and other objects. Most of them come from an archaeological site called Graufesenque, about 1km (½ mile) outside the town to the south, where excavations have revealed a village where 400 potters worked. There was a main street, a canal, houses for slaves, and giant furnaces capable of baking 30,000 items at the same time. It is known that pottery from this village was exported all over Europe, to the Middle East, and as far afield as India.

Another short excursion from Millau is to **Montpellier-le-Vieux**, which is reached by the D110 from Millau, 16km (10 miles). From the Auberge de Maubert a private road 1½km (1 mile) long leads to a parking place. From there a signposted path leads anti-clockwise through this amazing site of huge eroded rocks in grotesque shapes, often looking like ruined houses and castles. The rocks are partly bare, but the site as a whole is clothed in rich vegetation of trees and shrubs. Until the late nineteenth century this chaotic site was masked by thick forest, and the superstitious locals called it a 'cursed city haunted by the Devil'. It was certainly haunted by packs of wolves, and any sheep or goats that strayed into it were soon despatched. But in the 1880s the site was partially cleared and many trees were cut down and the wolves went away. The site was explored and in 1885 the great cave explorer, EA Martel, made a map of it. It takes about an hour and a half to follow the recommended route and it is very easy to get lost, if you stray even a short way from it. The path has some good viewpoints, as well as many named and recognisable rock formations, a cave where Martel found the bones of bears, and a pot-hole 53m (174ft) deep.

Millau lies at the confluence of the rivers Tarn and Dourbie. Though not as large as the better known Gorges of the Tarn, those of the Dourbie are extremely beautiful and dramatic. The drive from Millau to Nant, 32km (20 miles), by the D991 is very picturesque. From the first village there is a narrow road up to the Chaos of Montpellier-le-Vieux. A little further on there is a prettily sited mill on the right of the road, and not much further on a view on the left of the perched village of **Veran**. The tower that can be seen is all that is left of the château which was the home of the Marquis of Montcalm, who died in September 1759, fighting General Wolfe on the Heights of Abraham, in Quebec. At the confluence of the Dourbie and the Trevezel, about 10km (6 miles) further on there is a view of another perched village, Cantobre, with its houses teetering on the edge of a rock which juts out into space from the cliffs of the Causse Noir.

The road continues to Nant, at the end of the first gorge of the Dourbie. From there to St Jean du Bruel the road, now the D999, runs through a wide and fertile valley, with vines, orchards and market gardens, first cultivated by Benedictine monks in the seventh century. From St Jean du Bruel the roads are narrow and tortuous but with some spectacular views. The most practical, which is not saying a lot is the D341 which leads, with the D47, after 12km (7 miles) to Treves village and then the narrow and chaotic gorge of the Trevezel, deep but in places only 30m (98ft) wide. For those who love rugged and beautiful scenery, every road in this area is rewarding, but motor-cyclists may well feel more at ease than most car drivers.

The intrepid who follow the road through the Gorges of the Trevezel to Meyrueis will find themselves in a charming small town at the junction of three mountain rivers, the Betuzon, the Breze, and the Jonte. Its pure air, it is over 610m (2,000ft) up, and its proximity to a number of interesting sites, including the Aven Armand, one of the world's most remarkable potholes, the Grotte de Dargilan, and the Abyss of Bramabiau, make it a must to visit. The picturesque Gorges de la Jonte begin just beyond Meyrueis and can be followed on the D996 throughout their length of 21km (13 miles) to Le Rozier where the Jonte flows into the Tarn. The trip is best done in this direction because the gorge becomes more and more spectacular as it approaches the Tarn.

It can hardly be said that the **Gorge du Tarn**, 80km (50 miles) long and in places flanked by cliffs more than 500m (1,640ft) high, is off the beaten track, and certainly not in the summer high season, when the road which runs the whole length of the bottom of the gorge from Le Rozier to Florac is packed nose to tail with cars in both directions. But at other times of the year it becomes itself, towering and impressive. Even in high summer there is a way of seeing it which only a few people undertake. The whole area of these great gorges is criss-crossed by clearly marked footpaths, among them the Grand Randonnée routes GR6, GR6A, GR60, GR62, and GR62A, but many others are so well maintained and signposted that people who want to go only a short way can probably manage without maps. Serious walkers, planning longer trips, should have the appropriate rambler's maps and be properly shod and equipped, and should take

The Gorges du Tarn

enough water with them. Though there are springs on most of the routes, they do sometimes dry up in summer. Even the River Jonte itself sometimes disappears in hot spells into cracks in its own bed. A number of good walks start from the church at Le Rozier.

As a change from walking or driving, there are several villages where it is possible to take boat trips through the Tarn gorges. Probably the best place is La Malene where the river enters a particularly impressive part of the gorge. The system is that you drive to a parking place near the disembarkation point and leave the car. Passengers are then taken by bus back to the departure point and come down river by boat to join their car again. It is also possible to hire and paddle your own canoe.

Some of the gorges mentioned are in Aveyron, others like the Gorges du Tarn are in the Lozère department, but Millau, in Aveyron is one of the most convenient bases from which to explore what is, after all, one of the great natural marvels of Europe, and it would be a pity to miss it to because it happens to cross the boundary of another department. It is a fitting climax to a tour which began with the wonderful man-made marvels of Albi, only 120km (74 miles) away.

Further Information
— Rouergue-Albigeois —

Museums and Other Places of Interest

Abyss of Bramabiau
Via Meyrueis
Open: all day from April to end September. Visits restricted according to conditions in October and November.

Albi
Musée Toulouse-Lautrec
Palais de la Berbie, adjacent to St Cecile Cathedrale.
Open: am/pm, except Tuesdays from October to March.

Hôtel du Bosc
Birthplace of Toulouse-Lautrec, Rue Toulouse-Lautrec.
Open: am/pm from July 1 to mid-September.

Aven Armand
Cave
Via Meyrueis
Open: for accompanied visits from end of March to 1 November. All day from June to end August, am/pm at other times.

Bosc
Château
5km (3 miles) south of Naucelle-Gare, Vallée de Viaur, Aveyron.
Open: am/pm for guided visits from Easter to Christmas. A childhood home of Toulouse-Lautrec.

Dargilan
Cave
Via Meyrueis
Open all day for accompanied visits from Easter to All Saint's day, and Wednesday afternoons for the rest of the year.

Millau
Musee Archaeologique (Roman pottery)
Hotel Pegayrolles
Place Foch
Open: am/pm June to September. Rest of the year Wednseday and and Saturday afternoons.

Maison de la Peau et du Gant (Leather and Glove Museum)
Rue Droite
Open am/pm June to end September.

Chaos de Montpellier-le-Vieux
Via Millau
Open all day until sunset from Easter
to mid-October.

Najac
Château
Open: every day am/pm from Easter
to October. Sundays only in April and
October.

Roquefort-sur-Soulzon
The caves where the famous cheese is
matured are open am/pm for accompanied visits. Warm clothing advised.

Salles-la-Source
Musée de Rouergue
Open: am/pm in July and August.

Villefranche-de-Rouergue
Former chartreuse St Sauveur. Guided
visits in July and August.

Tourist Information Offices

Albi
Office de Tourisme
Palais de la Berbie
Place St Cecile
81000 Albi
☎ 63 54 22 30

Rodez
Office de Tourisme
Place Foch
12000 Rodez
☎ 65 68 02 27

Millau
Office de Tourisme
Avenue A-Merle
2100 Millau
☎ 65 60 02 42

Villefranche-de-Rouergue
Pavillon de Tourisme
12200 Villefranche-de-Rouergue
☎ 65 45 13 18

In towns and villages where there is no
Office de Tourisme or Syndicat
d'Initiative the local Mairie acts in this
capacity.
For booking accommodation and
particular leisure activity holidays:

Service Loisirs
Accueil de l'Aveyron
APATAR
Carrefour de l'Agriculture
12006 Cedex
☎ 65 73 77 33

Comité Departemental du Tourisme
du Tarn et Service Loisirs Accueil
Hotel de Departement
81014 Albi Cedex
☎ 63 47 56 50

Horse Riding
Comité Departemental de l'Equitation
33 Avenue Victor Hugo
12000 Rodez
☎ 65 68 27 72.

Motoring
A guide suggesting routes for car tours
in Rouergue (Aveyron) can be bought
in tourist offices or local Syndicats
d'Initiative.

10 • The Cévennes

The mountain chain of the Cévennes has been known since ancient times, for Strabo speaks of 'Kemménnon Oros', Pliny of 'Gebenna' and Caesar of 'Cevenna'. They all referred to the south-eastern edge of the Massif Central, which stretches from the mid-Rhône valley to the Montagne Noire.

In the seventeenth century, the Lieutenance Général of the area consisted of the Gévaudan, Vivarais and Velay, but after the revolt of the Camisards (Cévennes Protestants) in 1702, this was replaced by the Pays de Cévennes, which was the land between Mont Aigoual and the southern slopes of Mont Lozère with Florac (then in Bas Gévaudan) as its chief town. In 1790 the Pays was divided between the departments of Gard and Lozère.

However, even in the late nineteenth century, outside of the Cévennes proper, the word referred to a much larger region. Then the name became familiar to English-speaking readers through the journey of Robert Louis Stevenson as described in his book *Travels with a Donkey*.

Today, the official geographical region of the Cévennes proper (1947), is the northern slopes of Lozère, Montagne du Bougès, the region of the Gardons (rivers) and the southern slopes of Aigoual. This region is bordered to the west and south by the limestone Causses; eastwards lies the Alès coalfield, and to the north are the Margaride and the Vivarais. This with minor changes, is the region described here.

In 1970 most of the Cévennes, and parts of the adjoining Causses became the Cévennes National Park to safeguard the landscape already deteriorating due to rural depopulation, and to and try and improve the life of the remaining Cévenols. There is a central pro-tected zone of 84,200ha (207,480 acres) surrounded by a larger pe-ripheral zone. The central zone is subject to certain regulations, such as camping and caravan parking, but although the park seems to have been an environmental success, there exists some dissatisfac-tion — indicated by unwelcome anti-park slogans daubed on walls

209

etc, in western areas of the park. This may be due to hunting restrictions, reafforestation and banning of unsightly buildings, voiced by people who have been away from the region for a long time, and have returned to live there. Thus, it appears the term Cévennes means all things to all men.

The physical landscape of the south-eastern edge of the Massif, and hence the Cévennes, is sharply defined by a huge fault line scarp — a fracture of the earth's crust exposed as a steep face — which runs from north-east to south-west. Eastwards another great fault meets it running southwards from Villefort, and along this fault line are several Cévenol small towns and villages from Ste Cécile d'Andorge to La Bastide Puylaurent.

East and north of these fault lines are the mountains of the Cévennes, which are a rolling tableland of crystalline rocks — granites and schists — at about 1,300m (4,264ft), with gently flowing streams on the western side like the Tarn and Lot. Northwards the granite mass of Mont Lozère reaches 1,700m (5,576ft), its bare slopes scattered here and there with great piles of granite blocks; whilst southwards is another *massif*, Mont Aigoual, reaching 1,565m (5,133ft), where the granite overlaps schists, and the summit has a meteorological observatory which gives magnificent views.

The eastern or Mediterranean slopes of the Cévennes are in complete contrast to the west or Atlantic side, as they are steep and abrupt with deep ravines called *valats,* separated by narrow rocky ridges known as *serres.* Down these deep valleys rush torrential streams called Gardons, which flow to the Rivers Cèze, Hérault and Gard. They are fed by a high rainfall, over 2,000mm (80in), which comes in great bursts and sometimes destructive downpours.

For centuries, this landscape contrast reflected the way of life but there was always a struggle between pasture and woodland (*cebenno* in patois meant a wooded slope). For the people gradually cut into their once thick forest of beech, Scots pine and ash, and their sheep and goats finished off the destruction. By the 1870s the landscape was almost bare, deforested and suffering from soil erosion, but in 1875, George Fabre, a state forester, began a long-term scheme on Mont Aigoual of reafforestation. It was not without, at times, savage opposition.

On the Mediterranean slopes with a more benign climate it was a different story. There on the lower terraced slopes were mulberries — grown for a once prosperous silk industry — olives, vines, and, in stone-walled orchards, apricots and peaches. Higher up were apples and little irrigated market gardens. Still higher, up to 950m (3,116ft),

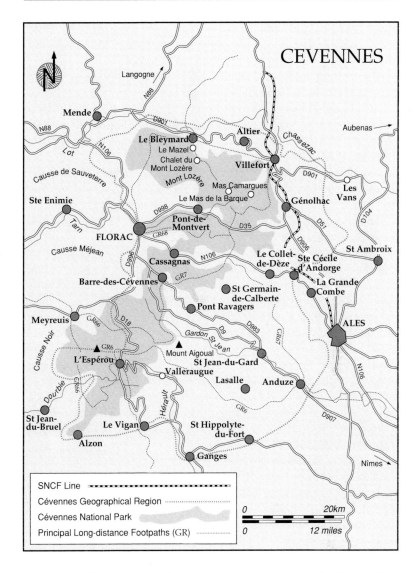

CEVENNES

Langogne

Mende

N88

Lot

N106

Causse de Sauveterre

Ste Enimie

Tarn

FLORAC

Causse Méjean

D998

D996

Le Bleymard
Le Mazel
Chalet du
Mont Lozère

Mont Lozère

Mas Camargues

Le Mas de la Barque

Pont-de-
Montvert

GR68

Cassagnas

N106

GR7

Barre-des-Cévennes

Altier

Villefort

D901

Génolhac

D35

Le Collet-
de-Dèze

St Germain-
de-Calberte

Pont Ravagers

Chassezac

Aubenas

Les
Vans

D104

St Ambroix

Ste Cécile
d'Andorge

La Grande
Combe

ALES

Meyreuis

GR66

D18

Causse Noir

GR66

Dourbie

St Jean-
du-Bruel

GR6

L'Espérou

Le Vigan

Alzon

Gardon St Jean

D9

D983

GR67

Mount Aigoual

St Jean-du-Gard

Vallèraugue

Lasalle

Anduze

Hérault

GR6

St Hippolyte-
du-Fort

Ganges

N106

D907

Nîmes

SNCF Line	▪▪▪▪▪▪▪▪▪▪▪
Cévennes Geographical Region	··················
Cévennes National Park	
Principal Long-distance Footpaths (GR)	············

0   20km

0   12 miles

were carefully cultivated chestnut groves; some actually flourishing on bare outcrops of schist, and even today the still remaining trees are the glory of the Cévennes.

The chestnut was a veritable breadfruit tree — for the people ate them raw, roasted or boiled in harvest time, but most were dried in special small stone buildings called *clèdes* which smoked for months. When dry and peeled, porridge was made from the flour, used at all meals or for fattening pigs. Livestock grazed on the ungathered nuts, sheep and goats ate the leaves, which were also used for litter; branches were made into baskets, and the wood for rafters and furniture — it was almost a chestnut 'civilisation'!

The undergrowth and suckers were always cleared before the harvest, but unfortunately nowadays many trees are untended, dead branches pile up, and diseases spread. However, many trees have been replaced by grafting the smaller Japanese chestnut, and the swiftness with which the chestnut regenerates suggests that it will be there for a long time.

Another former industry was mining; silver, lead and zinc from the granite mass of Mont Lozère at Le Bleymard and Vialas; and lead at Villefort and Cubières. Now uranium has been discovered at several places on Mont Lozère, but the National Park has opposed the exploitation.

There has been an inevitable rural exodus on both sides of the Cévennes, and the way of life has obviously changed with the spread of cars and holiday homes, but there is still much to see, and many opportunities to explore. These Cévennes landscapes are of great variety depending upon the geology, vegetation, aspect and human history. They range from granite moorland with peat bogs, the beech forests of windy Aigoual, the superb gorges on the border of the Causses to the sierras and deep valleys of the schist regions, where to discover them you must get off the road and follow the rivers or lanes from valley to valley. However, wherever one goes in the Cévennes there is a reminder of one historical event which remains in men's minds — the War of the Camisards — and the spark which ignited it took place at Pont-de-Montvert.

The background to this event was the revocation of the Edict of Nantes in 1685 by Louis XIV in a misguided attempt to unify his kingdom by forbidding the cult of the Protestant religion. This meant destruction of their churches and the exile of their pastors. But in the Cévennes, the Protestants, in spite of great danger, practised their faith secretly, often deep in the mountains — known as the Desert — both literally and figuratively. The revolt was also a mystical one, for the leaders were often prophets, known as the 'Fous de Dieu' ('God's Fanatics').

In 1702 the Abbé Chayla, 'Inspector of the Missions in the Céven-nes', arrested a small group of fugitives and had them imprisoned in the presbytery at Pont-de-Montvert. They were rescued by a group of armed rebels; and in the ensuing mêlée, the Abbé was killed. This was the signal for a general revolt of the mountain people, henceforth to be known as the Camisards (from the patois *camiso*, a shirt), for many were poor. The war was ferocious and lasted 2 years with 3-5,000 Camisards fighting never less than 30,000 troops under three marshals. They had two celebrated leaders: Roland and Cavalier, but one was betrayed and the other submitted, later taking service with England. Finally, after some years of persecution, in 1787 Louis XVI signed the Edict of Tolerance.

The wild life of the Cévennes has been greatly reduced by man in the course of history, most of the larger mammals having disappeared. In the twentieth century the wolf, hazel partridge and the griffon vulture were eliminated, although wild boar still exist and birds of prey like the golden eagle remain. The National Park has been active in re-introducing the beaver and griffon vulture, and protecting many others. As for the flora — a third of all French species flourish in the region — but some are under threat like the Carline thistle, St Bruno lily and orchids.

Undoubtedly the main attractions of the region are scenic and outdoor, although there are some very interesting buildings and museums worth visiting. For the long distance walker the region contains fourteen Grandes Randonnées, and several *gîtes d'étape*. Opportunities are plentiful for riding, kayak-canoeing, fishing, swimming, tennis and skiing. The climate varies according to altitude, but generally during the summer months everywhere is dry and hot with occasional storms. The contrast between the two slopes — Oceanic and Mediterranean — is shown in the seasons of late autumn and early spring when there is an abundance of rain in heavy brief outbursts on the eastern side, and more steady rain in the west. The winters can be severe with frost, high winds and snow on the high Lozère plateau with heavy rain on the Mediterranean slopes (especially Mont Aigoual with 2,250mm (90in) on the summits plus winds, snow and ice). But it is often sunny; although the European climate has changed, as 1987 showed, so the seasons are less regular.

Access to the Cévennes is quite good, both by road, and rail for so remote a region:

Road: N9 (Paris)-Clermont Ferrand-Béziers to Marvejols thence N108 to Barjac, N88 to Balsiège, N106 to Florac (633km, 392 miles), *autoroute* A7 (Paris) to Bollène, Pont d'Esprit, Alès exit then N86 to Bagnols, D6 to Alès then N106 to Florac (767km, 475 miles).

Rail: Paris (Gare de Lyon) via Clermont Ferrand to Villefort, Génolhac and Alès June to September. Fast train 'Le Cévenol'. Paris (Austerlitz)-Béziers line to Marvejols (connection to Mende and La Bastide Puylaurent). Paris (Lyon) by TGV to Avignon($3\frac{1}{2}$4hrs) then road to Alès by N100, D981 or TGV to Nîmes (4+hrs), then train to Alès.

Nearest Airports: Nîmes (Garons): then D42, N106 to Alès (2¹/₂ hrs) then to Florac. Montpellier (Fréjorgues): D66 to A9, then Vendargues exit, N110 to Sommières, D35 to Anduze (2¹/₂hrs), and then St Jean-du-Gard (D907).

In the Steps of Stevenson

The publication of Robert Louis Stevenson's *Travels with a Donkey* not only fascinated English speakers on both sides of the Atlantic, but later great interest was shown in France itself. For Stevenson was a pioneer in more senses than one — he virtually invented the sleeping bag — and probably outdoor camping as we know it. In modern times the publication of the complete diary of the trip (*The Cévennes Journal*) in 1979 has stimulated further interest in his journey, especially the last part through the Cévennes proper.

Here, it is proposed to follow his route from the Trappist monastery of Notre Dame des Neiges (Our Lady of the Snows) on the border of the old regions of Gévaudan and Vivarais (now Ardèche) to its end at St Jean-du-Gard in the Cévennes. To reach the monastery by road from northwards (Le Puy) take the N88/N102/N106 to Langogne, the D906 to La Bastide, then the D4a to the monastery. Southwards (Alès) take the N106/D906 to La Bastide. But a far more interesting and exciting journey is to arrive by train ('Le Cévenol') as it follows Stevenson's route closely at times and can be picked up *en route* either southwards or northwards. Alternatively one can arrive by branch line from Mende to La Bastide. Besides using D roads the route often follows 'Sentiers de Grandes Randonnées' (GRs), the long distance footpaths waymarked by white and red bars.

The monastery of Notre Dame de Neiges has changed somewhat since Stevenson's day. The original buildings were burnt down in 1912, and Stevenson's small guest-wing for travellers and those in retreat (including, nowadays, the monks' relatives) has been replaced by a modern building and a souvenir shop. There is a large group of buildings devoted to the sale of local products like cheese, chestnuts and wine. Not only sacramental wine, but there are cellars for the ageing of wine brought up from the Midi (Gard), and the making of table and sparkling wine and liqueurs. It seems that keeping wine at this altitude (1,081m, 3,545ft) produces a remarkable ageing and all these products can be tasted!

From the front of the monastery, where there is an enormous vegetable garden, the footpath GR7/72 leads past some Douglas firs to a narrow paved road, later a track which in July is bordered by a mass of flowers like small gentians, harebells, heartsease and wil-

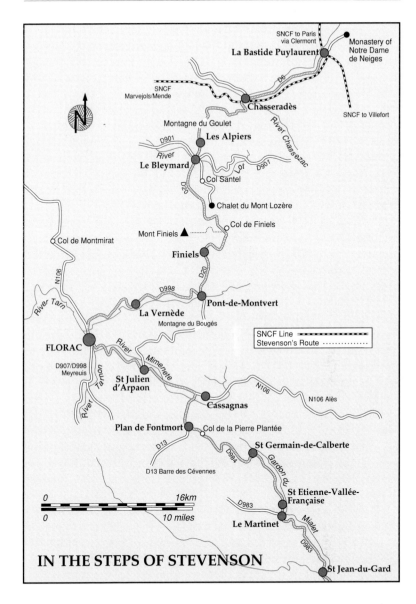

La Bastide Puylaurent

SNCF to Paris
via Clermont

Monastery of
Notre Dame
de Neiges

SNCF
Marvejols/Mende

Chasseradès

River Chassezac

SNCF to Villefort

Montagne du Goulet

Les Alpiers

D901

River Lot

Le Bleymard

D901

Col Santel

D20

Chalet du Mont Lozère

Col de Finiels

Mont Finiels

Col de Montmirat

Finiels

D20

River Tarn

N106

D998

Pont-de-Montvert

La Vernède

Montagne du Bougés

SNCF Line
Stevenson's Route

FLORAC

River Mimente

D907/D998
Meyreuis

River Tenon

St Julien
d'Arpaon

Cassagnas

N106

N106 Alès

Plan de Fontmort

Col de la Pierre Plantée

D13

St Germain-de-Calberte

D984

Gardon du

D13 Barre des Cévennes

0   16km
0   10 miles

St Etienne-Vallée-
Française

D983

Mialet

Le Martinet

D983

IN THE STEPS OF STEVENSON

St Jean-du-Gard

lowherb. After $3^1/_2$km (2 miles) La Bastide is reached, a rather dour town, which possesses one unusual feature — a stained glass teaching centre. Stevenson left it by following the River Allier to **Chasseradès** along what is now the D6 road ($9^1/_2$km, 6 miles). An alternative rural route is from near the church by GRs 72 then 7A to Chasseradès station on the line to **Mende**, and an appropriate place to reflect that Stevenson spent the night here (11 km, 7 miles).

From here Stevenson set out for Le Bleymard across the Goulet mountain, by its summit with no marked road, but the GR7A leads through Mirandol, then crosses the Chassezac — here a brook — and runs near the railway to reach L'Estampe with its *gîte d'étape* (3km, 2 miles). Then there is a very pleasant forest road over the mountain by a col (1,413m, 4,634ft), and descends to the hamlet of Les Alpiers. From here the GR7A goes by an old bridleway and emerges near a bridge over the infant River Lot on the main D901 (Mende to Villefort). Along the D901 and by the D20 to **Le Bleymard**, and this is almost the Cévennes proper. Stevenson left here, taking the ancient *draille* or drover's road up the northern slopes of Mont Lozère.

These ancient droving routes are prehistoric, and were made originally by wild animals long before they became the great transhumance routes for sheep in later centuries. This route begins on the left side of the cemetery in Le Bleymard, and climbs upwards, sometimes beside low walls and rejoins the GR7, which goes to the Col Santel (1,200m, 3,936ft), where it crosses the GR68 (Tour de Lozère). Then the GR7 climbs gently through the forest to the Chalet du Mont Lozère at 1,412m (4,631ft) with its chalet-hotel and *gîte*. From here the route takes the *draille* again which becomes the D20 and climbs up to the Col de Finiels (1,511m, 4,956ft) Here is granite country indeed, and an alternate route to the col is by the GR7 and up the Montjoie Heights — heaps of granite marking the way. From the col, the summit of **Mont Lozère** can be reached, the highest point in the Massif Central outside the volcanoes of Le Puy and Mézenc. It was here that Stevenson, coming up in the clear morning air, saw the blue hills of the Cévennes at his feet and remarked 'only this confused and shaggy country ... has any title to the name ... these are the Cévennes of the Cévennes'.

One will have noticed that the grassland which covers this high plateau and its crests is of the mat variety — the result of a thousand years of pastoral pressure and transhumance, but the latter has declined, and already bilberries, heather and shrubs are beginning to establish natural forest cover. Returning to the col the road southwards is now the D20, and on the left as the descent is made can be seen great piles of granite blocks and boulders called *chaos* in French. In English they are known as tors.

The road now winds round the plateau to reach the village of **Finiels**. Then it follows the Rieumalet stream to the confluence of the River Tarn and the Martinet, to **Pont-de-Montvert** (32km, 20 miles from Chasseradès).

Pont-de-Montvert, with the old toll house on the bridge over the River Tarn

The first thing Stevenson saw, as he came down the path to the village (which can be seen today as it leads to the Mont Lozère Eco-Museum) was the Protestant church. On going further: 'The place, with its houses...wore an indescribable air of the South'. The village is undeniably attractive with its seventeenth-century humped-back bridge upon which is a old toll tower, now the information office of the Cévennes National Park which was entered after Le Bleymard. Here, of course was the event which started the War of the Camisards — the Abbé Chayla's house is still there, but rebuilt, although it is now a souvenir/grocer's shop, but the cellar and kitchen-garden remain.

The way from Pont-de-Montvert to Florac is by Stevenson's 'smooth sandy ledge', now the paved D998 for 21km (13miles) (there is an infrequent bus service). It follows the valley of the Tarn, and is a very pretty route. Later Stevenson had breakfast in the hamlet of **La Vernède** with its Protestant chapel perched on a knoll. Soon on a rocky point the fourteenth-century château of Miral is seen, and about here the rock changes from granite to schist, and two villages appear, **Cocurés**, and further down on the opposite bank, **Bedoués**, with its collegiate church and behind it the beech oakwoods and conifers of Mont Bougés. Beyond here is the confluence of Tarn and Tarnon, and soon the picturesque old town of Florac is reached, just below the confluence in the Tarnon valley.

Florac is most impressively sited at the foot of the huge dolomitic cliffs of the Rocher de Rochefort. The town is near the entrance to the gorges of the Tarn, close to the Causse Méjean and not far from Mont Lozère and the southern Cévennes. It is therefore a good central point for exploring the region on foot, horseback or car. It was sited here on account of its water supply,like other villages, at the rock junction of limestone or dolomitic and impermeable schists. In consequence a stream called the Source de Pêcher, a principal resurgence from the Causse Méjean, flows gaily through the centre of the town with little waterfalls giving it an unusual character. This small river is much used for fishing, its real name being Pesquié (fishpond).

The original population of Florac was 'English', ie, Anglo-French from the English-held provinces of Aquitaine and Anjou, but the town's history has been a stormy one with the religous wars of the sixteenth century followed by the War of the Camisards, when the seventeenth-century château was fortified by palisades,'*cheval de frise*' (iron spikes set in wood to stop cavalry) and cellars. Before leaving, note the large severely classical Protestant church in the Place de Souvenir, which in spite of its puritanical appearance holds many cultural activities including concerts with musicians from Canada and the USA.

The town is left by the D907 (Avenue Jean Monestier), and the Tarnon crossed by a stone bridge (Pont de Barre), and the valley of the River Mimente entered by the N106. This can be followed via the village of Salle-Prunet or a path on the left bank overlooking the village and going via the hamlets of La Borie and Ventajols; and then **St Julien d'Arpaon** with its ruined castle on a rocky peak is reached. The road following the river now goes through a landscape of craggy schist, but from the church at St Julien the old railway line (if not too tangled with scrub) can be followed to the village of **Cassagnas** (off the main road). This gives good views of the river, and soon the cluster of Cassagnas' roofs are sighted perched on the slopes of Mont Bougès and surrounded by chestnut trees. Nearby, in the caves of the mountain was one of the five arsenals of the Camisard legions, where they stored arms, food and forged their weapons, and also where their sick and wounded were visited secretly by surgeons. A more pleasant reminder of history is an inn called the Relais de Stevenson.

Here Stevenson crossed the Mimente, and realised he was on the divide of two vast watersheds; behind him all the streams flowed into the Atlantic, before him they led to the Mediterranean. Our route crosses the river by the D62, and then shortly by the D162 up a very steep little road to the Plan de Fontmort (896m, 2,938ft) where there

The château at Florac

is a monument to the Camisard's revolt erected in 1887. From here the old road to St Germain de Calberte is taken, which is the GR7/67 to a junction (3km, 2 miles), where the right-hand fork (GR67A) is followed to the Col de la Pierre Plantée (891m, 2,922ft) where as its name suggests, there is a menhir. Descend quickly to **St Germain de Calberte** (14km, $8^1/_2$ miles from Cassagnas).

This small town is surrounded by terraced gardens in a Mediterranean-like vale with ilex, maritime pine and chestnuts. It has an old twelfth-century church with a fine doorway — a historical monument — and the Abbé Chayla whose murder started the Camisard's War is buried here. He had been an early missionary in China (seventeenth century), suffered martyrdom, then became a Christian persecutor. He lived here with his missionaries, and the town became a little Catholic metropolis enclosed by Camisard legions.

Stevenson left here for **St Etienne-Vallée-Française** besides the Gardon de Mialet along the modern D984, then at **Le Martinet** the D983 is joined. After here there is a long climb to the hill of St Pierre. Then comes a long and wooded descent to **St Jean-du-Gard**, and the journey is ended. The town is a very pleasant one in the heart of the 'Mediterranean' Cévennes, and the Camisard country, but the Gardon — here called St Jean — is subject to floods (*cardonnades*) due to heavy rains caused by clouds coming from the Mediterranean in contact with the Cévennes mountains. There is a very interesting museum here inside a seventeenth-century *auberge*, called Musée des Vallées Cévenoles, dealing with all aspects of life in the region including chestnut culture and the old silk industry.

Finally, Stevenson left here for **Alès** by diligence and we can continue by taking the tourist steam train to Anduze. It is an extremely picturesque route alongside the Gardons de St Jean and Anduze, and passes by the Bambouseraie de Prafrance (Bamboo Forest). Here a stop can be made to visit 34ha (84 acres) of exotic parkland, a giant bamboo forest including trees imported from Japan, China and USA, an Asiatic village and gardens. It was created by Eugène Mazel in 1855 after a voyage to the Far East to study mulberry trees for the silk industry. The line continues by a long tunnel to Anduze. From here (if wished) one can go to Alès by bus (13km, 8 miles).

Mont Lozère and Bougès Mountain Region
Eastern Lozère

Begin at the small village of **Ste Cécile d'Andorge**, just off the main N106 (Alès to Florac), and along the narrow winding wooded D276 above the railway from Alès to Villefort (on the line of the Villefort fault) to the Col de Bégude (510m, 1,672ft) at the head of the Andorge valley. Turning right at the col on the D52, equally wooded and sinuous it meets a very ancient highway, the Régordane, which linked Nîmes to the Ile de France. This road (D906) leads to the pleasant little resort town of Chamborigaud, in the valley of the Luech, where by turning on to the Pont-de-Montvert road (D998) this valley is climbed under the flank of Mont Lozère, which here is tree-clad almost to the summit of Bouzèdes (1,235m, 4,050ft).

Some way along and below a rocky ridge, known as the Rocher de Trenze, where Lozère granite meets the schists of the southern Cévennes is the village of **Vialas** with its narrow streets on two levels, and apples and vines on the slopes above. This is a splendid little unspoilt place, with its old low granite Protestant church (1612) on the outskirts, very peaceful with hollyhocks, lavender and petunias, belying its stormy history of religious strife. Here alleyways join the different levels, and in the upper street is a small traditional restaurant, Les Sources, which serves tiny ungrafted pears ($1^{1}/_{2}$in) from its garden. From the village, a footpath (3hrs) leads to Bourdouze, joining the GR68 (Tour of Lozère). On to **Les Bastides** where honey, cheese and beeswax can be bought, and soon the infant Tarn is crossed and **Pont-de-Montvert** reached with its tall old grey houses. The village is usually busy in summertime, especially if it is a Wednesday (market day) when leather goods are on sale.

The Protestant church at Vialas, with the Rocher de Trenze behind

From the village the D20 is taken, but immediately afterwards turn right towards Villeneuve (*gîte d'étape*), and continue to **L'Hôpi-tal**, a ruined and abandoned hamlet (1975). Its granite buildings were also the religious home of the House of St John of Jerusalem (Knights of Malta) who managed much land on Lozère; later the buildings were burnt and pillaged during the Wars of Religion (1615) and the Camisards revolt (1702). On to Mas Camargues, a vast farm building (used up to 1922), restored by the Mont Lozère Eco-Museum (information centre). From here is a walk (GR72) following one of the great sheep trails crossing the Tarn, and over pastures and peat bogs farmed co-operatively by tenants of the National Park. There is a special flora here of mosses, sedges and flowers like sundew and bogbean; also birds like the lapwing and the sandpiper. Returning via GR7 and 68 to L'Hôpital, the route goes by the road (without tarmac) to **Salarials** (one of the highest hamlets in the Massif Central at 1,412m, 4,631ft), and through wild scenery, to rejoin the D20 striking northwards over the Col du Finiels (see Stevenson's walk).

The D20 now descends to **Le Mazel** (information centre, *gîte d'étape*) where there are old silver and lead mines; then on to **Le Bleymard** with its thirteenth-century Benedictine priory and the D901 road is joined. The valley of the Lot is left, and the route passes through wild country to the watershed of the Lot and the Altier at the Col de Tribes (1,131m, 3,701ft). Then take the road left for Cubières (old lead mine), by the Altier River, and climb again into the higher valleys of Mont Lozère with hamlets, meadows and beechwoods to the Col de Bourbon, and down to **Pomaret**, where houses are built of three Cévennes rocks: limestone, granite and schist. Then the valley of the Altier is rejoined (D901), wooded and with apple orchards (Canadian 'reinettes'), then past the medieval Château du Champ to **Altier**, an old fortified village. Soon the granite towers of the Renaissance (1578) Château de Castanet appear, which can be visited during July and August (all day). It seems incredible that this beautiful building was only just saved from demolition in 1964, when water was being put in the hydro-electric power lake of Villefort, upon which it now stands (watersports).

On to **Villefort** itself (information centre); this little town is on the Régordane fault line which was crossed earlier, and lies in a ravine. It has many old houses (Rue de l'Eglise), and fifteenth-century town hall. From here the D66 is taken via the villages of Palhère and Costeilades in a glacial valley with terraced gardens, and houses covered with roofing stones called *lauzes*, actually mica-schists (Lozère is derived from this word). The views are good, with the Alps sometimes on the horizon. As the road rises, the landscape becomes covered with great blocks of granite, then passes through a relict wood of beech and firs, and soon, a turn on the right appears, leading to **Le Mas de la Barque**, a ski station with a *gîte d'étape* (horse-riding as well and GR72). Back to the road, now D362, and it climbs to the Belvédère de Bouzèdes (above at Vialas), which at 1,235m (4,050ft) presents a fine panorama. Then comes a tremendous winding descent, plunging 800m (2,632ft) to **Génolhac** far below. With its red tiled roofs, the view is distinctly that of the Midi. The town (information centre) is on the Régordane Way, and is interesting architecturally: façades of old houses, and shady promenades by the River Gardonette. Its history is linked with the locally born Camisard leader, Nicolas Jouany, who often 'occupied' the town during the rebellion.

From Génolhac the route now goes southwards on the D906, and crosses the D998, where the tour began earlier. Continue southwards to Chamborigaud, and the junction with the D52, and you can either return to Ste Cécile d'Andorge or continue direct to Alès.

The Cèzarenque (Upper Cèze Valley)

This short diversion shows the contrast between the high plateaux of Mont Lozère and the Cèzarenque with its sub-Mediterranean climate. It is a foray into rather unknown country.

From Génolhac the steep and winding D134 is taken south-westwards, and followed until it crosses the Cèze, a valley full of orchards and sunflowers. The route then rises steeply to the village of **Aujac** (D51), on a kind of sandy ledge above the river (caused by a fault). There is a backdrop of sunny wooded rocky slopes of the 'Cham' (plateau) of Bonnevaux. From Aujac go eastwards for half a kilometre, and perched on a hill among stumpy ilex trees above the valley is the fine Château du Chaylard. Already one can sense the Mediterranean-like atmosphere.

Returning to Aujac, the route continues along the D51, and glancing westwards, the massive bulk of Lozère dominates the skyline. The landscape gradually becomes more and more rocky with the trees a mixture of conifers and holm oaks, until the ruined Château de Bresis is reached at a road junction, and near the bridge over the Cèze. It is right on the fault here, and this extraordinary twelfth-century building is perched on a pile of shattered schists, its old square tower intact, and the rest ruined, although part seems to be used for a farm and lived in. It is possible to walk round, but one side falls steeply to the river. The high bridge is crossed and the road followed to **Vielvic**, with its sixteenth-century houses; then the D451 is taken to the main D906, and after a short way along, the red roofed village of **Concoules** is reached by turning right on to the D315.

Here on the eastern flank of Lozère was a little Catholic community, which along with others, organised themselves into armed bands, called 'Florentins' to combat the Camisards. The church has a twelfth-century bell tower from the Auvergne, and there is an agreeable restaurant here. Further south past the hamlet of Aiguebelle was the tile works of Nicolas Jouany, the Camisard leader, and one can see ruined tile-ovens along the road to Villefort. After this return to Génolhac, and so the contrast is complete.

The Bougès Mountain

This *massif* lying between Lozère and Aigoual, has its northern granite face separated from Lozère only by the Tarn valley, but the southern slope of schists is Midi in character. A further contrast on that side is the watershed between the Mimente (Atlantic) and the Gardon d'Alès (Mediterranean).

The route starts at Pont-de-Montvert, and the D20 is followed southwards as the road mounts the forested slopes of Scots pine. About 3km (1.8 miles) on the left is a forest track leading to the Col du Bougès (1,362m, 4,407ft, 4hrs) and GR72 (Barre-des-Cévennes). The road goes on through the Bois de Altefages (beech and conifers:

the name means 'high beech'). In this wood the capercailzie (grouse) is being reintroduced. We have now crossed from granite to schist, and just before the Col de Sapet is a panorama which contrasts the two faces. At the col the GR68 leads to the highest point of Bougès (1,421m, 4,660ft). The road, now narrow, winds down to St Julien d'Arpaon on the N106, and then the route goes eastwards. After passing the Col de Jalcreste the route follows the Gardon d'Alès (Vallée Longue), and continues for 16km (10 miles) until on the left is a narrow lane winding upwards (unnumbered) 1km (half a mile) before Collet-de-Dèze.

This is indeed 'off the beaten track', and rather hazardous, but will show the Midi side of Bougès with its chestnut groves, ilex trees, herds of goats, two hamlets (Loubreyroux and Pénens) and a way of life, apart from cars, which is little changed. An alternative route is by the D29, 6km (4 miles) past the Col de Jalcreste via St Frézal-de-Ventalon.

The two routes converge some way below the summit where the D35 is taken to the left to the Col de la Baraquette with good views, then to the Col de Berthel, where the GR7 goes to the summit of Ventalon (1,350, 4,428ft) not far along an old sheep trail. After this take the D998 to Pont-de-Montvert.

Between the Causses and the Cévennes

This route shows the great contrasts in the landscapes of the area. Coming from the north, ie Mende, the Cévennes are entered via the N106, the Florac road. On entering the Bramon valley the first glimpse is seen of the spurs of Mont Lozère, then the Truc de Balduc (1,100m, 3,608ft). This is an isolated small limestone *causse*, wooded with abrupt slopes. At the hamlet of Molines turn left on the D125 to the village of **St Etienne-du-Valdonnez**, interesting for its unusual shop fronts, and an old farm. At the southern end of the village a forestry road along the upper Bramon Valley is used to reach the junction of the GR44, where after a walk of half a kilometre the hamlet of **La Fage** is approached.

Here is a surviving traditional Lozère granite bell tower, formerly very much apart of life in the community. Not only tolling noon and angelus, but summoning schoolchildren and recalling harvesters, and also guiding lost travellers, shepherds, pedlars and pilgrims in fog or snowstorms. By its side are some restored objects: a village oven, fountain and a *trave* (for holding oxen while being shod).

From here the forest road is regained, until the D35 is met. Turning left, and taking a lane after 2km (1.2 miles) on the right and going down it, some menhirs will be passed, and then **Les Bondons** reached. This is a hamlet, and a group of strange limestone hillocks, where uranium has been found recently. In the hamlet itself, the architecture is interesting as houses are built of sandstone, limestone, dolomite and granite — the geology of the region in one building!

Returning to the D35, and turning left, the route is continued to the Col de Montmirat (1,046m, 3,430ft). From here, between Mont Lozère and the Causse de Sauveterre, is a superb panorama. Ahead is the Tarn valley, and beyond, the great scarps of the Causse Méjean, whilst on the left are the sharp crests of the Cévennes, and if it is clear — Mont Aigoual.

After this there is a fine descent along a corniche above the Tarn in its valley carved out of schist. Enter **Florac** on the right over the Tarn bridge on to the D907 (see Stevenson's walk for Florac). Continue on the D907 southwards out of Florac along the valley of the Tarnon (where beavers have been reintroduced), and under the lee of the Causse Méjean, and past old bridges built of schist to the village of **Salgas** where there is an eighteenth-century château. But it's not the original, as that was demolished by order of Louis XIV, and its owner, the Baron, sent to the galleys for collusion with the Camisards.

The route continues past a series of villages sited along a spring line on the slope where the limestone rests on non-porous rocks like marl or schist giving a water supply. At Les Vanels the road becomes the D996 and climbs through **Frassinet de Fourques** with its Romanesque church, and winds up to the Col de Perjuret (1,028m, 3,370ft). Here is the meeting point between the limestone Causses and Mont Aigoual schists, with fine views of the Méjean escarpment, towards Florac and Mont Lozère. Here also the GR60 (Draille d'Aubrac — sheep trail) crosses on to the D18, both going to Mont Aigoual. The way now descends along the upper Jonte valley and reaches the pleasantly sited town of **Meyrueis**, within the National Park, but outside the Cévennes proper. It was famous for its weavers and serge cloth, and pioneered tourism, as its hotels catered for people visiting the gorges in the nineteenth century. It has some superb sixteenth- and seventeenth-century houses with carved mullioned windows (*gîte d'étape*, GR66 Tour of Aigoual).

Mont Aigoual and Lingas Mountain Region

The granite and schistose *massif* of Mont Aigoual is the highest point of the southern Cévennes (1,567m, 5,141ft). It is in effect a huge water tower, being the meeting point of damp Atlantic and Mediterranean winds; hence its name — derived from the Latin *aqualis* (watery). On the Mediterranean slope precipitous valleys alternate with sharp crests, and on the Atlantic side gentle slopes merge into the limestone Causses.

It was always heavily forested with beech and Scots pines until the nineteenth century, when there was a vast increase in the transhumance of sheep on its slopes, and shepherds and farmers increased pasture at the expense of the forest. After some diastrous floods in the lower Mediterranean areas due to heavy rainfall and soil erosion in the 1850-60s the forest was virtually recreated by the State, and the efforts of George Fabre. His idea was to leave the good farming land, and have a mixed forest of beech and pine. So he thinned the meagre beech copses to grow thick tall trees, and planted hardy conifers like mountain pine on the higher degraded land, Scots and Austrian pine on the limestone soils westwards, and used Norway spruce and larch. This was achieved in spite of hostile communes, and shepherds who sometimes burnt the young plants. But he not only reafforested, but created footpaths, arboretums to study the different species, restored forestry houses and instituted an observatory.

The Atlantic Side of Mont Aigoual

The route begins at the small town of **Meyrueis**, at the confluence of the Rivers Bétuzon, Brèze and Jonte whose upper valleys are covered by the great Aigoual forest (National Park information centre).

Taking the D986 road, a short diversion on the left leads to the fifteenth-century Château de Roquedols (National Park information centre), built of pink sandstone flecked with ochre, situated in verdant surroundings. The D986 now climbs through forest by the River Bétuzon to the Col de Montjardin, then passes into a larch forest, whilst on the right is the old arboretum of La Foux. This has a walk among species such as a huge Chile pine. It is worth going into because birds like the small-toed eagle, honey buzzard and black woodpecker might be seen.

Soon there is a change of rock from the schists, and the curious spectacle of an abyss on the side of a huge limestone cliff, from which cascades the Bonheur stream. This is also called the 'Bramabiau' (Bellowing Ox), because of the noise of its waters from the subterranean caverns in the small Causse de Camprieu (may be visited). Then on the left is the hamlet of **Camprieu** (*gîte d'étape*, ski station). The GR62/66A meet, and if the GR62 is followed up the Bonheur valley an eleventh-century ruined priory is reached. After this take the

D986/D269 to the Col de la Sereyrède (1,300m, 4,264ft and a watershed), where the huge gash of the Hérault valley falls away. Here also was where the great Draille du Languedoc (transhumance sheep trail) crossed from the arid *garrigues* to the pastures of Aubrac, Lozère and the Margaride.

From the col the road with superb views then plunges into magnificent beechwoods, and $1^1/_2$km (1 mile) from the summit there is a botanist's walk in the arboretum of L'Hort de Dieu (God's Garden), made by the botanist Charles Flahaut helped by G. Fabre. Not only are there exotic species to see, but the walk gives a wonderful series of views. Then the summit is reached with the 1887 meteorological station, which has important functions, notably giving warning of torrential rains. The views from here are exceptional, with an immense panorama. It is however, always windy, and in summertime often hazy, and early mornings in September are best. In the winter Mont Blanc and Maladetta (Pyrénées) have been seen simultaneously — a distance of 625km or 400 miles! There is an orientation table on the tower (views to the Alps, Cantal, Mediterranean etc).

From the summit the D18 is followed down to Cabrillac, with its forested slopes, sheep pastures and houses with porches for protection against snow. From here the narrow D119 is taken across rock strewn ground and dip down into the granite gorges of the Tapoul valley to the village of **Massevagues** (*gîte d'étape*) perched on the valley side. Here Henry Castanet, forester, wool-carder and Camisard leader, who established his '*quartier-général*' on Mont Aigoual, was born. Continue on through the gorges to Rousses, where the D907 can be taken to Florac.

The Southern Face of Aigoual and the Lingas Mountain

This route starts from the Col de la Sereyrède southwards on the D55, where on the left one can glimpse the cascade of the infant Hérault before reaching **L'Espérou** (ski centre and GR7). Here the D986 is followed as it descends in an incredible series of long loops to the valley floor. The contrast between the south facing slopes of chestnuts and ilex, and the northern ones forested with beech is well marked. The drop here from the summit is 1,200m or 4,000ft in only $6^1/_2$km or 4 miles. Near the bottom is a very pleasant restaurant/camp site (two-star) called Le Mouretou. Next visit the very Midi-like charming old town of **Valleraugue** with very tall houses, some six or seven storeys high, and the River Hérault opening out to form a waterfront as it passes through. There is a huge Protestant church here. It was a much bigger town once with 4,000 people, now 1,050.

Off the Beaten Track: Southern France

From here there is a tough walk to the summit of Aigoual, called '4,000 steps' (in name only), very scenic, though wild with heather and broom, taking a day up and down. On to **Le Mazel** where there are an impressive spinning mill, and on the road very tall houses with a sheepfold, living space and silkworm rearing houses in successive storeys.

Eventually the route leads to Pont d'Hérault, turning left on the busy D999, and 6km (4miles) later reaches **Le Vigan**. Here is really a lively and interesting Midi town, in a picturesque setting, with a beautiful promenade of huge old chestnut trees, an old Gothic bridge, and a museum in an eighteenth-century silk mill; devoted to all aspects of Cévennes life (park information centre).

The route leaves the town on the D999, and turns right on to the D48 up the Coudoulous valley — very Mediterranean in aspect with vines, olives, mulberry trees, cypresses and scattered houses — then begins to climb the chestnut-covered slopes. Somewhere amid these hills is a small herd of mouflons (Corsican wild sheep) introduced in the 1950s. Soon on an enormous hairpin bend at La Cravate, there is a viewpoint of wooded ridges, Languedoc and the Arre valley. On climbing higher into beechwoods, certain butterflies like the rosalie alpine (blue-black, long antenna) might be glimpsed. Then the Col du Minier (1,264m, 4,145ft) is reached, and the route left on to a forest road. At first through beeches, and then there is complete change of landscape as the road passes on to an open grassy plateau encircled by distant trees. It is bright with flowers: yellow gentian, clover, daisies, toadflax, tiny buttercups, yarrow and scabious. This is the granite *massif* of Lingas, not well known, for as one goes on further the terrain becomes difficult with unpaved forest roads, but the route goes on to Pont du Lingas, across the Lingas stream. Then beyond, the road goes through woods of mountain pine and spruce to the open Col de Homme Mort (1,300m, 4,264ft) with eroded granite scenery of boulders and patches of sand, where the paved surface ends. There is a great deal of country to explore in this region, either by forest tracks or the GR66 (Tour of L'Aigoual) and GR71 or simply walking where you choose.

Return to the Col du Minier, and continue on the D48 through forest, where there are some very tall beeches, and into open land again where herds of fine Aubrac cattle graze. Below westwards can be seen the meanders of the River Dourbie. At a road junction, the D151 is taken to follow the valley of this river with Lingas rising to the south. Then the village of **Dourbies** is reached (accessible from Lingas by forest road), and the gorges begin, cut into schist, but the high cliffs of the Cade rock are made of that most resistant rock quartzite (metamorphosed or altered sandstone). At the Col de Pierre Plantée, the route turns north to the village of **Trèves** via D157, famous for its February carnival of the 'Pétassou', who walks the streets clad in coloured rags carrying a pig's bladder, which the villagers try to burst, while he wards them off with his broom. Then comes the narrow defile of the Trévézel Valley with massive limestone cliffs — at one point only 30m (98ft) apart. Then on the left the D252 takes one up a steep little road past the old silver mines of Villemagne to the D986, where left goes to the Meyrueis, and right goes to Mont Aigoual.

The South-Eastern Cévennes Valleys

This is the region of ridge and vale, '*serres et valats*', where erosion has cut countless crests and ravines in a mass of schists (with occasionally other rocks), but it is one of the most rugged landscapes in all France.

The Can de Hospitalet and the Corniche des Cévennes

The route leaves Florac south by the D907, then D983 to St Laurent de Trèves, on a limestone spur, where the footprint of a dinosaur was discovered, dating from 190 million years ago (protected site; may be visited). At the Col de Rey, continue down the D983 for a diversion to **Barre-des-Cévennes** (3km, 1.8miles). This small town has a high street with tall dark houses, that seems unchanged since the sixteenth century. Behind is a small limestone hill, the Castellas, on which was a fort; lower down is the twelfth-century church, Notre-Dame de l'Assomption; the Protestant church is at the entrance from Florac. Barre had a garrison during the War of the Camisards, which stayed for many years. It has a scenic site, and access to all the roads along the Gardons (*gîte d'étape*: GR7, 72, 67, Tour of Gardons, information centre).

Returning to the Col de Rey (992m, 3,253ft), take the D9, and here the Corniche begins across the windswept limestone plateau of the Can de Hospitalet. Reaching the Col de Farsses (1,026m, 3,365ft) a panorama of the Gardon St Croix in the upper Vallée Française can be seen. On to **L'Hospitalet**, where there is an old farm (*gîte d'étape*, GR67), behind which, among beech trees and rough blocks of dolomite, was a famous Camisard secret assembly point. Continuing along the plateau with views southwards of Aigoual, the road descends to the village of **Le Pompidou** amid chestnuts and schist, with its two churches not far apart. The road now runs along a ridge through chestnut woods and meadows, which in spring are bright with narcissii.

As one looks across eastwards over the Vallée Française there is a great line of crests, at much the same height, which are sometimes termed 'an accordance of summit levels'. This means here, many millions of years past it was almost a plain, then it was covered by a sea (Jurassic), and later slowly eroded to its present state.

Then the pleasant village of **St Roman-de-Tousque** appears with its equally pleasant L'Auberge de la Patache. The route changes so that it overlooks the Borgne valley, and at the Col d'Exil (705m, 2,312ft), it again alters with superb views of Mont Lozère and the Cévennes crests. And thus, on to the Col de St Pierre (597m, 1,958ft). Here is a marked rocky path (blue/white) to a viewpoint and an orientation table, where one can see Aigoual, towards Nîmes and the distant Mediterranean.

Now the road begins a picturesque winding descent to St Jean-du-Gard, and as the Gardon is reached, the schists are left behind, and the river is seen as a beautiful meander enclosed in a steep valley of very hard ancient rock (gneiss). Soon the town with its old humped-back bridge comes into view, and the journey ends.

St Jean-du-Gard to Anduze via Mialet

This route is an alternative to the D907 along the Gardon St Jean, and the steam railway. Incidentally, for the enthusiast, No C27, a large freight locomotive (2-8-0), built in 1917 at Glasgow (French design), works the line well in spite of its 70 years service. Leave St Jean-du-Gard by D983, and soon on the right is a track (GR61, 4km, 2.4 miles) direct to **Mialet**, but by road continue until on the right is a narrow steep lane D50, that leads to Pont des Abarines on the Gardon de Mialet, and Mialet itself (*gîte d'étape*, GR61/67). Further along, and on the left is a road leading to the hamlet of **Mas Soubeyran**. Here amid rather severe scenery of the surrounding mountains is the house where Roland, the Camisard leader was born (although of humble origin, he was always referred to as 'Count Roland', by the English Queen Anne, who resolved to help the Camisards). In this house, now the Museum of the Desert, is the history of the Protestant struggle, and particularly in the Cévennes. Each year, at the beginning of September, under the nearby trees is held a huge 'assembly' of up to 20,000 Protestants.

Continuing up the road for 3km (1.8 miles) now in limestone scenery, is the Grotto of Trabuc — the largest in the Cévennes. It has a long history of occupance from Neolithic times through brigands and refugee Camisards. But its deep exploration is quite recent, and now 12km (7.4 miles) of huge galleries are known, along with lakes, and curious calcite underground landscape. There is a mysterious group of stalagmites, known as the '100,000 soldiers', giving the illusion of a besieging army (may be visited). Returning to the D50 (GR61) the road goes by the Gardon with good views past the confluence of the Gardon St Jean, and a railway bridge until the village of Générargues and D129 is reached. Turning right the route passes close to the Bambouseraie de Prafrance, and then through a narrow defile of towering limestone cliffs ('Porte de Cévennes') to **Anduze**.

This charming small town — very busy during summer — is a good centre for exploring the southern Cévennes, but with its narrow streets, alleys and fourteenth-century clock tower, near the old château is worth exploring in its own right. In the seventeenth century it was known as the 'Geneva' of the Cévennes, being fortified by the great Protestant leader, the Duc de Rohan, who also built an embankment to protect the town against flooding. Later it became the great supply town for the Camisards; afterwards achieving much prosperity through the silk industry, fruit, vines, distilling and potteries. Around it are some very good marked walks (yellow and white):

1. To viewpoint of St Julien, from the old château, 1 hr.

2. To Peyremale, cliffs above the Gardons, from the bridge (Alès Road), 2hrs.

3. To dolmens of Pallières, from 'Vitrine Cévenol' $1^1/_2$km (a mile) from Anduze D907. (Smoking is forbidden on these walks!)

The Vallée Longue (Gardon d'Alès)
Ste Cécile d'Andorge

Ste Cécile, although near the N106, is little visited, but there is plenty to explore in the remote valleys of its hinterland. This village, high up, is reached off the D276 (2km, 1.2 miles), Catholic and nowadays rather sleepy, but has an interesting church, and had 104 houses burnt by the Camisards in 1702. (Hardly that number exist now!) Later, the villagers became (as others did) *mineurs-paysans*, working their land and going to the mines, either coal at Alès or lead-silver locally, usually by train, for years until the mines closed (1950-75). From the village the route on the left is followed (possible by car, but better to walk) along an intensely wooded track above a valley, which is eventually reached, Valussière, with terraced vines, fruit plus acacia, ilex, chestnuts and pine. This can be then taken far to its

Ste Cécile d'Andorge

head past remote farms, or on the left is a track which climbs steeply to a crest giving fine views of the HEP lake far below in the Gardon. This area in summer is full of butterflies: Apollo, clouded yellow, marbled white and orange fritillary — species long gone from other areas.

Returning to the village, descend to the level crossing, then on turning immediately right a track is taken down to the floor of the stony Andorge valley, and continue up past the massive railway embankment. Here the line of the great Villefort fault is clearly visible, and going on further under a remarkably fine disused railway viaduct, the valley can be explored passing the odd large old farmhouse with not so old red roof tiles — a feature to be explained later. For the adventurous the disused narrow gauge line to Florac can be followed from the viaduct via a tunnel, until tangled vegetation stops all progress. One can return to Ste Cécile via the road that leads from the hamlet of St Julien des Points.

From Le Collet-de-Dèze to St Germain de Calberte

From Ste Cécile follow the N106 for 6km to **Le Collet-de-Dèze** a village with an interesting Protestant church below the road level, where most of the old village lies. It escaped demolition during the War of the Camisards by the villagers giving it to the Marquise de Portes; today it is a light, airy building with clean lines, and obviously used. Here one can reflect on these Cévenols — austere, hardworking craftsmen, literate — and realise that even until the 1960s Protestants rarely inter-married with Catholics, in most villages they lived harmoniously — but separately.

From here just beyond Le Collet, the D13 is taken, a narrow winding, but picturesque steep lane, with, off on the right, another 'hidden' hamlet of **St Michel-de-Dèze** that has an excellent bar-restaurant, La Rivière. Continuing, the D13 climbs steeply to the Col de Pendédis (666m, 2,184ft) a kind of mountain crossroads, with steep schistose valleys on all sides. From here there is a good view of surviving traditional cultivation terraces, (*bancels* or *faisses*), laboriously enriched with baskets of earth. Nearby is a hamlet (*gîte d'étape*, GR67), and an old farm with red roof tiles, and the reason for these is that during the last war, Lozère prospered, and afterwards the heavy roof slabs (*lozes*) were replaced by tiles, as roofs were often damaged. Turning left for a short way (D54), there is an abandoned '*clède*', adjacent house, and untended chestnut groves, mute evidence of rural exodus.

The D54 can be taken in the opposite direction to the hamlet of **Les Ayres** amid its orchards and sheep, where curious rural fairs were held for labourers to get work in silkworm rearing, harvesting chestnuts, threshing wheat or the *vendanges* (ripening of vines). Returning to the col and the D13, the road continues upwards through remote country to the Col de Pradel (785m, 2,574ft) (GR67), where there is a splendid vista of serried ridges and valleys to the far horizon.

The road now descends in a series of tight hairpins to the Gardon de St Germain, past the restored ancient château of St Pierre perched on a knife edge ridge. Here in Gardons like these the beaver has been re-introduced, but he is a nocturnal, and only a silhouette of this majestic animal in the gloaming is all that is often glimpsed. Likewise the slough of the couleuvre de Montpellier, the region's largest reptile (2.5m, 8ft long) is all one would normally see of this snake on exposed slopes.

Soon the village of **St Germain de Calberte** is reached in the heart of the Mediterranean Cévennes (see Stevenson's journey) (park information centre).

Further Information
— The Cévennes —

Museums and Other Places of Interest

Anduze
Bambouseraie de Prafrance (Générargues)
Open: March-October 9.30am-12noon, 2-7pm. Steam railway station.

Meyrueis
Château Roquedois
☎ M. Bonnet (66) 45 62 81
Open: July-August daily.
At other times contact M. Bonnet.

Mialet
Desert Museum
Open: July/August 9.30am-6.30pm; March-October 9.30am-12noon, 2.30-6pm.

Trabuc Grotto
☎(66) 85 33 28
Open: June-September, guided visits lasting 1 hour.

Mont Aigoual
Brambiau
☎(67) 82 60 83
Open: all day April-September, restricted October-November. Closed mid-November-March. For ski station Prat-Peyrot ☎(67) 82 60 17; Camprieu ☎(67) 82 60 26.

Pont-de-Montvert
Eco-Museum
Open: June-September and school holidays daily. Rest of the year Thursday, Saturday and Sunday.

St Jean-du-Gard
Steam railway station
☎(66) 85 13 17
Trains: May-September in steam Thursday, Friday and Sunday and public holidays.

Cévenol Valleys Museum
☎ M. Vriet (66) 85 10 48 Tuesday and Thursday
Open: June-September daily except Monday and Sunday morning.

Le Vigan
Cévenol Museum
Open: April-October inclusive except Tuesday.

Tourist Information Offices (Syndicat d'Initative)

Anduze
Plan de Brie ☎ (66) 61 98 17
Open: June-September all day.

Florac
National Park HQ
BP 15 Le Château 48400.
☎(66) 45 01 75
Information centre for all activities within the park.
Open all day July/August; September-June every day except weekends.

Syndicat d'Initiative
Ave Jean Monestier
☎(66) 45 01 14

Génolhac
Mairie ☎ (66) 61 10 55
Open: 9am-12noon and 2-6pm.

Meyrueis
Mairie
Rue Apies ☎ (66) 45 62 64

St Jean-du-Gard
Place Rabot ☎ (66) 85 32 11

Valleraugue
Mairie ☎(67) 82 22 78

Le Vigan
Syndicat d'Initiative (National Park Information)
Place du Marché ☎(67) 81 01 72
Open: daily except Sunday afternoon and Monday morning.

Villefort
Mairie
Rue Eglise
☎(66) 46 80 26

11 • Ardèche

The publicity issued by the Comité du Tourisme de l'Ardèche describes six regions of Ardèche which are summarised here. The department is the ancient province of Vivarais, hence some of the terms used:

The Rhône Valley
The Rhône flows south from Lyon to the Mediterranean and forms the eastern boundary of the department. This is a fertile, alluvial plain, with vineyards, orchards and small industries. Old cities were established to repel invaders. This area has the highest population.

Haut Vivarais
This is the area of high plateaux at 500m (1,600ft) plus. Cattle breeding and cereal growing are predominant—do look at the farms, both large and small. Annonay, the former *préfecture*, is the main town; it was a centre of printing and parchment due to the purity of water from the River Cance. Today it is involved with the textile and car industries.

La Montagne (The Mountains — the Massif Central)
On the high plateau, Mont Mézenc 1,754m (5,753ft) is the highest mountain at the north-western point. The River Loire rises at Le Gerbier de Jonc, but had it risen a few miles further south it would have flowed into the Mediterranean. The watershed between Atlantic and Mediterranean is nearby, and clearly marked on most main roads (*Routes Nationales*). In this area, there are many extinct volcanoes, lakes, rock formations and man-made barrages or dams.

Le Moyen Vivarais
This area extends from the middle of the Ardèche Valley to the Rhône and includes the valleys of the Eyrieux and Doux and the plateau of the Coiron. Many geological variations may be seen, mostly limestone and sandstone.

Les Cévennes
This area shows where the stalwart people of the Ardèche managed

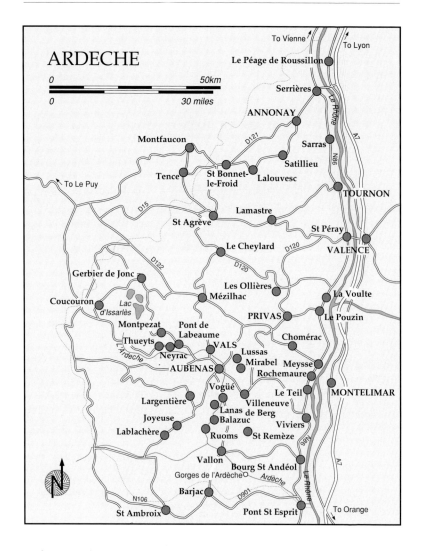

to farm on the terraces without the use of modern implements. They survived on chestnuts and vines, and olives on the southern slopes. Largentière had a silver mine until 1985, but this was the only real 'industry'. Most people work on the land or as entrepreneurs in building and domestic services.

L'Ardèche Meridionalè
This is where the 'Midi' begins, therefore approaching the climate of the Mediterranean. There are olive groves in profusion; spectacular rock formations through the Gorges of the Ardèche (with caves to

visit); the Bois de Païolive (a limestone 'forest'); the valley of the Chassezac; dolmens and old ruins from prehistoric times.

The climate of the Ardèche is mild to the north, warmer as it passes southward into the 'Midi' and not as hot as Provence but warmer than further north. In July and August it is hot and dry, excepting thunderstorms in the mountains which are intermittent and short-lived. The seasons of spring and autumn are generally very mild although temperatures drop a lot after sunset; even then eating out-of-doors can be a real pleasure.

Watch out for 'Le Mistral', particularly in the Rhône Valley. It emanates from the cold air over the Massif Central and affects mostly the eastern part of the department. It can last 3, 6 or 9 days according to local information. If you are stuck with it, seek sheltered valleys. The consolation is that when it does blow, the sky will be clear. 'Le Midi' is the south-west wind which tends to bring heavy rain. In winter (December to February) the temperature drops dramatically the higher you get, snow being most prevalent in January/February.

The developed areas are mainly the Rhône, the Ardèche and the valley of the Eyrieux. In spring, the blossoms of peaches, apricots, cherries, pears and apples are a spectacular sight and apples and pears are frequently grown in cordons and recently kiwi-fruit. Buy fruit in season from roadside stalls or fruit co-operatives — cheap by the *plateau* or box. Grapes are cultivated mostly on small plots. In the period of harvest (*le vendange*) it is most interesting to see the local farmers taking their grapes on their tractors to the local *cave co-opérative*. (It is quite an experience to see how this operates — if you ask nicely, most *caves co-opératives* will let you stand by and watch.)

On the hills there is a mixture of deciduous and coniferous woods — oak, beech and chestnuts. In autumn you are likely to run over the fruit of the latter on the road. Don't gather them near a village or farm, as this is part of their livelihood. There is wild cherry blossom in spring and wild flowers are abundant including daffodils, pansies, violets, cowslips and orchids; hillsides are covered with many varieties of wildflowers in summer including broom and heather. There are also numerous varieties of wild mushrooms, but be warned: do not offend local people by gathering at random near villages; and if you find them, check with *pharmacies* who are very knowledgeable and usually display charts of those which are safe and those which are not. There are three particularly good varieties — *ceps*, *bolets* and *chanterelles*, all of which are quite safe, and delicious. They are often available in markets.

If you like dried flower arranging, the thistles are pretty (and prickly). Several variations: one much sought by the Ardèchois (therefore difficult to find) is one which grows close to the ground. It is called *porte bonheur* (bring-good-luck) and may be seen pegged to doors of houses in the countryside.

This is an area rich in wildlife. There are buzzards in the mountains, occasionally kites and eagles and also kestrels and magpies. Flocks of goldfinches are quite common, as are wheatears and stonechats in higher areas. Jays have colonies in some valleys. Blackbirds and thrushes have been hunted in the past and are less common (though hunting is now more restricted); black redstarts and bluetits, great-tits and robins are fond of leftovers. There are rabbits, hare and some deer in the forest though these are not easily seen. Local hunters also seek pigeon and wild boar, though the wild boar are rare and their haunts are only known to the locals, so don't expect to come face to face with one!

Several varieties of grasshopper can be seen; praying mantis, which are beautiful and harmless; large black flying beetles and small green ones, and large 'ladybird' types, fascinating for the observer. Cicadas 'sing' loudly in hot weather, and frogs may give you a chorus near streams and under bridges.

With a lot of water around, there are inevitably some mosquitoes, but these are not generally troublesome; flying ants may get attracted to outdoor lights at night. Lizards scamper everywhere over stone walls, mostly tiny, but there are some large green ones which are very beautiful and very shy. If you walk on hillsides and on scree, wear sensible shoes — there may be adders, but usually they are more afraid of you!

Most beautiful are the butterflies in summer. There are many varieties — they feed on the wild flowers and they are always attracted to washing lines. It is worth finding an identification book from a library if you are interested in the subject. Beautiful moths are also attracted by the lights at night, and there are many varieties which are not seen further north.

The history of the Ardèche goes back to the Neolithic age, evidence of which can be found in the valleys leading to the Rhône (the Ardèche and Chassezac in particular), and Neolithic cave paintings and dolmens can be found. The Gaulois, the Helvians and the Romans followed: the old city of Alba and the town of Les Vans are important archaeologically.

The Middle Ages provided many fortified sites, towns and châteaux, though many of the châteaux are now, regrettably, only ruins, having been destroyed in the Wars of Religion between 1562 and 1629. (It is common to find both Catholic and Protestant churches in some towns and villages.)

The department of Ardèche is bounded by the Rhône Valley in the east, the Massif Central in the west, the Cévennes in the south-west and Languedoc in the south. It is an area of great contrasts, and is a paradise for anyone interested in geology.

The Rhône Valley is an alluvial plain, most land being devoted to fruit and vegetables, and vines, though maize and sunflowers are also important. Climbing to rockier areas, lavender fields and small market gardens can be seen, on land carefully terraced to extract the maximum from inhospitable ground. Sunflowers are not grown as a commercial crop.

In the north — Haut Ardèche/Haut Vivarais — there is pasture-land for cattle and sheep. This is a granite area, reflected in the construction of buildings with 'fish-scale' roofs (of split stone). This feature is in contrast to the split pots (clay) roofs of the more southerly parts of the Ardèche. It is indeed a green and pleasant land, being a mixture of pasture and mixed woodland. Here, timber is the most important source of heating in winter and it is interesting to see the neat piles of logs alongside the farms and in the villages. Snow is all-pervasive in winter and villagers must be very self-sufficient. However, the snow brings some benefits because there is now an increasing interest in cross-country skiing.

Further south volcanic areas are encountered — still high pasturelands interspersed with volcanic peaks and sources of rivers from this immense watershed between Mediterranean and Atlantic. In spring the meadows are carpeted with wild daffodils, narcissi, orchids and pansies, which seem to appear overnight when the snow disappears. Once seen they are never forgotten. In autumn, the colours are spectacular because of the mixed varieties of woodland, and in summer, wildflowers abound.

The Ardèche in its early stages flows through some really wonderful basaltic formations, as do some of its tributaries. Visitors who are adventurous enough to follow some of these will be rewarded with some fantastic sights. South of the volcanic area 'Le Tanargue' is a mountain range composed of a mixture of granite and crystalline rock and has many interesting rockfalls. It forms the southern boundary of the river, and is transformed when broom is in flower in early summer.

To the east and south of Privas is limestone country — the Plateau du Coiron is fascinating in this respect, and there are unusual strata to be seen. It is a harsh area for agriculture, though there are sheep and goats, with maybe the surprise of a field of lavender or small farms in unexpected places. Travelling southwards to reach the Gorges of the Ardèche, observe what water does to limestone! Further south and west is a very dry limestone area with spectacular rock formations, caves, dolmens and prehistoric sites.

The Ardèche is not as well known gastronomically as many regions of France, but many of its wines are now available in the UK, and local produce is described in the next paragraph.

Charcuteries (delicatessens) are a feast for the eyes and the palate. Try *saucisson de montagne* — rather dry in texture but full of flavour and not too strong; *boudin* — a sausage, red or white (the red akin to black pudding), delicious boiled or sautéed, served with local vegetables; *sanglier* (wild boar) — sometimes possible to buy cuts in wine sauce which are tender and delicious. Also *pâté de sanglier*, pigs' trotters and *jambon cru* (raw ham) — deliciously prepared and presented; *pâtés* — local *pâté de campagne* (*not* heavily laced with garlic) and many local specialities also to seek out.

Cheeses are available from all regions of France, but for local specialities try: Tome, a hard mountain cheese; Fromage de Chèvre (goat cheese) from farms, markets or supermarkets; Cantal, Bleu d'Auvergne, Tôme and Roquefort from neighbouring departments.

It is a statutory requirement to state the source of vegetables with prices, so look for '*Pays*' for local produce on price tickets. In season, asparagus is quite cheap, and very good. Look out for huge cauliflowers for economical meals; also leeks, onions, carrots and white turnips. *Bettes* (or *blettes*) — more commonly known as Swiss chard — can be found in shops and markets. Tomatoes grown locally are usually better flavoured than those from other regions. There are also lots of courgettes and aubergines. Occasionally you may find something strange which looks like giant celery called *cardons*, traditionally used in the region at Christmas braised like celery.

Local chickens are fed mostly on maize and the skin is yellow — don't be put off — the flavour is very good. Guinea fowl (*pintade* or *pintadeau*) are delicious and an extremely good buy in both markets and supermarkets — quite a small one easily serves four people. Turkey (*dinde*) and pheasant (*faisan*) are readily available; rabbit (*lapin*) and hare (*lièvre*) can be found in markets. Quail (*caille*) are available in *charcuteries*. (*Caillettes* are something different — almost a French version of haggis!) Sometimes you will see '*grives*' or '*pâté de grives*'. This is wild thrush so don't buy if you don't like the shooting of these lovely birds.

The *boucheries* are excellent and offer cuts of beef, lamb and pork with no waste. Offal is good and, if you like the stronger taste, ox liver (*foie de génisse*) is excellent value. Those partial to hamburgers may choose their piece of meat and have it ground specially — ask for *hachée* — perfect for barbecues. If you are so inclined, there are horse-meat butchers (*chevalines*) in many towns.

Markets usually have stalls run by those whose source of fish is the Mediterranean. There are many varieties which are not usually found outside France — do try them even if the name is unfamiliar. Fresh tuna (*thon*) and mixtures for *bouillabaisse* can be found at these stalls. Try smallfry (*fritures*) and cook like whitebait, sautéed in a little butter. Oysters are available in profusion in season — they are regarded as a special dish for New Year (Réveillon).

Eggs from small shops and supermarkets are very good but those from markets are even better. Butter from farms may be found in markets, either unsalted or lightly salted.

The first purchase most people make at *boulangeries* is bread. Small local shops are better than those in towns. In the Rhône Valley area try *pognes* which are slightly sweet. Elsewhere *pain de campagne* or *campagnard*, or *pain de sièglе* (rye bread, a tough texture but delicious when eaten fresh). For local *pâtisserie*, try *tarte au châtaignes* (chestnuts), Ardèchois biscuits with almonds, or *beignets* (miniature doughnuts — a Christmas speciality).

The Ardèche is not specially known for vintage wines, but the term 'Côtes du Rhône' encompasses the eastern limit of the department. However, St Péray and Cruas produce good sparkling wine and St Joseph is reasonably well known. If you wish to try the wines from local vineyards, select from: Côtes du Vivarais (from the Gorges de l'Ardèche); Vins de Pays de l'Ardèche; and Vin d'Orgnac, or otherwise visit local *caves co-opératives* and take advantage of any *dégustation gratuit* offered before you buy — they are mostly cheap and very pleasant. If you are so inclined, you can buy in quantity, 5 or 10l (about 1 or 2gal) of the lowest alcohol content at incredibly low prices. Look for signs saying *vins en vrac* — take your own container or buy one there, tasting first! A *vrac* is a 5 or 10 litres container, usually plastic, but a water bottle would suffice.

In season, eat all you can of peaches, cherries, pears, greengages, redcurrants and melons (*Charentais* type). *Pêches blanches* (white peaches) are particularly good, and the cherries are dark and sweet. *Fruit co-opératives* will sell by the box (*plateau*) and there are roadside stalls — the latter are better and cheaper off major roads.

Privas is the centre for *marrons glacées*, try them in various forms:

crème de marrons; — tins or tubes; boxed and sweets (quite expensive); fruit bottled in brandy or *eau de vie* are specialities — not cheap but a delicious luxury; honey is a 'must' — preferably buy from farms or where you see signs for *miel de pays* (also available from *alimentations* and supermarkets). Flavours vary from one flower to another including acacia, heather, thyme, lavender or *'mille fleurs'*; *fromage de chèvre* (the goat's cheese mentioned above) is frequently signposted at farms. It is very good, rather dry in some forms, but sometimes you may find a very soft one (this is delicious eaten with a spoon with a sprinkling of sugar).

The Mountains and the North (Haut Vivarais)

Starting from Privas, take N104 to Aubenas/Le Puy. After about 10km (6 miles) just before Col de l'Escrinet, turn right on D122 (NOT N535) towards Mézilhac. This is a very winding road with splendid views into steep valleys and masses of broom in summer. At Col de la Fayolle there is a sign indicating that snow tyres are required in winter. Follow the road to Col de Quatre Vios at 1,149m (3,768ft), so you will be climbing all the way. This part of the road gets very icy in winter due to snow drifting onto the road. The *crêperie* here is a must, for pancakes and local produce and there is also walking in the woods, and a walk to a ruined château (signposted). In late summer bilberries may be gathered in the woods and near the roadside, but parking places are limited. Continue to **Mézilhac**, where there is a *teleski* (ski-lift) and walking tracks, and to Lachamp Raphaël — both have road junctions to Aubenas and Vals-les-Bains. Continue on D122 and junction with D378 to Le Gerbier de Jonc, 5km (3 miles). This is a volcanic peak which can be climbed on a marked footpath. There are several pleasant places to eat local specialities, and the source of the Loire — in an old farmhouse — can be visited (you may taste the water). Follow D378 to Mont Mézenc — the highest point is at 1,753m (5,750ft). There is a marked route — Les Pieds de Mont Mézenc — which can be followed for good views and Mont Mézenc itself can be climbed on footpaths by walkers.

A diversion can be made on D36 to **Les Estables** (the road to Le Monastier), a village which is expanding to accommodate those interested in skiing. There are also walking tracks (*Grandes Randonnées*) well marked in this area.

Next take the road to Fay sur Lignon (D410/D262). Here the route goes briefly out of the Ardèche, but not for long. Continue along the valley of the Lignon to join the road to **St Agrève** (D15) and turn right. After Mars you are back in Ardèche. The area around St Agrève is wonderful to explore: there are many woodland trails for walking and in winter it is described as a *Zone Nordique* with good cross-country skiing. Take time to look at the villages *en route* and note the change in buildings, from split pot roofs and thatch (*chaume*) in the south, to granite and 'fish-scale' (split stone) roofs in the north.

From St Agrève follow the D9 towards St Bonnet-le-Froid. At **Devesset**, there is a reservoir with sailing, wind-surfing, swimming and picnic areas. At St Bonnet-le-Froid 20km (12 miles) from St Agrève join N105 and turn right to Annonay, following the River Cance. **Annonay** was the original *préfecture* of the Ardèche, and it is a fascinating old town to explore. It boasts three heroes — Marc Séguin (1786-1883) who was a notable engineer (see Tournon), and the Montgolfier brothers (Joseph and Etienne) who were the first people to ascend in a hot air balloon. There are statues to these remarkable inventors in Annonay, and also a museum of local history which commemorates their work.

From Annonay go to Peaugres on N82 (towards Serrières) to visit a large safari park. It is not cheap as the entrance fee is per person, not per car, so it is worth allocating most of a day for the visit. There are picnic areas and restaurant and toilet facilities. From here, return to the Rhône Valley and N86 at Serrières, or find some minor roads which drop down into the valley.

The Ardèche: From Source to the Rhône

The Ardèche rises north of the road N102 from Aubenas to Le Puy near Le Col de la Chavade. The source is in the middle of scrub and on private property. However, it crosses N102 very soon and drops into the southern valley on the way to Aubenas. To see it in its infancy, take a small side road to **Astet** — a road not usually used by tourists — following the valley and then coming back to **Thueyts**. This is the best place to see the river. In the middle of an avenue of plane trees and opposite a *co-opérative des fruits* — follow, on foot, a sign to L'Echelle de la Reine. A footpath passes behind some houses and apartments and leads to a broad stone staircase (easy walking) dropping down to a Roman bridge (Pont du Vernade) where there is a deep pool for swimming and rocks for scrambling. Also a track (devious but fun) which goes over the hill on the south side. The basalt rocks here are very fine.

In Thueyts, park in a shady square and take advantage of the small shops and restaurants and pretty backstreets. As you leave, look for the *belvédère* at the eastern end, and park for an excellent view. There is also a marked footpath to L'Echelle du Roi, Le Pont du

A simple Ardèche village church

Diable (Roman bridge) and La Chaussée des Géants. It is not too difficult, but the ascent of L'Echelle du Roi is not for the overweight as you have to climb up through a small fissure in the rock — have good strong shoes and enjoy the effort! Towards Aubenas, it is possible to get to the river by taking a right turn, on a sharp bend, to **Mercier**. There is a pleasant camping site at the bridge and access to the river. A small road is signposted to Le Pont du Diable and La

Chaussée des Géants — note that parking is limited, but worth trying for a scramble down to the river where there is a sandy beach for paddling and deep pools. There are fine views of basalt formations here too.

From N102 a small diversion can be taken to **Neyrac-les-Bains**, a mini-spa specialising in the treatment of skin diseases. There is a good hotel/restaurant, camping, and pretty views. From this point, the visitor can continue to Aubenas through small towns, some with old textile mills, and with campsites on the river. However, if you wish to follow the river, there is an alternative: after the sign to Meyras (a small village possibly meriting a detour), when the road crosses the Ardèche, do not do so; go straight on (N536) to Montpézat and Burzet and the Château de Ventadour. At a corner, where the road bears left, there is a small parking area. Walk back a few yards to a gap in the wall and descend some steps to a sandy beach at the junction of the Ardèche and the Fontolière for a sandy shore, shallow swimming and a deeper pool. (This area can also be reached from the bend of N102 near to Pont de Labeaume, but you have to watch out carefully for it.) This is on the fringe of **Pont de Labeaume**, and in the village, off N102 is a Roman bridge and old church, dominated by the Château de Ventadour, which was important in the history of the area; it is being restored and likely to be open to visitors in the near future.

To follow the river from here, turn sharp right over the bridge and sharp right again to Vals-les-Bains via Arlix. There are several places to bathe and picnic, but you have to seek out parking spots. It is possible to climb up through Chirols to Vals — tortuous but with splendid views — or carry on through Arlix. **Vals-les-Bains** is a health spa and is quite sophisticated. Visitors don't need to take the waters — they may try them in kiosks in the main street. It is a good centre for touring, with numerous hotels, restaurants, two cinemas, a theatre, a casino, skating rink and gymnasium. It is the most important centre in France for the treatment of diabetes. In addition to all these facilities there are beautiful gardens to enjoy and shady cafés in which to while away your time, as well as good local shops and there is a *source intermittent*, a spring which appears every 6 hours. The therapeutic value of the waters was discovered in the seventeenth century and many famous people have been visitors. The climate is mild and dry.

Go now to **Aubenas**, a charming market town with a lot of history. From its hilltop site there are wonderful views over the valley of the Ardèche and there is a panoramic point/orientation table. The town

The château and Hôtel de Ville at Aubenas

is dominated by its château, the oldest part dating from the twelfth century; there is also the Dôme St Benoit (formerly a Benedictine monastery, dispersed at the time of the Revolution), a 25m-high (82ft) *donjon* (keep) with two large towers, a Renaissance courtyard and an eighteenth-century staircase. There is an excellent market in the square by the château (now the Hôtel de Ville) on Saturdays, with people coming from a wide area. Go early to find a parking place or be prepared to walk a little — it is worth the effort. The most interesting stalls will be out of stock by noon. The market spills over now into the pedestrian areas of the old town, but on other days these are pleasant to explore for shops with basic requirements, local specialities and good quality souvenirs. There are two good cinemas, one with four screens, the other with two. Programme times are, however, a little difficult to understand and are usually at 9pm but vary. One of them, Le Navire, also has a pleasant restaurant/bar. The Syndicat d'Initiative (Information Office) is at Centre le Bournot, an old school building, which also has a small theatre and exhibition space — check for details at time of visit. There are several pleasant restaurants which are reasonably priced and an excellent pizzeria for more casual food. (Here you will also find one of the few 'washeterias', ie launderettes.) Most French banks are represented as well as a large post office; a modern hospital; a bus station; and a whole street with agents of most European cars for service and advice. The cathedral is very fine and has occasional organ recitals and international concerts. There are several hotels and restaurants, and pleasant camping sites nearby (particularly on the hills southwest of the town).

This first section of the route will take some time if the diversions are followed, so if time is limited, the next section could be explored separately.

L'Ardèche-Aubenas to Rhône

To visit the Gorges de l'Ardèche, take N104 from Aubenas to Alès. At St Etienne de Fontbellon you may care to stop to visit the church where there is a splendid organ and sometimes recitals. Then, turn left on D579 to Vogüé, Ruoms, and Vallon Pont d'Arc. **Vogüé** is dominated by a château incorporating a seigneurial mill of 1458. There are medieval streets to explore, bathing, fishing, campsites and *gîtes rurales*. Do *not* cross the river here, but turn right on D114 to Ruoms. Halfway there take a diversion, turning right to **Balazuc**. This site was inhabited in prehistoric times; in the year AD1 it was discovered when the Roman road from Poitiers to Nîmes passed through. See the ruins of a Roman church, covered passages, ramparts and a *donjon*. The streets are narrow, therefore parking is limited, but by the river there is excellent swimming from a sandy shore.

Continue to Ruoms and see a beautiful example of limestone cliffs. The town itself is also very pleasant, with old ramparts and a Roman church. There are good beaches (and canoeing) between Vogüé and Ruoms as well as riverside camping and hire of *vélos* (two-stroke cycles). Nearby at **St Alban-Auriolles** is the Museé Alphonse Daudet at Mas de la Vignasse (Alphonse Daudet wrote *Lettres de mon Moulin* and other novels). It was his family home and contains many interesting documents as well as collections of old tools for milling grain, and shows the history of the silk industry and domestic life in the nineteenth century. Also nearby, the River Chassezac joins the Ardèche. To find the 'join' is a test for the map reader. It is quite complicated, but if you get there, well worth the trouble. The visitor can bathe on a shingle river bed with some deeper pools when the water is high.

From Ruoms proceed to **Vallon Pont d'Arc**. In July and August this is the busiest place in the Ardèche; enthusiasts for canoeing and naturism come from all over Europe and the population increases tenfold! However, the town itself has pleasant old streets and good restaurants; the campsites are numerous and excellent, and offer entertainment during summer. It is recommended to those who want to be involved in activity holidays and meeting other campers, but it is possible to bypass the town if you are touring and want to get to the Gorges. It is clearly signposted, near a factory processing grape skins for use as fertiliser! This is the 'Route Touristique des Gorges' (D579) with the ruins of 'Vieux Vallon' on the left merging into the hillside. Soon the Pont d'Arc 60m-high (197ft) is reached — formed through many centuries of erosion of the limestone. The river is normally very calm and camping sites in this area offer swimming, fishing, trips in canoes-kayaks and barges.

After the Pont d'Arc, the road winds for about 30km (18 $^1/_2$ miles); there are numerous places to stop to admire the view which are well signposted. (This road did not exist until the late 1960s, but it is now an accepted tourist route to those who know the area.) There are some interesting limestone caves to be visited around here and many places to visit, some of which will be briefly described.

The Château de **La Bastide du Virac** is a fourteenth and fifteenth-century château, partly furnished, which also contains a display of the life cycle of the silkworm, and historical documents and implements. A small shop sells lovely silk items — scarves, lampshades, pictures, etc — which are not cheap but are authentic. **Aven Orgnac**, an excellent cave, has easy access and good facilities. A museum of prehistory in course of preparation is due to open in 1988; near to Vallon, the Grotte des Huguenots, covers spelaeology, archaeology and prehistory. There is also a private museum covering the history of the silk industry. Also along the Gorges road is the Grotte de la Madeleine and, by turning off, towards St Remèze, is the Aven de Marzal (the latter now has an underground prehistoric zoo with life-size models). Also nearby is the Grotte de la Forestière which is signposted. If you wish to picnic, there are numerous tracks off into the bush, where you can be quiet, but there are no snackbars except for the occasional ice-cream van or *crêperie* in parking areas.

After all these distractions, continue to **St Martin d'Ardèche** where the river opens out into the Rhône Valley. Here there is a fine sandy beach which you can drive onto via a concrete ramp. There is a somewhat complicated road system here, but it is worth finding Route D901 to Pont St Espirit, which goes over the suspension bridge, to find the medieval village of **Aiguèze**. It is tiny, with old buildings, an interesting church view over the river from ramparts, small restaurant anbd ice-cream parlour. This is the border of the department, but there is one thing left to try — the confluence of the

Ardèche and the Rhône, though this is, in fact, just outside the limit of the department. Continue to the junction with N86 at St Just, then turn left towards Bourg St Andéol. After about 2km (6 $^1/_2$ miles), just before a level crossing and opposite a garage, turn right along a small road. Follow it to the end and then bear left. On the right is a stone gateway to a house called Les Mouettes. Park nearby and look for a little track to the right to a small bridge where there are some quite steep steps down to the river. Be warned, however, that it is not easy to find.

Privas to Aubenas and the Plateau du Coiron

This is not strictly a tour, because it dots around, but it does suggest points of interest.

There is a misleading sign at Le Pouzin concerning the road to Privas which shows straight on. This is via Chomerac. To go to Privas direct, follow the sign to Aubenas which also shows 'Privas par la vallée de l'Ouvèze'. The visitor will pass through a number of small villages on this route. As the road climbs, divert to **Coux**, a very interesting medieval village — it is necessary to park and then walk to reach it.

Privas is now the *préfecture* of the Ardèche. It has been the centre of production of *marrons glacées* since the reign of Louis XIV, the industry having been developed by Olivier de Serres in the nineteenth century. The history of Privas is closely connected with the Religious Wars. It was a fortified town for the Protestants after the Edict of Nantes in 1598 and was razed by Richelieu's troops. Diane de Poitiers inherited the sovereignty of Privas in the sixteenth century, although she never actually lived there. Most existing buildings are eighteenth century, classical in style and there are many sidestreets to explore and a beautiful eighteenth-century bridge. There are various *fêtes* during spring and summer, and at the beginning of December a *Fête de la Rôtie Géante des Châtaignes*, when chestnuts are grilled and offered to the public with *vin rosé*! There is sometimes a 'cherry auction' in June, but check locally. A cinema (three screens), a municipal theatre, and a good swimming pool can also be found here.

To explore north of Privas take D2/D344 to Les Ollières and St Sauveur. At **Pranles**, visit the Musée du Vivarais Protestant. This old house, birthplace of Pierre and Marie Durand, prominent Huguenots, contains many historic documents concerning the Protestant struggles.

There is much more to see south of Privas, and a choice of routes.

Mirabel and the Plateau du Coiron

The D2 goes to **Chomérac**, towards the Rhône — a pretty village, with an occasional market. The first silk mill in the Ardèche was established here in 1670. At **St Symphorien sous Chomérac** there is a museum showing the history of basketmaking, for domestic and commercial use. A few kilometres after Chomerac, on D2 to Meysse, take a small diversion, on left, to **St Vincent de Barres**, a small medieval village in a hilltop, with well cared for, ramparts of the old village, a pretty church and lovely views.

The D7 goes to **Villeneuve de Berg** to visit the Auberge Musée de Verdus. This is a private museum, in an ancient barn, displaying farming implements and domestic utensils from the eighteenth and nineteenth centuries; it is well worth a visit. Food and drink can also be bought there.

Starting again from Privas, cross the Plateau du Coiron and N104 to Col de l'Escrinet (787m, 2,581ft). At the Col there is a two-star hotel and restaurant with splendid views towards the south and south-west. However, regrettably, they do not have a bar for casual drinks at present. For this the visitor should seek bars on the way up or down. There are not many (a bar advertising 'Repas Rurale' is very popular and expanding) but the numbers may increase.

Those who like a good walk and a rough scramble should take D122 towards Mézilhac just before Col de l'Escrinet. Follow the second paved road on the left (after Maison Cantoniale de Cholet) through to a farm then park, and take a footpath to the Roc de Gourdon — it is a rough scramble but on a clear day you can see as far as the Alps and the Massif Central.

From the col, continue on N104 towards Aubenas. In about 6km (4 miles) go right on D536 to St Michel de Boulogne, a splendid ruined château with thirteenth-century *donjon* and seventeenth-century gateway. At the corner where the château is first seen a small track leads down to the tiny River Boulogne, where you can scramble on to the rocks, picnic and swim in a good pool when there is enough water. At **Vesseaux** there are tennis courts which can be hired (contact the Mairie); the *cave co-opérative* sells local wine; and the church has a simple interior and a beautiful tiled roof.

Carry on to St Privat, amid vineyards and peach orchards, and turn left by a sign for 'Garden Center'(*sic*) on D259 to Lussas. The garden centre itself is worth a visit for seeing local trees, but also for the fact that it is at the confluence of the small River Luol and the Ardèche. Walk to the end and turn left.

The climb to Eyriac and Lussas has many hairpins and stupendous views, and **Lussas** itself, though small, is quite lively. The Mairie is sometimes an art gallery and there is usually a weekend market. There are also local fairs and a film festival in May and September.

There are many things to see on the Plateau du Coiron, and here are some recommendations: at **Darbres** there is good camping; **Freysennet** is a typical village; **Mirabel** has a tower of volcanic rock, privately owned, which is being restored; there are also lavender fields and fossils on tracks. Spend some time meandering , you will be well rewarded.

Villeneuve de Berg (on N102) was very important in the eleventh to fourteenth centuries and there are relics of the Wars of Religion. Olivier de Serres (called the 'father of French agriculture') was born nearby; there is a statue to him in the town and a museum at his birthplace is signposted.

Lavilledieu (N102) has existed in its present form since the sixteenth century. In the eleventh century it had a Benedictine convent which was devastated during the Wars of Religion. In 1944, during the withdrawal of occupying troops, many houses were burned and their inhabitants killed. Nearby, there is Le Petit Musée du Bizarre — it is somewhat bizarre, but exhibits local art and sculpture by young artists.

Alba, just off N102, is a prehistoric and Roman site. Destroyed in the second century, it became important again in the fourteenth under the Bishop of Viviers. The present château is sixteenth century, and archaeological sites are being investigated, with some important finds. There are several small camping sites nearby and small hotels and restaurants. The villages around Alba are also well worth exploration.

The Western Ardèche

From Aubenas take N102 and follow it through Thueyts and Col de la Chavade. After another 10km (6 miles) stop at the Auberge de Peyrebeille. This now modern hotel/restaurant has a rather grisly history, for in the nineteenth century the proprietors regularly killed their visitors in order to get their money! The original building is preserved and for a small donation you will be shown the old rooms where this happened. The proprietors were eventually guillotined in the courtyard. The old building contains a shop selling local produce, in what was the kitchen, and the present hotel provides good food.

Just after this, turn right on D16 to Coucouron. A crossroads shows a sign to Lac d'Issarlès, the eventual destination of this tour, but in the village find a small road left to the Lac de Coucouron, a small reservoir, which is a good picnic spot, down a rather bumpy road. From the village, continue to Lac d'Issarlès on D16.

An alternative route from Aubenas would be to take the N102 to Pont de Labeaume, then go right on N536 over the bridge, to **Montpézat**, where there are some find old buildings and a twelfth-century church; also walking tracks, river bathing and a *fête* in mid-August. After Montpézat, in $7^1/_2$km ($4^1/_2$ miles) at Le Roux, take D160 through a tunnel to St Cirgues en Montagne. (The tunnel was originally designed for a railway but the plan was abandoned in World War I and it is now a road.) Follow to **La Palisse** where there is a large reservoir with some water sports. Continue on D116, a winding road, to the village of **Issarlès** and Lac d'Issarlès, which is a lake in a volcanic crater. There is swimming from sandy shores, sailing, a walk around the lake, and good camping shops and restaurants. There are also *fêtes* in June, July and August. This spot is very popular at weekends with the Ardèchois.

The visitor is now near the western limit of the Ardèche. See signs for Le Monastier where Robert Louis Stevenson began his *Travels with a Donkey in the Cévennes* (see chapter 8). Also, just in the Ardèche, near La Bastide-Puylaurent (south of Langogne on D906) is the Cistercian abbey of Notre Dame des Neiges where Stevenson sought refuge. It is now quite a commercial enterprise, with its own sawmill, farm and vineyard. The old buildings are preserved; the shop sells their own honey, wine, jams, and other local specialities. It is a very pleasant visit.

The Valley of the Doux: Tournon, Lamastre and Le Chemin de Fer de Vivarais

There are two ways to take this interesting trip, which follows the valley all the way and enables the visitor to enjoy the steam railway. It is not cheap, and will occupy a whole day, but should appeal to all ages.

The first way is to take the steam train from Tournon early in the morning, spend about 4 hours in the town of Lamastre which is interesting, and walking nearby, and return to Tournon in the afternoon. The alternative is to drive from Sarras, on N86 and follow D221 to Ardoix and St Romain d'Ay, following the small River Ay. There are pretty gorges and places to picnic by the river. Then continue to Satillieu (where the Salle Don Quichotte has interesting tapestries, and where there is an old town to explore). Next to Lalouvesc, where the *basilique* is a centre for pilgrims; there is a nineteenth-century convent and an orientation table describing the Cévennes and the Alps. This is a walking centre, bicycles may be hired, and there is tennis and fishing.

It would be possible to go from here to St Félicien on D532 (10km, 6 miles) where there is good camping, accommodation, a Friday market and a dog fair in July. However, the picturesque way to Lamastre is to go straight on where D532 turns east, on to the D236, where the views are wonderful. After 7km (4 miles), near Col de Buisson at the junction of C6 to Molières, is a miniature Ardèchois village, which is very beautifully executed.

Go then to Lamastre to pick up the steam train. An explanatory leaflet at the ticket office (produced in English) tells you what to look out for. The 33km (20 mile) route takes 2 hours, with a stop for refreshments half-way. This afternoon steam train gives a very short break at Tournon and return on a rail-car to Lamastre.

Le Tanargue

From Aubenas, take N102 towards Le Puy. After Labégude turn left just before Lalevade (D19 to Prades and Jaujac and 'Le Croix de Bauzon'). At Jaujac, take care: there is a conglomeration of roads in the village. For this tour, take D19 left to La Souche (ignoring Pont de Labeaume and Largentière). At La Souche, cross the River Lignon and then start to climb. At the top, after climbing over 800m (2,600ft) there is a small road to the *teleski* and the forest. Here, in summer, are numerous marked walking tracks through the forest; in winter, this is now a popular resort for both downhill and *ski de fond* (cross-country skiing) particularly during school holidays. It is also a wonderful place to walk and picnic, with many quiet places with spectacular views, and there are good restaurant facilities.

Return to the main road and continue west to a fairly major road junction. D239 to the right takes you back to N102 (Le Puy/Aubenas), but instead, turn left on D24 to Col de Meyrand. There are many places to stop for views and picnics on the south side of this mountain range and a very clear orientation table. The villages *en route* show the typical, and hard, rural life.

If you have exhausted your time, either take N104 back to Aubenas or your base or continue to Largentière (covered in another tour) via Valgorge, for walking and seeing the pretty River Beaume which offers swimming, fishing and camping.

The Valley of the Eyrieux

This valley enjoys the reputation of having planted the first peaches in France, in the late nineteenth century. They are delicious, and very cheap in season. From N86, north of La Voulte, at Beauchastel, take N103 towards Le Cheylard. In 3km (2 miles) **St Laurent du Pape** boasts two *châteaux* — du Bosquet (sixteenth century, a classified historic monument) and d'Hauteville. There are also two notable potteries, fishing, river, bathing, handball, tennis and *boules*, hotels/restaurants and camping. There is also Grande Randonnée 42 (GR42) for walking and horse-riding. Follow to **Les Ollières** at a bend of the river, a quiet village with pleasant hotels/restaurants and good walking. Here, either turn south towards Privas via Pranles, or follow this lovely valley to St Sauveur de Montagut. The road (and track of old railway) closely follow the river and views are excellent, but it is frustrating that access to the river is very difficult. If there is somewhere to park it may be possible to scramble down in places, so check in the villages with local people.

Nearer **Le Cheylard** the valley widens and there are camping sites near the river. This town is described as midway between the snow and the olive trees, and the climate is very moderate. It is an excellent centre for excursions on foot or on bicycle; there is fishing, bathing, tennis and a *boulodrôme*; municipal camping and small hotels and restaurants. There is a fair in mid-July, and regular organ concerts in the eleventh-century church.

Here, either turn north towards Lamastre on N578 or make your own way back to base.

Le Cascade du Ray Pic

From the northern end of Vals, take N578 towards Antraigues/ Mézilhac. After about $1^1/_2$km (almost a mile), turn left at a rather hidden turning onto the D243 to Labastide. This is the Route de Besourges. Cross the river and look for a place to bathe and picnic (there is limited parking and a scramble down to rocks, with a tiny waterfall and deep pool). Continue climbing to **Lachamp Raphaël**, stopping where you can to enjoy the views. On joining N535 to Le Puy, turn left, and almost immediately left again on D215 to Burzet, Vals-les-Bains and Aubenas towards the Cascade (signposted $7^1/_2$ km, $4^1/_2$ miles). Enjoy the sight of broom and heather in season. Approaching the Cascade, there is a small café/snack bar which is open in summer, and there is a marked parking area. This is a 20-minute walk along a good but sometimes rough track (so have sensible footwear). In spring, after melting snow or periods of heavy rain, the double waterfall falling over basalt rocks is really spectacular and is a paradise for photographers!

Continue on D215 to **Burzet** ($7^1/_2$km, $4^1/_2$ miles) which has a fifteenth-century church, a thirteenth-century *calvaire* (calvary) (with a procession on Good Friday) and a local fair at the end of August. There is also walking and fishing nearby. Continue to N536 and to N102 to get back to Vals or Aubenas.

The South — L'Ardèche Meridionalè

This area is particularly interesting geologically and archaeologically, but has charm for all visitors.

From Aubenas, take N104 towards Alès. South of Aubenas at **Lanas** is Aerocity, a theme park based at the old airport. Visit **Largentière** by taking a right turn, N103, via Vinezac (a pretty village with a château), and pass the silvermines (now closed) which gave the town its name. (It is also possible to get to Largentière from N104 via D5, after Uzer.) Do take the opportunity on the descent to the town to stop and look over the wall at the rooftops. There is good parking outside the entrance to the town, so do not attempt to drive around the narrow streets. Walk through the archway to find many interesting buildings as well as small shops and restaurants. There is a market in the square on Tuesdays. The château is twelfth century — check locally for visiting it — while the church is thirteenth century and well worth a visit. Much restoration of old houses, built of beautiful local stone, has been done recently and is still in progress.

Continuing south on N104, turn right on N104A at Lablachère to Les Vans, or after about 8km (5 miles) at Maisonneuve, take D252 signposted to Casteljau and Bois de Païolive. The latter is a 'limestone forest' with limestone rock formations which are named as resembling animals. It is possible to scramble here, but parking places are limited. The villages on this route are very pretty, particularly Banne and Casteljau.

Les Vans has many old streets and arcades and a *place* with plenty of parking. Shopping for necessities and souvenirs is good. The municipal museum is extremely interesting, covering archaeology, geology and local crafts as well as milling and farming machinery. A map in the museum shows the history of the area. On the main road, visit Grospierres — a very old village. Those interested can check at the local *mairie* where to see ancient dolmens.

As you reach the southern limit of Ardèche, on N104, visit Les Grottes de la Cocalière, south of St Paul-le-Jeune. These beautiful limestone caves may be seen on a conducted tour lasting just over an hour of easy walking. At the end of the tour the visitor returns to the start on a small train, and there is a good shop with excellent souvenirs of semi-precious stones (not cheap, but from the region), as well as a good restaurant and toilet facilities (including those for the disabled).

The Rhône Valley

Follow N86 from Vienne, west of the Rhône and enter the department at Le Péage de Roussillon. At **Charnas** there is a viewpoint across five departments on a clear day. There is also a beautiful church, *fêtes* in July, and clay-pigeon shooting (ball-trap) in August. **Limony** has two historic monuments: one to a slave adopted by his master; the second a remarkable silver cross.

Serrières is an old fishing village. Le Musée des Mariniers et de la Batellerie du Rhône, in the church of mariners shows some history of this area. Explore old parts of the town. Around Whitsun (*Pentecôte*) look out for *joutes* or jousting on canal barges, which is great fun. Four kilometres (2¹/₂ miles) further on at **Peyraud**, walk either from the church to Verlieux (2km, just over a mile), or from the old bridge, following the stream to a small waterfall. Nearby at **St Désirat** is an ancient cross behind the church and another superb view. The wine in this area is *appellation contrôlée*; St Joseph is excellent and not expensive. Look out for *dégustation gratuit* signs and try before you buy.

Ozon has a river walk and children's playground; a local *fête* in late August, ball-trap in May; and water skiing areas are being developed near the barrage. **Tournon** is dominated by the feudal château of the Counts of Tournon, perched on an enormous rock. This contains Le Musée de la Ville with many things of regional interest. Explore the town on foot — the old streets are pedestrianised: see the collegiate church with seventeenth- and eighteenth-century paintings; the Lycée Gabriel Faure with wonderful tapestries, and a Jesuit chapel. The original suspension bridge across the Rhône to Tain was the first iron suspension bridge in the world, designed by Marc Séguin of Annonay. It has been replaced by a more modern one, regrettably, but is still very fine. This is an excellent touring centre for both the valley and the mountains.

At **Châteaubourg** a medieval castle dominates the Rhône, and houses a pleasant and not too expensive restaurant. **St Romain de Lerps** has an orientation table, a château/hotel, camping and horse-riding. **Cornas** is grouped around its bell-tower, and there is a wine fair here on the first Sunday of December.

St Péray is famed for white sparkling wines. There are fairs in summer and autumn, and there are always *dégustation gratuit* signs on the roadside to tempt you to taste (and probably buy!) the local product. There are also riverside walks here, a heated swimming pool and many hotels and restaurants. Nearby, the ruined Château de Crussol is attainable by a marked footpath.

La Voulte sur Rhône is a commercial centre. Its fifteenth- and sixteenth-century château was badly damaged in 1944 and is in process of restoration. Park near the river and walk: there are many narrow streets and old houses. The church has a sixteenth-century bas-relief and the suspension bridge is said to be the longest in France. This is a sporting town and rugby, soccer, volleyball, basketball, motocross and *boules/petanques* are all enjoyed. There are also many hotels and restaurants, making it another good touring centre.

Le Pouzin was a Protestant stronghold during the Wars of Religion, and was burned and pillaged in 1628. In 1944 it was damaged again by American bombardment and burned by retreating German troops. The new Hôtel de Ville has an exceptional 'Salon de Mariages' decorated by a regional artist, and the church, though modern, has preserved the regional character. Nearby, sporting activities include water sports in a *bassin nautique* and there is tennis and a gymnasium. There are local *fêtes* in June and September and a torchlight procession on 14 July with folklore groups and fireworks. Many excellent camping sites and small hotels can also be found.

Viviers cathedral

Baix has ruins of a feudal château razed by Richelieu's troops; a seventeenth-century chapel; fifteenth- and sixteenth-century houses with frescoes; a Louis XIV fountain and a clocktower. Local *fêtes* are held during July and August.

Cruas has remains of eleventh-century buildings in the foundations of the church. (The abbey here was involved in the Huguenot struggles and suppressed by the Bishop of Viviers in the eighteenth century.) There is a nuclear power station development nearby (strongly opposed by local people). In summer there is a programme of guided tours, including walking to an old château at St Vincent de Barres (bearing the arms of Diane de Poitiers), camping, a swimming pool and *boulodrôme* and a *fête* at the end of July.

At **Meysse**, turn left to pass the old station to get to the Rhône. The track alongside is a very good place to picnic and watch the river.

Rochemaure should definitely be visited. It is a medieval town with a colourful history and a majestic château which is well-sign-posted. Pass under the Roman wall which runs down to the valley, park where indicated and do the last bit on foot. Also visit the Chapelle de St Laurent and Pic du Chenevari (507m, 1,663ft). These are pleasant and easy walks. This was an important centre for the silk industry for two centuries up to World War II, but now most people work in wool and synthetic mills, and at local crafts such as basket-making.

Le Teil was classified as a *bourg* (a small market town) in letters patent of Henry IV. There is a baptistry and old streets and the nearby church at Melas is ninth century. There are many hotels and restaurants, a municipal swimming pool, tennis and fishing, as well as camping, a *salle des fêtes*, cinema and dancing. Near Le Teil is the giant Lafarge cement plant, on both sides of the road, but it does not spoil the town and provides much local employment.

Viviers has existed since Roman times. The first cathedral and convent of Notre Dame de Rhône was constructed in the sixth century and the present cathedral is twelfth century. The Bishops of Viviers ruled a huge domain (hence Vivarais) and controlled all of the abbeys in the province. The old town must be visited on foot. From N86, turn on to the N86A towards Montelimar and then left to the parking area in the *place*. See the 'Maison des Chevaliers', with its beautiful stone carved façade of coats of arms. Off Grande Rue, climb the steps to the cathedral — the porch, choir and nave walls are all original. The altar and other parts are of marble. There are two splendid Gobelin tapestries, two huge chandeliers and fine stained glass windows. A very tranquil place.

Outside, walk to see the fine spire and take a path to the Vieux Château — its remaining tower looks over old rooftops and the Rhône Valley. It is sad that the town has become depopulated in recent years, but the remaining shops supply the essentials. The church of St Laurent has an interesting belltower; there are several hotels/restaurants; also facilities for tennis, *boules*, a swimming pool and canoeing/water skiing areas in course of development. Local *fêtes* are held in July and August.

After 7km (4 miles) turn west to **St Montan**. This very beautiful village is being lovingly restored by local conservationists. Park in the square and walk through the cobbled streets to see archways and buildings of beautiful golden stone. There is an eleventh-century château and two twelfth-century *chapelles* — all designated as historic monuments. Small shops sell locally produced articles.

Back to the main road, go to **Bourg St Andéol** — another Roman town. The body of St Andéol is interred in a sarcophagus in the twelfth-century church; a bas-relief of the god Mithra, a convent, a monastery and an ancient palace of the Bishops of Viviers can also be seen. There are markets on the quays of the Rhône on Wednesdays and Saturdays and a *marché aux puces* (flea market) on the first Saturday of each month. There are also wine fairs in July and September.

St Marcel d'Ardèche is described as 'still Vivarais but already Provence', as the valley and rugged country give way to olives, asparagus, citrus fruits, herbs. It is a charming and unspoilt village with good hotels, restaurants and camping sites nearby. Just before Pont St Esprit, the visitor leaves Ardèche and enters Gard. (See tour of the Gorges for confluence of Ardèche and Rhône.)

Further Information
— Ardèche —

Museums and Other Places of Interest

The Comité Départmentale du Tourism, Cours de Palais, Privas, 07002, can provide an excellent booklet entitled 'Musées d'Ardèche', published by the Conseil Départemental de la Culture.

Annonay
Musée César Filhol
Regional exhibits, featuring Montgolfier brothers and Marc Séguin.
Open: All year, Wednesday, Saturday, Sunday 2-6pm; July/August, every day. Allow 1 hour for visit.

Aubenas
Château and Dôme St Benoit
Open: Easter-July and September-October, Saturday 3-6pm, Sunday 10am to 12noon; July-end August: every day 10am-12noon and 3-6pm. Length of visit 45 minutes.

Aven Orgnac
Limestone Cave and Museum of Prehistory
Museum open: daily from 10-12 and 2-5pm. Open until 7pm July and August; caves 9am-12noon and 2-6pm in season. Wear warm clothing.

La Bastide de Virac (near Vallon)
Medieval *château,* partly furnished, showing life cycle of the silkworm.
Open: June-September every weekday, 10am-12noon and 2-7pm. Also Easter and Whitsun weekends

Bidon
Off route de Gorges
Prehistorama
History of Mans Evolution
Open: April to October 10-6pm. July and August until 7pm.

Chirols
On D253 above Vals les Bains
The Hill Museum
History of the use of rivers in the mill
industry in Ardèche.
Open: daily 3-7pm except Mondays
and Tuesdays June to October.

Davézieux
Near Annonay
Musée des Papiers de Canson et Montgolfier
The history of paper-making for which
Annonay was famous.
Open: All year, Wed and Sat 2.30-6pm.
July and August every afternoon.

Joyeuse
Near the church
La Chataignerie
Museum of daily life and customs and
particularly the many uses of chestnut
wood.
Open: May/June/September: 10am-
12pm and 3-6pm.
July/August: 10-12 and 3-7pm.
All year: Mondays 2.30 to 5pm. Open
until 7pm July and August.

Grospierres
Archaeological Museum
Open: July/August every day 3-7pm.

Lanas
Aerocity
Open: June to October from 10.30am.

Lavilledieu
Le Petit Musée du Bizarre
Modern art and sculpture.
Open: 10am-12noon and 3-6pm every
day in summer.

Marzal
Aven Grottes de Marzal
St Remèze
Underground museum of prehistory
and spelaeology, limestone cave and
now includes a prehistoric 'zoo' of life-
size models.
Open: May-September every day 9am-
12noon and 2-6pm.
March/November, weekends and
holidays; Wear warm clothing.

Pranles
Protestant Museum
Open: April-mid-June and mid-
September-November, Saturday and
Sunday, 2.30-6.30pm; mid-June-mid-
September every day, 10am-12noon
and 2.30-6.30pm except Sunday
morning.

Privas
Musée du Verdus
Agricultural and Rural Museum
Open: out of main season, Saturday
and Sunday 2-11pm; mid-July-mid-
September, every day, 2-11pm.
La Chapelle de l'Ancien Collège

Religious Museum (municipal)
Open: all year, Wednesday-Saturday,
3-5pm.

Municipal Museum
Geology and archaeology
Opening times not specified, check locally.

Soyons
Archaeological Museum of Digs in the Area
Open: May/June/September -
Wednesday to Sunday 10am-12noon
and 2-6pm.
(Picnic area available Sunday)

St Alban-Auriolles
(near Ruoms)
Musée Alphonse Daudet
Mas de las Vignasse
Family and local history.
Open: 10-11.30am and 3-4pm. July and
August until 6pm. Closed Tuesdays.

St Symphorien sous Chomérac
Art and history of basketmaking.
Open: April-October, every day except
Tuesday, 10am-12noon and 2-7pm.
Other times, weekends, or by arrange-
ment 2-5pm.

Serrières
Maritime Museum
Open: Saturday, Sunday and public
holidays-1st Sunday April-last Sunday
October 3-6pm. (Visit lasts $1^1/_2$ hours).

Thueyts
Place du Champ du Mars
'Ancient Ardèche'
History of life of farmers.
Daily visits all year round. Check locally.

Tournon
Museum of Regional History at the château
Open: April-end May, 2-6pm; September-end October, 2-5pm; June-end August, 10-12noon and 2-6pm.

Vallon Pont d'Arc
Grotte des Huguenots
Spelaeology
Open: June-September, every day 10am-7pm. One evening a week, there are slide shows and meetings, and occasional concerts.
Magnanerie

Silk museum, with guided tour.
Open: May-September 10am-12noon and 2-6pm.

Agricultural Museum
Historical tools and displays.
Open: Easter-end August, every day, 9am-12noon and 2-6pm.

Les Vans
Museum of Archaeology, Geology and Local History (Municipal Museum)
Open: July/August, Tuesday-Friday 10am-12noon and 1.30-5pm, Saturday 2-5pm. Other times, Thursday 2-5pm.

Villeneuve de Berg
Olivier de Serres Museum
In Mirabel Village
Developement of agricultural in Ardèche and tour of botanical.

The Bee World
Guided tours regarding history of bees and honey production. Open everyday.
For both of these, check Syndicate d' Initiative.

Vogüé Château
Old documents and archives of Ardèche
Open: Easter-July and September-October, Sundays 3-6pm; July-end August, every day 3-6pm.

La Voulte sur Rhône
4 Quai Anatole France
Musée des Fossiles
Outstanding collection. Closed Saturdays
Open: July/August 9-12.30pm and 2-7.30pm. Other dates 2-6pm.

Maps
Michelin: 969 Grandes Routes (for planning); 76 Aurillac-St Etienne; 80 Rodez-Nîmes both 1cm-2km; Green Guide-Le Vallée du Rhône gives very detailed information.

IGN — Institut National Géographique: 59 Privas/Alès 1cm-1km; see also Carte Topographique 4cm-1km — numbers 2836 to 3038.

Editions Didier et Richard: 21 L'Ardèche Méridionale: 2cm-1km (showing footpaths, etc).

Carte Département Orientation 07 — Editions Ponchet: This is a good overall map of L'Ardèche.

12 • Dauphiné

Starting with the Rhône Valley the province of Dauphiné progresses eastwards, through forested lowlands, pre-Alps and on to the high alpine regions close to the border with Italy. From Roche Bernaude, a 3,222m (10,571ft) peak on the Italian border, its northern boundary runs north-westwards towards but not encompassing Lyon, and joins the Rhône above Vienne. Dauphiné's eastern boundary follows the Italian border south to a point beyond Mont Viso, running roughly south-west towards the Rhône Valley.

Strictly speaking the term Dauphiné should have disappeared after the Revolution but as with the Savoyards to the north, the people who live in the three departments of Dauphiné insist on retaining the old region's name.

Grenoble is the capital of the Dauphiné and its three *départements* are: Hautes-Alpes in the east where, as the name suggests, one finds the highest mountains; Isère covers the Chartreuse, and the countryside of the Drôme is mainly the rolling forested hills of the Vercors.

Many of the wilder areas have been protected by being designated as either National or Regional Parks. To the east, the Parc Naturel Régional du Queyras is mostly high alpine pasture climbing to the foothills of 3,348m (10,985ft) Mont Viso. Many of the alpine flowers are protected species, blooming in profusion from the last snows to autumn, depending on their season. Road access is possible, but tricky. The Parc National des Ecrins covers the icy peaks surrounding La Meige and Mont Pelvoux. Road access is limited to a handful of very minor roads penetrating the park's lower valleys, and the N91 which skirts the northern boundary. The largest of the three parks is the Parc Naturel Régional du Vercors. Mostly wooded with pine, larch and beech forests, this is also a region of wide-open spaces and remote upland valleys topped by airy plateaux.

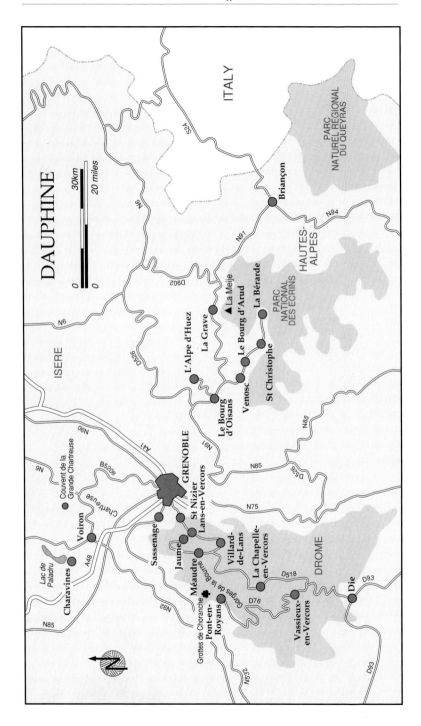

Hautes-Alpes

A high-level road the D902, often closed by snow until early summer, leaves Savoie and climbs southwards out of the Arc Valley towards the 2,642m (8,668ft) high Col du Galiber. All eyes will be pointed towards La Meije; 3,983m (13,064ft), the Dauphiné's highest mountain. This peak of almost vertical glaciers and jagged crags rears in splendid majesty above the headwaters of the Romanche. Intensely blue glacier ice contrasts with the blinding white of permanent snowfields; while through them carve shining black rocks, defeating, if only for a millennium or two, the inexorable advance of ever moving glaciers.

The D902 joins the busy N91 on the Col du Lautaret. Here an alpine garden run by the University of Grenoble contains many of the flowers found in the Alps and high mountains around the world.

One of the places where you might find the elusive delicate blue flower, King of the Alps (*eritrichium nanum*), is near the Refuge Chancel, an alpine hut which stands on a high crag above the little village of **La Grave**. The inhabitants of La Grave have come to terms with the grind of traffic as it slowly winds its way along the N91 towards the Col du Lautaret. Many of the roadside hotels, built when travel was more leisurely, have terrace restaurants which turn their backs on the road. Below are the rushing waters of the Romanche and a valley which fills with wild narcissi every spring. Above the river, the dark green of pinewoods lead the eye to rocky slopes topped by blinding-white summits. What better place to enjoy the local cuisine?

Seven walks around La Grave which are suitable for families are described in Brian Spencer's *Walking in the Alps*; published by Moorland Publishing. The guide also describes enough things to do to make an enjoyable 10 to 14 days holiday in the area.

A narrow side street climbs to La Grave's pretty fourteenth-century church and its sixteenth-century chapel with the graves of climbers, including Englishmen who died trying to conquer the cruel Meije. The church commands a clear view of the lower valley and local tradition links it with early settlers' attempts to avoid religious persecution. Certainly most of the surrounding villages seem to confirm this theory, built as they are on elevated terraces.

Roads leading to villages above La Grave peter out before reaching the limits of the high valleys. Beyond the road ends footpaths lead on towards remoter settlements or mountain huts. One of these paths, part of the GR54 long distance footpath around the Meije (the Tour d'Oisans), leaves the road at Le Chazelet Crossing the Valley of the Ga, the path climbs steeply towards the top of a ski-tow.

Admiring the scenery at La Grave

Beyond it a contouring path leads to the Plateau d'en Paris where a pool Lac Noir, creates a mirror image of La Meije. An alternative path for the return of Le Chazelet climbs the nearby eminence of Serre Bernard where a shaly ridge continues to Cime du Rachas. The ridge and plateau are particularly good areas for alpine flowers. Amongst the many varieties you should find several types of anemones, including the bright yellow sulphur variety.

Directly below Le Chazelet a fieldpath leads to an isolated oratory chapel built on a narrow ledge, the Chapelle de Notre-Dame de Bon Secours. A steep path descends the rocky hillside, past a dramatic waterfall, the Saut de la Pucelle, the Maiden's Leap, to join the main road at Les Freaux. The old road crosses over to the opposite side of the valley at this point. Now a simple cart track, where notices ban the unauthorised gathering of *escargots* (edible snails), the old track can be used to avoid walking along the main road.

Traffic frustrated by the slow uphill grind along the Romanche, thunders its way down the Guisane Valley on the opposite side of the Col du Lautaret. If, as by magic you could transport your car by itself, or more realistically, arrange local transport, there is an excellent way to avoid at least part of the N91. From La Grave a side track crosses the valley to join the old road. Turn left along the old road and follow it as far as a footbridge below the hamlet of Le Pied du Col.

Cross the bridge and immediately turn right to follow the Romanche river. This path gains close views of the eastern face of La Meije, and climbs steadily to the French Alpine Club hut of the Refuge de l'Alpe du Villard d'Arene. You could stay the night here, but it is only about 9km (5½ miles) over the Col'd'Arsine to reach the main road. The path onward from the hut leaves the Romanche and follows its tributary the Planche, almost to its source below the col. The path continues, steeply at first, downhill into forest, then out into meadowland near the village of Le Casset. The main road is only about a quarter of a mile away, beyond a belt of woodland. This walk which is about 21km (13 miles), has a total ascent of 898m (2,946ft), and the total walking time is about 6 hours.

The area to the west of the Guisane Valley and the N91 is certainly worth exploring by those in search of out of the way places. There are no through roads apart from the D994g which winds its way along the wooded Clarée Valley. Beyond Plampinet a right turn on the D1 climbs up to and over the little-used Col d'Echelle into Italy.

Tracks lead away from the Clarée Valley to mountain huts and a range of high peaks culminating at 3,178m (10,427ft) Mount Thabor. Unspoilt villages along the main valley will reward the attentions of all who explore this remote alpine region. Ancient chapels still watch over the daily lives of the inhabitants, and a waterfall at Queyrellin a few miles from the road-end more than justifies the long drive. As well as mountain huts, simple hotel accommodation can be found in one or two villages in the main valley.

Standing on the site of the Roman town of *Brigantium*, the oldest part of **Briançon** still commands the road to the Col de Montgenèvre, an important route into Italy. The highest town in Europe situated at 1,321m (4,334ft), it was fortified by Vauban the military engineer, in the early years of the eighteenth century. During the Napoleonic wars, British and Allied nationals, both soldiers and civilians, were held captive in Briançon. Many suffered the privations of incarceration, but those wealthy enough were able to live comfortably, and formed a lively society to ease the burdens of imprisonment.

The old part of Briançon, La Ville Haute, or High Town, is traffic free. There is a car park on the Champ de Mars and the best way to enter the old town is through the Porte Pignerol. Beyond it is the main street, the Grand Rue. Beautiful period houses line the precipitous street, down which flows a channelled stream known as the Grande Gargouille. Making an interesting foreground to the houses and popular with boat-sailing small boys, it has not always been so attractive. Its original purpose was as a convenient sewer!

Lac Noir and La Meije, the highest mountain in Dauphiné

The Church of Notre Dame stands to the right of the main street. Built by Louis XIV's great military architect, Sébastien Le Prestre de Vauban, it is part of the town's fortifications, and has twin towers and hardly any windows. To the left is the Citadelle which stands impregnable at the top of a rocky slope. Approached through the Porte Dauphiné, it dates from 1841. A large statue, *La France*, sits proudly above the Citadelle and close by it there is an orientation map showing all the peaks of the surrounding district. The statue is illuminated as part of a *son et lumière* which takes place Tuesdays to Saturdays in July and August. Details of this and tours of the town may be obtained from the Tourist Office on the Grande Rue.

Briançon marks the division between the main French Alps and the Southern and Maritime Alps. Three mountain torrents, the Guisane, Clarée and Cerveyrette join near Briançon to form the Durance, a tributary of the Rhône which it joins near Avignon. With the exception of the Cerveyrette, each valley is followed by a major road. The road along the Cerveyrette is the D902, which follows the valley east to Cervières. Here it leaves the main valley and turns south to climb the 2,360m (7,743ft) Col d'Izoard.

The col with its museum of cycling, marks the northern entrance to the Parc Naturel Régional du Queyras. The most isolated of all French National Parks, its title comes from the local dialect for 'the large crag'. With rolling forested hills to the north and west, and with moderately high peaks along the Italian border in the east, the park is a wildlife haven. In late June the alpine flowers bloom in profusion, each within its specific environment. In the lush meadows globeflowers, anemones, campions and cornflowers vie with each other to make a blaze of colour. With the increase in altitude carpets of forget-me-nots, cowslips and huge yellow gentians grow above the sparser grasses. The sharp flavour of the yellow gentian is used to make the aperitif *Suze*. Higher still and into the blue gentian zone, and beyond to the tiny cushion plants such as those of the saxifrage family. A special feature of the park is its butterflies, many not found anywhere else in Europe.

Traffic is banned from some of the more sensitive areas of the Queyras National Park. For example, in order to reach the high Couloir du Porc and the Refuge de Viso beneath 3,841m (12,602ft) high Mont Viso, it is necessary to park your car at the Petit Belvédère de Viso. A shuttle service continues along the rest of the surfaced road to the Belvédère where a footpath continues towards the alpine hut. Tunnels take the D902 westwards along the Combe du Queyras and out of the National Park, down to the Durance Valley and the busy N94. This road follows the valley as far as the huge man-made lake of Lac de Serrie-Ponson. In its pine-forested setting it makes a tranquil contrast with the snow-capped mountains to the north.

Joining the N85 at Gap, the N94 skirts the southern arm of the Ecrins National Park. Even though there are no through roads, valleys cut deeply into the park, and several of them can be used to gain access to many of the remoter areas.

The D994e leaves the N94 at L'Argentière-la-Bessée about 15km (9 miles) south of Briançon and follows the Gyronde Valley through the little market village of Vallouise to Ailefroide. From here a fairly easy path climbs up to the Refuge du Glacier-Blanc. As the title suggests, the refuge hut is at the foot of the glacier of the same name. From the hut an awesome river of convoluted ice and snow twists its way to a complex of summit ridges of the Barre des Ecrins.

Two other valleys give access to the southern part of the Ecrins National Park. The first is the Vallée du Drac de Champoléon, the headwaters of the north flowing River Drac, a river which appears to have been diverted from its original southerly course in post-glacial times. A flood plain and limestone strata below the forested hills of the Champs Aurm cause the river to temporarily disappear. The main road along the Drac Noir leaves the valley in order to reach the ski resort of Olcieres-Merlette, but a side road following the main stream, eventually becomes a footpath leading to the high-level, but accessible Champoléon hut.

The D985a, follows the Severaisse gorge along a narrow defile lined with ancient villages and where streams cascade vertically from the mountain sides. By using accommodation in the simple *Gîtes d'Etaps* in many of the villages, or mountain huts in the higher reaches it is possible to explore the southern part of the Ecrins National Park and the nearby Valgaudemar ridges. Food need not be carried in, most villages have a small shop. Even those without shops will have some system whereby basic supplies can be brought back by people who work outside their village. Almost every village has its own restaurant where you can sample the true *Dauphinois* mountain fare. Meals are simple but deliciously sustaining. Sausages, some with a mixture of meat and vegetables, called *pormoniers* are often served. *Polenta* a maize soup, is a good starter after a day on the hills, but the most sought after dish is *gratin Dauphinois*, a mixture of potatoes and milk sometimes topped by eggs and cheese and finished under the grill. The latter is considered by many not to be the genuine article. The real dish, according to purists should leave out the eggs and cheese, but whichever recipe is offered, it will be excellent. Bilberries (*myrtilles*), grow in profusion in the mountains, and a *tarte aux myrtilles* makes an ideal end to a memorable meal.

To the east of the N85 and north of the D994 near Gap, the upper rock strata is limestone. At Montmaur, the D937 climbs north from the D994 to an area where caverns attract specialist devotees to the sport of underground exploration. This area is a vast limestone plateau tilted upward to the north which ends at a precipitous cliff, the Crête de Samaroux. Using one of the few natural routes through this barrier, the road makes a dramatic plunge through the Défilé de la Souloise. Here the road, now the D537, enters the department of Isère by following the Souloise until its waters are arrested by the reservoir of Lac du Sautet.

Isère

The geography of the department of Isère is complex. Sharing the high summits of the Ecrins National Park at its most easterly point, it is roughly oblong in shape, aligned north-west towards the Rhône Valley. Westwards, mountain masses cut by deep and narrow valleys, gradually lose height until the deep trench of the Isère Valley marks the transition from alpine to the rolling sub-alpine ranges. Beyond this boundary, the hills become more wooded until agriculture takes over, with vineyards appearing on the steep south-facing valley slopes.

Grenoble, the administrative centre of Dauphiné and the capital of the Alps, fills a commanding situation, spilling beyond its original foundation around a tight bend of the Isère. The ancient city centre, now the commercial heart of the region, is traffic-free. The only vehicle allowed to cross the square is the *petit train de Grenoble* which threads its way around the city centre on a 35-minute run from the Place Grenette.

Grenoble along with neighbouring Vizille has a strong claim to be the birthplace of the French Revolution. In eighteenth-century Grenoble was the seat of government for the province. Fearing its power, on 7 June 1788 the king sent in troops to disperse its members, an act which so enraged the locals that they hurled roofing tiles at the soldiers, causing them to retreat in disarray. More troops were sent in to quell the riots, making it impossible for the Parliament to continue. Members moved out of the city and re-established Parliament at the Château de Vizille a few miles to the south-east along the Romanche Valley. In July 1788 the Parliament decreed that there would be 'No taxation without representation', and so began a national movement which culminated in the French Revolution of 1789.

The N91 crosses the departmental boundary between Hautes-Alpes and Isère near Lac Chambon, a reservoir held by a massively strong concrete dam built between 1927 and 1936. To the north of the dam tiny hillside villages reached only by steep alpine roads, once housed silver and lead miners.

One of the areas where silver and lead ore can still be found is around **L'Alpe-d'Huez**. Now a popular ski resort reached by a tortuously twisting road often used by the Tour de France, the village makes an excellent base from which to explore the archaeology of the district. Lumps of silver bearing barytes can be found near La Blanc. The lake marks the start of a steeply descending path towards Huez, passing several of the ancient mines, and can be reached by a cable car from the village. **Do not enter any of the mines. Long abandoned, they are dangerous**.

An archaeological dig on the Plateau de Brandes outside **L'Alpe-d'Huez** has discovered the remains of a medieval village, complete with its own defensive tower and chapel. Several of the important finds including a stone chesspiece, are on display in the village museum, La Maison du Patimoine. The museum has a permanent exhibition of silver mining, as well as temporary exhibits of village life in the Oisans district.

At the foot of the Gorges l'Infernet where the Romanche ceases to

The still waters of Lac Chambon

be an alpine river, a side road, the D530 turns south to follow the narrow valley of the River Vénéon deep into mountains of the Ecrins. The Alpine Centre of la Bérarde with its 5-star camp site sits at the road end. From there mountain paths radiate in all directions. Several climb high beneath the surrounding peaks, or wander beside glaciers, to welcoming alpine huts. At least five huts can be reached by walkers who want to enjoy the splendours of the high mountains, but without the need to become involved in any technical ice or rock climbing. The services of mountain guides can be arranged at the Alpine Centre in la Bérarde.

Moving back down the valley, many of the mountain guides live in **St Christophe**, home of Pierre Gaspard, who made the first ascent of the Meije in 1877. Lower still we come to the twin villages of **Le Bourg d'Arud** and **Venosc**. Marking the lower limits of the alpine course of the River Vénéon, the villages are home to the numbers of skilled artisans who have settled there over the years. Lute making is a speciality and on 11 and 12 August the Fête Artisanal shows off the locals' workmanship.

Le Bourg d'Oisans despite being the centre of tourism for the Central Romanche Valley, is still an important market town for the district's farming community. It is not uncommon to find haylofts at the end of the town's narrow streets, links with another era.

Valleraugue, with River Hérault, Cévennes

*Open-air market in
Aubenas, Ardèche*

Skiing in the brilliant sunshine, Savoie

The majestic peaks of La Meije, Dauphiné

Three side roads climb out of the Romanche Valley and into the mountains from points near Le Bourg d'Oisans. The well known road to L'Alpe d'Huez has already been mentioned, but there is another, less tortuous road which starts at Rochetaillée about 7km (4 miles) north-west of Le Bourg d'Oisans. This road climbs a gently wooded valley, by way of the Barrage Verney reservoir to the narrow pass of the Défilé de Maupas and the Combe d'Olle to the 1,924m (6,311ft) Col du Glandon, then down to join the Valley of the Arc in the Maurienne region.

A third road, the D526 leaves the N91 at La Paute to climb steadily south over sparsely forested hills and across high alpine pasture bordering the Ecrins National Park to the Col d'Ornon. Beyond and through Le Périer where a side road leads to the attractively situated waterfall of the Cascade de Conflens, the road leads to the attractively situated waterfall of the Cascade de Conflens, the road continues downhill and into the Bonne Maisanne Valley. This is the Valbonnais district and at the village of Entraigues, the road and side valley enter the Valjouffrey Valley in its gentler lower reaches and follows the river to the main road at La Mure.

The main road through La Mure is the N85, better known locally as the Route Napoleon. This is the road Napoleon took on his return to France from Elba in 1815. When he reached the village of Laffrey, Napoleon was met by a small army sent out from Grenoble under the leadership of General Dellessart. Seeing the troops, Napoleon strode forward, pulling back his greatcoat to expose the medal of the Légion d'Honneur pinned above his heart, crying, 'Soldiers, I am your Emperor! If there's one amongst you who would kill his general, here I am'. An equestrian statue of Napoleon, La Rencontre de Laffrey, marks the lakeside spot where this important meeting took place.

Grenoble may be a rapidly expanding industrial city, but as mentioned earlier, the central and oldest part has many traffic-free streets awaiting quiet exploration. The best way for first time visitors to view the old city is from the cable car, the Télépherique de la Bastille. From the Rue Berlioz beyond the Quai Créqui, cars rise from the river bank to the commanding heights of the Fort de la Bastille. From here the city spreads itself on the southern bank of a tight curve of the River Isère. Rooftops in all colours and designs indicate the age of their particular districts. Warmly hued pan-tiles on the irregular-shaped roofs of the oldest part of the city gradually give way to sharper outlines as the eye passes over centuries of architectural design to the present day.

There are numerous museums and ancient churches, and a maze

of narrow streets where the enquiring traveller can move on a voyage of discovery. Grenoble had its own Joan of Arc; Philis de la Charce who in 1692 helped save the Dauphiné region from attack. There is a statue of her near the gateway of the Port de la France, a tangible reminder that Grenoble was once a walled town. Moorland Publishing's *The Visitor's Guide to France: Alps and Jura* by Paul Scola has an easy to follow section devoted to the many facets of Grenoble.

On the eastern outskirts of Grenoble, a side road, the D524 climbs to the mountain resort of Chamrousse. Designed as a ski resort, with its proximity to Grenoble it becomes very crowded in winter, but less so in summer. A cable car from Le Recoin quickly reaches the summit of the Croix de la Chamrousse. This 2,257m (7,403ft) high mountain marks the southern limits of the Chaîne de Belledonne ridge which stretches north-eastwards for about 50km (31 miles) in an almost unbroken chain of moderately high summits and the inter-connecting ridges. There is a long distance high level footpath the GR549, linking Grenoble and L'Alpe d'Huez to the east. Taking 4 days to complete comfortably, the route passes mountain huts where overnight accommodation can be found without pre-booking.

The Belledonne range is dotted with numerous lakes, many secretively hiding in combes beneath the high peaks. One such lake, Lac Robert, can be reached by following a 3km (2 mile) footpath north from the summit of the Croix de Chamrousse. A longer walk, following the GR549 beyond Lac Robert to the Réfuge la Pra, where an overnight stay can be made, visits a number of small but attractive lakes and mountain pools. Keen walkers could continue along the Belledonne range for as long as time or ability allows, staying each night at one of the delightful mountain huts and remote inns along the way.

The land north of Grenoble rises rapidly into the Massif de la Chartreuse. The bed rock is limestone running roughly north-east-south-west. There is one major break in this mountain mass, La Grande Vallée de Chartreuse. Divided into *bassins* by ridges cutting across the main valley, each isolated commune within the region has developed its own distinct character. This is where St Bruno came in 1084 along with six companions to form a monastery, La Couvent de La Grande Chartreuse at the head of the Gorges du Guiers Mort.

It was the monks of La Couvent de La Grande Chartreuse who first developed the green and yellow 'Chartreuse' liqueurs, but since 1935 it has been made at the nearby town of Voiron. Still made from a secondary distillation of herbs and pine buds, the liqueur is stored in oak casks lining a 492ft (150m) long cave near Voiron. There is an interesting audio-visual show telling the history of the making of 'Chartreuse'. Open every day throughout the year, a visit to the caves also includes a free tasting of this exquisite liqueur.

The official *Zone de Silence* surrounding the monastery seems to extend well into the hills and forests of Chartreuse. There are footpaths and narrow winding roads galore, and high alpine meadows where brightly coloured flowers bloom before being sacrificed to the haymaker's scythe. This is a region for slow exploration, a region where each turning can offer something new, be it a quiet local village restaurant, or simply a scene which etches itself on the mind for ever.

North of the Isère valley and beyond Chartreuse, the character of the land changes from high mountain and pre-Alps to rolling forested hills which in turn give way to gentler slopes and plains towards the Rhône. **Voiron** marks this transition from mountain to lowland. An industrial town, nevertheless it has an interesting pedestrianised centre built around a Gothic style church and twin-spired town hall.

To the north of Voiron, the N75 leads towards Lac de Paladru where at the village of **Charavines** the well preserved remains of a medieval village were found in 1971. Interesting finds from this and earlier habitation going back to neolithic times, are on display in the Maison de Pays in Charavines.

From Charavines minor roads lead towards the A48-E711 autoroute. To the east and north of the motorway we come to the southernmost part of the Bugey. West of the motorway, the land is increasingly flatter, marked contrast to the highland zones further east. This is land flat enough to be used for the TGV railway track, so flat that unlike the standard mainline south along the Rhône Valley, the TGV super-fast track is mostly arrow straight, with only the widest bends to avoid unnecessary gradients.

Drôme

A region of high limestone plateaux, rolling forested hills and winding valleys, the Drôme department runs south from the Isère to the department of the Vaucluse. Its western boundary is the Rhône and to the east, the N75 roughly parallels its border with both of its sister departments, Hautes-Alpes and Isère.

The D93 Aspres-sur-Buech to Loriol-sur-Drôme road roughly divides the department in two, both politically and geographically. To the north the land is mainly high limestone plateau, and to the south tiny rural villages and the scattering of ruined châteaux speak evocatively of a land where time appears to stand still.

South-west of Grenoble, the **Parc Naturel Régional du Vercors** is a roughly triangular region of forested valleys topped by barren limestone plateaux, measuring about 64km (40 miles) from north to south and 40km (25 miles) from east to west. The Vercors is divided roughly in two distinctly differing zones by the River Vernaison. This river which rises somewhere beneath the 1,734m (5,689ft) Tête de Faisan has carved a deep trench through the surrounding limestone, and winds its way north to join the Isère. South and east of the Vernaison lies the highest and most arid of the two plateaux of the Vercors. That to the west of the river is lower and more lush, with beech and larch as well as the ubiquitous pine trees filling its ancient woodlands.

As would be expected the limestone rocks are riddled with caves and potholes. The most famous is in the north of Vercors, the Gouffre Berger above **Sassenage** to the west of Grenoble. The pothole and its related caverns have been explored by the Seine Caving Club to a depth of 1,200m (3,936ft), a depth which for many years was held as a world record. Although these are the restricted terrain of the specialist explorer, nevertheless there are many caves in the area which are illuminated and open to the public.

Farming is mostly dairy and beef, but sheep are reared both for their milk as well as wool. The local cheese made from ewe's milk is Fromage de Sassenage and is not unlike Roquefort.

The natural defence offered by the remote plateaux and high crags was used by the French Resistance during World War II. A constant threat to German troop movements, the Resistance harrassed the enemy so severely that in July 1944 the Germans mounted a massive attack on their mountain fortress. After heavy losses on both sides the Resistance were eventually defeated, mainly through lack of supplies. The graves of 193 Resistance fighters who fell in the battle of July 1944 are in the Cimitière National du Vercors near **Vassieux-en-Vercors** in the centre of the region. There is also a dramatic memorial at the head of a deep combe leading to the steep eastern escarpment of the eastern plateau.

Anyone staying at Grenoble can make the city their base when exploring the northern Vercors. Leave the N532 at Sassenage to the west of the city for the D531; this latter road leaves the town to climb a series of sweeping bends towards the Gorges de Furon. However, before venturing towards the high plateau country, time could be well spent exploring some of Sassenage's caverns and its stately home, the Château de Bérenger. Many of the caverns, some linked to the famous Gouffre Berger, have pools within their depths, known locally as *cuves*. One cave system near the château has a beautiful waterfall which is romantically associated with a mermaid called Mélusine who was murdered by her earthling husband. She is supposed to have lived in the waterfall, and that the *cuves* are her tears. Regretfully and for safety reasons, children under 6, even those accompanied by their parents, are not allowed into the cave.

The road follows the lovely River Furon where flowery riverside meadows are made for picnics, out of the valley to a low col marked by the village of **Jaume** where there is a museum of mechanical dolls, La Magie des Automates.

West of Jaume a side road the D106, winds through the Fôret de Guiney to the villages of Autrans and Méaudre. Both villages offer activity holidays ranging from caving to archery, and where the local terrain is ideal for cross-country skiing in winter. **Méaudre** prides itself in staging unusual events, which range from a Beer Festival in mid-July to goat-racing in late August. Details of these and other events in both villages can be obtained from the local Syndicat d'Initiative.

South of Méaudre the road follows a series of narrow gorges. The Gorges due Méaudret begin almost on the outskirts of the village, and join those of the Bourne at Les Jarrands. The side road also joins the D531 and a left turn quickly plunges into the deep recesses of the most spectacular route of the Vercors. Cliffs tower high above the road, almost blocking out the sunlight at times. Completed in 1872, the road replaced a tortuous mule track which crossed and recrossed the gorge by narrow cable suspended bridges. The modern road is cut into the side of the cliff at times, a triumph of nineteenth-century civil engineering. In places the River Bourne is 100m (330ft) directly below the road. The full impact of the work involved in building this road becomes apparent with the sight of the massive cliffs towering above the opposite bank of the river.

About half-way down the gorge a side road to the right the D35, leaves the main road at the tiny hamlet of La Balme de Rencurel to climb with forest on the right-hand and meadows to the left. Above the meadows and terraced by a series of limestone cliffs, forest again dominates the landscape. The road continues, over the Col de Romeyre, where side roads lead back towards the Bourne.

An old water mill marks the end of the Gorges de la Bourne. Where the gorge widens, a steep road on the right leads to a cave system known as the Grottes de Choranche. Open to the public, a major feature of the cave is the large number of needle-like, hollow stalactites which hang from the roof. Special lighting shows the almost transparent stalactites at their best advantage. A small museum attached to the cave describes the way they were used by different civilisations from as far back as 70,000 years ago.

Time spent in the village of **Choranche** is well worthwhile. The high cliffs of its gorge, rather than dominate, seem to add to the tranquil beauty of the place. Lower down the valley, **Pont-en-Royans** sits on either side of a narrow gorge, spanned by a single bridge centuries old. Houses are built perched on ledges to make full use of every scrap of the limited space available.

South of Pont-en-Royans along the D518, the road follows the twists and turns of the River Vernaison. At Ste Eulalie-en-Royans the river flows through a series of dramatic gorges. Known as *goulets*, the word closely translates as 'gullies' in English. Moving upstream, the first feature is the Petits Goulets, where tunnels and embankments carry the road through the gorge. At Echevis the road has to climb high above the river in a series of hairpins in order to find its way through the Grands Goulets. At one stage the river is 300m (984ft) directly below road level. The walls of the canyon seem to close in and the road has to thread its way through yet more tunnels as it winds it tortuous way towards the top village at **Barraques-en-Vercors**. This village was built to house the workers involved in the construction of this dramatic road which was opened in 1851.

South of the *goulets* and still on the D518, the village of **La Chapelle-en-Vercors** suffered dreadfully during that fateful July in 1944 when the Resistance took on the might of the German army. With the exception of the church, the village was completely obliterated. Every 25 July a moving ceremony known as the Cours des Fusillées remembers those who died during the fighting. The ground beneath La Chapelle is riddled with caves. Caving courses are organised locally, many of which are suitable for beginners. Some of the caves are entered by the novel method of climbing down one of the natural wells, or *scialets* which dot the surrounding countryside.

Anyone wishing to make more ambitious caving descents should contact the French National Caving Centre at St Martin-en-Vercors.

From La Chapelle a minor road, the D103 runs north to join the D221 near Les Barraques-en-Vercors. The road passes through the ruins of **Valchevrière**, deliberately never restored since World War II. Now a place of pilgrimage, Stations of the Cross lead to a memorial cross above the ruined village. From Valchevrière, the D221 follows the route of the Stations of the Cross, down through the forest of La Loubière and on to the upper part of the Gorges de la Bourne, then follows the River Bourne to **Villard-de-Lans**. Here the upper valley widens and the town has developed as a health resort with the emphasis on sporting activities, both in summer and winter. Surrounded by step-gabled houses, traditional to the Vercors, the town centre is traffic-free and the open-air market is a colourful feature. A cable car above the town climbs the surrounding wooded slopes to the beginning of a series of limestone ridges. Known as the Arêtes du Gerbier they provide miles of delightful high-level walking. South of Villard-de-Lans, another cable car from Clot-de-la-Balme can be used for further exploration of the limestone plateau and its surrounding ridges.

As well as being an interesting walking area, Villard-de-Lans and its neighbour Corrençon-en-Vercors are excellent centres for mountain biking. Maps and recommended route details can be obtained from tourist offices in the locality.

Turning back towards Grenoble, the D531 takes a scenic route above the Furon Valley to **Lans-en-Vercors** where there is a fine view of the Gorges du Bruyat. At **St Nizier** the Table d'Orientation covers a view ranging from the Chartreuse in the north to Mont Blanc further east. About 6km (4 miles) beyond the village the ground around the Tour sans Venin, the 'Tower without Poison', near the village of Paiset is supposed to have been purified by soil brought back from the Crusades. As a result no poison snake has ever been seen there.

On its way back to Grenoble, the D531 leaves the northern section of the Vercors by way of a wilderness of forest and rocks known as the Désert Jean-Jaques. This is where the French novelist and philosopher Jean-Jaques Rousseau (1712-1778) wandered and is supposed to have formulated many of his radical ideas. The views expounded in his *Social Contract* (1762) had a marked effect on the American Declaration of Independence and were wildly acclaimed during the French Revolution.

From La Chapelle-en-Vercors, the D518 continues south along the valley of the River Vernaison. Near **Les Chaberts** and about 8km (5 miles) south of the town, a signpost on the left points to the Grotte de la Luire. From the car park a footpath leads to the massive cave entrance and the public section of the cave; beyond this, there is a huge pothole which has been explored to a depth of 450m (1,476ft). During World War II the Resistance used the Grotte de la Luire as a hospital. On 27 July 1944 the cave was overrun by the SS. Fourteen wounded were immediately shot, eleven others were taken to the nearby village of Rousset and executed there. The doctors were executed in Grenoble and the nurses sent to a concentration camp in Germany.

In happier vein, the road climbs through Rouset on to the Col de Rousset where there is a superb view south along the Drôme Valley. A ridge to the east leads towards the Tête du Faisan and the barren upper reaches of the Vercors plateau. Unfortunately this is still an army training area where live firing takes place.

To the north-west and below the col, the plateau south of Vassieux-en-Vercors was used by Stone Age man in his search for flint. Many stone implements, in various stages of manufacture have been found. A cleverly designed museum has been built around this 'workshop', and together with information panels, the museum explains the lives of the people who inhabited the Vercors 5 to 6,000 years ago.

Vassieux has another museum. Linked with the Cimetière National, this also commemorates the horrific yet noble days of the Resistance in July 1944.

West of Vassieux-en-Vercors, the D76 winds its way through the Forêt de Lente, an area famous for its wildlife. To the left of the road and climbing out of the forest, a side road leads to the little ski resort of **Font d'Urle**. The village is backed by a steep ridge which is accessible only along a narrow track. A fine ridge walk can be enjoyed by following paths on either side of the col high above the village.

There is another cave nearby which is open to the public. This is the Grotte due Brudor and is found close to the D76 north of the turning to Font d'Urle. About 3km (2 miles) beyond the cave, a side road the D199 contours around an impressive rock ampitheatre which overlooks Val de Bouvante and is another good place for short walking excursions.

From the village of Lente, the D76 climbs to the Col de la Machine where there is a most impressive view into the Combe Laval. The road into Combe Laval is built of monumental proportions. For almost 5km (3 miles) it is actually cut into the cliff face, with a sheer drop of 2,460ft (750m) in places into the River Cholet far below. Not a place for the faint hearted! The best viewpoint is probably at the sharp left-hand bend a little beyond the Col de Gaudissart. On easier ground, the road reaches St Jean-en-Royans before joining the Bourne Valley. This village has a long tradition of woodworking, which is reflected in the Baroque panelling of its eighteenth-century church.

The southern boundary of the Parc Naturel Régional du Vercors is marked by steeply indented valleys and rolling forested slopes. Below the Col de Rousset, the D518 winds its way into the Comane Valley, then on to Die, the main high-level town in this area. **Die** has some interesting ancient remains. A few miles to its east, approached along a very minor side road through Sallières and its thermal waters, lie tranquil remains of the Abbeye de Valcroissant Pié Ferré. The D93 is the only major road to cross this part of the Vercors. It links Loiol-sur-Drôme with roads leading to the town of Gap, and follows the River Drôme for most of the way to the Col de Cabre, the boundary of the departments of Drôme and Hautes-Alpes. A side road the D593, leaves the main road at Pont de Quart la Salle. Winding its way along the valley of the River Gas, it becomes narrower as it climbs through gorges to its highest point on the Col de Grimone. Forest covers most of the lower slopes, but a side turning at Creyers turns left on to the D120. This road follows the Archiane Valley, leaving it at Menée to climb a twisting route to the Col de Menée before descending through pine forest to join the N75 at Celles.

A yet more minor road the D224, turns left at Menée, continuing along the Archiane to its namesake hamlet at the road end. Above the village and only reached by steep footpaths tower the steep limestone cliffs of the Cirque d'Archiane, the southern ramparts of the Réserve Naturelle des Hauts Plateaux du Vercors.

South of the D93, the countryside becomes less dramatic. Mixed pine and beech forests cloak the limestone ridges, bare in their upper limits, and dotted with sunny meadows where the forefathers of the present farmers cleared the original forest cover. Winding minor roads, used only by local traffic wend their way through the silent countryside. Ancient châteaux slumber in gentle tranquillity, still remembering their past glories, benevolently controlling life in their attendant villages: villages such as the one near **Marsanne** which now lies in preserved ruins. The remains of this feudal village have been restored and make an interesting insight into life in pre-Revolutionary France. To reach Marsanne, take the D6/D538 from the D93 at Crest for about 40km (25 miles), and follow one of the numerous side roads to the right which converge on Marsanne.

Marsanne is a typical village of the southern Vercors: sleepy, remote and yet offering its heart to those prepared to seek it out. These are the undiscovered places.

Further Information
— Dauphiné —

Museums and Other Places of Interest

La Chapelle-en-Vercors
Grotte de la Luire
Open: daily from May to September, 10am-12noon and 1.30-6.30pm.

Col du Lautaret
Jardin Alpin
Open: daily from end June to September daily except Tuesday from 9am-noon and 2-6.30pm. Closed on Fridays.

Grenoble
The following list is just a sample of things to do and places to visit around the medieval town centre of this ancient city. Museums are listed separately:

Cathédrale de Notre-Dame
An amalgamation of three differently-aged churches.

Palais de Justice
Ask the doorkeeper for admission.

Parc Paul Mistral
Modern town centre park named after one of Grenoble's most famous mayors.

Place Grenette
Lively pedestrianised town centre.

Place St André
Medieval centre of Grenoble.

Téléphérique de la Bastille
Cable car from riverside. Views of city.

Pont-en-Royans
Grottes de Choranche
☎ 75 48 64 92
Open: from June to September 9am-6.30pm.

Sassenage
Cuves de Sassenage
☎ 76 48 64 92
Open: daily in May, June and September except on Tuesdays, 9-11am and 2-6pm. August open every day 9am-6pm.

Château de Bérenger
☎ 76 27 54 44
Open: daily during July and August. Guided tours at 10.30am, 3pm and 4.30pm. Closed on Saturdays, Sundays and Holidays.

Voiron
Chartreuse
Open: daily May to October and weekends at other times.

Vizille
Château de Vizille
Place de la Libération
☎ 76 68 07 35
Open: October to April from Wednesday to Friday 2-5pm and on Saturday and Sunday 10am-12noon and 2-5pm. From May to September open Wednesday to Sunday 9.30am-12noon and 2-6pm. Closed on Mondays and Tuesdays.

Tourist Information Offices

Hautes-Alpes
Gîtes de France
Rue Capitaine de Bresson
05002 Gap

Grenoble (Isère)
Gîtes de France
Maison du Tourisme
14 Rue de la République
38019 Grenoble

Gîtes Ruraux
Maison de la Chartreuse
38380 St Laurent-du-Port

13 • Le Queyras

This isolated region lies in the extreme south-east of the High Alps bordering Italy on three sides, forming part of the Cottian Alps and within the old province of Dauphiné, which has been French since 1349. Today it is in the department of Hautes Alpes, and since 1977 the Queyras has been a regional nature park.

The heart of the region is the basin of the River Guil, the source and upper course of which is a splendid cirque dominated by the graceful Italian pyramid of Monte Viso (3,841m, 12,598ft). The middle of the river forms the meeting point of several high open valleys, their slopes covered with very fine larch woods. Lower down the river steepens and narrows its course into the Combe du Queyras and then flows through a high and precipitous limestone gorge to join the River Durance near the old fortified town of Mont Dauphin.

The Alpine landscape of the Queyras is dry, wild and rocky — though not austere — with bare crags and screes, especially in the east where the rocks are glossy schists glistening with flakes of mica, but there are high lakes, waterfalls and snow-capped peaks. The lower slopes and valley floors are green with woods and irrigated meadows mown for hay, but cultivation is scanty. Nevertheless, there are still some picturesque vestiges left of a much older mountain civilisation based upon the rhythm of the seasons, and there is also some transhumance practised, but the grand sight of long columns of sheep has long gone to be replaced by trucks. Above the valleys there are high grazing meadows often with a group of chalets set round an ancient chapel.

However, the jewel of the Queyras is its magnificent climate, an important consideration now that so much of Europe is in the throes of a climatic downturn. Here it hardly ever rains during the summer, the hazard of fog is unknown, and it is no exaggeration to say that 300 days of the year are sunny. Moreover the brightness of the southern sky added to the freshness of the high mountain air makes for a delightful feeling of well-being.

The alpine phenomenon of the south-facing sunny slope or *adret*, which is usually cleared for settlement or cultivation as opposed to the *ubac* or shady side — empty of man — and usually thickly forested is particularly emphasised in the Queyras where many valleys run west-east. This has been a factor in the development of skiing and tourism seized upon by the few remaining native residents who have supplemented their incomes from a land that yields only a moderate reward. But this pleasant combination of Mediterranean and alpine climates has had another effect, for the flora of the region is rich in variety as there are some 2,000 species found in stages, the Mediterranean plants grow at the foot of the slopes and gradually change upwards into alpine varieties towards the high summits. The flora of the Queyras as a result is of great interest to botanists the world over.

So, one may see typical Mediterranean flowers like blue or silvery-white thistles on a dry sunny valley pasture. Then higher up on thin hill grass you might come across the violet alpine pansy, and in the high alpine meadows see the bright yellow globeflower, and amongst the arid rocky summits the pink flowers of a variety of stonecrop called Jupiter's beard. Near the end of June is best when almost the whole of the Queyras is one mass of flowers. The attractive larch is the dominant tree, its bright green leaves throwing but a thin shadow, so that grass grows between the boles, and if you are walking amongst the larch woods on the shady or *ubac* side there is a pleasing brightness about the undergrowth, and often growing amid the grass are the flowers of the alpine pink family — typical of the Queyras.

The Queyras has its alpine animals too; high on the remote cols there is often a chance of seeing chamois, and on the slopes and mountain meadows the marmot is common, whistling like a kettle when they think danger threatens. With the coming of autumn the variable hare appears, so called because in summer he is brown and hardly visible, and then with a hint of snow in the air he is able to camouflage himself and becomes white to fool his enemies. There are typical birds as well, the small alpine grouse flits amongst the larch woods and myrtle bushes; and higher up the ptarmigan is seen near the lakes and rocky pools.

There are no towns in the Queyras as such, only the small one of Guillestre at the 'gate' or south-western entrance to the region. In spite of its size — less than 2,000 people — it is an interesting and lively place with plenty of shops, restaurants and hotels. It is a stage on the 'Grande Route des Alpes' from Evian on Lake Geneva to Nice

Le Queyras map showing Briançon, Montgenèvre, Cervières, Le Laus, Soubeyran, St Martin de Queyrières, Queyrières, Col d'Izoard, Pic de Rochebrune, Lakes of Malrif, Le Roux, Notre Dame de Clausis, Bouchet Stream, Col de Malaure, Col d'Urine, Brunissard, Col de Péas, Malrif, Abriès, Tête de Pelvas, Haut, Mouriare, La Chalp, ARVIEUX, Aiguilles, Ristolas, La Monta, L'Echalp, ITALY, Le Coin, Château Queyras, Molines en Queyras, Col de Furfande, Fontgillarde, Lac Foréant, Grand Belvédère, Col de la Traversette, Escoyères, La Chalp, St Véran, Montbardon, Le Grand Queyras, Bramousse, Pain du Sucre, Monte Viso, Col de Fromage, Ceillac, Col St Véran, Montdauphin Gare, Cristillan, Cime du Mélezet, Col Blanchet, Passo Chiaffredo, Guillestre, Pied du Mélezet, Tête de Noire, Barbein, Tête de Longet, Escreins, Lac Ste Anne, HEP Lake, Chianale, Vars, Font Sancte, Maljasset, ITALY, Les Claux, Blachière, **LE QUEYRAS**, Créoux

down on the Mediterranean, which passes through the region along the D902 from the Col d' Izoard to the Col de Vars. The nearest large town is the old fortress city of Briançon some 35km (21 miles) north of Guillestre on the N94 in the Durance valley. Nevertheless, villages are spread throughout the region, and some such as Abriès, Aiguilles, Ceillac, Molines and the best known — St Véran — have been expanded due to increased skiing facilities, regrettably neither improving on the vernacular architecture nor the environment.

Undoubtedly the greatest attraction of the Queyras is the way its superb climate makes outdoor pursuits such a pleasure, especially all forms of walking from gentle valley promenades to tough mountain hikes during late spring, high summer and early autumn. For long-distance walkers the Grande Randonnée GR5 (Amsterdam to Nice!) passes through by way of Brunissard, Château Queyras, Col de Fromage, Ceillac, Lac Ste Anne and the Col Girardin. Within the region is the GR58 Tour de Queyras circling the entire area with variations. These are waymarked and there are rest places along these routes in the form of high mountain refuges, *gîtes d'étape* (lodgings) and isolated unmanned simple camp sites and the use of alpine huts belonging to the local inhabitants. Thus a whole infra-structure is provided for walkers for whom the region is ideally suited.

A certain amount of riding is possible using the long valley tracks; and there is a climbing centre at Abriès, but most of the high peaks are on the frontier fringes such as the Pain de Sucre (3,208m, 10,522ft) with access from a refuge at Col Agnel. During the long winter season skiing is a great attraction with the sunlit slopes and brilliant light, but almost as popular and far less expensive, and suitable for all ages is *ski de fond* (using long narrow skis and low shoes) which is a speciality of the Queyras, Ceillac being the chief centre. However, a whole series of recognised skiing itineraries exist at some very high altitudes.

Most places are accessible by car except the extreme ends of some valleys where the road usually deteriorates to pot holes and then becomes a very rough track. Some of the roads are narrow, steep and sharply curved like the entrances to glacial hanging valleys such as the valley of the Cristillan (Ceillac), and now that the locals all have cars they seem to think that everyone knows the road so be cautious and don't drive at night unless forced.

All this plus the guaranteed sunshine and clear skies makes the Queyras the ideal region for exploration. There are many small side valleys and wooded combes with high paths that are rarely trodden, and one can penetrate into Italy on foot with the assurance that there is some sort of shelter if needed.

The Queyras is a little difficult to get to. There are four routes by road, but three are high mountain passes:

Col d' Izoard (2,361m, 7,744ft) from the north via Briançon (D902), closed by snow October to June; Col de Vars (2,116m, 6,940ft) closed by snow December to April. South from Nice via Italy or Barcelonette (Ubaye); Col Agnel (2,744m, 9,000ft) from Italy, but although a new route definitely not recommended, unless using 4-wheel drive, as road is in a bad state; Via Guillestre (1,000m, 3,280ft). Normal point of entry from Durance valley either Briançon or Gap (N94).

The easiest route by car is from Grenoble by the Route Napoléon (N85) to Gap, thence Embrun to Guillestre: 240km, 146 miles.

The shortest route from the nearest airport is from Turin (Italy) then via Susa and Col de Montgenèvre (1,850m, 6,068ft) open all the year round; thence Briançon to Guillestre: 144km, 88 miles.

Other airports are Marseilles (Marignane) — 244km, 149 miles; Lyon (Satolas) — 266km, 162 miles; Nice (Côte d'Azur) — 293km, 178 miles.

There are direct trains to Guillestre from Paris, Grenoble and Marseilles which stop at the Gare de Montdauphin-Guillestre, 4km (2.4 miles) from the town, and buses run from the station to Guillestre and main places in the Queyras.

Approach via Col d'Izoard to Château Queyras

By far the most interesting and spectacular route into the Queyras is from Briançon over the Col d'Izoard. From the town the D902 runs along a corniche above the gorge of the River Cerveyrette and past the village of Cervières, and then winds up to the col through a landscape that gradually becomes more arid.

Some little way below the summit on the left is a refuge built in 1858 by Napoleon III. But he is not the Napoleon it commemorates, for this is one of six refuges built on particularly exposed cols with money left by Napoleon I to the department of Hautes Alpes — in recognition of the enthusiastic welcome he received in Gap on his escape from Elba. At the summit (2,361m, 7,744ft) on the right is another monument to the French Alpine Army which built many of the roads and passes in the region.

The views from here are superb, and southwards is the first glimpse of the mountains of the Queyras. Away on the left of the road is a steep and rocky path leading to the **Col Perdu** and a dun-coloured mountain called Arpelin (2,601m, 8,531ft) which is really a fine arrêt flanked by massive screes. From the col is a full face view of the Grand Pic de Rochebrûne (3,325m, 10,906ft), a huge brown rocky pyramid that will not be seen again until far into the Queyras. Back on the road, the route passes along another corniche through a remarkable area called the **Casse Déserte**. This is a series of enormous screes descending from the crags above with needle-like pinnacles projecting through them like rows of obelisks. The whole region here is a classic example of erosion, the rocks being limestones and dolomites. This desolate scene in almost perpetual sunshine receives occasional publicity through press photos of many cyclists struggling up to the Col in the Tour de France.

The road now descends in steep narrow bends surrounded by trees and soon there is a magnificent view of the valley of Arvieux with its wide, flat, inclined floor and steep wooded slopes. Then, on the right is the hamlet of **Brunissard**, developed for skiing and where the Grandes Randonnées GR5 and GR58 cross. A new paved road leads north-westwards — the route of GR5 — and a few kilometres further on the right is an unfenced attractive camp site, manned only during summer months. The road ends in a track amidst the trees, but continue on the GR5 below it and reach the Chalets de Clapeyto (2,230m, 7,314ft). On the way is the huge square alpine meadow of Pra Premier with the massive peak of Haut Mouriare (2,810m, 9,216ft) behind it. All of which is a reminder of the old way of life here. Back on the D902, now very straight, the small hamlet of **La Chalp** appears on the left. Here another recent road turns off, very steep and curved at first, leading to a high wooded plateau 4km (2.4 miles) on, and the Lac de Rouet (1,854m, 6,000ft). From here are two remarkable views, eastwards to Château Queyras, and south-west-wards over the Combe du Queyras (valley of the River Guil).

The straight D902 now descends gently to the very pleasant village of **Arvieux** grouped around the fine tall building of its six-teenth-century church. This is a good place to stop, for here is a small friendly hotel-restaurant,'La Borne Ensoleillée', set in an old court-yard. Arvieux has a reputation for its cheese. A route to explore is behind the tiny hamlet of Le Coin off on the right as you enter Arvieux, where the Combe Bonne leads to a number of rarely trod-den paths.

From Arvieux, the D902 joins the D947 on the left, running through the Combe du Queyras, and soon a quite remarkable build-ing comes to view. This is the fortress of Château Queyras dating from the thirteenth century, when the region was part of a mountain republic including neighbouring Italy. The castle was later restored by Vauban, but the dungeon remains to remind one of those times. The site — the most impressive in the Queyras — is because it is a superb example of a *verrou* or remnant of the Ice Ages. This blocks the valley so completely that the river has to saw through it, and the road can only just squeeze past at the side of the rock through an old village.

Château Queyras to St Véran

From Château Queyras two hamlets, **Les Meyries** and **Rouet** (5km, 3 miles), can be reached by a side road (D444), which winds up on the left to what is the balcony of the River Guil, giving a beautiful view of the valley. Continuing on foot from the end of the road at Rouet, an old asbestos mine road leads to the Bergerie de Péas (sheep-fold) at 2,024m (6,638ft) by the Péas stream with a good view of the high valley of the Péas. The more energetic can continue by leaving the mine road, and going up to the Col de Péas (2,629m, 8,623ft), to be rewarded by an impressive view to the west by the pyramid of the Pic de Rochebrune (3,325m, 10,906ft).

A remote picturesque corner of the Alps, Dauphiné

Molines, bridge over the River Aigue-Agnel, Le Queyras

Agay, near St Raphaël, Côte d' Azur

On returning to the valley road (D947), it leads straight up the broad trench of the Guil past L'Iscle camp site, with splendid larch forests on the *ubac* slopes until the village of **Ville-Vieille** is reached. This forms one commune with Château Queyras known as Château Ville-Vieille. Here the road to St Véran (D5) turns right, and starts to twist up into the steep valley of the L'Aigue Blanche. On the first bend to the left, there is a forest route to the Bois Foran (1,804m, 5,917ft), which is a reasonable 2-hour walk. Continuing up the D5, the valley now becomes the Ravine de Prats, and on the right is a remarkable geological feature. This is a *demoiselle coiffé* (girl with a hat), a tall earth pillar topped by a large stone boulder.

Soon the view opens out, with the valley being dominated by the mountain of the Tête de Longet (3,151m, 10,335ft), and beyond lies the hamlet of **La Rua**, a very narrow street of some typical Queyras houses of half wood and half stone construction in seventeenth- to eighteenth-century style. Then follows the larger old village of **Molines**, which includes several outlying hamlets, where the road divides. A hundred and fifty years ago it was much larger with over a thousand people, when the Queyras reached its peak figure of 7,700, but the rigours of peasant life, and two World Wars led to a decline. However, in the last two decades, the almost inevitable development of skiing has stabilised the population, and even increased it — 243 in 1968, and 288 in 1975.

But the hamlet of **Gaudissard**, above the village, had another kind of emigration earlier — religious intolerance — and over 100 left Molines, amongst them the people of Gaudissard, who went afar. So that today in the Hesse province of Germany, there exists the village of Godihardessen (German for Gaudissard), believed to be founded by French Protestants. From here there is a walk leading to Prat Haut above the ravine, and one can continue along the forest road of Chanteloube, where there are picnic sites, and eventually right through to Aiguilles.

Our route leads through the narrow streets of **Molines** with its picturesque houses, then comes the long valley of the Aigue Agnel, with the most interesting hamlet of **Pierre Grosse** appearing. Here is a genuine survival of the typical Alpine house with its enormous *grenier* (loft), where the harvests of hay and forage are stored, but nowadays less and less. On the slopes above Pierre Grosse is the outlier hamlet of Le Coin — grossly, and incongruously expanded by chalets, apartment buildings, and a hotel.

But just below Pierre Grosse is a delightful small tranquil unguarded camp site by the river, in a charming setting, a leafy oasis in a rather stark valley. The valley road, however, is an ancient route to Italy, which is thought to be Hannibal's route, and above the hamlet of Fontgillarde is a massive boulder called 'Hannibal's stone'. The road has recently been revived as a through route, but it is not in a good condition. Although as a forest road it makes a good walk to the Col Agnel on the Italian frontier from Fontgillarde, where there is a mountain refuge, from which many high walks can be made. On the way there, you will pass the ruins of another refuge, one which is similar to that on the Col d'Izoard built with Napoleon's bequest. From the road above Fontgillarde, two mountain walks may be attempted: one to the Pas de Chai (2,790m, 9,150ft) in $2^1/_2$ hours, and the other to climb the mountain of Grand Queyras (3,114m, 10,217ft), which takes 4 hours.

Returning to Molines the D5 continues through forested meadows past the hamlet of La Chalp to **Le Raux**. Here is a very pretty walk, part of the GR58, by going down to the bridge over the Aigue Blanche, and following the path up by the wood of Bois du Moulin. Then comes a mountain stream, the Torrent de Lamaron, which is followed as far as a ravine, afterwards climbing up a steep zigzag path by a copse and a crest (2,380m, 7,806ft). Then, the stream is rejoined, and by its long upper valley the Col Estranques (2,651m, 8,695ft) is reached, with very good views, and a panorama which takes in Font Sancte (3,387m, 11,109ft). On the way down look out on the left for a fine distant view of the Pic de Rochebrune (3,325m, 10,906ft).

Back on the road (D5), at length the curious terraced village of **St Véran** is reached, and at 2,040m (6,700ft) is the highest in Europe. The houses with their vast *greniers* — mostly of wood — are arranged *en-echelon* to avoid being in each other's shade, and of course the risk of fire. The parish church is very interesting, with heavily gilded ornamental saints' statues, and an upper gallery for the choir and the old people of the village.

Outside is a marble porch with crouching lions, showing Italian influence, and rather similar to Guillestre and Embrun. A little further below on the edge of the village is the Protestant church, with its tall sombre steeple. The village has been largely developed for skiing in conjunction with Molines, which means expansion — so far it is not too spoilt — but the danger, and temptation is ever present.

From St Véran the D5 goes on a further 6km (3.7 miles), passing old copper mines and a marble quarry, to the Chapel of Clausis, a shrine to which there is an annual Franco-Italian pilgrimage on 16 July. This road is only open in the summer months before 9.30am,

St Véran (2,040m, 6,690ft), the highest village in Europe

and after 5.30pm, for it connects with important high alpine pastures, and is much used by cattle and sheep.

From St Véran, east of the village, an interesting and alternative route up the valley can be made. The route follows the D5 until the first ravine is reached, that of the St Luce stream, then it forks right going down to cross the Aigue Blanche. After crossing this river, it goes upstream on the left bank, which on a hot day can give some shade. At length past the old copper mines, another bridge is reached, which is the Pont sur l'Aigue Blanche (2,340m, 7,675ft), under the Chapel of Clausis.

Then the route continues to the confluence of the streams, and the junction of the footpaths. Here a choice can be made to the Col de Chamoussière (2,884m, 9,459ft). Either the direct route can be taken, or which is perhaps preferable, though a little longer, via the Col de St Véran, and passing through alpine meadows. When the Col (2,853m, 9,357ft) is reached, there is a surprise waiting, for the Italian side is steep and abrupt, opening on to the Chiantale valley, with its large blue hydro-electric power lake far below, and the peak of Monte Viso in all its glory. In this area are many marmots, for it seems to be quite a colony. Here it is interesting to reflect, that in October 1742 a Spanish army of 40,000 men crossed the Col de St Véran, but being surprised by the onset of sudden cold weather, abandoned their treasure chests to the south on Col Blanchet (2,897m, 9,502ft), and on the mountain known as Tête Noire (3,176m, 10,417ft); in spite of intense searching they have never been found. The way continues to the Col de Chamoussière, then down to the Col Agnel (2,580m, 8,462ft) and the Refuge Agnel, and a sizeable section of the GR58 (Tour of the Queyras) has been covered.

Ville-Vieille to the Belvédère de Monte Viso

Returning to the Guil valley, this route continues upstream in a fine open section forested with larch and pine, the Bois Foran. Then comes the village of **Aiguilles** set in a splendid site, and a most convenient centre for the High Queyras. The old village is most attractive, and seems full of fountains and balconies, while the character of the larger more recent houses is in harmony as well. It is a ski centre, and some of the outskirts lack the same taste, but all in all it is a very pleasant place.

From Aiguilles there are some good forest walks like the one to the hamlet of Peynin, which starts from the bypass road on the right of the village, and goes up through alpine meadows. A longer walk is to the Bergerie de Lombard (an ancient sheep-fold), some $3^1/_2$km (2.2 miles), and one can go on to the lakes of Malrif (described later).

Leaving Aiguilles by the valley road (D947), another 400m (1,312ft) further on, and over a bridge on the right is the municipal camp site of Le Gouret. Although, only rated two stars, it is one of the best sites in the region, with its situation in the Forest of Marassan, with acres of space, and myriads of alpine flowers all around.

On to **Abriès**, at the confluence of the Rivers Guil and Bouchet. This is an agreeable little place, rather more modern, having been rebuilt since 1945, and also, an important skiing centre. It has some excellent restaurants, one, also a hotel, La Mouffe, can be particularly recommended for its cooking, covering many French regions, especially Alsace, for there are no regional dishes in the Queyras, although the food is always fresh and good. Abriès offers a variety of routes to explore, with an easy way to have a fine view by taking the *telesiège* (chair-lift), open in the summer (July and August) to the intermediate station at 2,020m (6,625ft) and then an hour's walk brings one to the Colette de Jilly (2,366m, 7,760ft), where a perspective of the Guil valley, and Monte Viso can be seen.

A long walk, part of the GR58, starts by the picturesque and very steep Stations of the Cross, and then for nearly 5km (3 miles) is the most exhilarating in the Queyras, eventually to an old chapel above

Monte Viso (3,841m, 12,598ft) from one of the ski pistes near Abriès

Abriès. It then continues along a mountain shoulder, and round into the deep valley of Malrif. After some time the abandoned village of **Malrif** (1,841m, 6,038ft), appears with its curiously separated church dating from about 1830, and campanile perched apart on the sides of a deep ravine. Beyond are splendid flowery meadows, until two rushing streams meet at the Bergerie de Bertins (2,040m, 6,690ft). Here marmots are heard with a whistle similar to birds of prey, whilst falcons circle overhead. From here on the walk to the lakes is difficult but worth the effort, for the lakes themselves, as they seem continually to change colour, and also the panorama of the sea of peaks, inevitably dominated by the summit of Monte Viso. Here a curious phenomenon is sometimes seen, that of a distant curtain of smog behind Monte Viso, coming up from Italy — the industrial city of Turin is only 70km (43 miles) distant. Fortunately, the prevailing westerlies keep it from the Queyras, and it disperses at night.

Back at Abriès, take the D441 on the left to the hamlet of Le Roux, and here, turning sharp right, continue along the road until the chalets of Valpreveyre are reached, with good views of the pyramid of Bric Bouchet (3,261m, 10,696ft), and the Tête du Pelvas (2,929m, 9,607ft). There are two splendid walks here. The first through a larch-filled valley upstream of the Bouchet valley to the Col Malaure

Tête du Pelvas (2,929m, 9,607ft), Col d'Urine, Valpreveyre

(2,740m, 8,987ft), and the second to the Col d'Urine (2,525m, 8,282ft). This last walk could well represent the alpine flora of the Queyras. For the path passes by a stream, then through larches, and a large meadow full of buttercups, globeflowers, violets, pansies, white anemones, and Star of Bethlehem (starry flowers, glistening white tepals), then a ridge, and an open windy knoll with treacle mustard (small clusters of yellow flowers), as one approaches the col. Going down there is a path variation, that passes a bank massed with white St Bruno's lilies (a threatened species in some parts of France) and finally through a meadow full of globeflowers just before reaching Valpreveyre.

Returning to Abriès the road continues on upstream, the high valley now a little severe, to the village of **Ristolas**, badly damaged during the war, and now rebuilt. Along this stretch of road many high walks begin, from Ristolas up the valley of the Ségure to the Pic de Ségure (2,990m, 9,807ft) in $4^3/_4$ hrs. Further along is the hamlet of **La Monta**, another war victim, from where one can climb to the Col de la Croix (2,229m, 7,311ft) in $2^3/_4$ hrs. At length L'Echalp is reached, now the terminus of wheeled traffic. The road continues right up to the Belvédère du Cirque (9km, 5.6 miles), but is now cut (summer 1987) on account of many accidents. So all excursions to the various belvederes have to be on foot.

Starting with the forest route to the Chalets de la Médille, on the right, $1^1/_2$hrs from L'Echalp, which is an ancient alpine meadow full of flowers, and a good view of Viso, one can continue on to the Col Vieux (2,806m, 9,203ft) by way of two lakes, Lac Egorgéou first, and then Lac Foréant (2,618m, 8,587ft). Between them it is possible to see numerous chamois, and at Col Vieux, where Hannibal may have crossed into Italy, one can go on, and climb the Pain de Sucre (3,208m, 10,522ft) right on the Italian frontier. It is not difficult, taking but $1^1/_2$hrs, and the view takes in Savoy, the Italian Alps and even Switzerland — a vast panorama, which is accessible to non-climbers.

If the original road (D947) is taken, first after 3km (1.8 miles) comes the Petit Belvédère, and further along the Grand Belvédère, by a mountain hut, with already a magnificent view of Viso, and the high Guil valley. If the last 2km (1.2 miles) can be managed to the Bergerie-sous-Roche, the cirque and the majestic full face of Monte Viso is seen. It is possible to make a three stage tour of Monte Viso using refuges via the Col de Traversette (Refuge Sella), Passo San Chiaffredo (2,764m, 9,065ft) and at Castello, a hotel (1,660m, 5,444ft).

The Combe du Queyras — Château Queyras to Guillestre

From Château Queyras it is possible to go up to the Sommet Bucher (2,257m, 7,402ft) by road (11km, 6.8 miles), which starts on either side of the fortress. It was built by the Chasseurs Alpins of the French Army in 1934. The road is wide enough, but here and there are potholes, ruts and odd obstacles, which call for cautious driving. The views are superb of the Château Queyras, and the Guil valley as it winds up and up through pine, and larch woods carpeted with flowers. At the summit amid alpine meadows is a radar station, and an orientation table, as the view takes in a vast panorama of high peaks: Monte Viso, Font-Sancte (3,387m, 11,109ft), Rochebrune (3,325m, 10,906ft), and the Massif of Pelvoux westwards. On returning one takes the left fork at the bottom to rejoin the main road, thus avoiding the narrowness of Château Queyras. From here, the GR5 also climbs up cutting across the bends of the Sommet Bucher road to the Col de Fromage (2,301m, 7,547ft), a very long walk (4hrs), but the views are extremely good.

The valley road continues westwards to the junction of the route to Arvieux and the Col d'Izoard, becoming the D902, then begins the gorge of the Guil marked by the Rock of the Guardian Angel, and a war memorial to the men of the Queyras.

At the hamlet of **Chapelure** the gorge widens out, and in this area are three hamlets perched high above the valley: **Montbardon** on the left, further along is **Bramousse**, and right opposite, the ancient hamlet of **Escoyères** reached by a path. From these the GR58 offers high walking, but as can be imagined, climbing up from such a deep gorge, these routes are very steep!

The road now goes past pine-covered slopes to the Maison du Roy, and on the left the steep road (D440) leads up through the precipitous valley of the Cristillan, with many hairpin bends encased in trees.

On reaching the summit of the valley shoulder, for this is a classic glacial hanging valley, one sees **Ceillac** situated on a broad alp, enclosed by immense bare slopes, forming a Y-shaped valley feature. On the right is the larch-covered valley of the Mélezet, shut off by a huge cirque, and on the left the steep and bare valley of the Cristillan, with a long paved road, ending in a forest track and path to Col de Cristillan 2,961m (9,715ft). Ceillac has been heavily developed for skiing, and apartment blocks rather overshadow the pleasant old village, where the Mairie is dated 1558. The present parish church is a rather unusual building, whilst the former church is a tall elegant structure, now the chapel of Ste Cécile, set amid the meadows of the alp in splendid isolation.

From the village the road up the Mélezet valley goes to the Cime de Mélezet past the hamlet of Pied de Mélezet close to a very fine waterfall — the Cascade de Pisse! From here the GR5 path winds up in a larch forest, near the chair-lift (open in the summer months), and crosses a ridge to a very blue cirque or corrie lake — Lac Ste Anne at a height of 2,415m (7,921ft) below some large screes. The nearby chapel (Ste Anne) has a pilgrimage each 26 July from Ceillac, and Maurin over the Col Girardin (2,699m, 8,852ft) in neighbouring Ubaye.

Another walk is to cross the river from Pied du Mélezet, and go up the left bank of the stream, there joining a path up the alluvial fan north of the waterfall, and rejoin the stream which feeds it, and you arrive at a delightful little lake, well named Miroir. The path from the lake goes down through a wood, and joins the route of the chair-lift.

If the Mélezet valley road is taken to its limit at La Raille, a walk from there through a larch wood, and among half-ruined hamlets with a curious chapel, brings a good view of Font Sancte (3,387m, 11,109ft).

Ceillac is the crossing point of the GR5, and GR58, offering many high walks to the Col de Fromage (2,301m, 7,547ft), Col des Estron-

Limestone screes, Casse Déserte, Col d'Izoard (2,361m, 7,744ft)

ques (2,651m, 8,695ft), and a forest walk along the Cristillan valley to the Bergerie de Bois Noir. It may be noted here that these routes can be used by good skiers between December and March — Ceillac being the chief centre for *ski de fond*.

Returning to the Maison de Roy, the gorge proper is entered, with its towering sides of Triassic limestone and dolomite, along a corniche with many tunnels until the Pied la Viste is reached. Here is an orientation table on a high rock giving good views of the upper Durance valley, and the far-off majestic peaks of the Massif of Pelvoux.

Just before entering Guillestre, there is a very agreeable tranquil camp site, within an old farm, off a bend in the road. From here there is an extremely pleasant walk up the valley of the Escreins — a splendid mountain stream — leading through orchards and meadows, giving fine distant views of the Ecrins, and then passing through woods and screes.

Guillestre is really a crossroads town between three regions: Embrunais, Queyras and the Ubaye, but it is an ideal starting point for the Queyras because of its facilities. It has an interesting sixteenth-century church, inspired by the ancient twelfth-century cathedral of Embrun. The porch has four columns of rose marble, having at the base two crouching lions in the style of Lombardy. This rose marble, quarried locally, which was used to make all the pavements in the town, unfortunately much has been replaced by rather soulless cement. However, good specimens still exist, an example being the steps outside an ironmonger's shop (Ets Favier) in a small square off the main street.

One place worth visiting, 6km (3.7 miles) from Guillestre, is the old fortified city of Montdauphin on top of a scarp, which dominates the confluence of the Guil and Durance. Its construction was ordered by Louis XIV in 1693 following the campaign against Savoy, and duly built by Vauban, who fortified Château Queyras, and Briançon at the same time.

Further Information
— Le Queyras —

Museums and Other Places of Interest

Seasons: Summer June to September. Winter late December to mid-April. Most hotels are shut outside these periods. Those open all the year are sometimes closed in November.
Office Hours: for SIs (Tourist Bureaux): normally 9.30am-12noon and 2.30-5pm.
Shops and restaurants are often shut out of season.
GTA = Grand Traversée des Alpes.

Abriès (05460)
Gîte d'étape: Di Marco (50pl) GR5 GTA, open all year ☎ (92) 45 71 14
Tourist Office: ☎ (92) 45 72 26 morning/afternoon
Sport: Tennis Courts ☎ (92) 45 72 26
Ski School ☎ (92) 45 71 47
Taxis: Soissons ☎ (92) 45 75 66 and winter , Frendo ☎ (92) 45 71 16
Market: Friday

Aiguilles (05470)
Gîte d'étape: Mme Simon (20pl) GTA ☎ (92) 45 70 40, open all year
Tourist Office: Mairie ☎ (92) 45 70 34

Office of Tourist Promotion in Queyras:
☎ (92) 45 76 18
Sport: Tennis Courts
☎ (92) 45 76 38
Ski School ☎ (92) 45 73 73/77 19
Skating Rink ☎ (92) 45 76 68
Market: Thursday

Arvieux (05350) (Château Ville-Vieille)
Gîte d'étape: (Brunissard 3km, 1.86 miles north) (24pl) M. Faure
☎ (92) 45 73 85 GTA all year
Tourist Office: On main D902, open 9.30am-12noon and 2-5pm
☎ (92) 45 75 76
Sports: 2 Tennis Courts at Brunissard; Minigolf; Volleyball; Kayak-Canoe
☎ (92) 45 72 73 , Ski School ☎ (92) 45 71 69

Ceillac (05600)
Gîte d'étape: M. Fournier GTA (80pl)
☎ (92) 45 00 23
Tourist Office: ☎ (92) 45 04 74
Sport: 2 Tennis Courts
☎ (92) 45 04 74
Ski School ☎ (92) 45 10 58
Market: Wednesday (summer)
Taxi: Favier ☎ (92) 45 01 91

Château Ville-Vieille (05350)
Relais de Charpenal
☎ (92) 45 71 70
Tourist Office: ☎ (92) 45 70 70
Taxi: Audier ☎ (92) 45 70 61
Sports: 2 Tennis Courts, Volleyball
☎ (92) 45 70 70

Guillestre (05600)
Tourist Office: Pl. Salva, open 9am-
12noon and 2.30-7pm (6pm non-
season) ☎ (92) 45 04 37
Sports: Swimming pool (heated), 4
Tennis Courts, Mini-golf, Horseriding,
Ski de Fond and Ice Rink

Molines (05390)
Tourist Office: ☎ (92) 45 83 22
Sports: 2 Tennis Courts
☎ (92) 45 83 80/29
Ski School ☎ (92) 45 81 51
Taxis: E. Garcin ☎ (92) 45 83 01; Taupin
☎ (92) 45 83 70

Pierre Grosse
Gîte d'étape: At Fontgillarde M. Bonnet
winter/summer
☎ (92) 45 83 17

Ristolas (05460)
☎ (92) 45 76 07
Gîte d'étape: La Monta M. Frendo
☎ (92) 45 71 35 (60pl)
Sports: 2 Tennis Courts, Volleyball
☎ (92) 45 71 54
Tourist Office: ☎ (92) 45 72 76

St Véran (05490)
Gîte d'étape: M. Brunet (30pl) GTA
☎ (92) 45 82 19
Tourist Office: ☎ (92) 45 82 21
Sport: Ski School ☎ (92) 45 81 20
Taxi: Frendo ☎ (92) 45 71 35

14 • Provence
and the Côte d'Azur

Provence is the sun-drenched part of France that runs east from the Rhône estuary to the Italian border. It is most famous for the Riviera, the playground of the rich and those who want to lap up the sun on crowded beaches. Places like Cannes, Nice, St Tropez are renowned but there are many other towns and villages inland with much to offer the visitor and without the teeming crowds.

The coastline is divided into the Riviera and the Côte d'Azur. Originally the Riviera was the name given to the coastline around Nice, and the name Côte d'Azur was introduced in 1888 to distinguish the French Alpes-Maritimes coastline from the Riviera dei Fiori in Italy. Inland there is a glittering array of things to see and do, and after a day spent exploring you can still have time to drive down to the beaches and enjoy a swim when most of the crowds have left. It takes only 2 hours to travel from the Mediterranean to the alpine peaks. Along the 112km (70 mile) stretch of beaches there are twenty-six major resorts and every conceivable kind of sport on offer from fishing and scuba diving, to flying and pot holing. There is golf, horse riding, pelota, archery and even fencing.

This region was colonised by the Greeks in about 600BC. It is typical Mediterranean countryside. The rocky soil affords scrub vegetation and olive trees but little else, except in those small patches where vines can be grown. As one climbs into the hills, however, the vegetation becomes sub-tropical and there are orange trees, oleanders, cacti and eucalyptus. The best time for plants is in the late spring, when the rains have passed and the flowers, especially the bougainvillaea and mimosa, are out. It is really the only time of the year when the countryside can be said to look pretty, although the resorts maintain some magnificent gardens throughout the year. As the sun rises higher in the sky during the summer, the plants die away, the grass turns to hay and the earth is baked hard. In the summer, temperatures on the rocky coastal plain can rise to unbear-

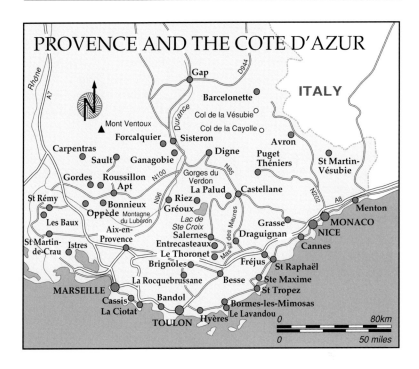

PROVENCE AND THE COTE D'AZUR

Rhône
A7
Gap
D944
ITALY
Barcelonette
Col de la Vésubie
Mont Ventoux
Durance
Col de la Cayolle
Forcalquier
Sisteron
Avron
Carpentras
Digne
Puget
Sault
Ganagobie
Théniers
St Martin-
Vésubie
Gordes
Roussillon
N100
Gorges du
Verdon
Apt
La Palud
Castellane
N85
St Rémy
Riez
N96
Bonnieux
Gréoux
Oppède Montagne
du Lubéron
Menton
Les Baux
Lac de
Ste Croix
Grasse
MONACO
Aix-en-
Salernes
Draguignan
NICE
St Martin-
Istres
Provence
Entrecasteaux
Massif des Maures
Cannes
de-Crau
Le Thoronet
Brignoles
Fréjus
La Rocquebrussane
Besse
St Raphaël
MARSEILLE
Ste Maxime
Cassis
Bandol
St Tropez
La Ciotat
Bormes-les-Mimosas
TOULON
Hyères
Le Lavandou
0
80km

0
50 miles

able levels, but there is usually a welcome breeze to be found on the
beaches and in the pine-coloured hills if you venture further inland.
The region boasts up to 2,800 hours of sunshine a year and fewer than
75 rainy days. Nice has about 3 days of frost a year and Menton claims
to have a foggy day once every 10 years. While the summer days are
hot, the evenings are warm and balmy. One can see why they are
known as 'velvet nights'.

Although the Greeks established Marseilles as a trading settlement little remains of their presence today except the vineyards. It
was the Greeks who introduced the first vines and while the wines
of Provence are still not widely known outside France, great efforts
are being made by the producers to promote sales in Britain and
North America.

There is a wine tour which you can follow which passes close to
Toulon, France's largest naval base, and follows a large circle,
through most of the wine producing areas of Côtes de Provence.
Even in the summer, this wine trail is not overcrowded, except in the
more famous production areas like Bandol and Cassis.

It is much better to follow your nose and to visit those producers
off the official route. Their wines are every bit as good and they will

welcome you with open arms. A wide variety of wines are produced and there is no difficulty finding the right one to go with the cuisine of the region, almost a reason in itself for visiting Provence. Marseilles has given the world the famous fish soup *bouillabaisse*, which is usually a meal in itself. Fish figures prominently on the menus of restaurants while the farther east you travel, the greater the influence of Italian cooking becomes, with pasta dishes and a French version of the pizza.

If you are interested in getting off the main tourist routes you can explore some of the beautiful, picturesque villages inland, go walking or horse riding in the hills or caving. There is much of antiquity to be discovered as well. Although the Greeks were the first foreigners to colonise the area, it was the Romans who have left their mark. It was they who built the great towns which now dominate the east of the region but Provence is still basically a place to relax in, for leisurely explorations, for bathing, basking in the sun, eating some fine food and drinking some very agreeable wines — what more could anyone want?

Provence consists of six *départements*, three along the coast — Bouches-du-Rhône, Var and Alpes-Maritimes, and three inland — Vaucluse, Alpes-de-Haute-Provence and Hautes-Alpes. The areas of the French Alps that fall in Provence include some marvellous walking, at both low and high altitudes. The Alps really plunge into the sea at Menton, close to the Italian border. From here they climb gradually throughout Provence with their highest peaks being about 2,000m (6,560ft), in the Hautes-Alpes. The Alps also boast many excellent national parks where you can walk all day long without seeing another soul. National parks include those of Barre des Ecrins, Queyras and Mercantour. For higher altitude walking some experience is necessary and a degree of fitness, but there are wonderful routes for the hiker and backpacker. Travel throughout the region could not be easier. There are fast toll *autoroutes* to speed the tourists to the beaches, but a good network of secondary routes to take you inland for exploring.

There are daily flights into Marseilless, Nice, and Nîmes from Paris and international flights to Marseilles and Nice. Nice-Côte d'Azur is France's second largest airport. It takes $10^1/_2$ hours to fly from New York to Nice and just over $1^1/_2$ hours from London. The rail link between Paris and Avignon, Marseilles, Toulon and Nice is also excellent. You can sleep the night away as you travel down from Paris with your car safely aboard the daily motorail service. It takes $10^1/_2$ hours by train from Paris and 20 hours from London. There is also the famous Blue Train plying between Calais and the Côte d'Azur, with sleepers and couchettes. There is a direct Paris-Nice motorway, and frequent coach services from Paris and other leading towns in France and Europe to the Côte d'Azur.

Car hire is available at all airports, near most main railway stations and in all large towns and cities. For the energetic bicycles can be hired, and for those not so keen, mopeds or motorbikes.

There is a large network of bus services to different parts of the region, but most provide only a daily service to villages.

In Provence you can enjoy the journey aboard the Chemin de Fer de la Provence, which runs from Nice to Digne. The train stops frequently and is an excellent way of exploring the countryside, especially the mountains. At many of the stops you can catch a connecting bus service to take you even further afield.

If you want to take in a little of the coastline, the following two tours will enable you to see something of the tourist spots while allowing you to enjoy the countryside inland, and let you stretch your legs with some walking.

Tour of Hyères and Surrounding Area

Start the tour at Hyères to the east of Toulon, just north of the airport into which you can fly from Paris. Drivers may take the N7 or the toll Autoroute de Provence. Trains run from Marseilles or Toulon where car hire is available. Local transport in this area is available, but not to be relied on for getting to, and more important, getting back from the outlying districts.

Hyères is the oldest resort on the Riviera which is why it deserves a visit. Cathérine de Medici planned to build a summer palace there in the sixteenth century, but the plan came to nothing. Queen Victoria visited it regularly, and novelist Robert Louis Stevenson lived there for a time. The town is a few miles inland from the coast, and there are palm tree-lined avenues and well irrigated flower gardens. There are the ruins of a castle on the hill overlooking the town, and a municipal museum which is worth visiting because it houses many remains found locally from the Greek and Roman occupations.

The townspeople are rightly proud of their parks and gardens and you should visit them, especially the Jardins Olbius Riquier and Parc St Bernard. Other things to see are the Place St Paul and the Chapel of Notre-Dame de Consolation. There are many good hotels and restaurants both in and around the town, and it is a pleasant place to make a base, close to the sea and giving easy access for exploring inland.

The beaches are found about 7km (4.3 miles) to the south at the end of the peninsula. The drive down the Route du Sel goes past the salt pans at Les Pesquiers to La Tour-Fondue. From here, the islands of Ile de Porquerolles, Ile de Port Cros and Ile du Levant are just offshore. Together the islands are known as the Iles d'Hyères and can be reached by a 15-minute boat crossing from La Tour-Fondue. The peninsula on which the beaches are situated used to be another island in this chain, but it became landlocked many centuries ago. Severe storms still occasionally sweep the area in winter, and in 1811 a fierce storm actually forced a channel through the peninsula, separating it again from the mainland briefly, but the sands quickly returned. Even today, if the weather is bad, this road can be closed. There are vineyards on Ile de Porquerolles, and many charming walks on all three islands, although the Ile du Levant is in part occupied by the French Navy and access to some of their land is restricted.

From Hyères, take the N98 to **Le Lavandou**, which gets its name from the lavender fields cultivated along the banks of the River Batailler; it is a charming little fishing port. There are good beaches along the coastline here, and inland the Massif des Maures dominates the landscape and does so until Fréjus is reached. The coastline here is known as the Côte des Maures, which is named after the hills, which in turn were named after the dark-coloured pine trees on their slopes. The densely-wooded hill slopes have some marvellous walks, and the villagers from the many hamlets of the Massif still earn their income in part from gathering the sweet chestnuts that thrive here, and collecting the bark from the cork trees.

Just north of Le Lavandou is the hilltop village of **Bormes-lès-Mimosas**, which is worth a visit. There is a sixteenth-century chapel to St Francis, and in front of it there is a statue to Francesco di Paola, who is said to have saved the village from the plague in 1481. The village, with its large tree-lined square and old houses, has been little changed by the tourists who now visit in growing numbers.

Circular Tour from St Tropez to Toulon

This tour starts in Bormes and the next stop is St Tropez which can be reached by either taking the coastal road through some marvellous little resorts with splendid beaches, or the higher road a little way inland, through Cogolin. On the lower route, are the beaches where the Allies landed in 1944; and if the higher road is chosen you can do a little wine tasting along the way. There are cellars and tasting centres at Bormes, La Môle, La Croix-Valmer and Cogolin.

The rocky coast of the Esterel corniche near St Raphaël

St Tropez is, of course, a legend. It is one of the most famous resorts in the world, bursting with fine hotels, restaurants and nightlife. It has always attracted artists because of the near-perfect light, and many of their works are now housed in the town's museum of modern art. There is also a maritime museum in the citadel with many exhibits from the old town. It was only 80 years ago that St Tropez got its first proper road into the town; before then people used the narrow-gauge railway, or the ferry from St Raphaël.

The harbour at St Tropez still houses the traditional fishing boats, but they are now dwarfed by the luxury yachts of the rich, while the quays are packed with artists dashing out oil paintings to sell to the tourists. The main sights to see are the sixteenth-century chapel of Ste Anne, just outside town; and also the statue of the French Admiral Bailli de Suffren, who, with a tiny fleet of five ships, managed to harass the Royal Navy around the globe in the mid-eighteenth century. His home was Château Suffren, in the old town, near the town hall.

St Tropez is surrounded by huge beaches, and the new marina-holiday complex of Port Grimaud. Cars are not allowed, and it is a little like a mini-Venice, to be visited only on foot or by boat, with conducted tours available through the maze of canals.

Continuing along the N98, the family resort of **Ste Maxime** is popular throughout the year with lively evening entertainment, and many sporting facilities. It also has many good restaurants, and a fine reputation for its food. Detours are also possible from here into the hills, to sample more of the local wine around Plan-de-la-Tour and La Garde-Freinet.

Fréjus, once a Roman harbour, is now a couple of kilometres inland, and there are some fine ruins to explore. They include the remains of a fifth-century baptistry. There is an incomplete Roman theatre to the north of the town, now used for French bullfights, and there are guided tours of the thirteenth-century cathedral and cloisters of Notre-Dame-de-Victoire in the town centre. There is a museum containing antiquities found in the area. **St Raphaël**, Fréjus' neighbour, has a twelfth-century church of the Knights Templars and a fine archaeological museum.

From Fréjus and St Raphaël the route turns inland, away from the beaches and into the hills and the vineyards. **Draguignan**, a small town with a reputation for good food, both in its restaurants and its shops, is the first main town. It has many fine old buildings and fountains, and the centre is dominated by the seventeenth-century Tour d'Horloge. There is a medieval gateway and the façade of a thirteenth-century synagogue in the Rue de la Juiverie. A museum is housed in the eighteenth-century former summer palace of the Bishops of Fréjus.

Nearby is the spectacular area of gorges and plunging waterfalls known as the Verdon Gorges. There are wine tasting cellars in Draguignan and in many of the villages on the road to Brignoles, especially Les Arcs, Vidauban and Le Luc.

Brignoles is another market town and agricultural centre, famous for its museum, which houses amongst other things, the oldest Gaulish Christian sarcophagus, dating from the third century. Just south of Brignoles is **Besse**, the home of Gaspard de Besse, a sort of eighteenth-century French Robin Hood. He was finally captured and executed at Aix-en-Provence. There is also a beautiful Cistercian abbey at **Le Thoronet**, and many of the original twelfth-century buildings have been restored to their austere splendour. Other places to visit in the area are **Salernes** with its thirteenth-century castle ruins; **Entrecasteaux**, a medieval village with château and fortified Gothic church; and **Tourtour**.

From Brignoles, drive in a sweeping curve back down to the coast using the N560 and taking in **La Roquebrussanne**, and a small detour off to La Ste Baume, where legend has it that Mary Magdalene lived in retreat in a cave for the last 30 years of her life. The cave,

The spectacular chasm of the Verdon Gorges

Grotte de St Pilon, can be reached on foot from the D80.

Continue on the D80 down to **Glémenos** with its eighteenth-century château and nearby chapel of St Jean de Garguier, with its collection of religious paintings dating back for the last 500 years, and then on to **La Ciotat**, on the coast, a former Greek settlement. The Musée Tauroentum, built on the site of a Roman villa, and housing many of the Roman finds discovered nearby should be visited. Then it is just a short drive to Bandol.

Bandol is the home of one of the region's most famous wines, and you can sit out at one of the many beach cafés and sample it at leisure. Just off the coast is the Ile Bendor, now a tourist trap with art gallery, museum, zoo and the World Museum of Wines and Spirits.

The final point of call before returning to Hyères should be to **Toulon**, a bustling, crowded city, with few attractions having survived the heavy bombardments during the last war. There are some good restaurants, however, and the fish and vegetable markets are worth visiting, as are the maritime and archaeological museums.

Walking in Provence

No other area in France affords the walker so much choice of countryside to travel through. If you want to get away from the crowds there are high mountains to walk in the summer, shaded woody hills to get out of the heat of the sun, vineyards to explore and the wine to taste, and it is still possible to walk along the coastline so you can plunge into the sea if it gets too hot. There are walks and climbs to suit all levels of fitness and skill, in almost every part of Provence.

It is best to divide the walking into two groups, the lowland and the highland sections. Gradually as you move both east and north the altitude rises and you switch from rugged hills into towering mountains. The lowland walking starts as soon as you cross the Rhône. As you travel east from the river there is the large plain known as the Crau, dealt with in more detail later, but an excellent place both to walk and birdwatch. It is the home of the little bustard and the majestic red kite. To the north of the Crau the land rises as you approach Les Baux. There is excellent walking here and especially north of Carpentras where the countryside is dominated by Mont Ventoux, which rises to 1,909m (6,260ft) above sea level. This area, known as the Baronies, is rugged but great walking and backpacking country.

If you proceed east you reach Aix-en-Provence, another great base for walking trips. To the north is the National Park of Lubéron through which runs the River Verdon. The Gorges of the Verdon, especially between the eastern boundaries of the national park and Castellane are spectacular with many walks, although some are only for the more experienced hikers. The locals refer to the gorges as the Grande Canyon, and while it is not as large as its American namesake, it is still impressive. There is also good walking in the Alpes-de-Haute-Provence, and Alpes-Maritimes, and both walking and mountaineering opportunities in the Hautes-Alpes. North of Le Lavandou is the range of the Massif des Maures, a ridge of hills rising up to 600m (1,968ft). The ridge runs in a north-eastern line between Toulon and Fréjus and from most points there are views of the Mediterranean. Around Grasse, world famous for its perfumes, the hills of the Alpes-Maritimes start to rise. The rolling hills are between 1,000 and 1,200m (3,280 and 3,936ft) and there are marvellous panoramas. North-east of Grasse is the Gorges de la Vésubie, also worth exploring, and then it is on and up into the mountains near the Italian border, where the air gets thinner and the walking tougher.

There are remote villages like St Etienne, St Martin-Vésubie and Auron, and more gorges to walk, such as the Gorges de Daluis and the Gorges du Cians. The mountains along the border rise to almost 3,000m (9,840ft), the highest being Mont du Grand Capelet at 2,935m (9,626ft) and Mont Neillier at 2,785m (9,134ft). There are many quiet alpine villages to stay in if you want a base from which to walk.

Apart from some tricky sections in the Gorges du Verdon and in the higher regions close to the Italian border there is nothing to daunt the serious, reasonably fit walker. Heat can be a major problem in the summer with temperatures regularly in the 'nineties' (30°C) and often going higher. The mistral normally blows in the spring and during the winter, but can occasionally occur in the summer, and a few fierce thunderstorms sometimes roll around the hills. The main rule for the summer walker is to be careful of the heat. It can get blisteringly hot as the sun pounds down on bare rock, so wear a cap and carry some liquid refreshment. Apart from the Gorges du Verdon, where you will find other tourists, most of the walking areas of Provence are still pretty deserted, and you can enjoy your solitude.

Carpentras and Sault make great bases from which to walk around Mont Ventoux to the north, and the Lubéron National Park to the south. The Lubéron is fast becoming one of the best wine-producing areas of the south of France, so you can combine your walking with a little tasting along the way. If you just want to concentrate on the Lubéron area, Apt makes a good base. The Lubéron National Park is an area of pine-covered hills. For centuries the area was used for grazing sheep and they would then be driven across country to the markets. There are still scores of old drove trails criss-crossing the park, usually following the highest land, and beside them you will spot derelict inns and old shepherds' huts. La

Garde Frénet is a good base for walking in the Var if you don't want to stray too far away from the coast. From here you can make a number of excursions into the Massif des Maures, and because you are so close to the coastal towns, there is a reasonably good local bus service to get you to and from your starting and finishing points. If you want to be more intrepid and tackle the Gorges du Verdon over three or four days — why rush it if you are on holiday — there are a number of places to base youself, such as Moustiers-Ste Marie, Gréoux or Castellane.

Walkers are welcome in Provence and almost all the local Syndicats can supply details of interesting routes which they have waymarked well. The tourist office in Aix has produced a very good handbook of local walks, many of them around Mont Ste Victoire. There are a score or more of waymarked routes around Menton ranging from a 2-hour stroll to a good day's hike.

Long-distance Grande Randonnée routes include the GR6 Alpes-Océan, which runs from Sisteron through Vaucluse to Beaucaire, the GR Tour du Lubéron, a walk covering a number of trails totalling about 160km (100 miles), the GR9 and 98 Var and Bouches-du-Rhône, a walk taking you round the coastline, and the GR91 Vercors-Ventoux, a walk of just over 160km (100 miles) through the Drôme, Hautes-Alpes to Mont Ventoux. The GR4 Méditerranée-Océan takes you from near Grasse in a 160km (100 mile) trip to Lubéron before leaving the region, while the hardest walk is the GR5-52 Hollande-Méditerranée, which runs from Larche to Menton through the Parc Naturel du Mercantour, in the highest parts of the Alpes-Maritimes.

The Mercantour park is really in the highland walking section which covers the Hautes-Alpes and Alpes-de-Haute-Provence, where many peaks are 2,000m (6,560ft) or more. Snow can be expected from October on and lies on the highest peaks well into June, and sometimes July. There are many glaciers in the area.

This is real rugged, backpacking country where you should be really fit and have a reasonable knowledge of mountain craft, map and compass reading and basic survival, just in case you are caught out by the weather. Sudden storms, low cloud and mist can all be problems.

In the Hautes-Alpes there are two nature parks, the Ecrins, famous for its alpine plants and flowers, generally between 2,000m (6,560ft) and 3,000m (9,840ft), although rising to 4,102m (13,454ft) on the summit of the Barre des Ecrins; and Queyras, which straddles the Italian border. There are many routes both in and around these parks. There are camp sites on the edges or near the parks.

You should also spot quite a lot of wildlife as there are chamois, marmot, golden eagles and many other species of mountain birds.The Alpes-de-Haute-Provence stretches from the hills around the Gorges du Verdon in the south to peaks 2,500m (8,200ft) and more in the north. It is a great place for backwoods camping and backpacking. A small railway line, the Chemin de Fer de Haute Provence climbs its way into the hills and you can choose any one of its many stopping places to start your walk.

The newest park is the Parc National du Mercantour which opened in 1979. It lies close to the Italian border and varies in altitude between 1,000m (3,280ft) and 3,000m (9,840ft). The whole park is worth exploring and there are very many waymarked trails.

The whole of the Alps are criss-crossed by a large number of long-distance footpaths, and many of them pass through the mountains of Provence. Most demand a high state of fitness and are rated as hard or difficult walks.

But, don't let that put you off. As the crowds squeeze on to the beaches, why not enjoy the peace and quiet of the mountains and hills.

Exploring the Crau

The Crau is a stone desert, a vast flatland to the east of the Rhône, rich in wildlife, yet hardly visited by tourists to the south of France. It is well known to ornithologists but most head for the Camargue, so this little corner of Provence is well worth exploring. The area is bordered in the west by the river, in the north by the Alpilles, in the east by the Etang de Berre and in the south by the sea.

St Martin-de-Crau just to the north, or Istres on the eastern shores of the Etang, make good bases for exploring the area, although it is only a short drive from Arles, Salon or Aix-en-Provence. The N568 runs diagonally across the Crau to Fos on the sea and from this road there are many lanes to follow to give you access to most of the area. There is a French air base just outside Salon and the jets do come screaming overhead, but the birds seem to have got used to it.

The Crau is all that remains of the alluvial flood plain of the Durance, a river which flows down from the Massif des Hautes-Alpes. Thousands of years ago, it forced a deep channel through the Alpilles, a valley known now as the Pertuis de Lamanon, and flowed straight into the Mediterranean. Today the Durance is a tributary of the Rhône, and the Crau is what remains of the mountain debris once deposited by the river as it rushed into the sea.

In some places the stones are 15m (50ft) deep but much of the

Crau, which covers more than 50,000ha (123,550 acres), has been converted into agricultural land.

A complicated series of canals in the north and east of the Crau has enabled vineyards and olive groves to be planted. The grazing here is much lusher than in the rest of the Crau where the sheep roam the flat, drab landscape looking for something to eat among the sparse vegetation. What makes the Crau so interesting is the wide range of birds that gather there, especially many rare breeding species. There are many reptiles to be seen if you are careful, including five species of snake, none of them dangerous to man. Alas, snakes are no match for motor vehicles and you will see many crushed on the road. If out exploring you may also see scorpions and tarantula spiders — two creatures which seem to strike fear into many people quite unnecessarily. The tarantula belongs to the wolf spider family. In Italy it was thought that a bite from a tarantula turned you insane unless you performed a feverish twirling dance to shake out the poison — the origin of the tarantella dance. Tarantulas will bite if attacked, and while painful it is not in the least bit dangerous. While tarantulas generally hunt by night, they do like to spend the day sunning themselves outside their homes, usually a camouflaged hole in the ground. Scorpions are quite common in the Crau. They like to shelter under stones or wedges in behind the bark of a tree during the day because they too, are nocturnal hunters. It is possible to find them by gingerly turning over stones with your boot or a stick.

There are two sorts of scorpion found in the Crau. The first species grows to about 10cm (4in) in length and the sting in the tail is no more irritating than that of a bee or wasp. The second species is larger, usually coloured a yellowish-brown, and its sting is much more painful, but still not fatal.

On a stifling hot summer's day it is quite possible to see a posse of different birds of prey soaring majestically over the Crau, using the thermals that rise over the hot stones. The Montagu's harrier swoops close to the ground in the hope of driving small birds up into the air where it can catch them. Several pairs breed on the Crau, laying their eggs on a carpet of trampled down grass which serves as a nest. Other birds of prey to be seen include Egyptian vultures, which nest in the Alpilles, the northern edge of the Crau; golden and Bonelli's eagle, sparrow hawk, goshawk, black kite, all the harriers, short-toed eagle, osprey, peregrine, hobby, kestrel and lesser kestrel. One part of the Crau has been used as a rubbish tip to dispose of the garbage from neighbouring towns, and it attracts thousands of birds, both birds of prey and many species of gull looking for easy pickings.

Another rare breeding bird that is ideally suited to the Crau is the stone-curlew. It is quite a large bird, up to 40cm (16in) long, with large eyes. If it is disturbed during the day it will run to escape or will flatten itself against the ground, and its colouring allows it to merge into the stony background. Even its eggs are camouflaged to look like stones, and are laid in a stony nest on the ground. Some of the other rare species that can be spotted are the little bustard, the great spotted cuckoo, Calandra lark, lesser grey shrike, short-toed lark, subalpine warbler, black-eared wheatear, pratincole, and pin-tailed sandgrouse. All the other colourful birds of the Camargue can also be seen here such as the roller, bee eater and hoopoe.

The most magnificent of the five species of snakes, none of which is dangerous, is the Montpellier snake which can grow to almost 2.2m (7ft) in length. The Montpellier is found all along the Mediterranean but its numbers are falling. The southern smooth snake grows to about half a metre (about 2ft) long, and while it can give you a nasty bite if cornered, it tends to slither away out of trouble rather than seek a fight. The viperine water snake can grow to more than a metre (3ft) in length and while its markings resemble those of the common adder, it does not bite (the adder is not found this far south). If surprised, however, it might release the stink glands at the base of its tail.

The other snakes that can be seen are the harmless grass snake and the ladder snake which likes to lie out on an exposed piece of rock lapping up the sun. It grows to about 1.5m (5ft) long and constricts its prey.

If you are lucky, you may spot pond tortoises and terrapins, mud frogs and natterjack toads. You should certainly see the magnificently coloured green tree frog, and there are edible frogs and laughing frogs about.

The Crau is certainly not a beautiful landscape, except perhaps where it starts to climb into the limestone hills of the Alpilles. Even here it is spectacular rather than pretty, with its densely wooded valleys and lower hill slopes. Despite this, however, it has an enormous amount to offer whether you just want to go walking or want to observe the wildlife. There may be thousands of birds to be seen, but you won't see many other people.

Exploring Upper Provence

The Verdon Gorges are France's answer to America's Grand Canyon but on a smaller scale. In places the cliffs tower more than 620m (2,000ft) above the narrow river floor and the green waters of the river after which it was named. The walking possibilities in this area have already been mentioned, but if you are less energetic but still want to explore this spectacular countryside, there are many routes which you can drive.

Castellane, is a small but bustling health resort at the eastern end of the gorges. It nestles in a natural river basin surrounded by mountains and makes an ideal base for touring the area by car. There are a number of hotels in Castellane and some pleasant cafés and restaurants, but few other points of interest. There is the Chapel of Notre-Dame du Roc, the Romanesque church of St Victor, and a pentagonal tower, but the main sights are beyond the town.

There are a number of routes to follow through the mountains. Many of the mountain roads are narrow, most are twisty and in some places there are near heart-stopping sheer drops just a few feet from your wheels, but the careful driver has nothing to worry about.

All the tours start in Castellane, and a map of the area is essential.

Tour 1   The Gorges du Verdon (about 128km, 80 miles)
Take the road out of Castellane leading to Draguignan, this follows the north or right bank of the gorges and gets you used to looking down on the river. Travel through the small village of Porte de St Jean and then follow the curve of the river round to Pont de Soleils. For the first part of this trip the road runs parallel to the GR4 long-distance footpath, so you can get out and stretch your legs provided you can find somewhere safe to park. Just before Pont de Soleils you will pass the Clue de Chasteuil where the gorge narrows and the sides become even more steep.

Stay on the D952 and follow the river round to Point Sublime passing by another constriction, the Clue de Carejuan. The road at this point is almost 930m (3,000ft) above sea level.

Continue on through La Palud, the Col d'Ayen, and up to Moustiers at the head of Lac de Ste Croix. The return journey follows the left bank of the gorges by leaving Moustiers on the D952 then turning off on to the D957 to cross the river over the new road bridge. The road takes you through Aiguines along the route known as the Corniche Sublime. After the Balcons de la Mescala and La Cournuelle, you turn off right on to the D90 through Trigance to rejoin the D955 which takes you back north to Pont de Soleils and then Castellane.

The mountain village of Tourette-sur-Loup, north-west of Nice

The tour is one of the most beautiful and scenic you can take from Castellane and the locals proudly claim it is one of the most spectacular sceneries in the world. The road on both banks overlook the Grand Canyon with cliffs between 279 and 651m (900 and 2,100ft high.

Tour 2   The Northern Bank of the Gorges du Verdon (80km, 50 miles)

It is possible to make a shorter tour of the northern bank of the gorges by following the Route des Crêtes. Take the road leading to Draguignan to Pont de Soleils, then on to La Palud. About 1km (about half a mile) before the village turn left on to the new road to La Palud just after La Maline. This route takes you through some of the highest mountains and there are many fine vantage points and spots to stop and picnic. Many of the picnic spots are in the forests and tables and benches are provided. On the way back just after Point Sublime there is a track down to the bottom of the gorges. The Martel track is just over a mile and strong shoes are essential as well as a torch because you have to walk through several dark tunnels. The walk down is the easy bit!

Tour 3   To Ste Croix Lake (56km, 35 miles)

Follow Tour 1 until you reach the bridge and then take the new road which follows the artificial lake on its left bank to the newly rebuilt village of Les Salles. Cross the lake by the bridge over the Ste Croix Dam, and drive on the village of Ste Croix. You can then reach Moustiers by the right side of the lake, or go to Riez.

Tour 4   The Upper Verdon Valley (64-72km, 40-5 miles)
This tour takes you up into the Provence Alps. From Castellane take the road to St André-les-Alpes. The road goes over the top of the impressive Castillon Dam, 90m (300ft) high and sheer drops on either side, so not for those who suffer from vertigo, and then along the side of the artificial lake to St André, about 16km (10 miles) on.

Take the road to the Col d'Allos which winds its way through wild scenery to the village of Allos. It is a popular summer centre with walkers but mainly a winter resort affording very good local skiing. If you have the time it is worth making the detour to the Allos lake, which is at an altitude of almost 2,017m (6,700ft). From the village it takes about 45 minutes driving and then 20 minutes on foot to reach the lake.

The road winds its way through large fields which are used as the ski runs during the winter. Barcelonnette is the most northerly point of the tour. It is in the Ubaye valley and from here you have a choice of three routes back to Castellane: La Lauzet and its lake, Serre Ponçon lake, the Clue de Barles, Digne and then the Route Napoléon back to Castellane; the Col de la Cayolle and the Vallée du Var; Jausiers, the Col de Restefond, the Col de la Bonnette with its marvellous views, and the Vallée de la Tinée.

Tour 5   The Gorges du Cians and Gorges du Daluis (about 193km, 120 miles)
From Castellane take the road to St André and at St Julien turn right on the Nice road to Pont de Gueydan. Go to Guillaumes through the famous Gorges du Daluis, carved out of red schist. Take either of the roads to Valberg and Beuil and then drop down the mountain to Puget Théniers through the Gorges du Cians. You can then go back to Castellane either by Entrevaux, Les Scaffarels and St Julien, or, if you have time, via the Clue de St Auban and Le Logis du Pin.

Tour 6   The Lavender Fields (about 180km, 112 miles)
From Castellane take the road going to Draguignan up to the Pont de Soleils and then on to Moustiers, Ste Marie and Riez, following the right bank of the Grand Canyon du Verdon. Go to Valensole, then down to Gréoux-les-Bains, up to Mesel and back to Castellane by the Route Napoléon. This tour takes you through the typical scenery of northern Provence and through many lavender fields which are at their most scented in the summer.

Tour 7   The Gorges du Loup (about 140km, 87 miles)
From Castellane take the Grasse road. At Le Logis du Pin take the road to Thorenc and Gréolières. The Gorges du Loup are situated between Gréolières and Gourdon. You can see them from either bank and can return to Castellane by St Vallier or Andon. These gorges are cut vertically into the mountains of Grasse. Gourdon is a delightful village at the entrance of the Gorges which also overlooks the Mediterranean.

Tour 8   The Vallée de l'Asse and L'Issole (about 80km, 50 miles)
From Castellane go up to Barrême and take the Nice road. About 2km (1.2 miles) after Barrême turn right on the road to Clumans, and then on to Tartonne and St André, before returning to Castellane past the dam.

Tour 9   The Gorges de Robion and Lachens (about 72km, 45 miles)
From Castellane take the road to Le Bourguet then down to Le Logis du Pin. At the crossroads take the road which leads to the top of Lachens for the most spectacular views. From here you can return to Castellane either by the Le Logis du Pin road or by the La Bastide and Comps road. This is a short trip but well off-the-beaten-track so you shouldn't meet very much traffic. From the top of the mountain you have views to the Italian border in the east and the Mediterranean in the south.

Tour 10   The Lakes of Castillon and Chaudanne (40km, 25 miles)
From Castellane, take the road to Grasse and after about 3km (1.8 miles) turn left on the Demandoix road. Before reaching the village, turn left again on to the new road which takes you past Lake Chaudanne to Lake Castillon. Just after crossing the Paontas bridge and before the road starts to descend, you have views of both lakes. When you reach Lake Castillon, turn right for St Julien and then back to Castellane by Barrême. If you do not have much time, you can go back directly by turning left and crossing the Verdon over the dam. There are also excellent vantage and photographing points of the lakes and dam from the small villages of La Beaume and Blaron.

Tour 11   The Forests (about 77km, 48 miles)
From Castellane take the Grasse road and after about 3km (1.8 miles) turn left on the Demandoix road. On the way, you can visit the skiing centre at Vauplane. Go down to Soleilhas and St Auban, through the Col de Blaine and then back to Castellane via the Logis du Pin.

Tour 12   The Col des Champs (about 161km, 38 miles)
Take the Allos road (see Tour 4) and when you get to the fortified city

of Colmars take the road up to the Col des Champs through the forest. The Col is just under 1,953m (6,300ft high). You can reach the valley of the Var River at St Martin d'Entraunes, and return to Castellane through the Gorges de Daluis by following the route in Tour 5. This tour is a quickie but it is through marvellous countryside and you can make a day of it by walking in the woods and picnicking.

The Durance Valley

Thousands of years ago the Durance used to flow south straight into the Mediterranean and how it came to be diverted to become a tributary of the Rhône is not certain. What is sure, however, is that this part of Upper Provence and the Durance valley in particular is worth a visit. It does attract tourists but not in huge numbers because most seem to prefer the attractions to the east such as Arles, Orange and Avignon, and to the south —Aix-en-Provence and the coast. The Durance flows south through the mountains of Upper Provence, past Sisteron, and then it starts to sweep westwards in a great curve, as it passes south of the Montagne du Lubéron, on its way to the Rhône.

There are a number of places for a base from which you will be able to explore the whole area. There is the Montagne de Lure to the west of Sisteron, the Plateau du Valensole to the south of the Durance, and the whole of the Lubéron range with its delightful walks and promising vineyards. A road, the Mourre Nègre, runs along the crest of the Lubéron hills, and this follows the traditional path along which sheep were driven to market for centuries. To the north of this road there are many lanes to venture along which will take you to delightful villages such as Ménerbes, Bonnieux, Gordes, Roussillon and Oppède-le-Vieux, a lovely village which has been faithfully restored by the many artists and craftsmen who have moved in.

One of the most noticeable things about this region is the red rock, and in Roussillon, the red stone of the houses blends with the red rocks all around. The village is surrounded by old quarries from which the rock was excavated, and these are worth noticing just to see the remarkable differences in the colours of the stone.

Ménerbes is an ancient village with an old church, citadel and spectacular views. At **Bonnieux** there are many old houses, twisting narrow streets and fountains to see and two famous churches. One dates back only to the last century but houses several fine fifteenth-century paintings of the Old German School, while the other church dates back to the twelfth-century. At **Gordes** there is a Renaissance château which has a collection of more than a thousand works of art by Victor Vasarély, a French painter of Hungarian origin born in 1908 and the originator of Op Art in painting and sculpture. Just to the north-west of Gordes is the Abbaye de Sénanque, remarkably well preserved and tranquil. Built by the Cistercians in their simple, almost austere style, the abbey was one of the 'three famous sisters of Provence', the others being at Le Thoronet and Silvacane. Occasionally during the summer, concerts are held there. The abbey also houses an exhibition of the Sahara desert. All over the area you can find the remains of *bories*, simple huts made by the shepherds, and to the south-west of Gordes there is the **Village Noir**, a complete village of these drystone shelters long since deserted. To the south-west of the abbey are the great water-filled caverns which give rise to the Fontaine de Vaucluse, said to be one of the most powerful springs in the world. The underground caverns are filled by the waters of the River Sorgue and it surfaces in a large lake, on whose shores a *son et lumière* is staged during the summer.

The village of the same name nearby, dominated by the ruins of an old castle, was for a time the home of the fourteenth-century Italian poet Petrarch, and there is a small museum in his memory, built, it is thought, on the site of his home. There is also an interesting caving museum in the village

Apt is one of the oldest villages in the area and became a Roman colony during their occupation of Provence. It was known as *Hath* but was renamed *Apta Julia* after Julius Caesar, which over the years contracted to its present name. Its most interesting building is the cathedral of Ste Anne built over two crypts. One crypt lies over the other and the upper one was carved out of the rock in the eleventh-century. It contains an altar which pre-dates the crypt, and six thirteenth-century sarcophagi rest in recesses around the walls. In the lower crypt are the relics of Ste Anne, the mother of the Virgin Mary. The sacred remains are said to have been found in 776 when Charlemagne consecrated the original church on the site.

There has certainly been a church on the site for at least 1,400 years, the first being built on the site of a Roman temple. Archaeological digs around Apt have also discovered a number of sarcophagi dating back to the fourth century AD.

After the discovery of the relics of Ste Anne, Apt became a pilgrimage centre and Anne of Austria came to worship in the crypt in 1623 praying for a child. The valuable gifts she bequeathed to the church are still kept locked in the treasury. Further evidence of the rich history of this area can be gained by visiting the archaeological museum nearby It contains many items dating back to Roman times which were found locally. Pont Julien is claimed to be the best preserved Roman bridge in France and is found 5 miles west of Apt crossing the River Coulon. The three arched bridge was built in the first century BC.

Cavaillon in the west lies alongside the Durance and is another good base for touring the region. It has a bustling fruit and vegetable market which is worth an early morning trip. The town itself lies in a fertile plain, the Petit Lubéron, and there are field after field of lush melons for which the area is famous. In the town itself there is the Romanesque cathedral of St Véran, an eighteenth-century synagogue and a museum of local Jewish history. The cathedral was built in the thirteenth century and has an octagonal tower, a feature found in many churches in Provence, as well as many fine religious paintings and carvings in wood and stone. In the Grande Rue there is the town museum featuring many Roman exhibits and ancient coins from many civilizations which shows the area must have been on an important route for traders. The Jewish synagogue is in Rue Chabran. There were a number of strong Jewish communities in the region with papal patronage which did not end until the French Revolution. The other communities were in Avignon, Carpentras and Isle-sur-la-Sorgue.

Above the town is **Colline St Jacques**, a flat rocky area which used to be the site of many civilizations. Traces of Neolithic and Ligurian settlements have been found, and these were followed by the Celts, then the Greeks, and finally the Romans who eventually founded *Cabellio* below the rock, later to become Cavaillon.

The **Lubéron Hills** provide excellent walking and there are many roads to drive along which will take you through some of the prettiest parts of this regional park. The Lubéron range extends for about 64km (40 miles) and is divided at Bonnieux into the Grand Lubéron in the east and the Petit Lubéron in the west. The people of the Lubéron are immensely proud of their region and its past. They still live in tight-knit communities in small villages that can trace their ancestry back hundreds of years, back to the bloody persecutions of the sixteenth century. In the fourteenth century, the Lubéron became the centre for the Vaudois sect which had fled Italy to escape persecution. The Avignon popes, presumably because the sect was so close, decided that a lesson had to be taught to the Vaudois. They were declared heretics and papal troops were ordered to destroy all trace of them. Entire villages were destroyed and thousands of people killed. The former capital of the religious sect was Old Mérindol, and it is still preserved as a heap of stones. Today, the Lubéron is a delightful area of rolling hills, many of them densely wooded and the ideal habitat for hare, deer, woodcock and partridge. In the more remote woods there are still wild boar.

The summer heat is intense and the land is baked hard so it seems a strange place to find one of France's most impressive vineyards — the result of a £6 million dollar dream which has now become a reality. The vineyard of Château Val Joanis lies in a valley of the same name on the slopes of the Lubéron mountains. The château has had many famous owners and in 1730 was in the possession of Jean Joanis, secretary to King Louis III of Naples, and it still bears his arms today. It can trace its history back to Roman times, and the first vines may have been planted then, more than 2,000 years ago.

Jean Louis Chancel, a self-made millionaire born in the Lubéron, has always had a dream — to make the wines of Lubéron famous throughout the world. In 1978 he bought the château, 12 acres of badly run down vineyards, and 650 acres of scrub and woodland because soil analysis had shown the ground was capable of producing quality wine grapes. The hillsides were cleared, the land drained and planted with vines, a new winery built — altogether an expenditure of over £4 million — more than enough to have bought a leading Bordeaux vineyard had he wished. Today the vineyard produces marvellous red, white and rosé wines, and his efforts have encouraged other producers to raise their standards as well, so much so in fact, that in 1987 the Lubéron gained full *Appellation Contrôlée* status for its wines. You must try them.

If you want to base yourself at the other side of this region, **Sisteron** makes a good base. Its massive citadel rises above and dominates the town. There is an imposing cathedral started in the eleventh century, and a delightful colonnade of covered arches down to the river. The town has always held a strategic importance because of its position immediately below the Dauphiné mountains to the north and guarding the way to the plains and coast to the south.

Work is still going on to repair some of the medieval buildings damaged and destroyed during bombing by the Allies in 1944. Many of the buildings have already been carefully restored. Near the town hall are four fifteenth-century towers, part of the old town's fortifications. There is also an archaeological museum nearby. The citadel was started in the eleventh-century but work on the fortifications continued for centuries. It is worth the walk to the citadel for the views it affords.

There are scores of quaint and interesting towns and villages to visit in the Durance valley or immediate vicinity. There is the small spa town of **Digne**, in the heart of the lavender country. In July an international lavender-essence fair is held. It has not much else of interest but many good hotels and restaurants, so could make a base.

The mountains of **Lure** are really an extension of the Mont Ventoux range, an area full of steep hills, caves and springs, and an excellent place for spending a few days walking. There are many paths to follow, and places to explore. The Lure has certainly not yet been discovered by the crowds.

There is a small Romanesque chapel surrounded by lime trees, built on the site of the Lure Hermitage founded in AD500 by St Donat. A road does cross the mountains, but the best way is to get out on foot, although the walk to the summit, at the Signal de Lure at nearly 1,700m (5,500ft) is a tough one. There are beautiful flowers, including several species of orchid to see, as well as a wide range of butterflies, and the views from the top are breathtaking.

Between the Lure mountains and the Plateau de Valensole is **Forcalquier**, another ancient town, known as *Furnus Calcarius* in the Middle Ages because of the local lime furnaces (kilns). There are a number of interesting things to see including the curious cemetery with carved yew trees, the Romanesque church of Our Lady in Provençal and the convent of the Franciscans. The church of Notre Dame was started at the end of the twelfth century and in front of it stands a fifteenth-century fountain bearing a plaque which commemorates the marriage in 1235 of Eleanore of Provence and Henry III of England. The Franciscan convent was founded in 1236 and has been restored well. The cemetery is just north of the town, and is an oddity as far as French cemeteries go. Yew trees have been cut and trimmed to form arches along the terraces on which the *cabanons*, or small dry-stone buildings, were erected.

A little to the north-east is **Ganagobie**, with its marvellous Benedictine monastery founded in 980, but rebuilt on a number of occasions since then. It is famed for its carvings, sculptures and paintings which start as you enter the building. Even the lintel above the imposing gate is decorated.

A final point of call, if you have to tear yourself away, should be to **Riez**, once important as an administrative centre during the Roman occupation. Just outside the town there are the remains of a temple, believed to be to Apollo, with four columns of grey granite remaining. The stone for the temple must have been hauled at least 112km (70 miles) because this is the nearest known quarry with such granite. Another interesting visit is to the baptistry, again on the outskirts of town on the Allemagne-en-Provence road. Nobody knows exactly when it was built, although the experts agree that it was some time between the fourth and seventh centuries. Although square outside and capped with a dome which was added later, it is octagonal inside and divided into four chapels. It contains many sarcophagi, an altar and many columns and carvings.

To the north of Riez is the desolate Plateau de Valensole which is cut in two by the valley of the River Asse. There are some minor roads crossing the plateau but many walks, and it is a rugged but exciting place to backpack.

The whole of the Durance valley is really off the normal tourist route and it has something to offer everyone, whether you want to explore ancient monuments, get out and walk, or hunt out an exciting new wine maker and sample the product.

The Gastronomy of Provence

Olive trees that hug the hillsides and parched plots of land throughout Provence provide the basic cooking ingredient for most of the region's dishes. There are plentiful supplies of fresh vegetables, fresh fish from the Mediterranean, and meat and game from the hills in the north.

The people of Provence have strong fiery tastes which is why garlic, peppers and raw onions all figure strongly in dishes. Marseilles is the home of the fish soup *bouillabaisse*, but soups and stews of fish and meat abound.

Garlic is extensively used. As one moves nearer the Italian border the food changes, and there are many pasta dishes, especially around Nice. There is *canelloni*, *ravioli* and *gnocchi*, and a French version of pizza called *pissaladière*. There is game, including venison, hare and rabbit, and the beef, which tends to be reared locally needs long, slow cooking in stews, or *daubes*, to be at its best. Garlic soup is offered everywhere. There is *aïgo*, a straightforward garlic soup usually poured over bread in a bowl, and *aïgo bouido*, with olive oil and eggs added together with cubes of fried bread. *Aïgo à la ménagèrie* is garlic soup with onion, leek, tomatoes and poached egg, and *aïgo saou*, or *sou*, is garlic soup with fish and sometimes potatoes. Other regional soups include *soupe d'épautre* made with mutton, vegetables and garlic, and you will often find *méjanels* added; this is a thick pasta made in Provence and added to soups and stews. Accompanying soups of all types you will find *aïoli*, a mayonnaise sauce flavoured with garlic and occasionally breadcrumbs.

Regional speciality fish dishes include anchovies, often served cold with a beetroot salad, sea bream and saddled bream. Look out for *boutargue*, a paste made from dried and salted tuna roe, and *capoum*, the local name for scorpion fish. Eeels are popular, especially when cooked in tomatoes and garlic. Fresh sardines, sea bass, mussels and squid are usually excellent. *Bouillabaisse* is a thick fish stew with conger eel, gurnard and many other species, cooked with saffron, garlic, tomatoes, onions, oil and wine. It is universally popular.

Many meat dishes are served as stews, or *daubes*. Dishes cooked *à la Provençale* means they have been cooked with tomatoes, oil, with herbs and garlic, while *à la Barigoule* indicates they have been cooked with mushrooms, ham, onions, wine and oil. *A la Marseillaise* indicates the dish has been cooked with tomatoes, anchovies, onions, olive and garlic. Snails are popular and there are many local names for them. There are also many vegetable stews featuring artichokes, spinach, cabbage and broad beans, while *porchetta* is a mouth-watering delicacy of suckling pig, stuffed and spit roasted. *Pieds et paquets* is a Provence speciality of sheep's tripe and trotters, cooked with tomatoes in white wine, and there are a host of salads, including *salade Niçoise* made from tomatoes, onions, broad beans, lettuce, olives, tuna, anchovies and hard boiled eggs.

There are sweet fritters, marzipan sweets, raisin cakes and a number of mild local cheeses made from both sheep's and goat's milk, including Banon, usually wrapped in chestnut leaves, and Brousse de la Vesubie, a soft cheese which goes wonderfully with fruit.

Further Information
— Provence and the Côte d'Azur —

Museums and Other Places of Interest

Bandol
Wine Exhibition
Open: 10am-12.30pm and 2-6pm, closed Wednesday.

Sanary — Bandol Zoo
Le Castellet
Open: 8am-12noon, 2-7pm, closed Sunday morning.

Bargème
Romanesque Church
Visiting between 10 and 11.30am Monday, Thursday and Saturday after collecting key from town hall.

Bormes-lès-Mimosas
Museum
Open: weekdays.

Brignoles
Museum (with sarcophagi)
Open: March to September 9am-

12noon and 2.30-6pm; October-March
10am-12noon and 2.30-5pm.

La Ciotat
Museum
Open: weekdays.

Draguignan
Museum
Open: 10-11.30am and 3-6pm.

Medieval Library
Open: 10-11.30am and 3-6pm.

Fréjus
Archaeology Museum
Open: 9.30am-12noon and 2-6pm,
closed Tuesday.

Buddhist Pagoda
Open: June-September 3-7pm.

Fifth-century Baptistry
Rue de Fleury
Guided tours 9.30am-12noon and 2-
6pm.

Roman Theatre
Open: April-September 9.30am-12noon
and 2-7pm, closed Tuesday.

Thirteenth-century cathedral
Open: 9.30am-12noon and 2-6pm,
closed Tuesday.

Zoo
Open: 9am-6pm.

Glémenos
Cistercian Abbey Ruins
Open: April-September 9am-8pm;
October-March 10am-6pm.

Hyères
St Paul's Church
Open: 2.30-5pm.

Notre-Dame de Consolason Chapel
Open: 8.30am-2.30pm.

Museum
Open: 10am-12noon and 3-6pm.

St Raphaël
Archaeological Museum
Open: June-September 10am-12noon
and 3-6pm; rest of year 11am-12noon
and 2-5pm.

St Tropez
Modern Art Museum
Open: June-September 10am-12noon
and 3-7pm; rest of year 10am-12noon
and 2-6pm.

Maritime Museum
Open: June-September 10am-6pm; rest
of year 10am-5pm, closed Thursday.

Le Thoronet
Cistercian Abbey
Open: May-September 10am-12noon
and 2-6pm, closed 5pm February to
April and 4pm November-January.

ACCOMMODATION AND EATING OUT

All hotels are required to show their room rates, remember that the rate will be for the room, and not per person, and a menu if they have a restaurant, in their reception area. It is normal practice to visit the room before finally agreeing to take it, though this practice is not always followed, especially if you have booked your room from the local Tourist Information Centre and it is the last one in town. The Tourist Information Centre will usually charge you the price of the phone call to enquire/book the room, but that is a small price to pay. In most hotels breakfast will not be included in the price of the room. Check to make sure, and if it is not ask what breakfast will cost: you may well find that it will be cheaper to go to a local café or bar.

In advance of your stay it may also be worthwhile obtaining a copy of *Logis et Auberges de France*, from the French Government Tourist Office in your own country. This is an association of family-run hotels which offer good service and food at the lower end of the price spectrum.

Many other more modest, non-tourist, hotels exist in most towns and villages, as do furnished room and flats to let. Properly equipped country houses, villas, cottages and farms (or self-contained parts of them) can be rented as holiday homes (*gîtes*). *Gîtes* are usually rented by the week and are competitively priced, so much so that you will need to book early. All *gîtes* are inspected annually and are invariably in excellent condition. As they are usually in superb rural settings they offer a peaceful base, though having your own transport is likely to be a necessity.

When choosing a restaurant use a combination of three methods to ensure a good meal at the right price. The first is to consult the guide books, preferably in advance. The second is to ask, at hotel, camp-site, local Syndicat d'Initiative or bar, for a recommendation. The third is to study the menus which all restaurants must display, with their prices, outside their premises. These will show one or more menus, or fixed-price meals, as well as a list of *à-la-carte* dishes. Menus are always better value than going *à-la-carte* in French restaurants unless you want only one dish (the *plat du jour*) or a light snack. They offer three or more courses at a range of prices, from the cheaper *menu touristique* to the expensive and copious *menu gastronomique*. Gourmet restaurants may also offer a *menu dégustation*, which gives you a chance to taste smaller portions of a larger number of the chef's specialities.

The first course is usually a starter: often soup, pâté, cold meats or *crudités* (raw salad vegetables). In a four-course meal the second course will usually be a fish dish, and the third course a meat dish. This may be lightly garnished with vegetables, or they may be served as a separate course. If you want a steak well-done, ask for it *bien cuit* or even *brulée* (burnt). *À point* is rare-to-medium, *saignant* (bloody) or *bleu* is hardly cooked at all. The fourth course with be either cheese or a sweet, or both if you are lucky. If so, the cheese will be served before the dessert. A choice of both cheeses and sweets is offered, with the *tarte maison*, or house fruit-flan, an alternative for dessert. Cheaper menus often include a drink in the price.

French restaurants are usually friendly and casual. Children are welcomed and accommodated, often with special menus. The French like to take their time over their meals, and there is sometimes a wait between courses. Lunch, often their main meal of the day, is taken early, at around 12noon, and is finished by 2pm — so get there in good time. Dinner starts at about 7.30pm, but you can go much later. Sunday lunch is the most popular eating-out time for the French, so you should book in advance for this. Sunday evening is very quiet and many restaurants are closed then.

At the other end of the scale, a good place for an *en-route* lunch is a transport café or *relais routier*. They are popular with the general public, and provide a simple but substantial meal at a reasonable price. You can easily recognise them by the distinctive blue and red circle displayed outside.

Currency and Credit Cards

All major credit cards (Access, Visa, American Express etc) are taken at most large restaurants, hotels, shops and garages. Eurocheques and traveller's cheques are also accepted. Banks are normally open from 8.30am-12noon, 1.30-4.30pm Monday to Friday only.

The French unit of currency is the French *franc*. There are no restrictions on the import of French or foreign currency. The export of currency valued at up to 5,000 French *francs* in any currency (including French *francs*) is permitted. Amounts worth in excess of 5,000 French *francs* may be exported, providing that the money has been declared on entry. The French *franc* (abbreviated for FF) is divided into 100 *centimes*. Current coins include 5, 10, 20 and 50 *centime* pieces as well as 1, 2, 5 and 10 *franc* pieces. Bank notes come in denominations of 20, 50, 100, 200 and 500 *francs*.

Telephone Services

Telephoning in France is very simple. There are only two regions, Paris and the Provinces. All subscribers have an 8-figure number, and to dial from province to province, or from Paris to Paris, you simply dial that number. From Paris to province you dial 16 then the 8-figure number; from province to Paris, dial 16 (1) then the 8 figures. All Paris numbers should begin with a 4, and in the outskirts a 3 or 6.

Telephoning France from the UK, you start with the international dialling code (010 33) then (1) plus the 8-figure number for Paris and its outskirts, or simply the 8-figure number for anywhere else in the country.

The international dialling code for the USA and Canada is 011 33 and for Australia 0011 33.

Cheap rates give you 50 per cent extra time: on weekdays between 10.30pm and 8am, and at weekends starting 2pm on Saturdays.

Phonecards, called *télécarte*, operate in most booths. You can buy them from post offices, tobacconists, newsagents, and where advertised on telephone booths. Incoming calls can be received at phone boxes with a blue bell sign shown.

Tourist Offices

Larger resorts will have an Office de Tourisme, smaller ones a Syndicat d'Initiative, and their staff are usually only too willing to dispense local information, help and advice. Brochures are usually attractively produced, and often in English. Some of the major tourist offices now have an Accueil de France (Welcome to France) facility to help you with hotel bookings. For a small cover charge they will make hotel bookings for you throughout France on the same day you call or up to 8 days in advance. They are open from 9am to 8pm every day of the year except 25 December and 1 January. Tourist offices at main railway stations in Paris and a few other large towns are open daily except Sundays and Bank Holidays (8am-9pm Easter to October, 9am-8pm in winter).

The main French tourist offices are:

UK
178 Piccadily
London W1V 0AL
☎ 071 491 7622

USA
610 Fifth Avenue Suite 222
New York
NY 10020-2452
☎ 212 757 1683

Canada
1981 Avenue McGill College
Tour Esso Suite 490
Montreal
Quebec H3 A2 W9
☎ 514 288 4264

Australia
Kindersley House
33 Bligh Street
Sydney
NSW 2000
☎ (2) 231 5244

Tipping

Most restaurants make a service charge, either included in their prices or added on at the end. Cafés include it in the price of drinks if you sit at a table. Tips are customary to taxi-drivers and helpful hotel porters. When public toilets are guarded, an entrance charge will usually be made. When garage attendants clean your windscreen and check your oil, they will welcome, but not expect a tip.

Museums and Other Places of Interest

Wherever possible opening times have been checked, and are as accurate as possible. However, during the main holiday period they may be extended. Conversely, outside the main season, there may be additional restrictions, or shorter hours. Local tourist offices will always be able to advise you.

Generally all churches, and abbeys and monasteries still in use, are open every day from 9am-6pm, except during services. You should remember that these are places of worship as well as historical monuments, so dress and conduct should be appropriate.

Accommodation and Eating Out

✳✳✳ Expensive
✳✳ Moderate
✳ Inexpensive

Chapter 1 •
Aquitaine

Accommodation

Arcachon
Arc Hotel ✳✳✳
Boulevard Plage 89
☎ 56 83 06 85
No restaurant.

Les Ormes ✳
Rue Hovy 1
☎ 56 83 09 27

Les Vagues ✳✳
Boulevard Ocean 9
☎ 56 83 03 75

Ascain
Parc Trinquet-Larralde ✳
☎ 59 54 00 10

Barbotan-les-Thermes
La Bastide Gasconne ✳✳
☎ 62 09 57 61

Blaye
La Citadelle ✳
In the citadel
☎ 57 42 17 10

Cauterets
Bordeaux ✳✳
Rue Richelieu
☎ 62 92 52 50

Ste Cécile ✳
Boulevard Latapie-Flurin
☎ 62 92 50 47

Dax
Du Lac ✳✳
St-Paul-lès-Dax
☎ 58 91 84 84
Provision made for disabled guests.

Splendid ✳✳
Cours Verdun
☎ 58 56 70 70

Eugenie-les-Bains
Les Prés d'Eugénie ✳✳✳
☎ 58 05 06 07

Etauliers
Relais de L'Estuaire ✳
Place de la Halle
☎ 57 64 70 36

Guéthary
Brikétenia ✳
Rue de l'Empereur
☎ 59 26 51 34

Mimizan
Parc ✳
Rue Papeterie 6
☎ 58 09 13 88

Mont-de-Marsan
Richelieu ✳
Rue Wlerick 3
☎ 58 06 10 20

Le Renaissance ✳✳
2km on the Route
Villeneuve
☎ 58 51 51 51

Orlon-Ste-Marie
Alysson ✳✳
Boulevard Pyrénées
☎ 59 39 70 70

Pau
Continental ✳✳✳
Maréchal-Foch 2
☎ 59 27 69 31

Commerce ✳
Rue Maréchal-Joffre 9
☎ 59 27 24 40

Sabres
Auberge des Pins ✳
Route de la Piscine
☎ 58 07 50 47

St-Etienne-de-Baigorry
Arcé ✳✳
☎ 59 37 40 14

St-Jean-de-Luz
Chantaco ✳✳✳
2 km (1 mile) on the D918
☎ 59 26 14 76

St-Jean-Pied-de-Port
Pyrénées ✳✳✳
Place Charles-de-Gaulle
☎ 59 37 01 01

Central
Place Charles-de-Gaulle
☎ 59 37 01 01

St Palais
Trinquet ✱
☎ 59 65 73 13

Sare
Arraya ✱
☎ 59 54 20 46

Tarbes
President ✱
Rue Aristide Briand
☎ 62 93 98 40

Eating Out

Aire-sur-l'Adour
Les Bruyères ✱
1km on the N124
☎ 58 71 80 90
With accommodation.

Condom
Table des Cordeliers ✱✱✱
Rue des Cordeliers
☎ 62 28 03 68

Dax
Moulin de Poustagnacq ✱✱
St-Paul-Lex-Dax
☎ 58 91 31 03

Mimizan
Au Bon Coin ✱✱✱
35 Avenue du Lac
1½km (1 mile) at
Mimizan-Bourg
☎ 58 09 01 55
With accommodation.
Includes apartments.

Mont-de-Marsan
Le Midou ✱
Place Porte-Campet
☎ 58 75 24 26

Nerac
D'Albret ✱
Allees d'Albret 42
☎ 53 65 01 47
With accommodation.

Pau
Chez Pierre ✱✱✱
Rue Barthou 16
☎ 59 27 76 86

L'Agripaume ✱✱
Rue Latapie 14
☎ 59 27 68 70

St-Jean-Pied-de-Port
Ipoutchainia ✱
1½km (1 mile) on the D15
☎ 59 37 02 34
With accommodation.

Chapter 2 •
Agenais-Perigord-
Quercy

Accommodation

AGENAIS

Agen
Hotel Campanile ✱
ZAC d'Agen Sud
☎ 53 68 08 08
One of a modern chain of
sound, functional hotels
with good value restau-
rants. Like many of them
situated on the edge of an
industrial estate but
pleasant, nevertheless.
Children under 12 free in
their parents' room.

Casseneuil
Hotel Les Trois Rivieres ✱
Place St Jean
☎ 53 41 10 66
Typical French family
hotel in a picturesque old
village, recently modern-
ised bedrooms, bar with
terrace. Sound regional
restaurant.

**Castelnaud de
Gratecambe**
10km north of Villeneuve-
sur-Lot by N21
Hotel du Golf ✱✱
☎ 53 01 60 19
Pleasant modern hotel
beside a golf course (18 &
9 hole courses) in
scenically-attractive
countryside. Small

swimming pool, tennis.
Good restaurant.

Le Temple-sur-Lot
Hostellerie du Plantie ✱✱
☎ 53 84 37 48
3km outside village in
pleasant grounds beside
the River Lot, this is a
small comfortable mod-
ern hotel in a tranquil
situation. Swimming
pool, meals on the
terrace. Sound restaurant.

Pujols
4km south of Villeneuve-
sur-Lot
Les Chenes ✱✱
☎ 53 49 04 55
A comfortable country
hotel just outside the old
bastide village of Pujols.
Pleasant views, swim-
ming pool. No restaurant
(see La Toque Blanche
under restaurants).

Puymirol
L'Aubergade ✱✱✱
52 rue Royale
☎ 53 95 31 46
A small luxury hotel in a
converted thirteenth-
century house in the
heart of a hilltop village
and with a superb
restaurant. Michel Trama,
the owner, is considered
one of the finest chefs in
France. Ten rooms.

St Sylvestre-sur-Lot
Château Lalande ✱✱✱
☎ 53 36 15 16
A well-modernised old
château (9km from
Villeneuve-sur-Lot by
D911) converted to a
luxury hotel in its own
pleasant grounds, with
swimming pool, tennis,
exercise room, air condi-
tioning. Good restaurant.
Twenty-two rooms.

Villereal

Hotel du Lac ✳
Rte d'Issigeac
☎ 53 36 01 39
Pleasant Logis de France
with sound regional
cuisine. 25 rooms.

Eating Out

Bonaguil

Les Bons Enfants ✳
☎ 53 71 23 52
A good regional restaurant. Meals also served
on the shady garden
terrace, facing the famous
old château. (Also has a
few bedrooms).

Lagarrigue

(Near Aiguillon)
Auberge des Quatre Vents ✳✳
☎ 53 79 62 18
Refined cuisine and
pleasant ambience in a
dining room with picture
windows overlooking the
Lot valley, or on the
terrace. Closed Sunday
evening and Monday.

Laugnac

Le Relais ✳
☎ 53 68 87 16
Country village restaurant/hotel (6 rooms).
Spacious garden, option
of meals on the terrace.
Good country cooking.
Open for dinner every
evening in June/July and
August.

Poudenas (Near Nerac)

La Belle Gascogne ✳✳✳
☎ 53 65 71 58
Marie-Claude Gracia, one
of the best known woman
chefs in France, produces
the rich dishes of Gascony with a light touch
and a warm heart. The
number of places is

limited, so book ahead.
Closed Sunday evening
and Monday, except July
and August.
Across the road she has a
small hotel (✳✳ 7 rooms)
converted from an old
water mill on the Gelise.

Pujols

(Near Villeneuve-sur-Lot)
La Toque Blanche ✳✳✳
☎ 53 49 00 30
One Michelin star. Fine
food in a comfortable
dining room with cross-
country views. Closed
Sunday evening and
Monday, except July and
August. Next door to
Hotel Les Chenes (see
above).

Puymirol

L'Aubergade ✳✳✳
☎ 53 95 31 46
Two Michelin stars.
Superb food in luxurious
but intimate surroundings. Closed Mondays.

PERIGORD

Accommodation

Bergerac

Hotel Climat de France ✳
rte de Bordeaux
24100 Bergerac
☎ 53 57 22 23
One of this big modern
chain of reliable and
inexpensive hotels, with
good value restaurants.
46 rooms (children under
12 free in their parents'
room).

Brantome

Le Moulin de l'Abbaye ✳✳✳
24310 Brantome
☎ 53 05 80 22
Delightful small luxury
hotel, beautifully furnished, with splendid
views of the river and its

fifteenth-century elbow
bridge. Renowned
restaurant and wine
cellar. 9 rooms and 3
suites.

Domme

L'Esplanade ✳✳
24250 Domme
☎ 53 28 31 41
Very comfortable hotel
with top class restaurant.
Some rooms have sublime views of the Dordogne and its valley.

La Roque-Gageac

Hotel La Belle Etoile ✳
24250 La Roque-Gageac
☎ 53 29 51 44
Charming family hotel
between the cliff and the
Dordogne, with some
rooms overlooking the
river. Good, sound
restaurant. (Closed in
winter).

Le Bugue

Château Hotel ✳✳/✳
Campagne
24260 Le Bugue
☎ 53 07 23 50
Nice modern hotel with
simple but comfortable
rooms and a very good
value restaurant. 17
rooms.

Montignac

Château de Puy Robert ✳✳✳
24290 Montignac
☎ 53 51 92 13
A bright and lively hotel
with comfortable rooms
both in the Napoleon III
château and a very
attractive annexe. Excellent restaurant. 33 rooms
and 5 suites.

Siorac-en-Perigord

Hotel Scholly ✳✳/✳
24170 Siorac-en-Perigord
☎ 53 31 60 02

Simple but comfortable rooms, and good but relatively expensive restaurant.

St Julien de Crempse
(Near Bergerac)
Manoir de Grand Vignoble ✳✳
24140 St Julien de Crempse
☎ 53 24 23 1
Beautiful Louis XIV manor in its own extensive park. Stables with 60 horses, deer. Swimming pool, tennis. 44 rooms.

Tremolat
Le Vieux Logis ✳✳✳
24510 Tremolat
☎ 53 22 80 06
Beautiful old house in a lovely old-fashioned garden crammed with flowers. Stylish comfort in the rooms, and a first-class restaurant. 14 rooms and 8 suites.

Eating Out

Beaumont de Perigord
Chez Popaul ✳✳/✳
☎ 53 22 30 11
Remarkable restaurant in the Hotel des Voyageurs. Most menus include an as-much-as-you-like buffet with a choice of forty different dishes as the second course. Essential to book in advance, as the wonderful value for money is known throughout Perigord. Closed Mondays.

Champagnac de Belair
(Near Brantome)
Le Moulin du Roc ✳✳✳
☎ 53 54 80 36
Charming old water mill with a garden and terrace beside the Dronne. Good

food (one Michelin star) and wines. Closed on Tuesdays and Wednesday for lunch. Also has ten very comfortable rooms and four suites.

Les Eyzies de Tayrac-Sireuil
Le Centenaire ✳✳✳
☎ 53 06 97 18
Perigord cuisine at its finest with one of France's best chefs, Roland Mazere. (Two Michelin stars) Expensive but very good value. Closed for lunch on Tuesdays, and from November to April. (Also hotel with 21 rooms. Heated pool ✳✳)

Hotel Cromagnon ✳✳
☎ 53 06 97 06
Country hotel with heated pool, well-known for its excellent restaurant (one Michelin star). Closed for lunch on Wednesday, except public holidays, and in winter.

Monbazillac
La Grappe d'Or ✳✳
☎ 53 58 27 67
Sound country restaurant, much used by business men of the local Sigoules vineyards. Closed Mondays.

Perigueux
L'Oison ✳✳✳
31 rue St Front
☎ 53 09 84 02
Very good regional cuisine (one Michelin star) accompanied by an excellent wine cellar, warm welcome and pleasant ambience. Closed on Sunday evening and Mondays.

Sarlat
Hotel La Madeleine ✳✳
Place de la Petite Rigaude
☎ 53 59 10 41
This venerable provincial restaurant maintains its traditions with excellent cuisine, fine wines, and thoughtful service.

Hostellerie Marcel ✳
8 Avenue de Selves
☎ 53 59 21 98
Very good value menus at low prices. (Also has a few simple rooms). Closed Mondays, except in July and August.

QUERCY

Accommodation

Gramat
Château de Roumegouse
✳✳✳ - at Rignac
46500 Gramat
5km north of Gramat
☎ 65 33 63 81
Small, luxury hotel with delightful rooms.

Lacave
Château de la Treyne ✳✳✳
46200 Lacave
☎ 65 32 66 66
Comfortable and elegant but exceptionally expensive hotel with terrace above the Dordogne.

Hotel Pont de l'Ouysse ✳✳
46200 Lacave
☎ 65 37 87 04
Charmingly situated country hotel with delightful rooms, and a first-class restaurant (one Michelin star).

Mercues
Château de Mercues ✳✳✳
46090 Mercues
9km from Cahors
☎ 65 20 00 01
Luxury hotel in the former castle of the

Counts of Cahors. Rooms
recently decorated.
Swimming pool and
tennis courts. Extensive
views.

Rocamadour
Le Beau Site ✳✳
46500 Rocamadour
☎ 65 33 63 08
In the centre of the
famous village, this hotel
has been run by the same
family for seven genera-
tions. Solid comfortable,
some rooms with views
over the valley. Very
good restaurant.

Souillac
La Vieille Auberge ✳
46200 Souillac
☎ 65 32 79 43
Small, comfortable
country hotel with a lot of
charm. (Very good
regional restaurant ✳✳).

St Cere
Hotel de France ✳
46400 St Cere
☎ 65 38 02 16
Very comfortable typical
French family hotel with
lovely garden, swimming
pool. Modern rooms,
terraces overlooking the
countryside. Very good
restaurant (see below).

Eating Out

Cardaillac (Near Figeac)
Chez Marcel ✳
☎ 65 40 11 16
Superb regional food in
the restaurant of an
attractive old village inn.
Low prices. Remarkable
value for money. Closed
Mondays. (Also has some
rooms).

Carennac
Auberge du Vieux Quercy ✳
46110 Carennac
☎ 65 38 69 00
A Logis de France in a
really delightful village.
Comfortable newly
decorated bedrooms. A
good restaurant known
for its regional specialities. Closed from Novem-
ber to February and
Mondays outside the
high season.

Lamagdelaine
(7km north of Cahors)
Marco ✳✳
☎ 65 35 30 64
Beautiful food, warm
hospitality, good wines,
altogether it represents
exceptional value at
reasonable prices. Closed
Sunday evening and
Mondays outside high
season.

Laroque-des-Arcs
(Near Cahors)
Les Deux Saisons ✳✳
☎ 65 22 16 28
An old building but a
very pleasant dining
room where the menus
are based on local reci-
pes, and the service is
good. Closed Mondays
and Tuesday lunch.

Montaigu-de-Quercy
Le Vieux Relais ✳✳
☎ 63 94 46 63
Generous helpings of
typical regional dishes
well prepared. Pleasing
rustic decor. Closed
Sunday evening and
Monday outside high
season.

Chapter 3 •
Limousin

Accommodation and
Eating Out

Argentat
Hotel Fouillade ✳
11 Place Gambetta
19400 Argentat
☎ 55 28 10 17
Genuine family-run
country hotel in a charm-
ing little town. Real
country cooking, gener-
ous helpins. 13 bedrooms.
Hotel closed November.
Restaurant closed Mon-
days out of season.

Bonnac-le-Cote
*Château Leychoisier (Camp
Site)*
87270 Bonnac-le-Cote
Couzeix
Haute Vienne
☎ 55 39 93 43
10km north of Limoges
via N20 and then D97 to
Bonnac-le-Cote, and 1km
outside village. Adequate
facilities without luxury
but in a lovely wooded
park next to the château.
Spacious, but reservation
advised from mid-June to
end August.

Brignac-la-Plaine
Manoir de Brignac ✳✳✳
Brignac-la-Plaine
19310 Correze
☎ 55 85 13 26
22km north west of Brive-
la-Gaillarde, via N89 for
15km, then D39. This is
an imposing manor house
in the Limousin style in
its own park, well-
furnished interior with 10
comfortable bedrooms.
Swimming pool. Good
cuisine.

Chaumeil
Auberge des Bruyeres ✳
19390 Chaumeil
☎ 55 21 34 68
Simple, and very reasonably priced hotel with Logis de France standards in the 14 bedrooms. Above average country cuisine in a restaurant with rustic decor and a huge fireplace. Situated in an attractive village in the Massif des Monedieres and within easy access of the Plateau de Millevaches.

Magnac-Bourg
Auberge de l'Etang ✳
Magnac-Bourg
87380 Haute Vienne
☎ 55 00 81 37
On the N20 halfway between Limoges and Uzerche, but in a quiet situation, this is a pleasant Logis de France, with excellent regional cuisine. Closed for two weeks in October and from mid-February to mid-March.

Nieul
Hotel La Chapelle
  St Martin ✳✳✳
St Martin du Fault
87510 Nieul
☎ 55 75 80 17
About 12km north of Limoges via N147 for a short distance and then D35, this is a modern country house in its own neatly maintained grounds, with tennis court and swimming pool. A member of the Relais and Châteaux group with the usual elegant and comfortable rooms (13 plus 3 suites). Cuisine well above average. Closed January and February.

Peyrat le Château
Au Golf du Limousin ✳
Auphelle
87470 Peyrat le Château
☎ 55 69 49 16
Pleasant situation close to Lac de Vassiviere. Tennis. Comfortable modern Logis de France in a quiet situation, with good regional cuisine. 18 bedrooms. Closed mid-October to end March.

Hotel La Caravelle ✳✳
Lac de Vassiviere
Peyrat-le-Château
☎ 55 69 40 97
Superb situation in large garden next to the lake with direct access to a beach. Twenty-one simple but comfortable bedrooms, all with views of the lake. Cuisine sound but uninspired and not quite up to the prices charged, best value in the cheapest menu. Closed 31 December to 1 March. Room prices are per person and include obligatory demi-pension.

Sadroc
Relais du Bas Limousin ✳
RN20 Sadroc
19270 Correze
☎ 55 84 52 06
Near N20, 17km south of Uzerche. Another attractive Logis de France with 24 rooms, proudly run by the Besanger family. Son, Philippe, provides first-class regional cuisine. Closed on Sunday evenings out of season.

St Hilaire le Château
Hotel du Taurion ✳✳
23250 Creuse
☎ 55 64 50 12
Off the D941 about 25km west of Aubusson, this is

a good Logis de France with ten comfortable bedrooms, and a really first-class regional restaurant. Closed January and February. Restaurant closed on Wednesdays.

St Merd-de-Lapleau
Au Rendez-vous des
  Pecheurs ✳
Pont du Chambon
19320 St Merd-de-Lapleau
☎ 55 27 88 39
Simple but comfortable country hotel (eight bedrooms) in an isolated position among wooded hills and beside the Dordogne, with a bar terrace directly overlooking the river. Exceptional situation. Good cuisine. Hotel closed 12 November to 20 December. Closed for Friday dinner and Saturday lunch in winter.

Eating Out

The hotels listed above have good restaurants open to non-resident clients. The restaurants below are therefore chosen from different geographical locations. Motorists should be aware that there is relatively little commercial tourism in the Limousin region as a whole and that in some areas restaurants are few. Assessment of prices is largely based on the cheapest menu offered.

Aubazines
Hotel St Etienne ✳
19190 Aubazines
Correze
☎ 55 25 71 01

Situated south of the N89 about 10km east of Brive, and in the valley of the Correze. This is along-established country hotel, run by the Duroux family for 150 years. A former priory with 40 bedrooms, the hotel has a restaurant which offers fine regional cooking at prices which are very good value. Meals can also be taken on the terrace or in the garden. Closed end November to end December.

Aubusson
La Tuilerie ✳
Fourneaux
23200 Aubusson
☎ 55 66 28 09
A pleasant hotel (24 rooms) with a good regional restaurant, 10km north of Aubusson on the D942. Closed Tuesday evening and Wednesday, and December, January and February.

Correze
Hotel La Seniorie ✳✳
19800 Correze
☎ 55 21 22 88
Well situated hotel with good classical cuisine and spacious, well furnished rooms (29). Good value for money all round. Closed Sunday evening, Monday, and 1 January to mid-February.

La Roche l'Abeille
Au Moulin de la Gorce ✳✳✳
87800 La Roche l'Abeille
☎ 55 00 70 66
Off the D704 about 20km south of Limoges, and 10km north of St Yrieix-la-Perche. The old mill slumbers in peace next to its millpond. There are

nine comfortable bedrooms in a separate building, but it is to its restaurant that the Moulin owes its renown. Top class cuisine and a good wine list. Closed Sunday evening, and Monday out of season.

Limoges
L'Amphitryon ✳✳✳
26 rue de la Boucherie
☎ 55 33 36 39
Comfortable, classic restaurant in the old style. Pleasant and efficient service, generous servings of splendid dishes each with a touch of originality, and a well-chosen wine list. Good value. Closed Sunday and Monday lunch.

France Grillades ✳
7 Avenue Garibaldi
Limoges
☎ 55 79 07 07
A good restaurant specialising in top quality meat dishes. Modern style, good range of menus at very reasonable prices.

Mezieres
Le Relais ✳
Mortemart
87330 Mezieres
Haute Vienne
☎ 55 68 12 09
15km south-west of Bellac on the D675. A simple country inn (6 bedrooms) in an attractive village. Above average regional restaurant. Closed Tuesday evening and Wednesday.

Pontarion
Rotisserie du Taurion ✳
23250 Pontarion
Creuse
☎ 55 64 50 78

Country-style restaurant with good range of menus of regional cuisine all at value for money prices. Good welcome and efficient service. Closed mid-November to 1 March, and on Sunday evening and Monday outside summer season.

St Yrieix-La-Perche
Les Voyageurs ✳
Coussac-Bonneval
87500 St Yrieix-La-Perche
Haute Vienne
☎ 55 75 20 24
A delightful, well-run Logis de France near the château. Good choice of menus at reasonable prices, all excellent value, and nine small, but charming bedrooms. Closed Sunday evening and Monday out of season, and January.

Tarnac
Hotel des Voyageurs ✳
19170 Tarnac
Correze
☎ 55 95 53 12
A traditional regional restaurant with cooking by the patron. Well-balanced menus at reasonable prices. A real country inn on the edge of the Plateau de Millevaches. Sixteen simple but comfortable bedrooms. Closed 20 December to 20 January, and Sunday evening and Monday out of season.

Chapter 4 • Auvergne

Accommodation

Camp Sites
There is a wide range of camp sites available,

ranging from one to four
star. Most are within easy
touring distance of each
other. Almost every town
or large village has its
municipal camp site,
often with a luxurious
array of facilities.

Gîtes
The term applies to most
self-catering establish-
ments which range from
furnished country
cottages to *gîtes d'étape*,
which are more like
youth hostels.

Hotels and Restaurants
These can range from
multi-starred accommo-
dation to small, family-
run *auberges*. Room prices
are by law, displayed on
the back of the bedroom
door, and only the most
expensive restaurant will
not indicate the price of
its menu. Other accom-
modation may be found
in *chambres d'hôtes* or
tables d'hôtes where guests
have their own room in a
private house, but
usually eat with the
family.

Chapter 5 •
Lyonnais-Bresse

Accommodation and
Eating Out

HOTELS
As in many provincial
towns in the south of
France many of the hotels
do not have restaurants,
and this is stated where
appropriate.

Amberieux-en-Dombes
Les Bichonnieres ✳✳
route de Savigneux
01330 Amberieux-en-

Dombes
☎ 78 42 75 75
A pleasant, peaceful,
countrified Logis de
France with a very good
regional restaurant.

Bourg-en-Bresse
Hotel Ariane
Blvd Kennedy
01000 Bourg-en-Bresse
☎ 74 22 50 88
Pleasant modern,
functional hotel within
500m of Brou church.
Half-board obligatory in
high season.

Hotel de France ✳✳
19 Place Bernard
01000 Bourg-en-Bresse
☎ 74 23 30 24
Attractive traditional
hotel in the centre of
town, good service and
comfortable rooms.
Excellent restaurant
Jacques Guy next door.

**Chatillon sur
Chalaronne**
Auberge de la Tour ✳
place Republique
01400 Chatillon-sur-
Chalaronne
☎ 74 55 05 12
A sound Logis de France
restaurant with 12
bedrooms, and a good
restaurant, in the centre
of this pleasant little
town.

Corcelles-en-Beaujolais
Hotel Gailleton ✳✳
Corcelles-en-Beajolais
69220 Belleville
☎ 74 66 41 06
Sound Logis de France
with good value restau-
rant.

Lyon
Cour des Loges ✳✳✳
6 rue du Boeuf

69005 Lyon
☎ 78 42 75 75
One of the world's most
unusual hotels. Stylish
luxury. A group of
Renaissance houses in the
Florentine style around a
courtyard, beautifully
converted with superb
furnishings and decor.
Indoor pool like a Roman
bath.

Sofitel ✳✳✳
20 quai Gailleton
69000 Lyon
☎ 72 41 20 20
One of the well-known
upmarket chain reputed
for their excellent
restaurants. Close to the
centre.

Royal ✳✳✳
20 Place Bellecour
69002 Lyon
☎ 78 37 57 31
Traditional hotel with
some modern, some
period rooms. Reason-
ably priced grill room.

Hotel des Artistes ✳✳
8 rue Andre
69002 Lyon
☎ 78 42 04 88
Pleasant hotel, near the
Pont Bonaparte and
handy for Vieux Lyon
across the Saone. No
restaurant.

Hotel Bayard ✳✳
23 Place Bellecour
69002 Lyon
☎ 78 37 39 64
Modest hotel right in the
centre of town. No
restaurant.

Hotel des Savoies ✳✳
80 rue Charite
69002 Lyon
☎ 78 37 66 94
Moderately priced hotel
near the main railway
station. No restaurant.

Perouges
*Ostellerie du Vieux
Perouges* ✳✳✳
01800 Meximieux
☎ 74 61 00 88
Old and attractive inn in
the middle of this
picturesque restored
village. Modern comfort
in spacious well-
furnished rooms. Good
regional cuisine and
sound wines.

Vienne
La Pyramide ✳✳✳
14 Blvd Fernand Point
38200 Vienne
☎ 74 53 01 96
Very comfortable hotel in
modern style with a
restaurant carrying on
the great traditions of its
founder, Fernand Point.

Hotel de la Poste ✳
47 cours Romestang
38200 Vienne
☎ 74 85 02 04
Well-placed modest hotel
with reasonably priced
restaurant. Rooms not
expensive.

Eating Out

There are countless
restaurants in the
Lyonnais region,
hundreds in Lyon itself,
all offering good value
for money. They would
not survive, if they did
not. The following is a
brief selection.

Annonay
La Halle ✳✳
place Grenette
07100 Annonay
☎ 75 32 04 62
Simple restaurant with
good meals at reasonable
prices. Closed Sunday
evening and Monday,
and last week in August.

Bourg-en-Bresse
Le Poulet Gourmand ✳✳
7 rue Teyniere
01000 Bourg-en-Bresse
☎ 74 22 49 50
Very good value lunch
time menus. Attractive
decor and friendly
service. Closed Saturday
lunch and Sunday, and 1
to 21 August.

Collonges-au-Mont-d'Or
Paul Bocuse ✳✳✳
pont de Collonges
69660 Collonges-au-
Mont-d'Or
☎ 72 27 85 87
It has become fashionable
among the gourmet-
critics to say that this
great restaurant and its
master, Paul Bocuse, are
past their best. But it still
has its three Michelin
stars, and for those who
care about food it will
remain a place of
pilgrimage for some
years yet.

Fleurie
Auberge du Cep ✳✳✳
place Eglise
69820 Fleurie
☎ 74 04 10 77
A first-class restaurant (2
Michelin stars) among
the vineyards of Beaujo-
lais. Closed Sunday
evening, Monday, and
Tuesday lunch.

Le Bois d'Oingt
Hotel de France ✳✳
Le Bourg
69620 Le Bois d'Oingt
☎ 74 70 60 61
Country restaurant with
several specialities.

Lyon
La Tour Rose ✳✳✳
22 rue du Boeuf
69005 Lyon
☎ 78 37 25 90

Luxurious restaurant in a
seventeenth-century
mansion in Vieux Lyon.
Closed two weeks in
August.

La Mere Brazier ✳✳✳
12 rue Royale
69001 Lyon
☎ 78 28 15 49
Traditional Lyonnais
'bouchon' with very good
value menus. Advisable
to book. Closed mid-July
to mid-August.

Brasserie Georges
30 cours Verdun
69002 Lyon
☎ 78 37 15 78
Typical brasserie.

Vienne
Le Bec Fin ✳✳
7 Place St Maurice
38200 Vienne
☎ 74 85 76 72
Superb food generously
served in a pleasant old
house opposite the
cathedral. Good value.
Closed Sunday evening
and Monday.

Villars-les-Dombes
Jean Claude Bouvier ✳✳/✳
83 rte de Lyon
01330 Villars-les-Dombes
☎ 74 98 11 91
Modern but with
pleasing touches inside.
Excellent regional cuisine
at moderate prices, sound
wines, and charming
service. (There is also a
modern hotel (Ribotel),
with small but welcom-
ing rooms.

Chapter 6 •
Beaujolais
Accommodation

Belleville
Hotel Ange Couronné ✳
18 Rue République

69220 Belleville
☎ 74 664200

Charolles
Hotel Lion d'Or ❋
6 Rue Champagny
71120 Charolles
☎ 85 240828

Cours
Hotel Le Pavilion ❋❋
69470 Cours
☎ 74 898355
Hotel is 5km (3 miles)
east of the town, on D64
at the Col du Pavilion

Fleurie
Hotel Grands Vins ❋❋
69820 Fleurie
☎ 74 698143
The hotel is a short
distance south of the
town, on the D119.

Juliénas
Hotel des Vignes ❋
Route St-Armor
69840 Juliénas
☎ 74 044370

Mâcon
Hotel Bellevue ❋❋❋
416 Quai Lamartine
71000 Mâcon
☎ 85 380507

Quincie-en-Beaujolais
Hotel Mont-Brouilly ❋
69430Quincie-en-Beaujolais
☎ 74 043373
The hotel is 3km (2 miles)
east of the village, on the
D37.

Romanèche-Thorins
Hotel Maritennes ❋❋❋
71570 Romanèche-Thorins
☎ 85 35 51 70

Salles-Arbuissonnas-en-
   Beaujolais
Hotel St-Vincent ❋❋
69460 Salles-
Arbuissonnas-en-Beaujo-
lais
☎ 74 67 55 50

Taponas
Auberge des Sablons ❋
69220 Taponas
☎ 74 663480

Villié-Morgon
Hotel Le Villon ❋❋
69910 Villié-Morgon
☎ 74 691616

Villefranche-sur-Saône
Hotel Plaisance ❋❋
96 Avenue Libération
69400 Villefranche-sur-
   Saône
☎ 74 653352

Eating Out

Beaujeu
Anne de Beaujeu ❋❋
69430 Beaujeu
☎ 74 048758

Beauregard
Auberge Bressane ❋❋
01480 Beauregard
☎ 74 609392

Blacaret
Beaujolais ❋
69460 Blacaret
☎ 74 675475

Chénas
Daniel Robin ❋❋
69840 Chénas
☎ 85 367267

Cours
Chalets des Tilleuls ❋
Thel
69470 Cours
☎ 74 648153
The restaurant is at Thel,
a hamlet about 10km (6
miles) north-east of
Cours, on the D64.

Fleurie
Auberge du Cep ❋❋❋
Place Eglise
69820 Fleurie
☎ 74 041077

Odenas
Christian Mabeau ❋
69460 Odenas
☎ 74 034179

St Georges-de-Reneins
Hostelerie St-Georges ❋❋
69830 St-Georges-de-
   Reneins
☎ 74 676278

St Vérand
Auberge St Vérand ❋
71570 St Vérand
☎ 85 371650

Tarare
Jean Brouilly ❋❋❋
3 Terrace Paris
69170 Tarare
☎ 74 632456

Villefranche-sur-Saône
La Fontaine Bleu ❋❋
18 Rue Moulin
69400 Villefranche-sur-
   Saône
☎ 74 681037

Viry
La Monastère ❋
71120 Viry
☎ 85 241424

Chapter 7 •
Savoie
Almost every town and
reasonable sized village
has its own Syndicat
d'Initiative, or Office de
Tourisme. Simply write to
M. le Directeur, Office de
Tourisme at the town or
village of your choice, but
try to include the five
figure post code. For
example, in Savoie all
codes start with 73 and
those in Haute Savoie
with 74. They will be able
to give you updated lists
of *gîtes, Chambres d'hotels*
(rented rooms), as well as
campsites and hotels.

Chapter 8 •
The Midi

Accommodation and Eating Out

Aigues-Mortes
La Camargue ✳✳
19 rue de la République
☎ 66 51 86 88
Traditional restaurant,
marvellous location,
good food.

Arles
Arlatan ✳✳
City centre off Place
Forum
☎ 90 93 56 66
Spacious, comfortable
hotel, ideal base for
sightseeing.

*Le Relais Du Passage a
 Niveau* ✳
Ave de la Libération
☎ 90 96 06 64
Comfortable, inexpensive
hotel and restaurant.

Avignon
Hôtel Innova ✳✳
100 rue Joseph-Vernet
☎ 90 82 54 10
Small, friendly, good
value hotel.

Banyuls-sur-Mer
*Hôtel Restaurant
 Les Elmes* ✳✳
Plage des Elmes
☎ 68 88 03 12
Friendly, popular restau-
rant-hotel overlooking
the sea. Good value.

Carcassone
Le Relais de L'Avenir ✳
93 ave Francklin-Roosevelt
☎ 68 25 09 39
Good value hotel and
restaurant

Air Motel Salvaza ✳✳
Close to the airport
☎ 68 71 64 64
Comfortable modern
hotel, good restaurant.

Narbonne
Le Novelty ✳✳
33 ave des Pyrénées
☎ 68 42 24 28
Welcoming, value for
money small hotel with
good restaurant.

La Toupine ✳✳
3 route de Coursan
☎ 68 65 11 01
Good touring base, good
value restaurant with
four bedrooms.

Nîmes
Novotel ✳✳✳
Périphérique Sud, D42
☎ 66 84 60 20
Modern large hotel, good
value, restaurant and
snack bars.

Impérator ✳✳✳
Place Aristide Briand
☎ 66 21 90 30
Luxury hotel in delightful
gardens, good but pricey
restaurant.

Orange
Le Moulin A Vent ✳✳
Pont de l'Aigue
☎ 90 34 02 41
Good value restaurant,
interesting wine list.

Perpignan
Parc Hotel ✳✳
18 blvd Jean-Bourrat
☎ 68 35 14 14
Reasonably-priced,
convenient hotel, with
good restaurant.

Polygone Nord ✳✳
10 rue Beau de Rochas
☎ 68 61 35 15
Small, friendly restaurant.

Le Relais St Jean ✳
Place de la Cathédrale
☎ 68 51 22 25
Good value, local cuisine
in historic surroundings.

Valence
*Logis de France Grand St
 Jacques* ✳✳✳
9 Faubourg St-Jacques
☎ 75 42 44 60
Very comfortable
upmarket hotel.

Chapter • 9
Rouergue-Albigeois
Accommodation

COUNTRY HOTELS

Aveyron
Chateau de Creissels ✳✳
Creissels
route de St. Affrique
12100 Aveyron
☎ 65 60 16 59
A charming chateau by
the Tarn. Rooms fairly
simple by chateau
standards but some in
course of redecoration.
Classical regional
restaurant, very good
value.

Fontvialane
La Reserve ✳✳✳
Route de Cordes
☎ 63 47 60 22
Three kilometres north-
west of Albi, this is a
pleasant Relais et
Chateaux hotel in its own
park on the banks of the
Tarn, swimming pool
and tennis. Very good
restaurant. Open from
1 May to end October.

Rodez
Le Parc Saint-Joseph ✳✳✳ /
 ✳✳
route de Rignac
12000 Rodez
☎ 65 67 03 30
Four kilometres north-
west of Rodez by N140. A
former summer residence
of the bishops of Rodez,
this is a comfortable hotel

with spacious bedrooms, and a park with lovely old trees. Good cuisine.

Villefranche de Rouergue
St Remy
Le Relais de Farrou ✳✳
12200 Villefranche de Rouergue
☎ 65 45 18 11
Four kilometres outside Villefranche on the Figeac road, this is a good Logis de France, with attractive rooms and good regional cuisine. Swimming pool, and tennis. Ask for a room overlooking the pretty garden. Closed for 2 weeks mid-April, mid October, and mid-December.

OTHER HOTELS
Albi
Campanile ✳✳/✳
Avenue Jean de Lattre-de-Tassigny
81000 Albi
☎ 63 47 18 80
One of a modern chain of pleasant but functional hotels which offer good standards at very reasonable prices. Restaurant offers particularly good value.

Hotel Chiffre ✳✳
50 rue Sere de Riviere
81000 Albi
☎ 63 54 04 60
Efficiently run family hotel near the town centre. Comfortable rooms, good restaurant, parking.

Conques
Hotel St Foy ✳✳✳/✳✳
12320 Conques
☎ 65 69 84 03
In a renovated seventeenth century house in the middle of this lovely village. Comfortable rooms, good restaurant.

Espalion
Le Moderne ✳✳/✳
27 Blvd de Guizard
12500 Espalion
☎ 65 44 05 11
Nicely placed near the old chateau, this is a family run Logis de France with a very good restaurant, father and son are keen anglers and the kitchen benefits. Small but comfortable rooms.

Millau
La Musardiere ✳✳
34 Avenue de la Republique
12100 Millau
☎ 65 60 20 63
Small, comfortable, traditional hotel with a very good restaurant. One place to try the best Roquefort cheese.

Rodez
Hotel du Midi ✳
1 Rue Beteille
12850 Rodez
☎ 65 68 02 07
Also a Logis de France In the town centre but reasonably quiet at night. Good restaurant, good value all round.

Villefranche de Rouergue
L'Univers ✳
2 Place de la Republique
12200 Villefranche de Rouergue
☎ 65 45 15 63
Typical Logis de France, reasonable comfort and good local cuisine.

CAMPING
Aveyron
Les Rivages
Avenue de l'Aigoual
12100 Millau
☎ 65 61 01 05
About 2km from Millau on the D 991 the road to

Nant. Large camp with excellent amenities and sporting facilities on the banks of the river Dourbie. Open from Easter to September. Reservation advised.

Beau Rivage
12410 Salles-Curan
Nicely sited camp on the edge of the 1200 hectare lake of Pareloup which has equipped beaches, water sports etc. Good amenities at the camp. Open from mid June to mid September. Booking advised July and August.

Addresses of farms equipped to welcome campers are obtainable from local Tourist Offices.

Tarn
Les Clots
81190 Mirandol Bourgnounac
☎ 63 76 92 78
About 10 kilometres north of Carmaux by D905, rte de Rieupeyroux. Pleasant and spacious camp, with good amenities, 500m from the river Viaur. Open from Easter to mid-October. Reservation advised in high season.

Restaurants
(in addition to those of hotels listed above)

Albi
Moulin de la Mothe ✳✳
Rue de la Mothe
☎ 63 60 38 15
Beautiful site on the banks of the Tarn near the Cathedral. Attractive dining room and terrace, warm welcome, and very

good cuisine in the local tradition. Closed Wednesday except July and August.

Les Jardins de Quatre Saisons ✲✲✲/✲
19 Blvd de Strasbourg
☎ 63 60 77 76
Fine cuisine based on seasonal products, and an excellent wine list. Good reception and considerate service. Closed Mondays, except public holidays.

Cordes
Le Grand Ecuyer ✲✲✲
Rue Voltaire
☎ 63 56 01 03
High degree of comfort and first-class cuisine in this well run restaurant in a fifteenth century house once a hunting lodge of the Counts of Toulouse. Closed Mondays, except July and August, and from mid October to mid-March.

The Hostellerie du Vieux Cordes ✲✲
☎ 63 56 00 12
has the same proprietor, an equally fine setting (lovely terrace), but is slightly less expensive.

Espalion
La Mejane ✲✲
near the old bridge
☎ 65 48 22 37
A high standard of cooking at moderate prices in a pleasant little restaurant. Closed Sunday evening and Wednesday except in August.

Laguiole
Restaurant Michel Bras ✲✲✲
☎ 65 44 32 24
Tucked away in the north-east corner of the Rouergue on the edge of the Massif Central, Laguiole was famous in the past for its top quality knives, still made there, but in the past few years it has acquired a new fame as a place of pilgrimage for serious gourmets. The gastronomic critics of France are unanimous in classing Michel Bras as one of the greatest of all French chefs past and present. So, if your pocket is deep enough, it is worth making the detour. Very expensive but in demand, so book in advance in summer. Closed November to March inclusive, and Sunday evening and Monday except in July and August.

Meyrues
Grand Hotel Europe ✲
☎ 66 45 60 05
and
du Mont Aigoual ✲✲
☎ 66 45 65 61
Quai de la Barriere route de l'Aigoual
Two restaurants in different styles, rustic for the Europe, modern for the Mont Aigoual, but with the same talented chef, whose family have owned this property for ninety years. Closed November to March inclusive.

Millau
La Mangeoire ✲✲
8 Blvd de la Capelle
☎ 65 60 13 16
Reliable cooking at very moderate prices. Closed Sunday evening and Monday except July and August, and in mid-October for 2 weeks.

Najac
Hotel Belle Rive ✲✲/✲
au Roc du Pont
☎ 66 29 73 90
Two kilometres outside the village by D 39, in riverside woods beside the Aveyron gorge. Typical Logis de France restaurant, sound regional cuisine. (Also 30 reasonably comfortable bedrooms at moderate rates). Closed November to March inclusive.

Salles-Curan
Hostellerie de Levezou ✲✲
☎ 65 46 34 16
Restaurant in a chateau dating back to the fourteenth century, in the heart of this delightful village near the Lac de Pareloup. Excellent cuisine (one Michelin star) and stylish service at moderate prices. Also has some simple rooms at cheap rates. Closed mid-October to Easter, and Sunday evening and Monday except from end June to mid-September.

Sauveterre-de-Rouergue
Auberge du Senechal ✲✲✲/✲✲
☎ 65 47 05 78
A very good restaurant indeed in this delightful bastide, regional food presented with skill and originality. Moderate plus prices, but very good value. (Also has 14 comfortable rooms moderately priced). Closed Sunday dinner and Monday, except in July and August, and from November to March inclusive.

Chapter 10 •
The Cévennes

Accommodation

Alès
Hotel Mercure ✳✳
Rue Quinet
30100 Alès
☎ 66 522707

Anduze
Hotel Porte des Cévennes ✳✳
30140 Anduze
☎ 66 619944

Genérargues
Hotel Trois Barbus ✳✳✳
30140 Genérargues
☎ 66 617212

Génolhac
Hotel Mont Lozère ✳
30450 Génolhac
☎ 66 611072

Lasalle
Hotel des Camisards ✳
30460 Lasalle
☎ 66 852050

Le Vigan
Hotel Commerce ✳
26 Rue Barris
30120 Le Vigan
☎ 67 810328

Mende
Hotel Lion d'Or ✳✳
12 Boulevard Britexte
48000 Mende
☎ 66 491646

Meyrueis
Château d'Yres ✳✳✳
48150 Meyrueis
☎ 66 456010
The hotel is situated
1½km (1 mile) to the east
of the village.

Ste Enimie
Hotel Burlatis ✳
48210 Ste Enimie
☎ 66 485230

St Jean-du-Gard
Auberge du Péras ✳
Route Anduze
30270 St Jean-du-Gard

Valleraugue
Hotel Petit Luxembourg ✳✳
30570 Valleraugue
☎ 67 822044

Villefort
Hotel Balme ✳
48800 Villefort
☎ 66 468 014

Eating Out

Alès
Auberge St Hilaire ✳✳✳
30100 Alès
☎ 66 301 142
The restaurant is situated
about 5km (3 miles)
south of the town, on the
N106 to Nîmes.

Aulas
Mas Quayrol ✳✳
30120 Aulas
☎ 67 811238

Durfort
Le Real ✳
30170 Durfort
☎ 66 775058

Florac
Grand Hotel Parc ✳✳✳
48400 Florac
☎ 66 450305

Méjannes-lès-Alès
Auberge des Voutins ✳✳
30340 Méjannes-lès-Alès
☎ 66 61380

Mende
La Gogaille ✳
5 Rue Notre-Dame
48000 Mende
☎ 66 650879

Mialet
Auberge du Fer à Cheval ✳
30140 Mialet
☎ 66 8520280

Meyrueis
Mont Aigoual ✳
Rue Barrière
48150 Meyrueis
☎ 66 456561

St Ambroix
Auberge St Brès ✳✳
30500 St Ambroix
☎ 66 241079

St Hippolyte-du-Fort
Les Cévennes ✳
3 Boulevard de Temple
30170 St Hippolyte-du-
Fort
☎ 66 779020

St Jean-du-Gard
La Paillerette ✳
30140 St Jean-du-Gard
☎ 66 619944

St Paul-le-Jeune
Auberge de la Cocalière ✳✳
07460 St Paul-le-Jeune
☎ 75 398134
The restaurant is close to
the Cocalière Cave, a
short distance from St
Ambroix.

Chapter 11 •
Ardèche
All hotels have restau-
rants unless stated
otherwise.

Accommodation

Annonay
Hotel du Midi ✳✳
12 Place des Cordeliers
(centre of town)
☎ 75 33 23 77
Menus: variable accord-
ing to season.

Bar/Hotel de la Gare ✳
31 Avenue Marc Sequin
☎ 75 33 29 11

Hotel La Siesta and
   *Restaurant 'Le Don
      Quichotte'* ✳✳✳
At Davezieux, outskirts
of town

☎ 75 33 07 90
Closed in winter. Highly
commended; check with
local Syndicat
d'Initiative.

Le Ratelier ❊
Family Hotel
Place du Champ de Mars
☎ 75 33 20 48

Aubenas
Le Cevenol ❊❊
Centre of town
Boulevard Gambetta
☎ 75 35 00 10
Also has coffee bar and
cafeteria.

L'Orangerie ❊❊
7 Allée de la Guinguette
Centre of town
☎ 75 35 30 42
No restaurant.

Le Provence ❊❊
5 Boulevard de Vernon
Close to town centre
☎ 75 35 28 43
No restaurant.

La Pinède ❊❊
Route les Pins
Just above town
☎ 75 35 25 88

Chez Jacques ❊
9 rue Beranger de la Tour
☎ 75 93 88 74
Modest hotel, town
centre.

Col de l'Escrinet ❊❊
At the Col on N104
between Privas and
Aubenas
☎ 75 87 10 11
Two star hotel with mag-
nificent views and swim-
ming pool, good parking.
No bar for casual drinks.
Closed from November to
Easter.

Dunières
Valley of the Eyrieux,
between Les Ollières and
La Voulte, D12.

Hotel de la Vallée ❊❊
Centre of village
☎ 75 62 41 10
Local specialities.

Lanas
Off road from Ruoms-
Vogué near Vallon
Les Voutes ❊❊
Centre of village
☎ 75 37 72 07

La Voulte sur Rhône
On RN86, alongside river
Hotel le Musée ❊❊
☎ 75 62 40 19
Corner of RN86 and road
to town centre.

Hotel du Rhône ❊
On N86, just beyond
Hotel du Musée

Lavilledieu
Route de Villeneuve de
Berg from Aubenas, N102
Les Persèdes ❊❊
☎ 75 94 88 08

Les Ollières
North of Privas, on the
River Eyrieux
Auberge de la Vallée ❊❊
☎ 76 66 20 32
Centre of town (a 'Logis
de France')

Mezilhac
In the mountains,
between Col de l'Escrinet
and Le Puy
Au Bon Saint Bernard ❊❊
☎ 75 38 78 93
Pension and Demi-
pension, near to ski and
walking. Good centre for
mountain pursuits.

Pont de Labeaume
On N104 Aubenas to
   Le Puy
Le Ventadour ❊
☎ 75 38 05 10
No restaurant.

Privas
La Croix d'Or ❊❊
12 Cours de l'Esplanade
☎ 75 64 65 62

Hotel de la Chaumette ❊❊❊
Avenue du Vanel
(signposted)
☎ 75 64 30 66

St Etienne de Fontbellon
South of Aubenas on N105
Les Acacias ❊❊
☎ 75 35 02 98
Closed September.

St Jean Le Centennier
Off route from Aubenas/
Villeneuve de Berg
Hotel Le St Jean ❊❊
Centre of village
☎ 75 36 71 11
No restaurant.

St Privat
Route between Aubenas
and Privas
Auberge de St Privat ❊
☎ 75 35 13 36

Soyons
On Route N86
La Chataignerie ❊❊❊
Best Western Group
Restaurant: à la carte
☎ 75 60 83 55

Vals Les Bains
Grand Hotel Les Bains ❊❊❊
☎ 75 94 65 55
Open: Easter to Christ-
mas/New Year.
Menus à la carte.

Hotel du Vivarais ❊❊❊
Best Western Group, in
centre of town
☎ 75 94 65 85
Open: all year. Large
swimming pool between
the park and the river.

Touring Hotel ❊❊
88 rue Jean-Jaurès
☎ 75 37 44 36
Open: Easter to end
September.

Hotel des Celestins ✳✳
2 avenue Paul Ribèyre
☎ 75 37 42 20
Open: Easter to end
December.

Hotel la Clef d'Or ✳
Modest hotel
5 Place Gallimard
☎ 75 37 43 22
Open all year.

Vallon Pont d'Arc
Hotel Du Tourisme ✳✳
(Logis de France)
Centre of town
☎ 75 88 02 12
Menus à la carte

Hotel Du Parc ✳
Centre of town
Note: Unusually, the
above two hotels quote a
taxe de séjour of 2 francs
per person per night.
☎ 75 88 02 17

Villeneuve de Berg
Both of the hotels listed
below are on RN102 -
Villeneuve to Viviers/Le
Teil
Auberge de Montfleury ✳
Gare St Germain
☎ 75 94 74 13

Relais St Germain ✳
Montfleury
☎ 75 94 74 98
In what was the old
railway station. Good
parking.

Viviers
Hotel du Provence ✳
On corner at south edge
of town on N86
☎ 75 52 60 45

Vogué
L'Auberge ✳✳
Centre of town
☎ 75 37 72 59
Nicely placed for the
centre of Ardèche.
Limited parking —
narrow street.

Eating Out

Annonay
Auberge de St Cyr ✳
6km (4 miles) from
Annonay at St Cyr
☎ 75 67 46 39

Aubenas
Le Chat Qui Pèche ✳✳
6 Place de la Grenette
(near Donjon)
☎ 75 93 87 43
Small, interesting, local
cuisine.

Restaurant du Chateau ✳✳
5 Grand Rue. Off market
square by Town Hall.
☎ 75 35 31 24
Ardèchois specialities.

Pizzeria le Dugueslin ✳
1 rue Silhol (near Le
Navire Cinema)
☎ 75 93 48 46
Pizzas and grills au
choix. Panoramic view
from restaurant.

Le Centre ✳✳
8 rue du 4 Septembre
(near to Cathedral)
☎ 75 93 64 17
Small, but charming and
typically family-style
restaurant in old part of
town.

Darbres
On the plateau of the Coiron
Les Lavandes ✳
☎ 75 94 20 65
Country restaurant, local
specialities and fish.

Largentière
Le Grill ✳/✳✳
rue Maréchal Suchet
☎ 75 39 16 77
Local specialities à la carte.

Pont de Labeaume
Route d'Aubenas
La Truite Enchantée ✳/✳✳
Local dishes, especially
fish.
☎ 75 38 05 02

Privas
In Privas there are a
number of Parisienne-
style brasseries on main
street. Menus, à la carte,
from 50/60 francs.

St Étienne de Fontbellon
Cafeteria Le Cascadine ✳✳
At Centre Leclerc Super-
market
A good selection of
snacks and fast food. A
very pleasant atmos-
phere and good value.

St Remèze
Near to the Gorges de
l'Ardèche and the caves
Auberge de la Belle Aurore ✳
In countryside between
Bourg St Andeol and
Vallon Pont d'Arc
☎ 75 54 48 09
Rooms may be available.

Le Maronnier ✳
Centre of village
☎ 75 04 30 58

Vals Les Bains
Du Parc ✳
Centre of town
☎ 75 37 42 33

Le Tonneau ✳ (Relais 'Les
Routiers')
89 rue Jean Jaurès
☎ 75 37 45 36

Viviers
Auberge de Pont Romain ✳
Near old Roman bridge
at entrance to town on
D107
☎ 75 52 60 84

Chapter 12 •
Dauphiné

Accommodation

Most towns and
reasonably sized villages
have their own tourist
office or Syndicats

d'Initiative. Write to M.
le Directeur, Office de
Tourisme, adding the
town or village you
require. They will be able
to give you updated lists
of *gîtes, chambres d'hôtes*
(rented rooms), as well as
campsites and hotels.

Chapter 13 •
Le Queyras

Accommodation

Briançon
Hotel Altéa Grand'Bouche
❋❋❋
Avenue Dauphine
05100 Briançon
☎ 92 20 11 51

Park Hotel ❋❋
Central Parc
05100 Briançon
☎ 92 20 37 47

Hotel Edelweiss ❋
32 Avenue République
05100 Briançon
☎ 92 21 02 94

Ceillac
Hotel Cascade ❋
Mélezet
05600 Ceillac
☎ 92 45 05 92

Chantemerle
Hotel Plein Sud ❋❋
05330 Chantemerle
☎ 92 24 17 01

Commune de Château-
  Ville-Vielle
Hotel Guilazur ❋
Ville-Vieille
05350 Commune de
Château-Ville-Vielle
☎ 92 46 74 09

Crevoux
Hotel Parpaillon ❋
05200 Crevoux
☎ 92 43 18 08

Embrun
Hotel Mairie ❋
Place Barthelon
05200 Embrun
☎ 92 43 20 65

Guillestre
Hotel Catinat Fleuri ❋
05600 Guillestre
☎ 92 45 07 62

Les Claux
Hotel Caribou ❋❋❋
05560 Les Claux
☎ 92 46 50 43

Molines-en-Queyras
Hotel Le Cognarel ❋❋
05350 Molines-en-Queyras
☎ 92 45 81 03
The hotel is 3km (2 miles)
east of the village.

Ste Marie-de-Vars
Hotel Le Vallon ❋❋
☎ 92 46 54 72

Eating Out

Briançon
La Péché Gourmand ❋❋
2 Route Gap
05100 Briançon
☎ 92 20 11 02

Altéa Grand'Bouche ❋❋❋
Avenue Dauphiné
05100 Briançon
☎ 92 20 11 51

Chantemerle
La Fourchette ❋
05330 Chantemerle
☎ 92 24 06 66

Embrun
Hotel Lac ❋❋
Plan d'Eau
05200 Embrun
☎ 92 43 11 08

Guillestre
Epicurion ❋
05600 Guillestre
☎ 92 45 20 02

Les Claux
Caribou ❋❋
05560 Les Claux
☎ 92 46 50 43

Chez Plumot ❋
05560 Les Claux
☎ 92 46 52 12

Mont Dauphin
Gare ❋
05600 Mont Dauphin
☎ 92 45 03 08

Montgenèvre
Valérie ❋❋
05100 Montgenèvre
☎ 92 21 90 02

St Véran
Châteaurenard ❋❋
05350 St Véran
☎ 92 45 85 43

Villeneuve-la-Salle
Christiania ❋❋
05240 Villeneuve-la-Salle
☎ 92 24 76 33

Auberge Ensoleillée ❋
05240 Villeneuve-la-Salle
☎ 92 24 74 04

Chapter 14 •
Provence and the
Côte d'Azur

Accommodation and
Eating Out

Aix-en-Provence
Hotel Paul Cézanne ❋❋❋
40 ave Victor Hugo
☎ 42 26 34 73
Comfortable, attentive
good value hotel.

Des Augustins ❋❋
3 rue de la Masse
13100 Bouches-du-Rhône
☎ 42 27 28 59
Elegant, moderately
expensive hotel.

Bandol
La Ker Mocotte ✳✳
Rue Raimu
☎ 94 29 45 53
Comfortable small good
value seafront hotel with
inexpensive restaurant.

Brignoles
*La Mamma Auberge La
    Reinette* ✳✳
On RN7
☎ 94 59 07 46
Good value restaurant.

Draguignan
Le Penalty ✳✳
1 ave de la lre Armée
☎ 94 68 11 28
Good food, reasonably
priced.

Les Deux Cochers ✳
7 blvd Gabriel Péri
☎ 94 68 13 97
Traditional local cuisine
in rustic settings. Good
value.

Fréjus
Le Vieux Four ✳✳
57 rue Grisolle
☎ (94 51 56 38
A good value restaurant
with a few inexpensive
rooms.

Les Trois Chênes ✳
Route de Cannes
☎ 94 53 20 08
A good touring base,
comfortable rooms, good
food, reasonably priced.

Hyères
Relais du Gros Pin ✳
15 ave Paul-Renaudel
☎ 94 97 63 26
Comfortable, reasonably
priced small hotel and
restaurant.

St Raphaël
Le Relais Bel Azur✳
247 blvd de Provence
☎ 94 95 14 08
Friendly hotel and
restaurant. Good touring
base. Good value.

Hotel Moderne✳✳
329 ave de Géneral-Leclerc
☎ 94 51 22 16
Excellent restaurant and
small, comfortable hotel.

St Rémy
Le Mas des Carassins ✳
13210 Bouches-du-Rhône
☎ 90 92 15 48
Hôtel just out of town on
the Les Baux road.
Charming and inexpen-
sive.

St Tropez
Leï Mouscardins ✳✳
In the port
☎ 94 97 01 53
Good restaurant, popular
and not too expensive.

Les Santons ✳✳✳
At Grimaud 6 miles
(9km) away
☎ 94 43 21 02
Excellent innovative
cuisine, expensive but
worth the treat.

Index

Page numbers in **bold** type indicate maps

A Note To The Reader

The accommodation and eating out lists in this book are based upon the authors' own experiences and therefore may contain an element of subjective opinion. The contents of this book are believed correct at the time of publication but details given may change. We welcome any information to ensure accuracy in this guide book and to help keep it up-to-date.
Please write to The Editor, Moorland Publishing Co Ltd, Moor Farm Road, Airfield Estate, Ashbourne, Derbyshire, DE6 1HD, England.
American and Canadian readers please write to The Editor, The Globe Pequot Press, 6 Business Park Road, PO Box 833, Old Saybrook, Connecticut 06475, USA.

MPC

The Globe Pequot Press